DATA AND PRIVATE LAW

This collection examines one of the fastest growing fields of regulation: data.

The book moves debates about data beyond data and privacy protecting statutes. In doing so, it asks what private law may have to say about these issues and explores how private law may influence the interpretation and the form of legislation dealing with data.

Over five parts, it sets out an overview of the themes and problems; explores theoretical justifications and challenges in understanding data; considers data through the perspective of cognate private law doctrines; assesses the contribution of private law in understanding individual rights; and finally examines the potential of private law in providing individual remedies for wrongful data use, supplementing the work of regulators.

The contributors are specialists in their respective fields of private law with long-standing expertise in the challenges to data privacy posed by emerging digital technologies.

Volume 44 in the series Hart Studies in Private Law

Data and Private Law

Edited by
Damian Clifford
Kwan Ho Lau
and
Jeannie Marie Paterson

•HART•
OXFORD • LONDON • NEW YORK • NEW DELHI • SYDNEY

HART PUBLISHING

Bloomsbury Publishing Plc

Kemp House, Chawley Park, Cumnor Hill, Oxford, OX2 9PH, UK

1385 Broadway, New York, NY 10018, USA

29 Earlsfort Terrace, Dublin 2, Ireland

First published in Great Britain 2023

A catalogue record for this book is available from the British Library.

A catalogue record for this book is available from the Library of Congress.

Library of Congress Control Number: 2023942977

ISBN: HB: 978-1-50996-602-8
ePDF: 978-1-50996-604-2
ePub: 978-1-50996-603-5

Typeset by Compuscript Ltd, Shannon

FOREWORD

Ten years ago, V Mayer-Schonberger and K Cukier wrote that the 'era of big data challenges the way we live and interact with the world' (see V Mayer-Schonberger and K Cukier, *Big Data: A Revolution That Will Transform How We Live, Work and Think* (Boston, Houghton Mifflin Harcourt, 2013)). They began their book with the example of how, in 2009, Google was able to utilise search data and processing power to predict how a new flu virus, H1N1, spread in real-time. In particular, Google found that a combination of 45 search terms on the flu, when used together in a mathematical model, provided a strong predictor on where the virus had spread. In other words, Google's method was built on big data. This refers to society's ability to harness the information in novel ways to produce significant insights or products.

Viewed in 2023, Mayer-Schonberger and Cukier's example has turned out to be highly prescient. This is because, less than ten years later, at the height of the COVID-19 pandemic, scientists and health workers turned to big data to help them in their fight against the virus. They used big data to track the virus globally and came up with strategies to stop its spread.

Framed in this manner, it is almost intuitive to think only about the benefits that big data brings to society, as opposed to the risks of various kinds of harm. This may also explain why, when it comes to addressing the harms arising from the use of big data, the response has tended to be regulatory. There may be a sense that, given the large-scale impact that big data can have on society, any curtailment of the risks it brings should come from legislation as opposed to piecemeal development by the common law courts.

This collection of essays, helmed by three outstanding scholars in the field, Damian Clifford, Kwan Ho Lau, and Jeannie Marie Paterson, is therefore an important contribution to the question of whether private law doctrines can be adequately applied to transactions and interactions that concern data, as well as demands for data protection. As the editors rightly point out, the increasing patchwork of regulatory responses to the risks posed by big data clearly necessitates a transversal analysis. Private law, fueled by its conceptual structures and ability to respond swiftly to novel situations, may well be a worthy contender for facilitating such an analysis. However, private law is often not seen as a viable response except in discrete issues such as whether property rights should be attached to cryptoassets as a form of data. Marshalling expertise from distinguished experts from around the world, the editors and contributors are to be congratulated for an outstanding contribution to this larger question around the proper relationship between data rights and private law.

Building on this larger question, this collection explores five important and related themes, namely, (a) the capacity of private law to respond to the pervasive challenge of personal data and the technologies informed by that data, (b) the values and assumptions brought to the analysis of private law and data, (c) the interrelated or networked nature of the legal interventions in the field, (d) the ongoing need to embed law reform in the practical realities of access to justice and the balance with broader social goals, and (e) the question of regulatory design, such as the relationship between statutory and general law concepts, as well as the appropriate regulatory focus. These are all important themes and each deserves careful consideration. For example, in relation to the capacity of private law to respond to big data, the collection benefits from a characteristically thought-provoking chapter by Roger Brownsword, who frames this inquiry as a choice between 'regulatory' and 'coherentist' approaches to the law. More to that, whether private law can even respond coherently and clearly to data is an issue that divides the essays in this collection. It is impossible for me to do justice to the sheer breadth of expertise seen in the essays, nor should I attempt to do so. It suffices to say that it is a true mark of excellence in a collection to see the essays engaging with each other, whether intended or not, and the editors bringing them together by identifying clear themes for the reader to ponder about. On that count, and many others, this is truly a remarkable collection.

On a more personal note, I am delighted to see this collection in print. I am grateful to Damian and Jeannie for approaching me to collaborate on this project in early 2021. While the project faced its fair share of challenges posed by the COVID-19 pandemic, it is clear that the tenacity of private law scholars to debate the relevance of their work on an issue of our time knows no bounds. It is wonderful to see the fruition of this excellent book, and I am equally grateful to the editors for still giving me a voice in this collection by their generous invitation to pen this foreword.

Goh Yihan
Judge of the High Court
Supreme Court of Singapore

ACKNOWLEDGEMENTS

This book is a culmination of the efforts of many.

Beginning with initial drafts that were subsequently discussed and refined over two workshops, one conducted virtually and the other in hybrid format, we witnessed the intellectual nous of our stellar contributors at every turn. Each of them was unfailingly constructive and punctual. It has been a delight and privilege to work with them.

In addition to our contributors, the workshop discussants included Professor (now Justice) Goh Yihan and Professor TT Arvind. Their incisive commentary on various chapters has undoubtedly made this collection a better one. We express our gratitude to Justice Goh also for kindly agreeing to pen the Foreword.

That this book was published owes much to the team at Hart Publishing. Thanks are due to Victoria Broom for her careful editing work, as well as Tom Adams, Sasha Jawed, Sinead Moloney and Peter Warren for shepherding the process so efficiently. The chapters were also excellently handled in draft by Liam Harding at Melbourne Law School and Niamh Brazil at the ANU College of Law. Ashley Rogge lent invaluable assistance in the organising of the workshops.

We wish also to acknowledge our respective institutions. This project involving a talented group of scholars could not have flourished without the support, both tangible and intangible, shown to us by the ANU College of Law, the SMU Yong Pung How School of Law and Melbourne Law School. The resulting book is a testament to their vision and encouragement.

Finally, reflecting the contemporary nature of the debates at the centre of this collection, while it was in press the Australian Government published their responses to the Attorney General's review of the Federal *Privacy Act* 1988 (Cth). The government's responses include proposals to reform the Act but also agreement *in principle* to introduce statutory tort for serious invasions of privacy and a direct right of action to permit individuals to apply to the courts for relief in relation to an interference with privacy. The development underlines the importance of the contributions in this collection to private law scholars and also to policymakers navigating the complex intersections between statutory interventions and general law doctrines.

Damian Clifford
ANU College of Law, Australian National University

Kwan Ho Lau
Yong Pung How School of Law, Singapore Management University

Jeannie Marie Paterson
Melbourne Law School, The University of Melbourne

CONTENTS

LIST OF CONTRIBUTORS

Samuel (Shmuel) Becher Professor, Victoria University of Wellington

Roger Brownsword Professor, King's College London and Bournemouth University

Lee A Bygrave Professor, Norwegian Research Centre for Computers and Law, University of Oslo

Damian Clifford Senior Lecturer in Law, The Australian National University

Niva Elkin-Koren Professor, Tel-Aviv University

Jelena Gligorijevic Senior Lecturer in Law, The Australian National University

Kwan Ho Lau Assistant Professor, Singapore Management University

Eoin O'Dell Fellow and Associate Professor of Law, Trinity College Dublin

Jeannie Marie Paterson Professor of Consumer Protection Law, Director, Centre for Artificial Intelligence and Digital Ethics, The University of Melbourne

Maayan Perel Assistant Professor, Netanya Academic College School of Law

Andelka Phillips Senior Lecturer in Law, Science and Technology, University of Queensland and Research Affiliate HeLEX Centre, University of Oxford

Chris Reed Professor of Electronic Commerce Law, Queen Mary University of London

Megan Richardson Professor, ARC Centre for Automated Decision Making and Society, Melbourne Law School, University of Melbourne

Jerrold Soh Assistant Professor, Centre for Computational Law Yong Pung How School of Law, Singapore Management University

Ohad Somech Post-Doctoral Fellow, Tel-Aviv University

Kim Weatherall Professor, ARC Centre for Automated Decision Making and Society, University of Sydney and Fellow of the Gradient Institute

Sally Wheeler Professor of Law, Business and Society, The Australian National University

Normann Witzleb Associate Professor, The Chinese University of Hong Kong

TABLE OF CASES

TABLE OF LEGISLATION

Australia

Canada

China

European Union

International

Ireland

Hong Kong

Japan

New Zealand

Singapore

United Kingdom

United States

PART I

Introduction

1

Introduction to Data and Private Law

DAMIAN CLIFFORD,* KWAN HO LAU**
AND JEANNIE MARIE PATERSON***

I. Introduction

In our everyday lives, we leave a stream of data behind. From when our phone alarm goes off in the morning, to the messages and emails we send during the day, our supermarket shopping, the use of our service station loyalty card, and the takeaway we buy using our phones on the way home, our everyday movements and activities leave digital traces.[1] These traces may be valuable to a range of public and private sector entities as they reveal detailed insights into our behaviours and interests.[2] Insights are derived through the use of algorithms to aggregate diverse datasets and create digital profiles.[3] This intensive data processing brings benefits. However, the vast amounts of data generated, and the ubiquitous surveillance of our everyday lives, raise risks of various forms of harm.[4]

Concerns about both public and private uses of personal data are well established. Privacy and data protection legislation emerged in an era of socio-economic change and was a response to public concerns regarding the increasing digitalisation of our everyday lives from the second half of the twentieth century onwards.[5] More recently,

* Senior Lecturer, Australian National University.
** Assistant Professor, Singapore Management University.
*** Professor, University of Melbourne.

[1] On the ubiquity of data see: V Mayer-Schonberger and K Cukier, *Big Data: A Revolution That Will Transform How We Live, Work and Think* (Boston, Houghton Mifflin Harcourt, 2013).

[2] S Zuboff, *The Age of Surveillance Capitalism: The Fight for a Human Future at the New Frontier of Power* (New York, Hachette Book Group, 2019).

[3] See: P Quinn and G Malgieri, 'The Difficulty of Defining Sensitive Data – the Concept of Sensitive Data in the EU Data Protection Framework' (2021) 22 *German Law Journal* 1583; D Clifford, M Richardson and N Witzleb, 'Artificial Intelligence and Sensitive Inferences: New Challenges for Data Protection Laws' in M Findlay et al (eds), *Regulatory Insights on Artificial Intelligence: Research for Policy* (Cheltenham, Edward Elgar, 2022).

[4] For a discussion see: R Calo, 'The Boundaries of Privacy Harm' (2011) 86 *Indiana Law Journal* 1131.

[5] For a more elaborate discussion see: LA Bygrave, *Data Protection Law: Approaching Its Rationale, Logic and Limits* (The Hague, Kluwer Law International, 2002) ch 6.

similar concerns have emerged (or perhaps just re-emerged) and crystallised in the public consciousness given the widespread and seemingly increasing reliance on data. Repeated scandals and the rapid development of technology and business models reliant on intensive data processing have thrust data protection and privacy issues to the fore, and produced a suite of law reform proposals and inquiries.[6] Moreover, the speed of development of artificial intelligence ('AI') technologies, and the increasingly ubiquity of AI in business, government and social spheres, means that the data collected from individuals may be put to new and previously unimagined ends.[7]

The regulation of data (mis)use is, therefore, of paramount importance in mitigating the risks of harm to individuals and communities linked to the emergence of the digital economy. In recent years, law and policy debates have largely focused on how data protection/privacy legislation can and should be adopted or updated to respond to these risks. Indeed, the data protection/privacy rhetoric has seemingly subsumed the alternative, or at least supplementary and intersecting, inquiries into more substantive controls over data processing and use. In particular, the adoption of the General Data Protection Regulation (GDPR)[8] in the European Union and the reforms it introduced have set a legislative trend that has been followed across the world.[9] There is a mammoth literature elucidating the precise interpretation of legislative accountability mechanisms that such statutory instruments often contain. Here reference can be made to notions such as data protection/privacy by default and by design, and statutory tools such as the requirement to conduct a data protection/privacy impact assessment as particularly apt examples.

Far less has been written about the application of private law doctrines to transactions and interactions concerning data, and demands for data protection. Indeed, we would suggest that the application of private law to this domain has been drastically under-explored. This might be explained by the fact that expertise often exists in siloes, with experts sometimes failing to discuss the overlaps and gaps that may or may not exist and consider *intra*-disciplinary questions. Traditionally, the governance of digital technologies in the context of data has primarily been the domain of regulatory theorists and human rights lawyers interested in privacy, data protection and freedom of expression issues. Yet this kind of discipline focus has been changing. Given the increasing digitalisation of the marketplace, other areas of regulatory intervention, such as in consumer law and labour law, have evolved to consider companies' uses of data and the effects of individual rights and availability of remedies. This increasingly diverse patchwork of regulatory responses clearly requires a transversal analysis, and we suggest that an important part of this analysis must include recognition of the role played by

[6] In Australia for instance reference can be made to: Australian Competition and Consumer Commission, 'Digital Platforms Inquiry – Final Report' (2019); Attorney General's Department, 'Review of the Privacy Act 1988 (Cth) – Issues Paper' (Australian Government, 2020); Attorney General's Department, 'Review of the Privacy Act 1988 – Discussion Paper' (Australian Government, 2021).

[7] For example, at the time of writing, ChatGPT, an AI chatbot, has captured media and public attention.

[8] Regulation (EU) 2016/679 of the European Parliament and of the Council of 27 April 2016 on the protection of natural persons with regard to the processing of personal data and on the free movement of such data, and repealing Directive 95/46/EC (General Data Protection Regulation) [2016] OJ L119/1.

[9] See: G Greenleaf, 'Global Data Privacy Laws: 89 Countries, and Accelerating' (Queen Mary School of Law Legal Studies Research Paper No 98/2012); G Greenleaf, 'Countries with Data Privacy Laws – By Year 1973–2019' (10 May 2019); G Greenleaf, 'Now 157 Countries: Twelve Data Privacy Laws in 2021/22' (2022) 176 *Privacy Laws & Business International Report* 1, 3–8.

private law. We hope this work contributes to encouraging such a debate. The contributors to this volume provide different views on the role of and potential for private law in responding to the potential benefits and risks of harm arising from the collection and use of data. But the overall contribution, we hope, is to show that private law is at the least worthy of serious consideration, and may even make a significant contribution, in understanding how the law responds to data protection and the need for reform in this field.

II. Statute, Private Law and Data

The challenges raised by the increasing reliance on data and the exponential growth of data driven technologies have foregrounded the relationship between statute and private law in providing a response to new concerns about fundamental rights, and both interpersonal and transactional relationships. The answer cannot be as simple as assuming that legislation is needed to fill some void left by private law, or that private law will again prove its adaptability to new challenges. Rather we suggest the relationship is more complex.

Private law and statute relevant to data do not operate in isolation – they are not 'oil and water' in Beatson's terms.[10] They operate in tandem, and in ways that are often, although not always, complementary. Statutory regimes have an overt goal of influencing and even controlling the behaviour of the entities they regulate. The primary functions of private law are recognising, protecting and vindicating individual rights, and through this, have a secondary effect in influencing the on-going behaviour of those subject to its rules and principles. Moreover, private law concepts inform the statutory regimes, and the converse is also possible, with statute influencing the development of private law.[11] Private law is therefore a core part of the regulatory landscape. This collection aims to ask what private law may have to say about data protection, and also explore how private law may supplement and inform the application and even the form of legislation dealing with data.

Private law is the law of relationships between natural and/or legal persons and, beyond contract and tort, its boundaries may be elusive or disputed. The chapters in this work primarily focus on contract and tort, as well as intellectual property. We have not aimed for prescriptive coverage. Rather our aim has been to provide different perspectives on, and even challenges to, conventional assumptions about the divide between statute and private law regulating data or, at least, that private law may not be relevant to a field that is increasingly covered by a prescriptive statutory regime. For instance, we are interested in the way in which contract and tort doctrines may provide a way of illuminating the limitations on consent as a protective mechanism, notwithstanding its expanded requirements in these statutes, and promoting conversations about the

[10] J Beatson, 'The Role of Statute in the Development of Common Law Doctrine' (2001) 117 *LQR* 247, 259.

[11] E Bant, 'Statute and Common Law: Interaction and Influence in Light of the Principle of Coherence' (2015) 38 *University of New South Wales Law Journal* 367. See also A Burrows, 'The Relationship between Common Law and Statute in the Law of Obligations' (2012) 128 *LQR* 231.

boundaries of acceptable data use. And, when speaking about invasions of privacy, we are interested, for instance, in whether something can be learned from the various tests that courts have applied in the context of privacy torts to determine whether there has been an interference with privacy when interpreting protective statutes.

In our view at least, too often private law is not presented as a viable response to developments in data analytics, which fuels machine learning and other algorithmic processes, and is dismissed as irrelevant. Our intuition, which we seek to test in this work, is that private law provides a groundwork on concepts and a normative framework for addressing the challenges posed by emerging technologies in society. Equally, with only some limited exceptions, the proliferation of technology and the increasing awareness of its impact has been considered by private law scholars at the margins and/or in the context of some high-profile exceptions. Reference here for instance can be made to the debates and court judgments in various jurisdictions on whether property rights should be attached to crypto-assets as a form of data.[12] This is a specific example where commercial interests have driven scholarly consideration of a doctrinally thorny question. Smart contracts and electronic bills of lading and how they map (or do not map) onto existing contract law doctrines represent another instantiation.[13]

But these examples can be seen more as exceptions rather than the rule. They are also illustrations of an analysis that is directed by the challenges posed by a specific technology rather than a clear inquiry into the status of data in a more abstract sense. In contrast, this collection aims to leave such technology-orientated debates to one side to consider data more specifically. Our discussion is therefore not framed through the lens of a particular innovation and its associated socio-economic challenges. Instead, our focus is on the data that is generated by, fed through, stored on, or in some other manner processed by, a range of technologies that are often referred to through simplified buzzwords – ie AI, Blockchain, etc. The collection leaves the buzzwords to one side and instead interrogates how rights over data may be provided, recognised and protected by private law. Our view is that making particular technologies the regulatory target may prove futile given the speed of technological change. Data is the fuel of new digital technologies and so may itself be a potentially fruitful site of regulation.

Often the benchmark for data protection legislation is the comprehensive and far reaching GDPR. However, despite its prominence and scope, this regime does not remove the need for other perspectives. It is also important to acknowledge that, although comparable developments have been evident in many common law jurisdictions, not all countries have data protection/privacy legislation in place. Even when they do, there are still gaps in the scope of the statutory regimes. Moreover, even under the GDPR there remain areas of debate and uncertainty. For example, there has been an ongoing debate regarding the focus on, and overlaps between, 'consent' and 'contract' as conditions for

[12] See A Ray, D Clifford and H Roberts, 'Digital Assets as Property and the Challenges of Forced Judicial Activism' (2023) 12 *Modern Studies in Property Law* (forthcoming 2023).

[13] See S Wheeler, 'The possibilities of IF-THEN-WHEN' in M Findlay et al, *Regulatory Insights on Artificial Intelligence* (Cheltenham, Edward Elgar, 2022); P Todd, 'Electronic Bills of Lading, Blockchains and Smart Contracts' (2019) 27 *International Journal of Law and Information Technology* 339; F Wang, 'Blockchain Bills of Lading and Their Future Regulation' [2021] *Lloyd's Maritime and Commercial Law Quarterly* 504.

the lawful processing of personal data in the GDPR, and the performance of the GDPR in counteracting the effects of the asymmetric data processing environment.[14] There has also been ongoing discussion of the efficacy of other models, drawn from private law concepts such as the 'trust', for protecting the data rights of individuals. There are continuing discussions about the scope of both individual and collective responses to data harms, and the nature of relief in these circumstances. Reference can also be made to the role of privacy torts and breach of confidence as an equitable doctrine (under-explored in many jurisdictions) and the complementary roles these may play alongside (or arguably as a substitute for) data protection legislation in particular circumstances where there has been an interference with one's privacy. Our task is to better elucidate the role of private law to inform such discussions. This collection represents a forum for such discussions; we are fortunate to have assembled a stellar team of contributors, and are delighted by the diverse range of topics and themes explored.

III. The Themes

Engagement with data provides a way of thinking about the agility and currency of private law in responding to technological change. If you are not entirely convinced by this statement, then rest assured that neither are some of our contributors! One key theme of the collection indeed concerns the capacity of private law to respond to the pervasive challenge of personal data and the technologies informed by that data. We, as editors, are optimistic as to the role of private law doctrine in adapting to and addressing these issues. We are not alone in this view but nor are we in the majority. Roger Brownsword, in chapter two, for instance, opens the collection by framing the inquiry as requiring a choice between regulatory and coherentist approaches to the law. He argues that although we should not neglect private law given its obvious application to data rights debates, we need to be aware of its limits. The challenge, or critique, posed by Brownsword is that private law thinking tends to be, in his words, 'coherentist' in nature. This characteristic makes private law inappropriate to govern technological developments because the concern with coherence, over innovative regulatory responses, makes it unable to engage with the regulatory challenges posed. Brownsword concludes that we need 'regulatory', as opposed to 'coherentist' thinking to address the challenges of data driven technologies, which is a perspective found primarily in statute not private law. This view does not ignore the responsive flexibility of private law. Rather, Brownsword (and also in different ways, Lee Bygrave (chapter 4), Chris Reed (chapter 7) and Sally Wheeler (chapter 3)) is profoundly aware of the constitutional challenges posed by big tech and big data, which require legal responses that are directly policy based and democratically accountable. Nonetheless, we suggest that in addressing the harms to individuals and possible distortions in the market presented by the use of data and data driven technologies, private law remains credible, and viable. Moreover, private law

[14] D Clifford and J Paterson, 'Consumer Privacy and Consent: Reform in the Light of Contract and Consumer Protection Law' (2020) 94 *Australian Law Journal* 741, 749; W Hartzog, 'Opinions · The Case Against Idealising Control' (2018) 4 *European Data Protection Law Review* 423.

is inescapably relevant in informing and complementing more overtly policy driven statutory regimes.

The ability of private law to respond coherently and clearly in relation to data is a theme that continues throughout the collection, with contributors standing on both sides of the divide. Reed, for instance, believes that private law could be used to structure dispute resolution mechanisms, as statutory interventions for a number of reasons are doomed to failure. Reed uses examples of mechanisms created by e-commerce platforms such as eBay to resolve small consumer disputes, to question whether similar mechanisms could be relied upon to address the privacy and consumer protection concerns evident online. He concludes that although there is no conceptual reason why these mechanisms should not develop to control data collection, use and sharing, their development would come at a cost and that, therefore, their adoption depends on whether the cost-benefit calculus alters to render them of commercial interest to the intermediaries he identifies. Despite this qualification, Reed appears optimistic as to the potential for these mechanisms even if he remains unsure of whether we have reached a time when their development is likely.

Jelena Gligorijevic in chapter 9 too seemingly sees less of a distinct role for the statutory frameworks and argues that the various privacy torts recognised by the courts in different common law jurisdictions offer more doctrinal coherence and normative force in responding to intrusions of privacy or the misuses of personal data, than do statutory protections like the GDPR. Her argument is that compared to data protection legislation, tort law may have the capacity to offer, in her words, 'clearer, more internally coherent, and better protection for individuals' informational privacy', but at the very least offers a valuable additional means of protection. She understands the privacy tort to be normatively anchored in terms of its application and evolution with its scope determined by the value of individual privacy, and for these reasons concludes that it may be superior to data protection legislation.

Gligorijevic therefore seems to stand in opposition to Brownsword who, to reiterate, argues that the preoccupation with coherence may prevent private law in particular from dealing squarely with the public policy decisions inherent in attempting to regulate or respond to the uses of personal data for business purposes. Integral to Brownsword's argument is the discussion of the role of the courts, judicial restraint, and the legislature, in that he contends that the courts have neither the resources nor the mandate for expansive lawmaking or for setting new policies.

Turning to a specific context, Niva Elkin-Koren, Maayan Perel and Ohad Somech in chapter eight appear more open to the court's role in matters of public policy. The authors demonstrate the role social media platforms currently play in regulating the availability of the data that they collect, host and process and its ensuing impact on scientific research and innovation. In doing so, the authors explore the financial and reputational reasons why these platforms limit access and the mechanisms they employ (both technical and contractual) and suggest that these actions often exceed what is within the legitimate scope of legal protection. Elkin-Koren, Perel and Somech argue that this is contrary to the public interest in facilitating academic research and propose the use of common law contract doctrines pertaining to the enforcement and interpretation of contracts to advance a right of research as a response to the issues presented.

Damian Clifford and Jeannie Marie Paterson in chapter 5 fall somewhat in the middle of the coherentist/regulatory divide, seeing private law and the regulatory aspects of statute as performing different but commonly complementary roles. They explore the role of contract in grounding the key concepts used by legislative interventions, as a means of providing normative guidance on the role and the limits of individual consent in regulating data transactions. Clifford and Paterson consider the emerging debate regarding the intersection and alignment between data protection and consumer law in the protection of individual choices regarding data and what the authors refer to as the 'series of assumptions' as to the existence of a valid contractual relationship underpinning these debates.

Such assumptions reflect the second of our overlapping themes relating to the values and assumptions brought to the analysis of private law and data. For instance, Clifford and Paterson use the assumed existence of a contract to frame their discussion of the interface between common law contract doctrines and data rights to conclude that much is to be gained from an analysis that recognises the complementary functionalities of contract law, consumer law and data protection and privacy law. Samuel Becher and Andelka Phillips in chapter 6 explore the potential for these complementary functionalities through the lens of a specific case study: the market for personal genomics as a service industry posing several hidden risks, failures and challenges for private law. More specifically, the authors examine the complexity and sensitivity of this market and explore the potential legal and policy implications calling for regulatory intervention in the form of a Consumer Data Right. At the centre of Becher and Phillips' chapter are the challenges presented by frameworks structured in terms of notice and choice. Clifford and Paterson also address these concerns by focusing on the individualist/transactional rhetoric of private law generally and contract law in particular as legitimising a market-based perspective on data and avoiding confronting hierarchies or power and information that underlie this model. Although accepting such concerns, ultimately Clifford and Paterson suggest that a focus on empowering individual decision-making has a valuable role, albeit, importantly, where complemented and strengthened by statutory interventions that address abuses of bargain power and substantive unfairness.

Sally Wheeler also challenges the transactional approach to the debate, cutting across both regulatory and coherentist approaches as understood by Brownsword. Wheeler brings the work of Ian Macneil on relational contract and Actor Network Theory, as developed in Science and Technology Studies in the late 1980s in the work of Bruno Latour and John Law, together to explore the transfer and licensing of data through the lens of contract law. Her analysis offers a broader perspective than a conventional contract law or legal theory analysis allows and aims to provide a different angle on the relationships involved. Wheeler argues that Actor Network Theory offers relational contract in what she refers to as a much 'thicker' description of a relationship and its constituent elements, thereby allowing us to appreciate the constellations of actors, values/norms, practices and rules across the spectrum that are relevant throughout the lifecycle of our data. She concludes that this description creates the space to consider new approaches to data acquisition and use.

Another contribution illustrating these (understudied) assumptions and notions of contract and consent comes from Bygrave, who compellingly shows how contract, and the values it represents as both an ideological and legal tool, underlie much of the regulation in the field, ranging from governance of critical internet resources such as the domain name registration system and the interconnection arrangements at the core of the internet's 'backbone' to the variety of cloud services and social media platforms we rely on and use as consumers. He analyses the various functions that contracts play in order to demonstrate the downstream consequences, for instance in relation to the efforts to enhance accountability of governance mechanisms. In particular, Bygrave uses Meta's Oversight Board as a case study to argue that: (1) contract is a popular means of transnational private regulation because of its capacity to manage complexity, (2) there is a tendency to exploit this capacity aggressively, and consequently, (3) the accountability mechanisms are often weak and this affects their legitimacy.

Taking a slightly different approach, but still interrogating the assumptions about the scope and role of private law, Kimberlee Weatherall in chapter 12 explains that there is nothing fundamental about data that renders it impossible to 'propertise' given that property and, more specifically for the purposes of the chapter, that intellectual property is a highly malleable concept. To reach this conclusion, Weatherall systematically analyses the core objections to arguments in favour of property rights being attached to data and explains how the history and structure of copyright more specifically may provide important lessons. Importantly, she does not advocate for intellectual property rights in data, not because it is 'too hard' a subject matter or that intellectual property rights have specific characteristics, but because it is not the right frame of reference and does not effectively address key questions that new technologies of data use pose regarding the distribution of benefits. In doing so, Weatherall challenges the assumptions made in arguments against recognising intellectual property rights in data to more accurately frame the issue as one involving debates as to the appropriateness of intellectual property as a regulating response to the power imbalances we see today. Weatherall convincingly concludes that, even if they could be used, IP models do not offer useful resolutions for most pressing data challenges we face and that we should instead confront these challenges directly.

A third theme is the interrelated or networked nature of the legal interventions in this field. On one view the mix of statute and private law doctrine applying to data and governing data rights presents problems of coherence – and we should adopt a consistently regulatory stance, or at least be more imaginative about the role that private law might perform. Certainly, a number of the chapters showcase the potential for private law to respond to concerns about data protection and access, as well as to privacy invasions and misuse.

Megan Richardson in chapter 11, for instance, examines the role of the equitable doctrine of breach of confidence and argues that the doctrine is capable of acting as an important rights-protecting doctrine both now and in the future. She convincingly claims that if the doctrine is treated in a progressive manner it would reflect two important features of modernity: first, a clear focus on individuals or arguably groups and second, an acknowledgement that the seemingly indelible social order is a social construct that is capable of change. Richardson builds her argument while also charting the historical development of the doctrine to conclude that, if construed in a flexible manner and adapted where necessary, breach of confidence has the capacity to function in conditions of uncertainty and risk while offering significant protection for data rights in the digital age.

Jerrold Soh in chapter 13 also demonstrates the potential adaptability of private law and analyses the timely question of whether dataset providers should be held to owe duties of care to victims when the output of machine learning algorithms causes harm arising from errors in the training data. Soh uses the ImageNet dataset and the Generative Pre-trained Transformer (GPT) family of language models as case studies to argue that the common approach of centralising duties on system providers alone provides insufficient safeguards, and that dataset-specific duties should be seriously considered in order to incentivise effective precautionary steps to be taken in the preparation of a crucial machine learning input. He examines how dataset duties may be encompassed within existing tort law and thus how specific duties are more likely to be established. Soh concludes that although not all dataset providers should owe all potential victims duties of care, imposing duties of care in certain circumstances would plug a liability gap.

The need for progressive interpretation is, therefore, a common suggestion and so are calls for judicious reform, albeit while still working within the parameters of the existing law. Eoin O'Dell in chapter 10 for instance explores this in his analysis of the role for private enforcement in the context of data breaches, focusing on the tort of negligence as a means of protecting privacy interests in particular. O'Dell focuses on the failure of negligence claims in England and Wales following data breaches due to the statutory policy bar, ie the perception that there is neither room nor a need for a concurrent duty in negligence when there is a bespoke statutory regime for determining the liability of those processing personal data. O'Dell argues that the mere existence of a statutory cause of action should not automatically bar a negligence claim, that such a bar is illogical if other common law claims are not barred by statute (eg the tort for the misuse of private information), and that the absence of the threat of negligence claims removes an additional incentive to implement appropriate measures against breaches.

We note the pace of law reform is slow and it may be that even the coherence in the law is prompted by regulatory intervention to fill gaps and to clarify the reach of private law to more controversial applications. However, many of the contributors recognise and approve of the complementary operation of statutory and private law regimes (although as noted above some would prefer giving different emphasis to regulatory/statutory opportunities). Reference here can be made to the contribution of Becher and Phillips and their argument that, in addition to the need to utilise existing laws to improve the regulation of the personal genomics industry, there is a need to develop and implement a Consumer Data Right to improve the protection of consumers' autonomy and control, but also for instance to Normann Witzleb's contribution to this collection in chapter 14.

Witzleb provides a comparative analysis of direct rights of action in data protection regimes and relevant leading cases in a number of jurisdictions such as the EU, the US, China, Canada and Singapore. Direct rights of action are an integral part of data protection enforcement but Witzleb argues that they must be carefully designed to avoid interpretative uncertainty and to make clear what elements need to be established by the claimants and the type of relief that is available. Witzleb uses the example of Australia and the ongoing discussions there regarding the reform of the *Privacy Act* 1988 (Cth) as a case study to emphasise the significance of these points. He further points out that even with a well-drafted direct right of action, most individuals will be reliant on an accessible and effective complaints-based process.

A fourth theme is the ongoing need to embed law reform in the practical realities of access to justice and the balance with broader social goals. Elkin-Koren, Perel and Somech remind us of the value of data for research, while Weatherall pertinently reminds us that questions of the scope of regimes commonly rest in values or policy-based decisions about how rights are framed. Reed brings us back to the practical relevance of dispute resolution, which he argues may work better within a private law system than outside it. O'Dell explains how the existence of a statutory regime may – but should not – act as a barrier to accessing an alternative negligence claim and Witzleb describes how an individual cause of action must be understood within the broader regulatory scheme and should not detract from the need to improve regulatory enforcement. Kwan Ho Lau in chapter 15 also considers remedies and in particular explores the monetary remedies that a claimant may pursue following an inference with their rights to data or what he refers to as a 'data rights incursion' and the hurdles that need to be overcome by claimants.

Lau argues that consideration of this topic requires the relevant policy considerations to be taken into account. After referring to two main hurdles to be overcome by claimants when pursuing relief following a data rights incursion, namely, the need to first establish that the loss or damage suffered is legally cognisable, and second, to prove that content of that loss or damage to a legally satisfactory standard, Lau considers how legal and public policy considerations have been treated in developing and refining causes of action to compensate for novel types of harms. Lau arrives at the conclusion that, in the context of data rights incursions, the relevant policy considerations justifying the development of common law rules surrounding recovery of damages are significant and pressing. Concerns stemming from the 'floodgates argument' should not entirely forestall recognition of other important considerations such as the vast and ever-increasing volume of data being collected and processed (thereby increasing the risk of misuse), as well as the realistic possibility that meaningful redress will be unavailable without further development also of the rules of recovery and civil procedure.

Finally, the collection touches on the question of regulatory design, such as the relationship between statutory and general law concepts, and, more generally the appropriate regulatory focus. This issue is particularly evident in Witzleb's insistence that direct rights of action must be seen within the broader regulatory landscape and should not detract from the need to improve the regulatory enforcement mechanisms more generally. Weatherall also addresses this point of regulatory focus and, as described above, argues that trying to incorporate rights to control data in copyright runs against the trend of authority. As copyright is arguably ill-suited to the questions of distributive justice, accountability or authenticity posed by new technologies, Weatherall argues that these fundamental questions are better confronted directly.

IV. Conclusions and Areas for Future Consideration

For their sheer diversity of perspective – and this arising from principally a study of private law in the common law tradition – it is neither possible nor ideal to capture the import, and importance, of the contributions to this volume in one neat summary. It was suggested earlier that an appreciation of both private law and statute was essential to understanding the appropriate legal responses to data issues as well as the direction reforms in this area may take. That our contributors have not alighted at precisely the same balance to be struck between private law and statute in ordering those responses is hardly surprising considering the relative infancy of the debate, the transversal nature of regulation of data and the jurisdictional orientation (both subject matter and geographic) of the contributors. Indeed, an express objective of the editors was to assemble a cast whom they could be reasonably confident would offer a tableau of perspectives to give shape to the overall discussion.

A few conclusions (some firm and others tentative) may nevertheless be drawn at this early juncture. The first is that there *are* substantive divergences in approach, as our contributors make clear, and lawmakers and regulators would be better off confronting and understanding the differences than ignoring them. This book should not however be taken to suggest that any one approach is necessarily more meritorious than another. In that spirit, we invite you, the reader, to take in the ideas in individual chapters but also to consider how they relate to orthogonal issues that may also feature in the relevant section.

Secondly, this volume gathers an array of viewpoints which, however beneficent and deeply held they may be, can of necessity form but a cross-section of the possible analyses and approaches. Again, the caution must be issued that any charting of a path forward should take all reasonable viewpoints into consideration in a measured process involving the relevant stakeholders. Legal regulation and enforcement – the broader question with which this collection of essays is concerned – are not the less dependent on the context and practices of a particular jurisdiction simply because it is the issue of data rights that is being discussed. As the present volume demonstrates, the time is ripe for sharper deliberation on the application and interaction of private law doctrine to and with data as well as data protection. The editors are confident that the views contained in the present volume offer a springboard for that important exercise.

Thirdly, legal concerns over the recognition, protection and enforcement of data rights are intrinsically tied to policymaking in an area of arguably overwhelming importance for a digitised world. On that point our contributors agree. But their analyses disclose a variety of approaches to accommodate and address such concerns, a kaleidoscope which has fallen from the hands of exponents of (mainly) just the common law. This last point is of course a crucial anchor point of the book – the aim was to examine the issues using the richness of private law doctrines in the common law. We are therefore cognisant that those concerns transcend borders and do not lose sight of the possibility that private law systems in civil law jurisdictions have a number of lessons to offer as well.

Finally, allowing ourselves the luxury of future casting, what do we, the editors, consider to be the more pressing areas for future research? Certainly, there is a need for continued scrutiny of general law and statutory regimes, and the interaction between them; after all there are limits to what this collection could hope to achieve in light of the complex and varied issues at stake despite our excellent contributors. We believe that this collection has certainly demonstrated the value of exploring the challenges posed by technology in a transversal manner. The analyses of the complex socio-economic issues focused on in this collection require an approach that cuts across the inter and intra-disciplinary barriers to incorporate insights from a range of disciplines but also common law private law and, for instance, rights-based protections such as those provided in statutes like the GDPR. This requires scholars to stretch beyond their comfort zones and the traditional siloes in order to appreciate the role and value of different areas of research and types of regulatory interventions (and what they aim to safeguard).

Ultimately, we embrace an approach that recognises that no one intervention will be sufficient to address the many concerns in this field. The challenge for future research, as this collection demonstrates, is rather to recognise the different purposes of the varied private law and statutory regimes and to coordinate these regimes for a pluralist but effective network of responses. For instance, in recent years there has been an ongoing discussion regarding the value of consent in technology regulation. Various contributions in this collection have pointed to the challenges associated with its meaningful operation, but they have also shown that there is a rich body of private law literature incorporating both theoretical[15] and behavioural insights[16] to draw upon. These insights make it obvious that the issues with consent are not a new phenomenon, and that we have much to learn from private law and the statutory interventions that have been adopted, particularly in consumer law, to render consent more meaningful in the context of the provision of a whole range of consumer goods and services. What often goes missing in the more recent discussion regarding the regulation of decisions to give up data and, for example, 'dark patterns' as a shorthand phrase that has emerged to describe manipulative design, is that the law has been responding to these issues in pre-digitalisation form for decades.

Therefore, we need an approach to the regulation of technology that is mindful of history and its lessons. We also believe there is a tendency to see each new technology or alleged abuse of commercial power as novel, requiring new interventions that, if acted upon, would lead to reams of the new legislation with complex defining concepts, uncertain overlaps and navigational difficulties. Recent policymaking developments in the EU, and the explosion of internal market-making legislative proposals, that have emerged in the last few years are an important example of this concern.[17] To be clear,

[15] See Sally Wheeler discussing relational contract theory in chapter 3 of this volume.

[16] See Samuel Becher and Andelka Phillips, and Damian Clifford and Jeannie Paterson in chapters 6 and 5 respectively.

[17] See the proposed AI Act (Commission, 'Proposal of the European Parliament and of the Council Laying Down Harmonised Rules on Artificial Intelligence (Artificial Intelligence Act) and Amending Certain Union Legislative Acts' COM (2021) 206 final); Digital Services Act (Regulation (EU) 2022/2065 of the European Parliament and of the Council of 19 October 2022 on a Single Market for Digital Services and amending Directive 2000/31/EC (Digital Services Act) [2022] OJ L277/1); Digital Markets Act (Regulation (EU) 2022/1925 of the European Parliament and of the Council of 14 September 2022 on contestable and fair markets in the digital sector and amending Directives (EU) 2019/1937 and (EU) 2020/1828 (Digital Markets Act) [2022] OJ L265/1); Platform to Business Regulation (Regulation (EU) 2019/1150 of the European Parliament and of the Council of 20 June 2019 on promoting fairness and transparency for business users of online intermediation services [2019] OJ L186/57); updates to the consumer law acquis in the Modernisation Directive (Directive (EU) 2019/2161 of the European Parliament and of the Council of 27 November 2019 amending Council Directive 93/13/EEC and Directives 98/6/EC, 2005/29/EC and 2011/83/EU of the European Parliament and of the Council as regards the better enforcement and modernisation of Union consumer protection rules [2019] OJ L328/7); the Digital Content Directive (Directive (EU) 2019/770 of the European Parliament and of the Council of 20 May 2019 on certain aspects concerning contracts for the supply of digital content and digital services [2019] OJ L136/1); and the GDPR, etc.

we certainly believe that statutory interventions are important and often required to respond to the complex challenges posed by computational systems. Our point rather is that interventions must be carefully and precisely designed. Moreover, they should recognise the value of private law (ie that the aspiration of private law is worth protecting), and that private law should be seen as an integral part of, and be integrated in, any such regulatory scheme.

A significant part of this role of private law relates to the protection of our ability to make choices. Both private law and statute aspire to protect choice, and we believe that this should not be abandoned in a wholesale manner, despite the apparent calls to hard code rules thus removing our ability to make mistakes in the digital environment. This is not to say that the status quo is desirable or that there are no circumstances in which statute should provide more paternalistic black letter rules limiting or banning some forms of market conduct. The spectrum of responses between the empowerment of individuals and their safeguarding through paternalistic interventions should carefully toe a line when imposing limits. We believe that there is a need for future research exploring this spectrum of statutory responses to concerns about data harms, and the rationale behind the more extreme responses lying between no regulation and hardline bans. Our task as scholars is to research and recognise these problems and propose appropriately designed regulatory solutions.

V. How this Book is Organised

The collection begins with an examination of the theoretical justifications and challenges in understanding data rights, along with the role of private law in protecting such rights. The opening section is comprised of two thought-provoking chapters.

In chapter 2, Roger Brownsword starts our analysis with a rather bold (and perhaps for our readers, unexpected) thesis that private law is not the future in the governance by, and the governance of, technologies. Brownsword's contribution is then followed by Sally Wheeler who, in chapter 3, explores in novel ways the transfer and licensing of data.

Building on this first section, the next section then considers data rights through the perspective of private law doctrine. It considers the contribution of private law in understanding individual rights, in the first place, to deal with data, and then secondly, as protection against the harmful use of data. There are five chapters in the section focused on rights to deal with data.

In chapter 4, Lee Bygrave analyses the effects of the regulatory role of contract given that it underpins much of the regulation of the internet, ranging from the critical internet resources to the variety of cloud services and social media platforms we rely on as consumers thus affecting the accountability of the actors involved. In chapter 5, Damian Clifford and Jeannie Paterson consider the protection of individual choices regarding data in data and consumer law and the circumstances in which a valid contractual relationship may be formed.

The focus of the collection then shifts to a more context specific analysis in chapter 6 where Samuel Becher and Andelka Phillips explore the risks associated with the market for personal genomics as a service industry and hence, the challenges for private law. In chapter 7, Chris Reed examines how the creation of private law mechanisms to provide independent oversight of data collection, use and sharing, may offer alternative and perhaps better regulatory outcomes in the balancing the rights and interests of both consumers and commercial entities. Niva Elkin-Koren, Maayan Perel and Ohad Somech then explore the importance of scientific research and innovation and the gatekeeping role played by social media platforms in regulating the availability of the data that they collect, host and process in chapter 8.

In the section focused on the protection against harmful uses of data, there are five chapters. In chapter 9, Jelena Gligorijevic examines the value of tort law in protecting data privacy. Gligorijevic explores the informational privacy torts that have developed across most common law jurisdictions as a means of both recognising and addressing interferences with data privacy. Eoin O'Dell explains how the existence of a statutory regime may act as a barrier to accessing an alternative negligence claim in chapter 10. He argues that a negligence claim should not be automatically barred by the mere existence of a statutory cause of action. In chapter 11, Megan Richardson examines the role of the equitable doctrine of breach of confidence and argues that the already quite modern doctrine has ongoing significance as an important rights-protecting doctrine.

The challenges presented by the use of data in terms of the risks posed and the uncertainties presented for existing frameworks is a theme shared with chapter 12. In this chapter, Kimberlee Weatherall explains that as intellectual property is a highly malleable concept, data is not fundamentally impossible to 'propertise', but ultimately she is not an advocate for IP rights in data. In chapter 13, Jerrold Soh analyses the timely question of whether duties of care should be owned by dataset providers to victims when errors in the training data lead the outputs of machine learning algorithms to cause harm.

In the last part of the book, the analysis explores the possibility of direct rights of redress for wrongful uses of data and the possibility of remedies and redress, supplementing the work of regulators in protecting data rights. Two chapters make up this final section. In chapter 14, Normann Witzleb comparatively analyses direct rights of action in data protection regimes and relevant leading cases in a number of jurisdictions. Finally, in chapter 15, Kwan Ho Lau explores various difficulties surrounding the monetary remedies that may be pursued by a claimant following a 'data rights incursion'.

PART II

Data and Private Law – Theoretical Insights

2

Private Law, Technology and Governance

ROGER BROWNSWORD*

I. Introduction

In the landscape of Law 3.0,[1] which is one of legal, regulatory and technological governance, what role is there for private law? How salient is private law and how significant is private law thinking in engaging technologies that might invite being subjected to governance but also to being deployed as instruments of governance?

While we should neither neglect the clear applications of private law nor underestimate the inspiration (and potential repurposing of concepts) to be drawn from its rich jurisprudence,[2] we should recognise its two principal limits. First, to the extent that private law thinking is 'coherentist' in its nature, it is not significant because it fails to engage squarely with the 'regulatory' challenge of ensuring that law's governance *of* technologies is fit for purpose. Second, to the extent that governance *by* technologies, whether deployed by public or private bodies, needs to be 'constitutionalised'[3] – that

* King's College London and Bournemouth University. In addition to being presented at the ANU workshops in 2021 and 2022, this chapter was the basis for a keynote lecture at a workshop on 'Private Law and New Technologies' that was held at King's College London in May 2022. I am grateful to participants at these workshops for their comments; I am also grateful to Hans-W Micklitz, Przemyslaw Palka, Agnieszka Jablonowska, Giovanni Sartor and other members of the EUI 'Claudette group' for valuable feedback on an earlier version of this chapter; and, last but by no means least, I am grateful to the editors for their various comments and suggestions on drafts of the chapter. Needless to say, the usual disclaimers apply.

[1] See, R Brownsword, *Law, Technology and Society: Reimagining the Regulatory Environment* (Abingdon, Routledge, 2019); R Brownsword, *Law 3.0: Rules, Regulation and Technology* (Abingdon, Routledge, 2020); and R Brownsword, *Rethinking Law, Regulation and Technology* (Cheltenham, Elgar, 2022).

[2] On the former, see, eg, R Brownsword, 'Regulatory Fitness: Fintech, Funny Money, and Smart Contracts' (2019) 20 *European Business Organization Law Review* 5. On the latter, famously, see S Warren and L Brandeis, 'The Right to Privacy' (1890) 5 *Harvard Law Review* 193; and for a recent example, see J Fairfield, *Runaway Technology* (New York, Cambridge University Press, 2021) 54–59 (concerning judicial development of the old idea of 'trespass' to apply in cyberspaces).

[3] Compare the introductory remarks in H Micklitz et al (eds), *Constitutional Challenges in the Algorithmic Society* (Cambridge, Cambridge University Press, 2021), where the editors say: 'The development of data collection, mining, and algorithmic analysis, resulting in predictive profiling – with or without the subsequent potential manipulation of attitudes and behaviours of users – presents unique challenges to constitutional law at the doctrinal as well as theoretical levels. … [To meet these challenges] requires either the redrawing of constitutional boundaries so as to subject digital platforms to constitutional law or a revisiting of the relationship between constitutional law and private law, including the duties of the state to regulate the cybernetic complex, within or outside the jurisdictional boundaries of the state.'. For elaboration of these introductory

is to say, needs to be properly authorised, limited, and licensed – then it is public law rather than private law that is salient.

This chapter elaborates three aspects of my view. I start by specifying my understanding of 'private law' and 'private law thinking' and, most importantly, the distinction between 'coherentist' and 'regulatory' thinking; then, I respond to what I anticipate will be objections to my claim that private law coherentism is not what we need for the governance of technologies; and, finally, I sketch what I see as the licensing conditions for both governance by, and the governance of, technologies.

II. Private Law and Private Law Thinking (Coherentist and Regulatory)

A reasonable response to the questions posed at the start of this chapter would be that it depends on what we mean by 'private law' and by 'private law thinking'. In this part of the chapter, I specify what I mean by 'private law', differentiate between 'coherentist' and 'regulatory' types of private law thinking, and identify four articulations of private law.

A. Private Law

I take it that 'private law' refers to a broad sweep of rules and principles that govern the relationship between citizens (and other legal persons) in civil society. Some might understand 'private law' as covering only 'contract, agency, bailment, tort, unjust enrichment and restitution, property, trusts and succession'[4] but I am not restricting it in this way.[5] Thus, unlike public law which applies to the 'vertical' relationship between nation states and their citizens, the focus of private law is 'horizontal'. Much of private law is found in historic codes and cases but, increasingly, it is found in legislation – such as data protection legislation[6] that sets out a code of governance for the civil society processing of personal data (where the central relationship is between, on the one side, data subjects and, on the other side, data controllers and data processors) and the proposed Regulation on Artificial Intelligence (AI) that the EU is now legislating.[7]

Typically, private law recognises a set of legitimate interests (in person and property, regarding personality, and so on), along with relevant rights, duties and permissions.

remarks, see O Pollicino and G De Gregorio, 'Introduction' in H Micklitz et al (eds), *Constitutional Law in the Algorithmic Society* (Cambridge, Cambridge University Press, 2021).

[4] See Law Commission, *Smart Legal Contracts: Advice to Government* (Law Com No 401, 2021) para 1.13, fn 7, referring to the Wales Act 2006, sch 7B, para 3(1).

[5] Compare S Grundmann, 'The Inside and the Outside of Law?' in S Grundmann, H Micklitz and M Renner (eds), *New Private Law Theory* (Cambridge, Cambridge University Press, 2021) 35, where 'private law' is also 'understood in a broad sense, encompassing questions of regulation and rule-setting in particular'.

[6] In the UK, this is the Data Protection Act 2018.

[7] European Commission, 'Proposal for a regulation of the European Parliament and of the Council laying down harmonised rules on artificial intelligence (Artificial Intelligence Act) and amending certain union legislative acts' COM (2021) 206 final. In many such statutory regulatory regimes, including data protection and consumer protection regimes, we find a combination of both private law compensatory and public law punitive provisions.

This represents, so to speak, the 'baseline' legal position. Where there is wrongdoing relative to these interests – for example, an act of unjust enrichment, or a breach of contract or confidence or copyright, or a breach of trust, or the commission of a tort – the function of private law is to restore the parties by reference to their baseline position (whether by reversing or rectifying the wrong or, in the case of contract, by protecting the innocent party's baseline expectation).

For present purposes, the key distinction to carry forward is that between private law that is judge-made and private law that is made by a legislative body.

B. Private Law Coherentist Thinking

Characteristically, legal reasoning in areas such as contracts, torts and property, where the rules are based on general principles and concepts, displays a pervasive concern with doctrinal coherence. To think like a private lawyer is to apply historic legal principles and rules to all situations, regardless of whether those situations involve novel technologies or applications.

Spelling this out, we can treat private law coherentist thinking as being defined by the following five characteristics. First, for coherentists, what matters above all is the integrity and internal consistency of legal doctrine. So, for example, in its report on smart contracts, the Law Commission adopts coherentist thinking when it rejects the idea that reference might be made to pre-contractual negotiations in order to assist with the interpretation of the coded terms of a smart legal contract. Quite simply, this 'would create an unprincipled distinction between the courts' approach to interpreting traditional contracts, and their approach to interpreting smart legal contracts'.[8] Second, coherentists are not concerned with the fitness of the law for its regulatory purpose. Third, coherentists approach new technologies by asking how they fit within existing legal categories – for example, developments in a number of technologies have raised questions about the way in which fundamental concepts and distinctions in property law map onto a range of 'things', such as detached human tissue, gametes, cryptoassets and, of course, personal data. Generally, coherentist thinking is marked by a reluctance to revise established classificatory schemes. Fourth, coherentists believe that legal reasoning should be anchored to guiding general principles of law. Fifth, coherentists assume that the function of private law, together with its guiding principles, is largely concerned with *ex post* correction and compensation.[9]

C. Regulatory Thinking

Regulatory thinking, by contrast, is purposive and policy-guided; it aims for a desired outcome or state of affairs such that we can always ask whether the regulatory environment

[8] Law Commission, *Smart Legal Contracts* (n 4) para 4.102.

[9] To be sure, there might be limited preventive measures available to litigants but, for the most part, private law is geared to specifying which acts or omissions constitute wrongs and to remedying such wrongs as and when they occur.

is fit for purpose relative to that outcome or state of affairs. Regulatory interventions seek to channel conduct in a particular direction, inter alia by incentivising or disincentivising action.

For present purposes, the key characteristics of regulatory thinking are the following. First, the internal consistency of legal doctrine is of little or no concern – or, at any rate, it is not valued for its own sake. Second, the focus is entirely on whether the law is instrumentally effective in serving specified regulatory purposes, which might be of both an economic and a non-economic nature.[10] Third, regulatory thinking is not concerned with whether the law is 'coherent' – other than in the sense of asking whether a group of related interventions pushes in the required regulatory direction – but with whether it works.[11] Fourth, in regulatory thinking there is no reservation about enacting new bespoke laws if this is an effective and efficient response to a question raised by new technologies. For example, if the investment in databases cannot be properly protected by Intellectual Property (IP) laws, then a bespoke IP regime can be enacted.[12] Fifth, the anchoring points for regulatory thinking are not the general principles that are established in the jurisprudence but current policy purposes and objectives. Sixth, alongside its policy focus, regulatory thinking in relation to new technologies tends to be orientated towards striking an acceptable balance between benefits and risks. Seventh, the tilt of the risk-management mind-set that goes with regulatory thinking is towards *ex ante* prevention rather than *ex post* correction.

This kind of regulatory-instrumentalism is, typically, the (democratically) mandated language of legislators, policymakers, and regulatory agencies. While judges might have some responsibility for applying the spirit of policy driven legislation,[13] it is precisely the initiation and setting of regulatory policy, or the making of regulatory 'corrections' that we think falls beyond the mandate of unaccountable judges.[14]

That said, we should recognise that, in practice, there might be a considerable 'grey zone' in which judges, guided by regulatory thinking, do set the policy agenda for private law – arguably so, for example, in relation to consumer protection (in the absence of legislative intervention) and in determining the scope of negligence liability.[15]

[10] See T Prosser, *The Regulatory Enterprise* (Oxford, Oxford University Press, 2010) (underlining that regulation is no longer directed only at correcting market failure or other economic objectives).

[11] *cf* E Rubin, 'From Coherence to Effectiveness' in R Gestel, H Micklitz, and E Rubin (eds), *Rethinking Legal Scholarship* (Cambridge, Cambridge University Press, 2017) 310.

[12] See Directive 96/9/EC of the European Parliament and of the Council of 11 March 1996 on the legal protection of databases (On the Legal Protection of Databases) [1996] OJ L77/20.

[13] See, eg, the judicial reasoning in the Uber drivers' test-case, *Uber BV v Aslam* [2021] UKSC 5; [2021] 4 All ER 209.

[14] That said, there are occasions when coherentist-minded judges will respond in a more regulatory way to pressing policy concerns. See, eg, C Ford, *Innovation and the State* (New York, Cambridge University Press, 2017) 174, noting that, in the absence of railroad legislation, 'Courts were the primary public players, and it was courts that solved the railways' short-term cash flow problem(s). In view of the perceived public interest in keeping the railroads running, judges modified existing security contracts and the law of liens, *often to the bewilderment of the business community*' (emphasis supplied).

[15] See, eg, Ford, *Innovation and the State*, ibid, and generally, Brownsword, *Law, Technology and Society* (n 1) ch 10.

D. Four Articulations of Private Law

Given that private law can be made by legislators and by judges and that it can be guided by coherentist or by regulatory thinking, then, in principle, we have the following four articulations of private law:

- (PL1) private law, guided by *coherentist* thinking, that is *judge*-made;
- (PL2) private law, guided by *coherentist* thinking, that is made by a *legislative* body;
- (PL3) private law, guided by *regulatory* thinking, that is *judge*-made; and
- (PL4) private law, guided by *regulatory* thinking, that is made by a *legislative* body.

If one of these articulations is paradigmatic of private law, then I take it to be PL1 – or, at any rate, I take this to be the case in the common law world. I also take it that the ideal-typical case of PL3 is one in which the judge not only asks the regulatory question explicitly (ie asks whether private law is fit for purpose) but also addresses it and tries to respond to any lack of fitness in a fully regulatory way without the characteristic constraints of coherentist thinking.

Accordingly, if we imagine a spectrum running from ideal-typical PL1 coherentism to ideal-typical PL3 regulatory thinking, there will be a number of intermediate deviations and variations – for example, judges who do not make their regulatory thinking explicit and who operate in an apparently coherentist way, judges who ask the regulatory question (explicitly or implicitly) but then address it in a coherentist way, and judges who recognise that some action needs to be taken to render the law more acceptable or fit for purpose and who apply creative thinking to the principles, concepts and classifications to come up with novel doctrines that offer a limited response. Exploring this part of the legal landscape merits an article in its own right – in particular, we need to look more carefully at that part of the spectrum where coherentism allows for doctrinal correction when judges believe that the application of settled rules and principles leads to results which by common consent are unacceptable, and where judges thinking in a regulatory way make corrections that are guided by policy considerations – but I cannot undertake it here.

Restating the first limb of my opening response, my position is that, while PL4 is clearly salient and significant,[16] PL1, PL2 and PL3 are much less salient and significant.

III. Objections and Responses

Against my view that PL1, PL2, and PL3 are not particularly salient or significant in the governance of emerging technologies, I expect it to be objected that, while

[16] See, eg, Law Commission, *Electronic Trade Documents: Report and Bill* (Law Com No 405, 2022). The Commission signals its regulatory thinking early on in its Report. Thus, in para 1.5, the Commission rejects law's governance of current paper-based practice in international trade as 'clearly archaic, inefficient, and wholly unsuited to a world in which processes and transactions are increasingly in digital form. Allowing for electronic versions of certain trade documents could lead to significant cost savings and efficiencies, together with improvements in information management and security'.

I underestimate the capacity of private law and its practitioners – especially the capacity of PL1 – I over-state its limits. From a clutch of similar objections, I will focus on the charge that my view underestimates: first, the flexibility of private law (PL1) and the imagination of its practitioners; second, the extent to which there is judicial engagement with policy in private law disputes; and, third, the extent to which legislatures are involved in setting private law rules.

A. The Flexibility of Private Law and the Imagination of its Practitioners

According to Eliza Mik, contract law is 'not only form agnostic but also technology neutral'.[17] The cornerstone ideas of intention, exchange, reasonableness and so on, are flexible enough for contract lawyers to recognise a deal when they see one and to accommodate new technologies. Arguably, this kind of flexibility applies in a similar way to other areas of private law and other applications of private law thinking – for example, to the concept of 'property' and its associated concepts. We should not underestimate PL1.

Indeed, we should *not* underestimate the potential of PL1 to respond to perceived harms or to novel questions arising from emerging technologies. To underline this point, we need only recall Samuel Warren and Louis Brandeis' seminal article in which the authors pose a textbook private law question to which they respond by arguing for recognition of a right to privacy.[18] The question, in their own words, was 'whether the existing law affords a principle which can be properly invoked to protect the privacy of the individual; and, if it does, what the nature and extent of such protection is'; and, their response was that, thanks to 'the beautiful capacity for growth which characterizes the common law', such a principle could be found and, moreover, it could be relied on 'to afford the requisite protection, without the interposition of the legislature'.[19] This last point is worth emphasising: then, and perhaps even now, many practitioners of PL1 are reluctant to hand the task over to the legislature.[20]

The reason why the question needed to be asked was (as Warren and Brandeis judged it) the unacceptable use of 'mechanical devices' associated with the camera and photography which had led to the 'unauthorized circulation of portraits of private persons'.[21]

[17] E Mik, 'The Resilience of Contract Law in Light of Technological Change' in M Furmston (ed), *The Future of the Law of Contract* (Abingdon, Routledge, 2020) 112.

[18] Warren and Brandeis, 'The Right to Privacy' (n 2). Arguably, this is not a straightforward example of PL1 reasoning. Rather, it is an example of the regulatory question being asked, the law being found to be unfit, and then a creative coherentist solution being proposed. Compare, too, the discussion of platforms and power in S Kreiczer-Levy, *Destabilized Property* (Cambridge, Cambridge University Press, 2019) at 146–56 (esp concerning 'market-constituting fiduciaries').

[19] Warren and Brandeis, 'The Right to Privacy' (n 2) 195.

[20] Compare Law Commission, *Smart Legal Contracts* (n 4) para 3.146: 'Given our conclusion that smart legal contracts can satisfy the requirements for a contract, a legislative statement that smart contracts are capable of being legally enforced … seems unnecessary. In the absence of a real need for legislation, we do not think it would be justified.'

[21] Warren and Brandeis, 'The Right to Privacy' (n 2) 195.

In some contexts, it was not practical to take photographs without the consent of the parties who would sit for the photographer; here, the interest of the individual in their privacy could be protected either by contract law or by the law of confidentiality. However, because 'the latest advances in photographic art [had] rendered it possible to take pictures surreptitiously',[22] the answer needed to be based in tort law. Even though the unauthorised taking and circulation of photographs did not cause any injury or damage to a person or their property, Warren and Brandeis argued that a right to privacy was already implicit in the general principles of law relating to the protection of the interest in personality and the right to be let alone. The precise way in which the jurisprudence of the privacy right was to be developed would be left to the courts,[23] but the enduring message of the article is that the common law is flexible and has the capacity to be applied in ways that respond appropriately to technological applications that are unacceptable. Surely, it will be objected, this cautions against underselling private law, private law thinking, and private law practitioners; and, it cautions especially against underselling PL1.

Generalising this, when confronted by new technologies or by novel situations, private lawyers who are thinking in a coherentist way ask how the precedents and the historic principles of the law apply to, or fit with, the technology or situation. For example, we might ask how the general principles of tort law apply to defamatory content that is hosted online; or how the principles of contract law might be applied to those platforms in which the relationship between, the roles, and the responsibilities of the parties are not clear or, again, how those principles might be applied to so-called 'smart contracts'; or we might ask how copyright law maps onto creative works generated by AI or by those who engage in remixing; or we might ask how traditional concepts of property, assignment and novation map onto cryptocurrencies and transfers of tokenised assets. The list of potential questions is not endless, but it is long and it gets longer with each new technology and its applications.

Often, this kind of question will be asked (and answered) by lawyers who are advising clients on their best reading of the legal position. However, where such questions are referred to courts, the flexibility of the law notwithstanding, there is a tendency towards conservative rulings coupled with no more than incremental development of the law. So, for example, although patent offices were able to adjust their understanding of patentability and disclosure to accommodate new products and processes in biotechnology,[24] the courts were not so quick to recognise body parts, embryos and gametes as property in order to ground tort claims.[25]

[22] ibid 211.

[23] For that multi-pronged development in the jurisprudence, see W Prosser, 'Privacy' (1960) 48 *California Law Review* 383.

[24] A Pottage and B Sherman, *Figures of Invention: A History of Modern Patent Law* (Oxford, Oxford University Press, 2010).

[25] Leading examples of the reluctance to recognise detached body parts as either a property object or as the property of the source, include *Moore v Regents of University of California* 51 Cal.3d 120, 793 P.2d 479, 271 Cal. Rptr. 146 (Cal. 1990), and *Greenberg v Miami Children's Hospital Research Institute* 264 F. Supp. 2d 1064 (S.D. Fla. 2003). For general critique of judicial conservatism in the context of claims arising from the reproductive applications of modern biotechnologies, see D Fox, *Birth Rights and Wrongs* (New York, Oxford University Press, 2019).

This is not to say that practitioners of PL1 are uncritical of the state of the law. To the contrary, the 'coherence' of legal doctrine and its consistent and predictable application is central to the ideal of legality and this is a matter of intense and enduring concern. Contradictions and inconsistencies in the body of doctrine, unprincipled distinctions, and the like are not to be tolerated; precedents and principles should not simply be ignored; legal doctrine should not be distorted; law should be applied in a way that respects its integrity. Given this culture, it is understandable that there is a good deal of nervousness about stretching legal principles, or creating ad hoc exceptions, in order to accommodate a hard case, all of which merits study in its own right.[26]

In this context, while some coherentists are relatively formal and inflexible in their thinking, others recur to deeper principles to apply private law doctrines in more creative ways. For example, one of the questions considered by the Law Commission in its report on smart contracts is whether, in a fully coded transaction, an 'offer' could be 'accepted' without the shadow parties being aware that an offer had been made. One of the consultees argued that, because offer and acceptance is predicated on acts of human will, then there can be no acceptance where 'the accepter is ignorant of the very existence of the offer at the time it is made'.[27] Although the Commission takes a less formal approach, there is no guarantee that a judge would share the Commission's view that 'the operation of [a] program in making or accepting an offer can be considered a manifestation of [a] party's intention to be bound by the agreement'.[28] Similarly, at times of rapid economic, social and technological development, the concern for doctrinal coherence can inhibit major development of the law. While critics will say that the law should move with the times, judges will tend to exercise restraint and be mindful of being accused of assuming an unauthorised legislative role.[29]

We could argue to and fro about just how flexible private law is for some time. However, at best, PL1 is no more than what it is. In its pure coherentist form, PL1 does not at any stage ask the regulatory question; it does not ask whether private law is fit for purpose but only whether it can be fitted to novel technologies. Nor does PL1 free itself from the constraints of working with the present legal materials. Accordingly, while the courts will give an answer to the question that is put to them, they do not have either the resources or the mandate for expansive lawmaking or for setting new policies. This means that the burden of responding to questions that invite a serious overhaul of the regulatory environment moves elsewhere. To ignore these constraints would, I suggest, risk expecting too much of PL1.

[26] For classic studies in the last century, see: B Cardozo, *The Nature of the Judicial Process* (New Haven, Yale University Press, 1921) and K Llewellyn, *The Common Law Tradition* (Boston, Little, Brown and Co, 1960). For commentary linking both books, see: C Clark and D Trubek, 'The Creative Role of the Judge: Restraint and Freedom in the Common Law Tradition' (1961) 71 *Yale Law Journal* 255. For a general overview of the jurisprudence, see A Reichman and G Sartor, 'Algorithms and Regulation' in Micklitz et al (eds), *Constitutional Challenges in the Algorithmic Society* (n 3) 132–39.

[27] Law Commission, *Smart Legal Contracts* (n 4) para 3.36.

[28] ibid para 3.38.

[29] Compare Sir John Mummery's opening remarks in 'Property in the Information Age' in W Barr (ed), *Modern Studies in Property Law* (Oxford, Hart Publishing, 2015) vol 8, ch 1 ('Decisions by courts on novel claims, such as the assertion of property in the content of emails must be made in a principled way … If information is not property and cannot be owned at common law, only Parliament can provide that kind of protection in legislation …').

B. Policy in Private Law

To be clear, the question concerning 'policy' (qua the setting or advancing or prioritising of collective goals) in private law is not whether *legislatures* can (or should) debate and decide policy and then take a position which is translated into a private law framework; initially, policy-setting might be for the executive branch of government but we can take it that debating and deciding policy falls within the remit of legislatures. Rather, the question is whether *judges* can (or should) decide private law disputes on the basis of policy considerations. The question, in other words, is about policy and PL1/PL3 not about policy and PL4.

Famously, Ronald Dworkin proposed the thesis that 'judicial decisions in civil cases, even in hard cases like *Spartan Steel*, characteristically are and should be generated by principle not policy'.[30] Predictably, Dworkin's critics lined up to offer counter-examples to this thesis, starting with *Spartan Steel* itself, a case in which tort lawyers would see policy considerations looming large in the Court's careful delimitation of liability in negligence for economic loss.[31] In the present context, where private lawyers want to draw out the way in which PL1/PL3 can have policy on board, what should we make of this?

Taking private law cases at face value, while judges do sometimes steer clear of policy arguments,[32] there is no question that 'policy' figures explicitly and implicitly in judicial thinking. In some cases, judges go out of their way to flag up explicitly where they are considering matters of principle and where they are engaging with questions of policy. In other cases, it is not so explicit but, as Stephen Waddams has convincingly argued, the history of contract law reveals a complex entanglement of thinking that is implicitly guided by policy and by principle.[33] In cases such as *Spartan Steel*, where judges are cautiously extending or cutting back on the extent of negligence liability for purely economic loss, they are mindful of the burden on business, the need for clear lines of liability so that risks can be insured, and of the way in which losses can be distributed. Similarly, where judges in contract cases are setting the lines of liability for consequential losses arising from breaches of contract, they are thinking about clear lines of liability so that risks can be insured and about incentivising disclosure of unusual risks. The thinking here looks conspicuously policy-sensitive.

So, what should we make of this? In principle, we might want to differentiate between (i) the inception or origination of a policy, (ii) a policy adjustment (major or minor), and (iii) the application of a policy and the interpretation and application of

[30] R Dworkin, *Taking Rights Seriously*, rev edn (London, Duckworth, 1978) 84.

[31] *Spartan Steel and Alloys Ltd v Martin and Co (Contractors) Ltd* [1972] 3 All ER 557.

[32] See, eg, the policy-eschewing approach of the Court of Appeal in *Thaler v Comptroller General of Patents Trade Marks and Designs* [2021] EWCA Civ 1374 (especially Birss LJ at para 55), where it was held that, given both the history and the scheme of the Patents Act 1977, it was only a person who could be treated as the inventor. Humans could invent machines and be assisted by machines; but the machines (in this case, Thaler's AI machine, DABUS) could not qualify as inventors. In general, courts elsewhere in the common law world, including in Australia, have taken a similar position.

[33] S Waddams, *Principle and Policy in Contract Law* (Cambridge, Cambridge University Press, 2011). Compare, too: M Renner, 'Values in Private Law' in Grundmann, Micklitz and Renner, *New Private Law Theory* (n 5) 156 (specifically, on Dworkin at 160–62).

legislation guided by its underlying policy[34] (such as the interpretation of consumer protection legislation). Now, what I am treating as distinctively 'regulatory' is the origination of policy and major policy adjustment. In relation to emerging technologies, it is for regulators to make governance decisions about 'red lines', about what needs to be incentivised or disincentivised, about the management of risks, about the balance to be struck between the interests of stakeholders, and so on. Policy choices of this kind are not an articulation of PL1 or PL2; PL3 (even with the benefit of Brandeis briefs) is not really geared for this and, anyway, it might not be constitutionally mandated.[35] To my mind, this is where PL4 is and should be engaged.[36]

My point, then, is not that private law cannot 'do policy' (whether licitly or illicitly, covertly or openly) but that this should be done by competent bodies – that is, bodies which are able to ask the right questions, which have the right resources, and which have the appropriate constitutional mandate. Exceptionally, and *faute de mieux*, it might fall to judicial bodies to undertake policymaking responsibilities in relation to emerging technologies but, generally, we would expect this to be for the political branch.[37]

C. The Legislative Articulation of Private Law

Where private law is enacted in a legislative form, it might be guided by coherentist thinking (PL2) (for example, the reform of privity law in England and Wales[38]), or it might be guided by regulatory thinking (PL4). However, these are not mutually exclusive approaches. My tendency is to characterise unfair contract terms legislation as regulatory (guided by a policy of consumer protection) but the legislation might also be viewed as building on a sense that the application of traditional principles of contract law is unacceptable (suggesting a corrective jurisdiction within coherentist thinking); so, in this sense, we have overlapping or complementary coherentist and regulatory thinking. Moreover, there are also examples of legislative schemes that combine private law

[34] See, eg, *First Tower Trustees Ltd v CDS* (Superstores International) Ltd [2018] EWCA Civ 1396; [2019] 1 WLR 637, para 104 (Leggatt LJ).

[35] In some cases, the constitutional position might be reasonably clear in allocating certain questions or justificatory reasons exclusively to the political branch (whether because they involve 'policy' or are 'political') in which event the issues in question should be treated by the courts as non-justiciable. In other cases, though, the allocation of competence will be less clear and, as a result, there will be no unproblematic answer to the question of whether, relative to the constitution, there is a mandate for judges to reason in a policy-focused way in a particular case. Moreover, unless we have an agreed external reference point for resolving questions about the proper allocation of policy-related functions, the debate will go round in circles. See, further: D Goddard, *Making Laws That Work* (Oxford, Hart Publishing, 2022) ch 11.

[36] As reflected, for example, in the *Thaler* (n 32) case.

[37] Compare J Morgan, 'Torts and Technology' in R Brownsword, E Scotford and K Yeung (eds), *The Oxford Handbook of Law, Regulation and Technology* (Oxford, Oxford University Press, 2017) 522; and Goddard, *Making Laws that Work* (n 35) 99: 'If there is a significant change of policy direction – new goals or significant changes in how those goals are pursued – then that can and should be dealt with by the legislator. Basic constitutional and democratic principles require decisions of that kind to be made by the legislator with the legitimacy to make and political accountability for, those decisions.' Moreover, as Goddard emphasises at ibid 108, '[c]ourts are not generally well placed to determine policy issues'; and, famously, see: LL Fuller, 'The Forms and Limits of Adjudication' (1978) 92 *Harvard Law Review* 353.

[38] Contracts (Rights of Third Parties) Act 1999 (which is based on the principle that the intentions of the contracting parties should determine the scope of their obligations).

coherentist and regulatory thinking (for example, data protection legislation is backed by a policy objective of enabling personal data to be applied for beneficial purposes, but it also has echoes of private law principle in making the consent of the data subject a key element of the regulatory scheme).

Having said this and having defined private law broadly, I do not think that I can be accused of underestimating the extent to which private law might be articulated in a legislative form. However, this is not to say that *coherentist* private law thinking is salient or significant. What we need to consider is how far, in engaging with new technologies, private law legislation is, and should be, guided by coherentist thinking and how much by regulatory thinking. Generally, I think that we will find that regulatory thinking dominates private law thinking in legislative schemes that relate to new technologies – and, indeed, I would add 'rightly so'; regulatory thinking that addresses the kind of technologically-enabled communities that we want to be is what we need.[39]

To be sure, the judicial commitment to legality means that we can expect their employment of coherentist reasoning to be both rigorous and free from political influence or other lobbying. Nevertheless, coherentism simply does not ask the right questions and nor does it review the full range of governance options. On the other hand, it must be granted that it does not follow that the political branch, reasoning in a regulatory way, is a better bet. Regulatory reasoning poses the right questions and invites consideration of all governance options; but politics is politics. Even with better resourcing than the judicial branch, the political branch might not bring the same level of rigour and acuity to its reasoning as the judicial branch, and it certainly does not have the same independence or insulation against lobbying and other pressures. Moreover, regulators might overreach in trying to micro-manage matters that are better left to private agreement.

So my preference for *regulatory* and *legislative* private law in engaging with new technologies is subject to qualification. I accept that there is no guarantee that the regulatory reasoning of the political branch will not be compromised, and I am also mindful that the instrumentalism of regulatory reasoning can dominate consideration of whether our policies and ends are legitimate – a concern that leads me to the final part of the chapter.

IV. Legitimacy and Licensing

Whether we are thinking about the governance of, or governance by, technologies, we surely aspire to 'good' governance. But what are our criteria for good governance? We might start with the integrity of those who govern, or with some procedural requirements (relating to transparency, inclusiveness, and the like), or with considerations of effectiveness and efficiency.[40] However, I want to highlight the importance of governance being able to justify the positions that it takes (in other words, being able to defend what it prohibits, permits or requires as legitimate). In this spirit, let me suggest that

[39] Compare G Hadfield, *Rules for a Flat World* (New York, Oxford University Press, 2017) 151: 'Legal analysis can't exist off in a specialized corner by itself. It needs to be deeply integrated with business and policy thinking.'

[40] See, eg, H Addink, *Good Governance* (Oxford, Oxford University Press, 2019).

governance should be orientated to the following licensing conditions, namely, that the positions taken and policy choices in relation to new technologies should be (i) compatible with respect for the global commons, (ii) in line with the community's fundamental values, and (iii) socially acceptable within the community. In what follows, I will speak briefly to these three conditions.[41]

A. The Global Commons

I take it that no group or community of humans will be viable unless some baseline (generic) conditions are respected. These conditions generate three imperatives as follows: first, humans must protect the global commons – that is to say, they must respect the planetary boundaries and its resources lest human existence on Earth is no longer sustainable;[42] second, humans must observe the conditions for peaceful co-existence, both between humans in a particular community and between communities; and, third, humans must respect the conditions that support their agency and autonomy. Accordingly, the first, and paramount, licensing condition is that governance of, or by, technologies must be compatible with the protection of these generic conditions.

Ideally, humans would recognise and sign up to these imperatives before they have begun the process of forming their own communities and before they have invested in their own interests. However, the challenge now is much more difficult because, at all levels, humans have invested in current arrangements. Nevertheless, if any human were to challenge these imperatives – for example, by proposing that it should be permissible to deplete the global planetary resource at will and to undermine the possibility of communities forming around their own projects and developing in their own way – then this should be rejected as being so unreasonable that no reasonable human could hold such a view. Even the most sceptical of humans cannot coherently reject the importance of the preconditions for their own (sceptical) existence, or for the viability of human communities and their governance.

That said, the world does not stand still and there needs to be a constant dialogue about whether particular practices are compatible with the imperatives. For example, nation states might claim to be acting in line with the imperative of peaceful co-existence because they are not engaging in 'aggressive' acts while, at the same time, they engage in various kinds of hybrid and cybrid threats, disabling critical infrastructures and destabilising communities.[43] There is also much room for discussion about the nature of human agency and its supporting conditions (concerning human self-development and then for engagement in purposeful self-direction whether for oneself, with others, or in groups and communities). While we might be convinced that some modern technologies (such as mass surveillance systems) interfere with the conditions for agency, how precisely is agency inhibited or compromised?[44]

[41] These conditions constitute a 'triple licence' for new technologies: Brownsword, *Law 3.0* (n 1).

[42] Compare R Brownsword and H Somsen, 'Law, Innovation and Technology: Fast Forward to 2021' (2021) 13 *Law, Innovation and Technology* 1.

[43] See, eg, L Freedman, *The Future of War: A History* (London, Allen Lane, 2017).

[44] See further R Brownsword, 'From Erewhon to Alpha Go: For the Sake of Human Dignity Should We Destroy the Machines?' (2017) 9 *Law, Innovation and Technology* 117.

One very important limit on the imperatives is that they must remain neutral between particular humans, particular communities, particular projects, particular views of what is prudent or moral, and so on; these are imperatives that are foundational for the possibility of human community but, other than insisting that the foundational conditions themselves are respected, they are strictly impartial between particular humans, particular articulations of community, and particular preferences, positions and policies.

Over and above the imperatives, and given the non-ideal conditions in which we now seek to establish them, two practical measures need to be adopted. First, because self-interest is so much entrenched in both domestic and international relations, a precautionary buffer should be adopted.[45] This means that if there is any reasonable doubt about whether an imperative is being violated by some act or practice, it should be restricted or even cease. To those who protest at this inconvenience, we can concede that, after the event, we might find that our precaution was unnecessary. But we have to act on what we know at the time, and if the choice at the time is between a possible catastrophe and a possible loss of utility, then it is better to be precautionary than sorry.[46] Second, because the most dangerous violations of the imperatives are likely to occur on the international stage, global regulatory stewards need to be authorised to maintain respect for the imperatives. To be sure, the idea that the global powers would support such an initiative might be wishful thinking; but, when even the most powerful nations are threatened by a breakdown in the conditions for governance, who knows, we might be surprised.

B. The Fundamental Values of the Community

If the global commons is first base, humans start building their communities at second base. It is here that they declare their distinctive values, as well as their distinctive conception of cornerstone values (such as respect for human dignity) and define themselves as the particular people that they aspire to be. Where there are questions about the interpretation or application of these values, it will fall to the community's laws and legal institutions to respond.

It is, of course, essential that whatever the fundamental values to which a particular community commits itself they should be consistent with (or cohere with) the commons' conditions. It is the commons that sets the stage for community life; and then, without compromising that stage, particular communities form and self-identify with their own distinctive values.

It follows that the first priority for governance of, or by, new technologies is that it is compatible with the generic conditions; and the second priority is that it is in line with the fundamental values of the particular community. At this second level, there can be plurality; different communities can reasonably disagree with one another in identifying themselves with different values.

[45] See R Brownsword, *Rethinking Law, Regulation and Technology* (n 1) ch 11.

[46] Compare D Beyleveld and R Brownsword, 'Emerging Technologies, Extreme Uncertainty, and the Principle of Rational Precautionary Reasoning' (2012) 4 *Law Innovation and Technology* 35.

C. Social Acceptability

The third licensing condition, like the second, is applicable within each community (it is only the first condition that is applicable across all communities). Here, no governance position or policy can be considered socially acceptable if it fails the licensing conditions relating to the global commons or the community's fundamental values; but, otherwise, social acceptability depends largely on governance processes that have integrity. In other words, to satisfy this condition, governance must have given the members of the community a fair opportunity to present their views and, where there are conflicting views, the accommodation reached must be (relative to the community's own standards) not wholly unreasonable.

Consider, for example, proposals for the adoption of new technologies (robots, AI, digital doctors, and so on) in healthcare as a case in point. The functions performed by the technology might be in the nature of governance (such as making triage decisions) or they might be diagnostic or surgical, and so on. Whatever the function, while some persons, regretting the loss of the human touch, will insist that the application of technologies should always be 'human-centric', others will welcome smart governance and 24/7 intelligent care. More generally, while some will push for a permissive regulatory environment that is facilitative of beneficial innovation, others will push back against healthcare practice that gives rise to concerns about the safety and reliability of particular technologies as well as their compatibility with respect for fundamental values. Yet, how are the interests in pushing forward with research into and the adoption of potentially beneficial health technologies to be reconciled with the heterogeneous interests of the concerned who seek to push back against them?

In such a scenario, the first priority will be to pick out those aspects of the proposals that touch and concern the global commons or the fundamental values of the community. To the extent that the proposals are incompatible with respect for these conditions, they are 'non-starters'. However, assuming that the proposals can satisfy these licensing conditions, we get to the matter of their social acceptability. Let us assume that, following serious public consultation on the proposals and members of the community having had a fair hearing, regulators take a position on the proposals which they present as a reasonable (or not unreasonable) accommodation of the various interests. There are a number of ways in which we might think that such a model of social acceptability is less than ideal – for example, because it allows all interests (self-serving or community-serving prudential as well as other-regarding ethical) to be flattened in the balancing process; there is no ranking of interests, and there are too many positions that can be presented as reasonable.[47] Nevertheless, this might be the best that we can expect at this level.

[47] See, further, R Brownsword, 'Regulating Automated Healthcare and Research Technologies: First Do No Harm (to the Commons)' in G Laurie et al (eds), *The Cambridge Handbook of Health Research Regulation* (Cambridge, Cambridge University Press, 2021) 266; R Brownsword and J Wale, 'Testing Times Ahead: Non-Invasive Prenatal Testing and the Kind of Community that We Want to Be' (2018) 81 *MLR* 646.

V. Conclusion

This chapter opened with the following question: how salient is private law and how significant is private law thinking in engaging with new technologies? My response yields three particular take-home messages and, implicitly, a bigger picture of the de-centring of private law.

First, with regard to governance *by* technologies, no articulation of private law is particularly salient or significant. Here, private law simply is not the priority. What we need is public law authorisation, limitation and licensing for governance (public and private) that relies on new technologies. I have suggested that the key licensing conditions relate to the global commons, to the community's fundamental values and to social acceptability in the community.

Second, with regard to the governance *of* technologies, legislative measures backed by regulatory thinking are the most salient and significant articulations of private law. We look to legislators, having engaged in a regulatory assessment of the benefits and risks relative to agreed policy, to set the governance frameworks for new technologies. Whether or not their governance will be effective will turn to some extent on whether it is legitimate (and perceived to be legitimate); and that will depend on whether it meets the licensing conditions summarised above.

Third, without underestimating the flexibility of private law principles and concepts, judicial applications of private law backed by coherentist thinking should be treated as being of lesser salience and significance. Ahead of a PL4 intervention, there might well be early cases taken to the courts and there might be a satisfactory PL1 response.[48] However, this is not the hub of tomorrow's private law governance.

Summing up, it bears repetition that we should not underestimate the relevance of private law and the contribution that it can make to the governance of new technologies. However, the direction of travel as technologies become smarter and capable of 'out-performing' humans is for judges, courts and coherentist private law thinking to be de-centred by automated dispute resolution,[49] and for humans to be taken out of the regulatory loop by technological management.[50] As governance moves deeper into the era of Law 3.0, as governance by technologies takes over, private law and its practitioners are relegated to the margins. The authority of law as well as respect for law's governance will be challenged.[51] For better or worse, private law's rules and principles are not the future.

[48] See, eg, Reichman and Sartor, 'Algorithms and Regulation' (n 26) 177–78.
[49] See, eg, E Katsh and O Rabinovich-Einy, *Digital Justice* (Oxford, Oxford University Press, 2017).
[50] See Brownsword, *Rethinking Law, Regulation and Technology* (n 1) chs 8 and 9.
[51] See R Brownsword, *Technology, Governance and Respect for the Law: Pictures at an Exhibition* (Abingdon, Routledge, 2023).

give a more accurate picture of the place data occupies within exchange structures than that offered by more traditional approaches within contract. It allows us to see data as a powerful actor in and of itself and not simply as the by-product of contractual practices and internet use.

The contracts that I have in mind in constructing this analysis are consumer contracts for online purchases or cloud-based online services such as Facebook where knowledge of the contract terms (usually framed as Terms of Service) and assent to them is inferred from a 'click' on a clickwrap agreement. That 'click' might be on an 'I agree' button, on a 'buy now' icon or the equivalent of a box tick on a pop-up window. In any event, what it signals, alongside an acceptance of delivery terms and such like, is a consent to harvest personal data from the consumer. Data as a general concept has frequently been referred to as the 'new oil'[7] and, although the comparison is not entirely accurate,[8] the metaphor does offer an illustration of the importance of data. It underpins the information economy ecosystem that drives some of the largest firms in the world; Apple, Amazon, Microsoft, Google and Facebook for example.[9] Data is used to provide a variety of commercial income flows from its direct sale to its use in designing individualised services and its role in predicting or nudging behaviour change.[10]

Data generated by individuals, the data of daily life, I see as being both part of us and existing around us and our activities, but also distinct from us. What I mean by this is the conflict inherent in our data, revealing not only facts about us but also our preferences, our associations and our associates,[11] and so being at the very core of our identity[12] and this data not being owned by us and so protected as an ownership interest would be.[13] It is the significance of data to us as individuals that makes the relationship between contract law and data problematic. The focus of contract law is on the product or service we are buying. Whilst it uses non-product-based filters that focus on the promisor and promisee as individuals in areas such as good faith and unconscionable

[7] Like many popular metaphors the exact source is hard to attribute. For a discussion of sources, see A Mavuduru, 'Is Data Really the New Oil in the 21st Century' (*Towards Data Science*, 12 December 2020), towardsdatascience.com/is-data-really-the-new-oil-in-the-21st-century-17d014811b88.

[8] For two rather different critiques of the 'new oil' position, see S Taffel, 'Data and Oil: Metaphor, Materiality and Metabolic Rifts' [2021] *New Media and Society*, journals.sagepub.com/doi/abs/10.1177/14614448211017887 and M Mandel, *The Economic Impact of Data: Why Data is not Like Oil* (Report, Progressive Public Policy Institute, 2017).

[9] K Birch and D Cochrane, 'Big Tech: Four Emerging Forms of Digital Rentiership' (2022) 31 *Science as Culture* 44.

[10] S Viljoen, 'A Relational Theory of Data Governance' (2021) 131 *Yale Law Journal* 573.

[11] For an interesting argument on the negative social costs borne by those in our data collection ambit as a result of inferred preferences and tolerances, see P Palka, 'Data Management Law for the 2020s: The Lost Origins and the New Needs' (2020) 68 *Buffalo Law Review* 559.

[12] J Cohen, *Between Truth and Power* (Oxford, Oxford University Press, 2019) 38. Cohen supplies a definition of data that moves beyond those typically found in jurisdictional regulatory structures such as 'personal' or 'personally identifiable information' to one that encompasses data collected in the contexts of work, investment, socialising, conducting business and generally living. For Zuboff the extraction of our data represents the end of our private relationship with our sovereign self, we are thereafter commodified and colonised as the central input into the information economy: see S Zuboff, *The Age of Surveillance Capitalism* (London, Profile Books, 2019).

[13] For a comprehensive unpacking of the issues around data ownership see, V Janeček, 'Ownership of Personal Data in the Internet of Things' (2018) 34 *Computer Law and Security Review* 1039.

conduct,[14] those are concepts which sit on the periphery of the doctrinal structure. They are overspill valves at best to remedy a small number of situations where even bargain-based objectivity cannot infer that both parties assented to a contractual arrangement on the terms now presented by one of the parties. Contract law is most comfortable when the terms of our purchases elide into the product itself.[15] This elision, as Bygrave alludes to in his contribution to this collection,[16] is clearest in the use of standard form contracts. The point about data and its release is that it is tied to us as individuals not to a product or service that we might purchase.

We glibly 'click' our data away from our control for others to use through contract, or a licence derived from contract, in circumstances where our purchase might well be a singular event, but the harvesting of our data is a continuous process. Underpinning our 'click' is that most elusive of contractual concepts, consent. Consent carries the burden of contract's bargain theory, embodying as it does so the key values of freedom of choice, autonomy and efficiency that underpin so many propositions in liberal society.[17] In operational and contextual terms, though, consent fails to represent the positive actions that one might associate with entry into a bargain, such as an evidenced reading of the terms of the contract or a recognition that consent is often context-dependent rather than operating in a binary[18] 'yes' (click) or 'no' (leave site having made no purchase or not enrolled for a service) format.[19] Section II of this chapter looks at how consent operates in relation to data release and use.

At the points of data storage and data use there is a departure from traditional private law structures and our rights are safeguarded not through property or contract regimes but through privacy-based structures that are wrapped in the language of 'data governance'. The public nature of this regulation sounds in the very nomenclature of 'data governance' and the debates that surround it. Whilst the controls and obligations imposed in the name of 'data governance' on data processors are undoubtedly necessary protective measures, the absence of contract from the medium of redress reflects negatively on the appropriateness of its doctrines, as currently understood, to deal with the challenge posed by this type of technology use. The balance between public law and private controls on data governance is something that Brownsword reflects upon from a conventional jurisprudential standpoint in his contribution to this collection.[20] Section III of this chapter considers this issue from the rather different viewpoint of relational contract theory with its emphasis upon prior social relations, the limitations of planning and the importance of collaboration around *ex post* events. This section also integrates ANT into the ideas of Macneil's relational contract. ANT urges an analysis that is neutral towards existing explanations and theories and centres instead on

[14] R Craswell, 'Remedies When Contracts Lack Consent: Autonomy and Institutional Competence' (1996) 33 *Osgoode Hall Law Journal* 209.

[15] M Radin, 'Humans, Computers, and Binding Commitment' (2000) 75 *Indiana Law Journal* 1125, 1160–61.

[16] See Bygrave in chapter 4 of this volume.

[17] R Wright, 'Clicking Through Consent' (2018) 64 *Wayne Law Review* 315.

[18] For comment on the binary nature of much of contract law, see C Dalton, 'An Essay in the Deconstruction of Contract Doctrine' (1985) 94 *Yale Law Journal* 997.

[19] N Oman, 'Reconsidering Contractual Consent' (2017) 83 *Brooklyn Law Review* 215.

[20] See Roger Brownsword in chapter 2 of this volume.

the realities of what happens, what is situated where and the relationships between 'things'. This allows for a focus on data that sits within and alongside the contractual relationship irrespective of the view of contract law on the role of consent, personal identity and the terms of the bargain.

II. Data and the 'Work' of Consent

In their chapter in this volume, Clifford and Paterson explain how for many individuals data release is nested in contracts with their familiar array of requirements: formation requirements of offer and acceptance, the incorporation of terms and the intention to create legal relations.[21] Key to these markers of enforceability is consent.[22] The objective[23] theory of consent is the threshold indicator both for contract formation and for doctrines that might vitiate a contract or determine its legality; lack of capacity, duress, unconscionability and undue influence for example. These external defences or vitiating factors as negators of consent are in many ways more developed within the doctrinal model of contract than consent itself as an affirmative position.[24] Any judicial or arbitral attempt at contract interpretation goes first to an assessment of the parties' intentions as evidenced by their individual consent, which then becomes their mutual assent to the terms of the contractual relationship. Bargain[25] and, to a lesser extent, promise[26] doctrinal contract theorists focus on consent as the cornerstone of contract. It is an exercise of individual autonomy that underscores the move from status-based relationships to ones of choice and free will.[27] For Barnett, whose work offers the most thorough discussion of consent in contract, it is the cornerstone because it is consent that converts a promise into a legally enforceable arrangement; the promisor has 'voluntarily performed acts that conveyed her intention to create a legally enforceable obligation by transferring alienable rights'.[28] Consent has to be

[21] See Damian Clifford and Jeannie Marie Paterson in chapter 5 of this volume.

[22] We might go so far as to say that the search for agreement is really a search for consent, see C Leonhard, 'The Unbearable Lightness of Consent in Contract Law' (2012) 63 *Case Western Reserve Law Review* 57, 70.

[23] See *Byrnes v Kendle* [2011] HCA 26, (2011) 243 CLR 253. In what is essentially an Equity and Trusts issue the High Court of Australia could not have been clearer that what mattered was not what the parties subjectively intended even if those were their 'real' intentions, but what could be objectively determined as their intentions. See also R McClintock, 'Objectivity in Contract' (1988) 6 *Auckland University Law Review* 317.

[24] M Chapman, 'Common Law Contract and Consent: Signature and Objectivity (1998) 49 *Northern Ireland Legal Quarterly* 363.

[25] I am using 'bargain' as a shorthand for the theoretical (as far as it goes …) underpinnings of liberal contract doctrine without delineating the difference between its various strands, eg Atiyah's reliance school, Kimel's detachment theory and social choice theory-based law and economics. Some might also distinguish Barnett's consent-based position from 'bargain' theory. It is not from laziness that I use this shorthand but rather from a deep-seated irritation at the narrowness of these positions, notwithstanding the huge role that ideas of contract play in modern society, and their divorce, even within their narrow stance, from anything approaching an empirically-based reality.

[26] C Fried, *Contract as Promise* (Cambridge MA, Harvard University Press, 1981).

[27] The dangers of ignoring this link in the rush to expose the binary nature of current formulations of consent is explained in R Grossi, 'What Can Contract Law Learn from #MeToo' (2022) 49 *Journal of Law and Society* 263.

[28] R Barnett, 'A Consent Theory of Contract' (1986) 86 *Columbia Law Review* 269, 304–305.

objectively assessed according to Barnett because the 'rights and liberty interests of the other party would be severely limited if they were not entitled to rely upon things as they appear to be'.[29]

An objective interpretation of consent furthers certainty for the parties and encourages responsibility. However, those are not always the values that contractual relationships need in order to function for both parties, and it does mean that consent is not actual consent in terms of a knowledge of contractual terms, it is a manifestation of assent to terms. These are different things. Nancy Kim very helpfully breaks consent down into three components, all of which she advocates need to be present; a manifestation of consent, voluntariness and knowledge.[30] The problem with this is that the objectivisation of consent in the sense of the overarching concept means that contract law is pushed into assumptions and hierarchies. On top of this hierarchy sits manifestation which trumps knowledge. This is the only way that the absolute binding nature of Miss L'Estrange's signature[31] can be justified[32] – a rule that has been upheld by the Australian High Court subsequently.[33] It is the explanation for the starkness of the position taken in relation to the 'duty to read' cases, even if imposing that duty means making assumptions about literacy.[34] These are not 'meaningful' manifestations of consent. The balancing issue of 'notice of the terms' simply does not arise in many 'click' contracts. The terms are available; the issue is with the comprehension of those terms and whether consent to them is genuinely voluntary.[35]

Contracts from the perspective of contract doctrine often involve more than one time period; there is the moment of agreement where responsibility crystallises and there is then performance which may occur later and may be a continuing act. This is particularly true of 'click' contracts; agreement is constituted by the 'click' but the consent given to use data is continuous. What might be meant as a one-off transaction to purchase an item of clothing from an online retailer or to join a streaming service

[29] ibid 306.

[30] N Kim, 'Relative Consent and Contract Law' (2017) 18 *Nevada Law Journal* 165, 169. What this categorisation misses is the point that knowledge and voluntariness are invariably relative. Few choices are made with perfect information and most choices are made under the constraints imposed by scarcity, see M Trebilcock, *The Limits of Freedom of Contract* (Cambridge MA, Harvard University Press, 1993) 19–20.

[31] *L'Estrange v Graucob* [1934] 2 KB 394. The only positions open to Miss L'Estrange, despite the sympathy the Divisional Court expressed for her (Maugham LJ at 405), were to claim fraud, *non est factum*, or misrepresentation on the part of Graucob Ltd.

[32] See further J Spencer, 'Signature, Consent, and the Rule in L'Estrange v Graucob' (1973) 32 *CLJ* 104, where the author argues that a signature should not be relied upon in circumstances where the other party ought to know *inter alia* that the signatory had not read or understood the document before signing it.

[33] *Toll (FGCT) Pty Ltd v Alphapharm Pty Ltd* [2004] HCA 52, (2004) 219 CLR 165.

[34] See *Parker* v *South Eastern Railway Co* [1877] 2 CPD 416 and *Thompson v London, Midland and Scottish Railway Co* [1930] 1 KB 41. In *Parker* Mellish LJ expressly asserts (at 423) the right of the railway company to assume literacy and the exercise of literacy by those it contracts with, subject to the knowledge that there was writing on the documentation handed over and this writing might contain conditions. In *Thompson* (where *Parker* is cited with approval) only one judge in the Court of Appeal (Lord Hanworth MR) referred to the plaintiff's illiteracy and then it was to dismiss it as a relevant factor because of the authorities (presumably *Parker*) and the 'condition of education in this country' (at 46).

[35] This interplay between the presence of terms and their substantive content, is captured in the consumer protection legislation present in Australia and the UK, but also in other jurisdictions, see J Paterson and E Bant, 'Contract and the Challenge of Consumer Protection Legislation' in T Arvind and J Steele (eds), *Contract Law and the Legislature* (Oxford, Hart Publishing, 2020) 79.

to not be a member when social contacts are, is perceived as a life detriment.[53] Nancy Kim suggests that people *might* behave differently online; the requirement to accept terms for every transaction might habituate us to 'click' behaviour in the way that a requirement for a wet signature does not.[54] There is also the idea of digital resignation;[55] individuals, whilst still caring about data privacy, have become resigned to the fact that there is very little they can do given the power imbalance that exists if they wish to inhabit digital spaces. Even if either or both of these suggestions are true (they are not supported by empirical evidence), they are insufficient to support the proposition that consent to personal data access with all the consequences that brings, is given voluntarily with knowledge of the terms of the contract by a 'click' to purchase an item or to access a service.[56]

III. An Approach Grounded in Relationality

The objective standard of consent and its consequences cause discomfort amongst even its advocates.[57] Barnett, when read closely, resiles from an entirely objective stance on consent to make the point that objectivity and subjectivity in contract are inextricably bound together in a complex relationship that links individuals, culture and society.[58] Similarly, Leonhard talks about focussing not on objectivity but on 'the totality of the circumstances'.[59] Kim bemoans the fact that courts routinely enforce wrap contracts in circumstances where the consumer did not intend to enter into a contract.[60] Her position, which draws heavily on Eisenberg's[61] Dynamic Contract Law, is to see 'valid consent' as distinct from subjective or objective readings. For her consent is a process, a dynamic that depends upon the 'relative blameworthiness of the parties', their relationship, the effect on third parties and societal impact.[62] For all this, she fails to mention any of the studies on the non-reading of contract terms and the apparent manipulation of 'consent' in how terms of service are offered on web pages or the lack of alternative supply in many cases. Radin offers a strident critique of consent focussing exactly on contracts made by a 'click' and situated within the literature on terms of contract not being read. For her it is a distortion of the objective theory of consent to think that a contract can be made in these circumstances.[63] Her solution is to remove contracts of

[53] J Obar and A Oeldorf-Hirsch, 'The Clickwrap: A Political Economic Mechanism for Manufacturing Consent on Social Media' (2018) 4 *Social Media and Society*, https://doi/full/10.1177/2056305118784770.

[54] N Kim, *Wrap Contracts: Foundations and Ramifications* (Oxford, Oxford University Press, 2013) 59–62.

[55] N Draper and J Turow, 'The Corporate Cultivation of Digital Resignation' (2019) 21 *New Media and Society* 1824.

[56] D Clifford and J Paterson, 'Consumer Privacy and Consent: Reform in the Light of Contract and Consumer Protection Law' (2020) 94 *Australian Law Journal* 741.

[57] See generally O Gan, 'The Many Faces of Contractual Consent' (2017) 65 *Drake Law Review* 615.

[58] R Barnett, 'The Sound of Silence: Default Rules and Contractual Consent' (1992) 78 *Virginia Law Review* 821.

[59] Leonhard, 'The Unbearable Lightness of Consent in Contract Law' (n 22) 85–90.

[60] Kim, *Wrap Contracts* (n 54) 128.

[61] M Eisenberg, 'The Emergence of Dynamic Contract Law' (2000) 88 *California Law Review* 1743.

[62] Kim, 'Relative Consent and Contract Law' (n 30) 169.

[63] M Radin, 'The Deformation of Contract in the Information Society' (2017) 37 *OJLS* 505, 519–21 and Radin, 'Humans, Computers, and Binding Commitment' (n 15) 1128, 1133 and 1135.

adhesion in general from the realm of contract law and situate them instead within tort law and consumer protection law.[64]

We might sum up these criticisms as a plea for consent to be construed in a way that is more reflective of the actual situation in which contracts are made and goes beyond the idea of contract as product. Implicit here is a recognition that consent as a concept is a rigid tool and this rigidity is particularly significant in the context of data transfer which is a by-product of the agreement between the parties, not its objective, which is the purchase of goods or services. These remedial ideas lack any big picture descriptive framework within which a meaningful intervention could be constructed. This is where Macneil's Relational Contract offers a different approach.[65] Macneil saw himself as offering a general theory of exchange behaviour at the level of society, so exactly the macro approach that is lacking in the above discussions of the deficiency of the concept of consent.[66] He described this theory as creating a unified law of contract by moving it from solely the transactional principles which underpin the doctrinal model to a relational model. This relational model, which includes contracts enforceable at law, extended to embrace a much broader and richer social, or perhaps philosophical, context that more accurately explained how exchange takes place.[67]

Macneil's methodology was one that he defined as 'casual empiricism'. By this he means that whilst he did not generate empirical work, his ideas about relational contract were built upon a bottom-up approach of observing lived transactions.[68] A key source for these observations were empirical studies done by others.[69] For example, if Macneil were writing now he would be familiar with the empirical studies that highlight the length of terms and conditions and the routine non-reading of contract clauses in standard form contract settings. What Macneil offers is a sociology of the contracting process where contract is a social behaviour rooted in co-operation which is used to plan exchange into the future and help the parties attain their separate goals. He asserts that his sociological account is value neutral, or, perhaps more accurately, that his work has a 'relative social neutrality',[70] something that it shares with ANT.[71] As the following text

[64] M Radin, *Boilerplate: The Fine Print, Vanishing Rights, and the Rule of Law* (New Haven CT, Princeton University Press, 2013) 197–216.

[65] Macneil did toy with the idea of labelling his theory 'essential' as opposed to relational because he felt it better encapsulated his idea that exchange behaviour, and within that contract relationships, could only function within his framework. See I Macneil, 'Relational Contract Theory: Challenges and Queries' (2000) 94 *Northwestern University Law Review* 877 and I Macneil, 'Contracting Worlds and Essential Contract Theory' (2000) 9 *Social and Legal Studies* 431. However, the idea does not seem to have taken hold. The secondary literature even from Macneil aficionados such as David Campbell still uses the nomenclature of 'relational'.

[66] See I Macneil, *The New Social Contract: An Enquiry into Modern Contractual Relations* (New Haven CT, Yale University Press, 1980) 5: '[c]ontracts are about getting things done in the real world … building things, selling things, cooperating in enterprise, achieving power and prestige, sharing and competing in a family structure … If we wish to understand contract, and indeed if we wish to understand contract law, we must think about exchange and such things first, and law second.'

[67] I Macneil, 'Barriers to the Idea of Relational Contracts' in F Nicklisch (ed), *Der komplexe Langzeitvertrag: Strukturen und international Schiedsgerichtsbarkeit* (Heidelberg, CF Müller, 1987).

[68] I Macneil, 'Relational Contract: What We Do and Do Not Know' [1985] *Wisconsin Law Review* 483.

[69] ibid 508–11.

[70] I Macneil, 'Other Sociological Approaches' in B Bouckaert and G de Gees (eds), *Encyclopaedia of Law and Economics* (Cheltenham, Edward Edgar Cheltenham, 2000) vol 1, 694–718.

[71] ANT has been accused of ignoring the difficulties and issues raised by the presence of categories such as race and class and concepts such as neoliberalism. ANT theorists would answer that it is its role to explain how

demonstrates, Macneil's assertion becomes harder to support when viewed alongside the edifice of community that he builds around standard form contracts as a substitute for individualised consent.

Macneil's model of contracting behaviour is a tier made up of three horizontal levels. The top level contains the common bonds of 'society' such as shared meanings, language, etc. The second level contains the political bonds of polite society; for example, rules which outlaw theft as a way of acquiring resources. These two levels are the necessary foundations for exchange behaviour to take place. At the third level come Macneil's 10 external and internal norms which he asserts will be present to some degree or another in each exchange. More likely to be present in relational exchanges are the norms of role integrity, reciprocity, flexibility, contractual solidarity, power and the linking norms of reliance, expectation and restitution, propriety of means and harmonisation of the social matrix.[72] These will be generated in the relationship over time. Some norms will come to the fore when exchanges are more discrete,[73] namely 'implementation of planning' and 'effectuation of consent'. Whilst the model emphasises the need for co-operative goals, it is not suggesting that conflict between the parties does not exist. Macneil points out that conflict is inherent both within individual norms and between norms.[74]

Coherence in terms of consistency and clarity across Macneil's work sometimes suffered[75] as he battled for recognition of his model in the face of considerable opposition from some doctrinal scholars who viewed his work as overtly hostile and oppositional to theirs or at least presenting something distinctively different from them and thus othering in its ambit.[76] In other instances he encountered a straightforward ignorance of his work.[77] Despite these difficulties, Macneil's position on the way consent is used as a threshold concept for enforcement in liberal theories of contract and why it is incorrect is very clear. Not unexpectedly it was that exchange relations often have gradual and fuzzy beginnings and similar endings.[78] For him, any legal doctrine founded on freedom of contract and dependent on using a single moment as the trigger for *presentiation* to take effect was going to be fraught with difficulties. *Presentiation* was constantly

they are produced and why they endure. See B Latour, 'The Powers of Association' (1986) 32 *The Sociological Review* 264.

[72] I Macneil, 'Values in Contract: Internal and External' (1983) 78 *Northwestern University Law Review* 340.

[73] The 'discrete' and 'relational' parts of Macneil's analysis are the ones that are engaged with most frequently but also usually incorrectly. They are not particularly important for the analysis presented here and so they will not be engaged with. For a full description, see S Wheeler, 'Modelling the Contracts of the Future' (2017) 26 *Griffith Law Review* 593, 603–604.

[74] I Macneil, 'Exchange Revisited: Individual Utility and Social Solidarity' (1986) 96 *Ethics* 567.

[75] W Whitford, 'Ian Macneil's Contribution to Contracts Scholarship' [1985] *Wisconsin Law Review* 545, 555–57. Somewhat ironically in the very same issue of the *Wisconsin Law Review*, Macneil opined that Critical Legal Studies (CLS) scholarship was opaque and overly complex, see Macneil, 'Relational Contract (n 68).

[76] Despite views to the contrary, it is not the case that Macneil saw himself as a 'trasher', either in the CLS sense of the word, of doctrinal law or as an opponent of doctrinal structures. He saw them as a useful classificatory apparatus for some exchange relationships: see A Freeman, 'Truth and Mystification in Legal Scholarship' (1981) 90 *Yale Law Journal* 1229 and E Mertz, 'An Afterword: Tapping the Promise of Relational Contract Theory – "Real" Legal Language and a New Legal Realism' (2000) 94 *Northwestern University Law Review* 909.

[77] S Wheeler, 'Law in Action' in W Swain and D Campbell (eds), *Reimagining Contract Law Pedagogy* (Abingdon, Routledge, 2019) 79.

[78] I Macneil, 'The Many Futures of Contracts' (1974) 47 *Southern California Law Review* 691.

reconstituted as the relationship between the parties evolved and changed.[79] Consent and what is being consented to is a dynamically evolving process around commitment and choice preferences made over time. Choice preferences over time are exactly not what is enabled by 'click' contracts. This approach is absolutely aligned to the four-stage explanation of relational contract he gave that begins with the individual transaction and builds from there.[80]

The picture becomes less clear, as much by lack of familiarity with the concepts as anything else, when Macneil presents his views on the alternative to a fictional consent and moves away from the traditional underpinning societal level ideas of autonomy and freedom in contract. His replacements for these ideas are 'bureaucracy', in the context of which he expressly considers standard form contracts, and 'community'. Neither features heavily in his work or in the commentary on it. Bureaucracy for Macneil applies to both public and private sector actors[81] and denotes a form of generic governance and social organisation where reasoned and detailed planning exists. Bureaucratic organisations have internal and external boundaries, interconnections, purposes and goals. These features are not dissimilar to ones found in organisations and structures that are subjected to analysis by ANT. And in a connection to Macneil's model of exchange these internal boundaries separate the goals of the bureaucracy from the goals of interconnected sub-units or individuals within it. These individuals are bureaucrats as bureaucrats are defined as anyone who is a participant at any level and in any role. Consumers are key bureaucratic figures,[82] acquiring as they do goods and services from bureaucracies frequently through becoming parties to contracts of adhesion. Consumer law provides the constitution for this particular bureaucracy.

What needs to be considered is not the idea of individual consent to contracts of adhesion but the idea of joining a relation which can only be legitimised if it has received collective approval through the community. Community is the bulwark against bureaucracy and can be found both internal to bureaucracies (eg employee groups) and external to them (eg family groups or social clubs). Collective approval is based on deciding outer limits of tolerance where there is an acceptance of conflict between limiting principles. The community, the core of which is communal duties, reciprocity and a sense of belonging,[83] needs to decide how it regulates the relationship between

[79] *Presentiation* is explained by Macneil as the idea that the parties are bound in the future by what they have agreed at the time the relationship allegedly becomes binding: see I Macneil, 'Restatement (Second) of Contracts and Presentiation' (1974) 60 *Virginia Law Review* 589.

[80] I Macneil, 'Reflections on Relational Contract Theory after a Neo-Classical Seminar' in D Campbell, H Collins and J Wightman (eds), *Implicit Dimensions of Contract* (Oxford, Hart Publishing, 2003) 207. These stages were, in ascending order: that every transaction is embedded in complex relations; that to understand any transaction a requirement was also an understanding of any of the surrounding context that might affect the transaction significantly; that to analyse a transaction effectively all its relational elements had to be recognised and considered; and finally that a contextual analysis that combines an examination of relations and transactions is considerably superior to one that begins with a non-contextual approach to analysing transactions alone.

[81] In classic Macneil style, the breadth of 'bureaucracy' only becomes clear in a footnote: see I Macneil, 'Bureaucracy and Contracts of Adhesion' (1984) 22 *Osgoode Hall Law Journal* 5, fn 8.

[82] I Macneil, 'Bureaucracy, Liberalism, and Community – American Style' (1985) 79 *Northwestern University Law Review* 900, 904.

[83] ibid 934–37. Community is under-theorised by Macneil, not least because it is being used in an oppositional discourse to reject liberal theories of individual autonomy of action. For a discussion of Macneil

fluid and capable of multiple personalities and existing in numerous categories simultaneously. It offers us a much thicker description of relationship and its constituent memberships. It allows us to see constellations of actors, values/norms, practices and rules across the spectrum from data acquisition through consent to contract terms, to its various uses as aggregated information by numerous third parties. It is only this breadth of vision that creates the space (and the urgency) for new approaches and policies around data acquisition and use.

PART III

Rights to Deal with Data

4

The Predilection for Contract in Governing Digital Networks: Micro-Management's Face Off with Accountability

LEE A BYGRAVE*

I. Introduction

Contract has been a central legal mechanism for governing the internet and its attendant cyberspace(s) from the network's birth. United States' (US) government agencies used contracts in the form of co-operative agreements to fund the research efforts to develop the internet and its precursors.[1] When the US Government formulated its regulatory approach to internet-based commerce in the late 1990s, contract remained its preferred legal tool, with the Clinton-Gore Administration opining that 'governments should establish a predictable and simple legal environment based on a decentralized, contractual model of law rather than one based on top-down regulation'.[2] This stance fitted well with the contemporary preferences of numerous US policy entrepreneurs for a 'bottom-up' private ordering of the digital world that would permit emergent cyber-communities to constitute themselves with little interference from government. Libertarian ideology combined with concern for efficient governance helped ground these preferences.[3]

* Professor of Law, University of Oslo. Many thanks to Sebastian Schwemer, Emily Weitzenboeck, Rebecca Schmidt, Jeannie Paterson and Damian Clifford for helpful comments on previous drafts of the chapter, and to Rekha Dwivedi and Naomi Lintvedt for valuable research assistance. The usual disclaimer nonetheless applies.

[1] Zittrain aptly characterised the legal regime for early internet development as a 'Byzantine tangle of cooperative agreements offered by the National Science Foundation': J Zittrain, 'What's in a Name?' (2002) 55 *Federal Communications Law Journal* 153, 155–56. At the same time, these agreements rarely placed a clammy hand over the endeavours of the computer scientists who worked on the emerging internet's protocols.

[2] WJ Clinton and A Gore Jr, *A Framework for Global Electronic Commerce* (Washington DC, The White House, 1997) 5 (Principle 3).

[3] See, eg, I Trotter Hardy, 'The Proper Legal Regime for "Cyberspace"' (1994) 55 *University of Pittsburgh Law Review* 993 (concerned with efficient governance); DR Johnson and DG Post, 'Law and Borders: The Rise of Law in Cyberspace' (1996) 48 *Stanford Law Review* 1367 (concerned with libertarianism). See further section III of this chapter.

this regard may be summed up in terms of coordination, control, community and constitution.[18]

In respect of coordination, numerous internet-related contracts essentially aim at coordinating infrastructure and actors in order to enable efficient data transfer. This is best exemplified by the thousands of interconnection or 'peering' agreements between the network operators that are responsible for routing data between the various nodes or 'Internet Exchange Points' constituting the internet.[19] The contracts for the internet naming and numbering system are another key example.[20]

As for control, while an intrinsic function of contracting generally, it assumes a particularly salient role in the contractual mechanics of much of the digital world. The predominant purpose of many contracts for the provision of software and online services is to manage the use of the software and services to the advantage of the providers' economic interests and to restrict behaviour or norms that undermine those interests.[21] Technological-organisational measures frequently reinforce this control. Encryption and steganography mechanisms operating as part of so-called digital rights management systems are manifestations of such measures.[22] The control functionality is also evident in the form that many of the contracts take. A considerable number are essentially contracts of adhesion offering little chance to negotiate their core terms and laying down broadly formulated warranty and liability disclaimers, indemnity clauses and choice-of-forum clauses all of which typically favour the provider.[23]

Turning to community, some contracts govern digital spheres in which large numbers of people invest considerable time, energy and other resources, often for various ends of social interaction and self-realisation. A function of such contracts is to help create or strengthen a feeling of community for the people involved. Online social networks, such as Reddit and Facebook, are prime examples in point, and the contracts governing their usage are prime examples of 'community' contracts – a function that the latter themselves sometimes acknowledge.[24]

In respect of constitution, several of the above-noted community contracts have acquired a constitutional element in the sense that they create a set of fundamental rules for the governance of a digital community or network in a way that parallels the constitutional law of an ordinary country. Note that the concept of 'constitutional' as used

[18] Bygrave, *Internet Governance by Contract* (n 8) 38–40.

[19] See further DeNardis, *The Global War for Internet Governance* (n 6) ch 5.

[20] See further Bygrave, *Internet Governance by Contract* (n 8) ch 4.

[21] See, eg, A Jankowich, 'EULAw: The Complex Web of Corporate Rule-Making in Virtual Worlds' (2006) 8 *Tulane Journal of Technology and Intellectual Property* 1; JAT Fairfield, 'Anti-Social Contracts: The Contractual Governance of Virtual Worlds' (2008) 53 *McGill Law Journal* 427.

[22] See, eg, M de Zwart, 'Contractual Communities: Effective Government of Virtual Worlds' (2010) 33 *University of New South Wales Law Journal* 605, 608ff and references cited therein; E Bekker et al (eds), *Digital Rights Management: Technological, Economic, Legal and Political Aspects* (Berlin, Springer, 2003).

[23] See, eg, JD Michels, C Millard, and F Turton, 'Standard Contracts for Cloud Services' in Millard, *Cloud Computing Law* (n 9) ch 3; EY, 'Study on the Economic Detriment to Small and Medium-Sized Enterprises Arising from Unfair and Unbalanced Cloud Computing Contracts' (Brussels, European Commission, 4 November 2019), commission.europa.eu/system/files/2019-11/dg_just_cloud_computing_final_report_web_final.pdf.

[24] See, eg, the preamble to Reddit's User Agreement as last revised 12 August 2021 ('Reddit powers hundreds of thousands of distinct online communities. This User Agreement and your conduct make that possible'): 'User Agreement' (*Reddit*, 12 August 2021), www.redditinc.com/policies/user-agreement-september-12-2021.

herein is reserved for rules that provide a comprehensive, overarching framework for social behaviour in a community. Thus, Meta's terms of use for Facebook have a constitutional function whereas the terms for using a service such as Dropbox do not. At the same time, 'constitutional' has a constitutive dimension in the sense that contract is an important mechanism in the development and acceptance of such rules. This dimension may also be expressed using Rebecca Schmidt's concept of 'constitutionalisation effects' – that is, a process involving stabilisation and harmonisation of internal normative values and structural settings in a network such that actors in the network find it increasingly difficult to justify contrary positions.[25]

At the risk of spelling out the obvious, a contract or contractual framework may have more than one of the above-mentioned functions concurrently. Further, the division between each function is far from watertight in practice. For instance, a close connection frequently exists between the community, constitution and control functions, with the latter often linked, in turn, to the maintenance of a particular business model. Ultimately, the practical role played by each function will depend on the particularities of the governance structure that the contract in question both embeds and reflects. For example, a governance regime building on a strong degree of mutual trust, collaboration and respect between the involved actors – as is the case, say, with the 'bazaar governance' structure for distribution of open-source software[26] – is likely to generate a contractual framework with a relatively mild control function.

The profile of a function of a particular contractual framework may change over time. The profile's salience may increase in certain respects, or diminish. Over the last decade, for instance, some aspects of standard contracts for the provision of cloud computing services have altered in order to accommodate EU legislation on consumer protection and data protection.[27] This has softened the contours of their control function. A related point is that a function's *practical* impact may change as well. A contract may end up akin to a sleeping dog; sometimes even to a forgotten dog.[28]

Co-ordination, control, community and constitution are by no means the only functions played by contract in the digital world. Other functions come into play, depending on context. For example, contract may assume an important role in embedding the status of particular entities relative to others, and relative to alternative organisational forms. This function may be denoted using yet another term beginning with 'c': consolidation. The contractual web spun by ICANN illustrates the consolidation function well. That web embraces a multitude of stakeholders engaged primarily in management of generic Top-Level Domains. They include domain name registries, domain name registrars, domain name registrants/subscribers, data-escrow providers, regional internet

[25] R Schmidt, *Regulatory Integration Across Borders: Public-Private Cooperation in Transnational Regulation* (Cambridge, Cambridge University Press, 2018) 72, 95–96.

[26] B Demil and X Lecocq, 'Neither Market nor Hierarchy nor Network: The Emergence of Bazaar Governance' (2006) 27 *Organization Studies* 1447.

[27] Michels, Millard, and Turton, 'Standard Contracts for Cloud Services' (n 23) 96ff.

[28] T Dietz, 'Contract Law, Relational Contracts, and Reputational Networks in International Trade: An Empirical Investigation into Cross-Border Contracts in the Software Industry' (2012) 37 *Law and Social Inquiry* 25 (documenting that, in parts of the software industry, contracts are often drawn up only to be largely ignored in the ensuing business transactions).

registries, and the Internet Engineering Task Force.[29] Some of the stakeholders consist of a multitude of interest groups with differing agendas. The result is a hybrid regulatory regime that is 'easily chastised for its lack of a recognised pedigree',[30] long riven by strong tensions,[31] and repeatedly subject to attacks on its legitimacy.[32] Against this background, the contractual web does not simply function as a means of co-ordinating operational affairs; it also binds a large number of entities to ICANN, thus amplifying the corporation's importance for those entities and thereby its importance more generally. Any move to wind up the corporation will necessarily involve unravelling numerous bilateral contracts with other entities. Such a process is likely to become messy, especially were it to incur the demise of entities that are heavily ICANN-dependent.[33]

III. Why Contract?

A congeries of factors is behind the ascendancy of contract-based TPR in governance of digital networks. Some factors are rooted in ideology, some in legislative lag, some in the aforementioned functions of contract, while others are related to contract's special 'digital fit'. Before elaborating on each factor, it is worth noting that contract would inevitably have played *some* role in the governance of digital networks – for example, in private corporations' development and distribution of software – even if the networks had been subject to a high degree of legislative intervention from their birth. What this section explores is why contract-based TPR was able for many years to be the *primary* governance mechanism for digital networks, with legislation playing the role of 'second violin'.

Taking ideological factors first, the emergence of the internet from its academic chrysalis occurred concurrently with a deepening loss of faith in the efficacy of state-run, 'command-and-control' regimes, together with a growing belief in the ability of a competitive marketplace to deliver goods and services efficiently.[34] This helped to give relatively great latitude to private sector-led, contractual governance of the internet. The US being the home both of the internet and the leading innovators within the software industry and subsequent 'internet economy', reinforced this trend. In the US, *laissez-faire* ideology and a commitment to freedom of expression have traditionally had a firmer hold on government than in other countries. As part of this ideological mix, contract was promoted as a preferred legal tool because of its assumed strengths in enabling

[29] Mahler, *Generic Top-Level Domains* (n 5) 19ff; Bygrave, *Internet Governance by Contract* (n 8) 57.

[30] Bygrave, *Internet Governance by Contract* (n 8) 57.

[31] See, eg, ML Mueller, *Ruling the Root* (Cambridge MA, MIT Press, 2002) Pt III; ML Mueller, *Networks and States* (Cambridge MA, MIT Press, 2010) chs 4, 9, 10; DeNardis, *The Global War for Internet Governance* (n 6) 59–62.

[32] See, eg, N Palladino and M Santaniello, *Legitimacy, Power, and Inequalities in the Multistakeholder Internet Governance: Analyzing IANA Transition* (Cham, Palgrave Macmillan, 2021); J Weinberg, 'ICANN and the Problem of Legitimacy' (2000) 50 *Duke Law Journal* 17.

[33] Bygrave, *Internet Governance by Contract* (n 8) 137.

[34] See, eg, M Jänicke, *Staatsversagen: Die Ohnmacht der Politik in der Industriegesellschaft* (Munich, R Piper GmbH & Co KG, 1986); M Moran and T Prosser (eds), *Privatization and Regulatory Change in Europe* (Buckingham, Philadelphia, Open University Press, 1994); JP De Vries, 'The Resilience Principles: A Framework for New ICT Governance' (2011) 9 *Journal on Telecommunications & High Technology Law* 137.

private enterprise to flourish. For example, when the Clinton-Gore Administration advocated the use of contract in its aforementioned 1997 White Paper, it assumed that this would create a 'predictable, minimalist, consistent and simple legal environment for commerce'.[35]

Additionally, the informal, open, 'bottom-up' decisional culture of the internet's technical pioneers – manifest particularly in the operations of the Internet Engineering Task Force – became a benchmark for subsequent governance regimes, such as that established by ICANN.[36] The democratic ideals of the culture combined with its success in engendering innovation with obvious societal benefits gave it a high degree of legitimacy. This helped to head off recourse to more formal, 'top-down' regulatory approaches.

Turning to factors rooted in legislative lag, the internet's rapid growth as a global communications medium came as a surprise to many governments, leaving them initially struggling to regulate it and its attendant cyberspace(s).[37] The same goes for the business models quickly built on its back. The slow pace of legislative processes, along with the customary difficulties of reaching meaningful intergovernmental agreement, exacerbated these struggles.[38] Government caution was another contributory factor: 'move fast and break things' might have been a clever strategy for Facebook in its early days, but the mantra was (and is) patently inappropriate to guide the development of government regulatory policy. Governments have been generally conscious of digital networks' immense societal benefits and accordingly wary about upsetting 'the apple cart' through hasty regulatory control.

It also bears emphasis that the use of contract in the online environment has enjoyed broad support amongst parliaments, law reform committees, and courts across multiple jurisdictions. The comprehensive rounds of law reform over the last three decades aimed at fostering electronic commerce are testimony to this support. An important element of that reform was to give contractual transactions carried out electronically similar legal status to non-electronic transactions.[39] Courts in many jurisdictions faithfully followed through on this reform by recognising online forms of contracting. In so doing, they tended to apply relatively weak tests for finding party consent to contractual terms presented on websites.[40] They thereby undermined the ability of consent requirements to hinder online contracting in any significant way.

As for factors concerning contract's digital fit, these have indirect links to the functions of contract outlined in section II – particularly the control function. However, they have special pertinence for digital networks. The principal point is that contract is extremely adept in enabling flexible micro-management of the digital world. Contract can be closely tailored to the specific features of a particular technology

[35] Clinton and Gore, *A Framework for Global Electronic Commerce* (n 2).

[36] See, eg, AM Froomkin, 'Habermas@discourse.net: Toward a Critical Theory of Cyberspace' (2003) 116 *Harvard Law Review* 749.

[37] Mueller, *Networks and States* (n 31) 5.

[38] Bygrave, *Internet Governance by Contract* (n 8) 47–48.

[39] See especially the work of the United Nations Commission on International Trade Law (UNCITRAL) as manifest in its Model Law on Electronic Commerce (adopted 16 December 1996) particularly Articles 5–12.

[40] See, eg, MA Lemley, 'Terms of Use' (2006) 91 *Minnesota Law Review* 459; Leidö, *Realizing the Single Software Market* (n 7) 201ff.

Variations in nomenclature and possible normative punch have added to the challenge of making sense of them legally. For example, Facebook's original contractual instrument, simply titled 'Terms of Service' (ToS), was replaced by a set of 10 'Principles' and a 'Statement of Rights and Responsibilities' (SRR) in 2009. A raft of more narrowly focused codes (concerning, inter alia, advertising, data use and community standards) flanked them. While the SRR was legally binding, the legal status of the Principles was far from evident.[51] This hampered their operationalisation as accountability standards.

While the codes constituting lex Facebook are predominantly the call of Meta management, the latter is not their sole creator. Some of their norms derive from outside the Meta regime. For instance, the 13-year age requirement for Facebook membership derives from the US Children's Online Privacy Protection Act 1998.[52] A more recent example is Meta's public commitment in March 2021 to respect human rights in accordance with the UN Guiding Principles on Business and Human Rights (UNGPs).[53] The move injected Meta's internal accountability criteria with a comprehensive set of norms grounded in concerns differing in significant respects from those that first informed Facebook's contractual framework. Concomitantly, the move brought with it considerable potential to break open the hitherto largely self-referential normative circuitry of lex Facebook – as elaborated further on.

Nonetheless, the move was ultimately the choice of Meta management and did not fundamentally break with the corporation's pursuit of contractual 'command-and-control'. The Meta regime for Facebook continues to offer little room for formalised, bottom-up policy development. Although Mark Zuckerberg experimented with 'town hall' decision-making for Facebook users in 2012, the experiment was superficial and truncated.[54] This is not to suggest that Facebook users, app developers, advertisers, or operators of other websites that use the Facebook platform have no influence on how Facebook operates. At a fundamental level, the platform's commercial success hinges on Meta governing it in ways that the bulk of its users perceive as generally conducive to their needs.

Numerous factors hem in the ability of the actors that are part of Meta's 'ecosystem' to call the corporation to account. The forum to which Meta owes primary accountability as a business corporation is its shareholders. These are generally interested in maintaining a business model that generates enormous profits. They are reluctant to act as a brake on Meta if this would seriously damage that model. Meta's dual-class share structure compounds their difficulty.[55] As for Facebook users, their ability to act

files-xcheck-zuckerberg-elite-rules-11631541353 (revealing inconsistencies between Facebook's public content moderation rules and its internal 'cross check' programme that gave special privileges to certain high-profile users, such as Donald Trump).

[51] See further Bygrave, *Internet Governance by Contract* (n 8) 91–92.

[52] Codified at 15 USC §§ 6501–6506. See particularly § 6501(1) in combination with § 6502.

[53] See 'Our Commitment to Human Rights' (*Facebook*, 16 March 2021), about.fb.com/news/2021/03/our-commitment-to-human-rights/. The Human Rights Council adopted the UNGPs in Resolution 17/4 of 16 June 2011.

[54] Bygrave, *Internet Governance by Contract* (n 8) 97–99.

[55] Mark Zuckerberg has the majority shareholding in Meta's Class B shares, meaning that he alone controls more than 57% of votes: see further M Humphery-Jenner, 'Mark Zuckerberg Can Sack 11,000 Workers but Shareholders Can't Dump Him: It's Called 'Management Entrenchment'' (*The Conversation*,

as a brake is weakened by the fact that many are highly dependent on the platform for their self-realisation, whether professionally, personally, or both. This is despite their possible acknowledgement of the platform's problematic aspects. Meta employs various design strategies to cultivate such path dependency and to nudge users to choose options favouring its business interests.[56]

Advertisers operating within Meta's ecosystem clearly have the potential to exert significant pressure on the corporation to change tack, at least in respect of content moderation. In 2020, for example, a group of deep-pocketed advertisers, including Microsoft, Unilever and Coca-Cola, stopped advertising on Facebook over deficiencies in the removal of racist and hate content from the platform. This brought about a large drop in Facebook's share value and generated questions about its long-term viability.[57] However, while the event contributed to a series of scandals that, together, have indelibly damaged the reputation of Meta and Facebook, the resulting financial pain was short-lived. Meta and Facebook flagged measures to assuage the advertisers' concerns, the advertisers returned to the platform, and corporate profits made a healthy comeback.

The most high-profile actor in Meta's internal accountability structure, and one established specifically to enhance that structure, is the Oversight Board (OB). Its special profile and remit make it deserving of extra attention here. Set up in 2020 essentially in order to head off regulatory intervention from governments as a result of the deepening 'crisis of legitimacy' over content moderation policies for Facebook and Instagram,[58] the Board is currently composed of 23 experts from outside Meta with a variety of complementary sets of expertise in law, politics, journalism, ethics and technology.[59] The Board's overarching remit is to render independent, impartial decisions on the availability of certain types of contentious content on Facebook or Instagram and to issue advisory opinions on Meta's content policies, primarily with a view to upholding freedom of expression. Meta views establishment of the Board as a measure towards fulfilling its commitment to honour the UNGPs, particularly Principles 29–31 on grievance and remedial mechanisms.[60]

Board output takes four main forms: (i) a decision as a result of direct referral from Meta; (ii) a decision on appeal from a Meta decision by a Facebook or Instagram user; (iii) a decision as a result of Meta's request for 'expedited review'; and (iv) advisory policy statements on Meta's request. In addition, a Board decision may contain policy advisory statements with recommendations for Meta. The rules for each form of output

10 November 2022), theconversation.com/mark-zuckerberg-can-sack-11-000-workers-but-shareholders-cant-dump-him-its-called-management-entrenchment-194333.

[56] P Kallioniemi, 'Facebook's Dark Pattern Design, Public Relations and Internal Work Culture' (2022) 5(12) *Journal of Digital Media & Interaction* 38.

[57] See, eg, B Bambrough, 'Is This the Beginning of the End for Facebook?' (*Forbes Magazine*, Jersey City NJ, 30 June 2020), www.forbes.com/sites/billybambrough/2020/06/30/is-this-the-beginning-of-the-end-for-facebook/.

[58] E Douek, 'Facebook's "Oversight Board": Move Fast with Stable Infrastructure and Humility' (2019) 21 *North Carolina Journal of Law & Technology* 1, 2.

[59] See 'Meet the Board' (*Oversight Board*), oversightboard.com/meet-the-board/. The number of Board members shall vary between 11 and 40, depending on what is 'appropriate': see Article 1, section 1 of the Oversight Board Charter (version of February 2023).

[60] See 'Our Commitment to Human Rights' (n 53).

are enshrined in the Oversight Board Bylaws and Oversight Board Charter, and can be summarised as follows:

Figure 1 Case Submission by Meta

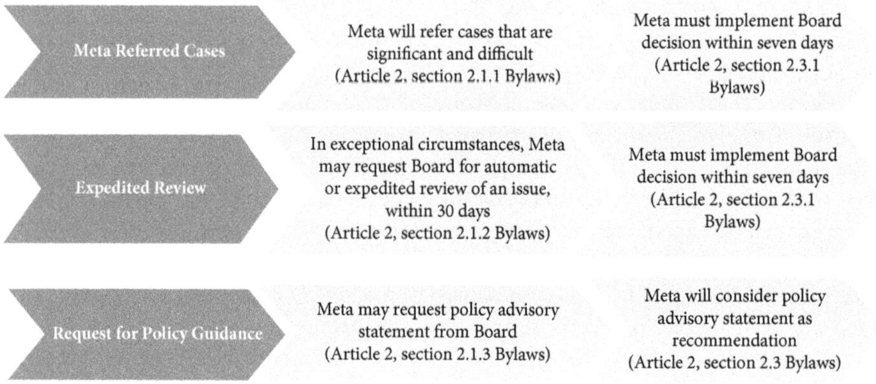

Figure 2 Case Submission by User

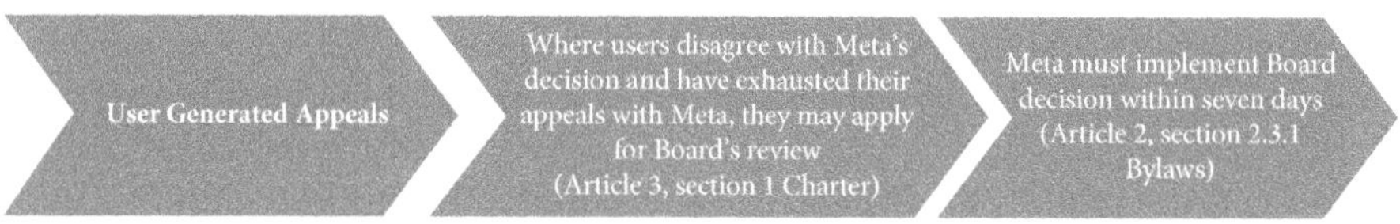

Of the four processes outlined in Figures 1 and 2, three lead to outcomes that are binding on Meta (except where their implementation 'could violate the law': Article 4 Charter; Article 2, section 2.3 Bylaws). Thus, the Board has teeth. As for policy advisory statements, although Meta does not have to comply with these (Article 3, section 7.3 Charter), it must 'transparently communicate' its response to them (Article 4 Charter; see also Article 2, section 2.3.2 Bylaws). Moreover, policy advisory statements with recommendations that are issued within decisions 'will be taken into consideration by Meta to guide its future policy development' (Article 3, section 4 Charter). However, Meta's response to recommendations has tended to be lukewarm at best.[61]

At the time of finalising this chapter (February 2023), the Board had published 35 decisions and two policy advisory opinions, overturning Meta's decisions in the majority (26) of cases.[62] Thus, the Board's teeth bite. It is important to bear in mind, though, that the Board has considerable discretion as to what and when it bites. The Board is not required to review all appeals submitted to it; rather, it selects cases that it deems

[61] VS Levy, 'Inside Meta's Oversight Board: 2 Years of Pushing Limits' (*Wired*, 8 November 2022), www.wired.com/story/inside-metas-oversight-board-two-years-of-pushing-limits/ ('Of the board's 87 recommendations through the end of 2021, Meta claims to have fully implemented only 19, though it reports progress on another 21. The company brushed off another 13 recommendations by saying, without elaboration, it is "work Meta already does." Other recommendations are outright refused').

[62] See overview at 'Case Decisions and Policy Advisory Opinions' (*Oversight Board*), www.oversightboard.com/decision/.

especially contentious and globally important, and that have 'the greatest potential to guide future decisions and policies' (Article 2, section 1 Charter).

While the quality of Board output is arguably not quite at the level one would expect of a proper court,[63] it is impressive for a non-judicial body. The Board's language is generally clear and its reasoning cogent, with judicious respect for precedent. The accretion and use of precedent is mandatory (Article 2, section 2 Charter), helping to ensure consistency and transparency in Board deliberations. Publication by the Board of documents elaborating the procedural steps it takes and of the overarching criteria it applies for case selection, augment decisional transparency.[64] Draft decisions of the five-member panels that customarily handle each case are subject to mandatory internal review (Article 1, section 3.1.8 Bylaws), further bolstering output quality.

Governance mechanisms (primarily in the form of a fairly well-endowed Oversight Board Trust) are in place to shore up Board independence. This independence is, nonetheless, relative: in the words of Andreas Kulick, 'the OB remains very much Meta's creature: set up, (initially) selected and financed by the corporation'.[65] There is also a requirement for global diversity in Board membership (Article 1, section 1.4.1 Bylaws), although fulfilment of this was initially imperfect.[66]

Freedom of expression constitutes the primary normative touchstone for Board decisions. This is evident at multiple points in the public presentation of the Board's mandate and reinforced in the Charter (see Article 2, section 2). However, the introduction to the Charter also recognises the need to balance freedom of expression against other legitimate considerations, such as 'authenticity, safety, privacy, and dignity' – a need also required by international human rights norms. In this respect, it is noteworthy that, for particular contexts, the Board has acted in large part to safeguard privacy interests.[67] Nevertheless, freedom of expression tends to have pride of place in Board deliberations.

Whether this points to a bias running counter to international human rights law is an issue falling outside the scope of this chapter.[68] More pertinent for present

[63] See further A Kulick, 'Meta's Oversight Board and Beyond – Corporations as Interpreters and Adjudicators of International Human Rights' (2023) 22 *The Law and Practice of International Courts and Tribunals* 1, 16–20 (criticising the Board's idiosyncratic and shallow approach to interpretation of international human rights law).

[64] 'Rulebook for Case Review and Policy Guidance' (Internal Policy Guidance of Private Judicial Body, *Oversight Board*, October 2022); 'Overarching Criteria for Case Selection' (Internal Policy Guidance of Private Judicial Body, *Oversight Board*, October 2022).

[65] Kulick, 'Meta's Oversight Board and Beyond' (n 63) 13.

[66] Of the first appointed Board members, a disproportionately high number (five) were from the US and a disproportionately low number (one) from India, despite India having by far the greatest number of Facebook users: see S Dixon, 'Countries with the Most Facebook Users 2023' (*Statista*, 24 February 2023), www.statista.com/statistics/268136/top-15-countries-based-on-number-of-facebook-users/. Some commentators also note lack of diversity along other parameters, such as sexual orientation: see D Wong and L Floridi, 'Meta's Oversight Board: A Review and Critical Assessment' (2022) *Minds and Machines*, section 4.4, doi.org/10.1007/s11023-022-09613-x.

[67] See, eg, 'Policy Advisory Opinion 2021-01 on the Sharing of Private Residential Information' (Advisory Opinion of Private Judicial Body, *Oversight Board*, 2021).

[68] Some scholars suggest the Board has a propensity to prioritise freedom of expression over other conflicting human rights and that this prioritisation aligns with Facebook's business model. See, eg, R Neuvonen and E Sirkkunen, 'Outsourced Justice: The Case of the Facebook Oversight Board' (2022) *Journal of Digital Media & Policy*, https://doi.org/10.1386/jdmp_00108_1.

purposes is the Board's energetic use of such law – in particular Article 19 of the 1966 International Covenant on Civil and Political Rights (ICCPR) – to subject Meta to extraneous accountability standards that have traditionally struggled to gain traction within the corporation's culture. This might seem surprising since the rules for Board deliberations cultivate an accountability regime that uses Meta's values as primary, if not exclusive, normative benchmarks (see Article 1, section 4 Charter and Article 1, section 3 Bylaws). However, when Meta publicly committed to adhere to the UNGPs, it effectively incorporated into its value system the requirement to respect the rights laid down in the ICCPR and other relevant constituents of the International Bill of Human Rights – a requirement articulated in the UNGPs. Meta thereby also opened up for the Board's operationalisation of these rights, probably to a degree beyond Meta's expectation.

The quantity of Board output is low in terms of the number of decisions and advisory policy recommendations published since October 2020 when the Board began hearing cases (ie over two years ago). Shortly after the Board's establishment, one critic disparagingly quipped that the Board 'is designed to move slowly and keep things intact'.[69] The Board's activity shows this characterisation to be a half-truth. While it is an exaggeration to claim this activity is 'changing Facebook's normative system almost beyond recognition',[70] the Board has shaken up elements of it significantly by insisting that international human rights law does not simply complement Meta's content moderation norms, but steers them. The Board's progress is also far from glacial. However, the pace of its output scarcely matches the urgency and scale of the need for its corrective eye. This is largely a function of the judicially slanted design of Board operations together with their narrow remit. The Board typically undertakes *ex-post* examination of individual posts; it is unable to rule on content moderation decisions regarding accounts or groups. Moreover, the criteria for Meta's use of OB decisions as precedent for its treatment of other posts are vague,[71] further undermining the decisions' generalisability.[72]

Although the Board carries out its permitted tasks well, its endeavour is poorly suited to addressing many of the systemic challenges of content moderation. As Evelyn Douek aptly states, '[c]ontent moderation cannot be made accountable post by post'.[73] She goes on to show how judicially inspired casuistic approaches to content moderation – as the OB endeavour exemplifies – risk missing systemic problems arising from the *ex-ante* design choices that platform operators make, the lack of transparency around those choices, and the aggregate harms they create. In this regard, the Board's remit does not permit it to strike at the heart of Meta's content moderation system. Moreover, significant facets of Facebook and Instagram operations, such as Meta's algorithmic settings for advertising and surveillance, fall formally outside the Board's purview. So, while the OB has teeth that bite, the reach of the bite is both shallow and narrow.

[69] S Vaidhayanathan, 'Facebook and the Folly of Self-Regulation' (*Wired*, 9 May 2020), www.wired.com/story/facebook-and-the-folly-of-self-regulation/.

[70] L Gradoni, 'Constitutional Review via Facebook's Oversight Board' (*Verfassungsblog*, 10 February 2021), verfassungsblog.de/fob-marbury-v-madison/.

[71] Meta shall apply these decisions to 'identical content in parallel context' where 'technically and operationally feasible': Article 4 Charter and Article 2, section 2.3.1 Bylaws.

[72] See also, eg, Wong and Floridi, 'Meta's Oversight Board' (n 66) sections 4.3 and 7.3.

[73] E Douek, 'Content Moderation as Systems Thinking' (2022) 136 *Harvard Law Review* 526, 568.

Fortunately, actors exist outside the Meta regime with a disciplining effect that is potentially greater than the Board. A pertinent example amongst US regulatory bodies is the Federal Trade Commission (FTC), which may impose penalties on corporate actors that engage in unfair or deceptive business conduct.[74] The FTC has exercised this power on several occasions against Facebook, forcing the platform to strengthen its data privacy regime,[75] and it is now in a lengthy antitrust battle to force Meta to sell Instagram and WhatsApp.[76] The FTC's recent successful suit against Epic Games evidences its ability to halt unscrupulous conduct in the provision of online services and to penalise unfair default settings for such services.[77] Nonetheless, it is too early to determine accurately the degree to which the FTC will be able to upend systemic elements of Meta's business model. And we must not discount the risk of a political backlash against the FTC should it be seen as overly aggressive in pursuing its mandate.[78]

Disciplinary regulatory oversight also comes from elsewhere, especially in Europe where Meta is engaged in a long-term struggle with regulators over putative breaches of EU legislation on data privacy and consumer protection. The outcome of this struggle is far from settled, but it involves clear threats to Meta's *modus operandi* and profit margins.[79] Moreover, the EU's Court of Justice has shown willingness to torpedo well-entrenched, profitable business practices in defence of fundamental human rights.[80] New legislative frameworks that, on paper, may significantly impact platform power and data use are emerging. Of these, the Digital Services Act (DSA) is particularly noteworthy as it subjects large online platforms to enhanced due diligence and fair design obligations, and establishes a sanctions and enforcement regime with potentially more punch than that of the General Data Protection Regulation (GDPR).[81] Nonetheless, experience with the GDPR suggests that it would be foolish to assume that the DSA will quickly cut serious inroads into the practices and profits of 'Big Tech'. The machinery of the GDPR's beefed-up sanctions and enforcement regime is still not firing with the efficiency and speed that many actors expected, despite its formal adoption back in 2016.[82]

[74] Section 5 of the US Federal Trade Commission Act 1914, codified at 15 USC § 45(a)(2).

[75] See, eg, Agreement Containing Consent Order In the Matter of Facebook Inc, No 092-3184 (Federal Trade Commission, November 2011; finalised August 2012). Further on the FTC's emergence as data privacy regulator, see DJ Solove and W Hartzog, 'The FTC and the New Common Law of Privacy' (2014) 114 *Columbia Law Review* 583.

[76] *Federal Trade Commission v Meta Platforms Inc*, No 3:23-mc-80074 (ND Cal 2022).

[77] Order of 7 February 2023, *United States of America v Epic Games Inc*, No 5:22-CV-00518-BO (EDNC Feb 7 2023).

[78] C Lima, 'GOP Uproar Over FTC's Khan Mounts as Lone Republican Calls it Quits', *The Washington Post* (Washington DC, 15 February 2023), www.washingtonpost.com/politics/2023/02/15/gop-uproar-over-ftc-khan-mounts-lone-republican-calls-it-quits/.

[79] See, eg, decision of 6 December 2022 by the European Data Protection Board directing the Irish Data Protection Commissioner to prevent Meta's Irish subsidiary from relying on a claim of contractual necessity under Article 6(1)(b) of the General Data Protection Regulation for the running of behavioural ads. Meta has appealed against the decision.

[80] See, eg, *Google Spain v Agencia Española de Protección de Datos (AEPD) and Mario Costeja González* Case C-131/12, ECLI:EU:C:2014:317; *Meta Platforms and Others* Case C-252/21, ECLI:EU:C:2023:537.

[81] See further M Husovec, *Principles of the Digital Services Act* (Oxford, Oxford University Press, forthcoming 2023).

[82] G Gentile and O Lynskey, 'Deficient by Design? The Transnational Enforcement of the GDPR' (2022) 71 *International & Comparative Law Quarterly* 799; MN Lintvedt, 'Putting a Price on Data Protection Infringement' (2022) 12 *International Data Privacy Law* 1.

V. Conclusions

The overarching conclusions of this chapter are as follows. First, the popularity of contractually based TPR of digital networks is primarily rooted in its ability to manage the complexity of these networks in an efficient, agile and flexible manner, particularly compared to the customary pace of legislative procedures. This capacity is largely a function of the special 'digital fit' between contracting as a governance mechanism and the way(s) in which data networks develop and operate.

Second, there is a tendency to exploit this capacity in aggressive pursuit of micro-management. The quest for micro-management results in the control functionality of contract looming large in this area of governance. It reinforces strong hierarchical elements in many of the contractual relations concerned, thereby underscoring Hugh Collins' general observation that 'markets and hierarchies are … not opposites, as they are sometimes presented, but rather markets create their own hierarchies through contracts'.[83]

Third, the attendant accountability mechanisms are often weak, at least as initially configured within the TPR regimes. This partly reflects an overriding concern for control that translates into a concerted attempt to achieve a type of normative self-sufficiency. At the same time, Meta's OB initiative shows the capacity of TPR regimes to engage in innovative bootstrapping processes to bolster their accountability, particularly in an effort to head off external regulatory intervention. The OB experience further shows that this can lead – somewhat paradoxically – to a rupturing of a regime's normative self-sufficiency, at least if the bootstrapping is accompanied by a public commitment to respect extraneous norms. Nonetheless, the OB experience also shows that bootstrapping will not necessarily lead to comprehensive enhancement of accountability. For example, the resultant mechanisms may remain deficient in terms of their scalability, and systemic problems with the TPR regime may stay unaddressed. This may maintain or deepen legitimacy deficits that are challenging for legislatures or the court system to correct.

[83] H Collins, *Regulating Contracts* (Oxford, Oxford University Press, 1999) 24.

5

Data Rights and Contract Law: Formation, Incorporation and Vitiating Factors

DAMIAN CLIFFORD* AND JEANNIE MARIE PATERSON**

I. Introduction

Underpinning much of the academic and policy debate about data rights are a series of assumptions as to the existence (or non-existence) of a valid contract, and the role that consent does and should play in managing that relationship. Consent and contract frame much of how personal data rights are conceptualised in commercial and regulatory contexts. In a formal, as opposed to substantive, legal sense we 'choose' to give up our data in a variety of settings on a daily basis, often by merely occupying or visiting certain spaces (virtual or physical). In publicly accessible, privately owned physical spaces such as shopping centres and supermarkets, on publicly accessible websites (whether or not requiring a user-account), we encounter intensive data gathering exploited for commercial gain.

Consent and contract are key themes of statutory data protection regimes. These typically rely on the presumed decision-making autonomy of the data subject by using notice and consent as key grounds for legitimising the collection and use of data, with contract as an alternative basis for legitimising these actions. Sceptics have criticised the assumptions underlying these models, and indeed the importance placed on individual choice, in data protection and privacy law.[1] In particular, it has been pointed out that the impact of factors such as standardised terms, complex legalese, bounded rationality and information or power asymmetries poses substantial limitations on the purported value of consent or contract in legitimating transactions over data.[2]

Notably, questions about what amounts to valid consent for the purposes of law, and the factors that might undermine consent have responses in other areas of law. Contract

* Senior Lecturer, Australian National University.
** Professor, University of Melbourne.

[1] See, eg, W Hartzog, 'Opinions · The Case Against Idealising Control' (2018) 4 *European Data Protection Law Review* 423.

[2] See further Sally Wheeler in chapter 3 of this volume.

law is focused on the circumstances in which promises, or agreements, become binding, and the circumstances in which that consent may be vitiated. Statutory consumer protection law complements, and constrains, the private law of contract in many jurisdictions by bolstering the significance and reality of consumer consent. This state of affairs is often forgotten in debates about the operation and reform of statutory data protection regimes. The risks of neglecting these key fields of law operating alongside data protection regimes include the possibilities that the overarching body of law becomes too complex to be effective, and that key gaps in the relevant regulatory regime, taken as a whole, are missed. The intersection and alignment between data protection, contract and consumer law in the protection of individual choices regarding data are therefore topics of vital importance, and the ones we set out to address in this chapter.[3]

We recognise that a focus on the private law of contract and consumer protection statutes in data protection might be criticised as perpetuating an individualistic and artificial vision of the capacity of individuals to make meaningful bargains about data rights, thereby reducing data rights to a purely transactional perspective.[4] We take the view that, although there is merit to this criticism, it underestimates the regulatory potential of consumer law, as well as the value of preserving conditions for genuine consent in data transactions.

The first section of the chapter explores the relationships between data protection law, the private law of contract and consumer protection regimes, including considering the various perspectives on consent. The second section analyses the details of the often-assumed contract for data – considering how certain legislative developments appear to place personal data as the 'price' in a consumer contract, and the intersection with the vitiating factors in contract and statutory consumer law protections, such as on misleading or unfair conduct. The third section considers the application of contract doctrine on incorporation of terms and the protections in consumer law that diverge from the private law of contract, primarily in policing unfair terms, including in data collection contracts. We conclude by broadening the perspective from doctrine, to address the question of the proper lens for considering the regulation of personal data collection.

II. Overlapping Legal Regimes

A. Data Protection, Contract and Consumer Protection

The adoption of the General Data Protection Regulation (GDPR)[5] in the European Union (EU) and the policymaking ripple effects it caused in other jurisdictions such

[3] See, eg, N Helberger, F Zuiderveen Borgesius and A Reyna, 'The Perfect Match? A Closer Look at the Relationship between EU Consumer Law and Data Protection Law' (2017) 54 *Common Market Law Review* 1427; D Clifford and J Paterson, 'Consumer Privacy and Consent: Reform in the Light of Contract and Consumer Protection Law' (2020) 94 *Australian Law Journal* 741.

[4] *cf* J Goldenfein and L McGuigan, 'Managed Sovereigns: How Inconsistent Accounts of the Human Rationalize Platform Advertising' (2023) 3(3) *Journal of Law and Political Economy*, 425.

[5] Regulation (EU) 2016/679 of the European Parliament and of the Council of 27 April 2016 on the protection of natural persons with regard to the processing of personal data and on the free movement of such data, and repealing Directive 95/46/EC (General Data Protection Regulation) [2016] OJ L119/1 (GDPR).

as the United States, Singapore and Australia, to some extent seeks to address concerns about the take-it-or-leave-it model of standard form contracting. Even in the EU, where data protection has a fundamental rights grounding, consent and contractual necessity are provided as bases legitimising the processing of personal data.[6] Therefore, individual choice remains a cornerstone of legislative data protection.

The GDPR and equivalent models impose requirements for what will amount to valid consent to satisfy those parts of the regime that rely on this requirement for data processing. These regimes also, at least to some extent, address concerns about substantive fairness, by requiring processing to be fair and/or reasonable, as a supplement to consent-based justifications for data processing, and also the accountability-based mechanisms often found in these frameworks.[7]

Contract also figures as a key element in statutory data protection regimes: as a justification for data processing, and as a conceptual basis for the core concept of consent and notice, which figure strongly in most statutory regimes for data protection.

The classical contract theory, which is commonly understood as providing the moral force of contract, positions contract as based on individual choice in the pursuit of human flourishing.[8] To support this key normative and functional role performed by consent, contract has a suite of techniques for overseeing the validity of that concept. In commercial contexts, and in contrast to data protection regimes, the requirements for the effective manifestations of contractual consent tend to be highly formal, being influenced by pragmatic concerns and the aim of maintaining certainty in market transactions.[9] The safeguard on this stance is found in doctrines, primarily vitiating factors such as misrepresentation or unconscionable dealing, which provide courts with the ability to scrutinise the probity of contract formation, and may even allow substantively unbalanced terms to operate as a reason for reopening the transaction.[10]

Consumer protection law aims both to promote consumer autonomy, primarily by improving the opportunities for consumers to exercise free and informed consent, and protect consumer welfare by making consumers better off, or at least no worse off, in transactions. These two aims are not co-extensive because while promoting autonomy is a primary goal of consumer protection law, it also commonly prohibits certain options regardless of the choices otherwise made by consumers on the ground they are contrary to the best interests of consumers, or even inconsistent with the domain of contract.[11] These doctrines are typically regulatory, in Brownsword's nomenclature,[12] but in so

[6] See ibid Arts 6(1)(a-b).

[7] See here in the context of the EU GDPR: D Clifford, 'The Data Protection Fairness Principle and the GDPR' in M Finck (ed), *Oxford Encyclopedia of EU Law* (Oxford, Oxford University Press, 2022); D Clifford and J Ausloos, 'Data Protection and the Role of Fairness' (2018) *Yearbook of European Law* 1.

[8] SA Smith, *Contract Theory* (Oxford, Oxford University Press, 2004) 56.

[9] See L Bernstein, 'Merchant Law in a Merchant Court: Rethinking the Code's Search for Immanent Business Norms' (1996) 144 *University of Pennsylvania Law Review* 1765. Also, J Morgan, *Contract Law Minimalism* (Cambridge, Cambridge University Press, 2013).

[10] See JM Paterson and E Bant, 'Contract and the Challenge of Consumer Protection Legislation' in TT Arvind and J Steele (eds), *Contract Law and the Legislature* (London, Bloomsbury Publishing, 2020).

[11] See discussion in M Chen-Wishart, 'Controlling Unfair Terms: Protecting the Institution of Contract' in L Gullifer and S Vogenaur (eds), *English and European Perspectives on Contract and Commercial Law* (Oxford, Hart Publishing, 2015) 105.

[12] See Roger Brownsword in chapter 2 of this volume.

much as they build on principles originating in contract or tort, they retain elements of coherentism.[13] This dual operation is particularly evident in the remedial sphere. Where enforced by regulators, statutory consumer protection law has an objective of influencing or deterring future behaviour but, like private law, may also be used by individuals to seek redress for wrongs.

The potential for consumer protection law to contribute to the protection of data rights is evident in at least two strategies: as a means of (1) bolstering the rights of consumers to exercise control over commercial data gathering and (2) providing protection against the unfair effects of personalised data driven commercial practices. For instance, we can think of personalised pricing and the discussion regarding digital market manipulation more generally as examples.[14] Additionally, consumer protection law exercises control over the substance of contractual bargains, prohibiting some practices and imposing mandatory standards of quality and performance in most business to consumer transactions. Consumer law may regulate the substantive fairness of contracts 'for data', potentially going beyond data protection regimes in terms of limits of the kinds of incursions that may be made on consumers' rights under those contracts.

We can see therefore, that statutory data protection and consumer protection regimes both have elements that operate in a welfare protecting manner, trumping formal manifestations of consent to circumscribe the options that can be presented to consumers. These interventions on what the parties can agree may be justified in different ways, as a rational readjustment of consumers' bounded rationality, upholding consumers' reasonable expectations of the bargain, or expressing fundamental social values of fair and just treatment. Hence, where a consumer enters into a contract which includes provisions dealing with the use of personal data/information, protections provided in consumer and data protection law may place boundaries on the agreement which would not exist in the formal law of contract. Nonetheless, assumptions about the existence of a contract arising from formal manifestations of consent may impact on the outcome for consumers, and are critical in understanding the application of the consumer protection regime. As we have noted, a concern with how consent is manifest by individuals is shared by all three regimes.

B. Perspectives on Consent

Consent is fundamental to contracting, and other key doctrines are effectively mechanisms to identify and formalise the manifestations of consent necessary to recognise a binding legal agreement. As we have already noted, consent in the law of contract is typically a formal standard – tied to objective manifestations of agreement – and softened by specific doctrines relating to vitiating factors. Consent in data protection under the GDPR and comparable regimes is set as a far more robust standard. For instance, taking

[13] Potentially leading to tensions in judicial interpretation, see Paterson and Bant, 'Contract and the Challenge of Consumer Protection Legislation' (n 10).

[14] D Clifford, 'Data Protection and Consumer Protection: The Empowerment of the Citizen-Consumer' in GG Fuster, R van Brakel and P De Hert (eds), *Research Handbook on Privacy and Data Protection Law* (Northampton MA, Edward Elgar Publishing, 2022) 234.

the GDPR as an example, in Article 4(11) consent is defined as 'any freely given, specific, informed and unambiguous indication of the data subject's wishes' with Article 6(1)(a) then stipulating it as a condition for lawful processing. Article 7 of the GDPR specifies the conditions for consent and in brief, states amongst other things that: the data subject should be able to withdraw their consent at any time, and in the assessment of whether consent is freely given, 'utmost account' is given to whether access to the service is conditional on consent.

Demanding requirements of consent for data are not found in all jurisdictions. For example, in the Singaporean Personal Data Protection Act 2012 (PDPA), sections 15 and 15A specify the elements necessary for demonstrating what is referred to as 'deemed consent'.[15] These provide that deemed consent arises when: (1) an individual 'voluntarily provides' personal data to an organisation for a purpose provided it is reasonable;[16] (2) it is necessary for the formation or conclusion of a contract;[17] or (3) notice is given and the individual does not opt out of the collection, use and disclosure of their personal data.[18] This is a separate notion from the consent generally required under the PDPA, and seems far more akin to the formal notion of consent evident in contract law.

Despite the contrasting approaches taken under the GDPR and the PDPA, they both demonstrate the complexities of a common issue, namely the difficulties in differentiating between contexts which require the satisfaction of a robust notion of consent and processing that requires some less burdensome form of legitimisation. In EU law, the uncertainty relates to complexities in terms of the overlaps between consent and other conditions for lawful processing, such as processing necessary for the formation or performance of a contract or in pursuit of particular legitimate interests. A reasonable interpretation of the EU regime would seem to suggest that a court may deem a valid contract has been formed without the offeree's conduct satisfying this legislative standard of consent. These complexities are also evident for instance in what appears to be the more 'business-friendly' PDPA, given that even in addition to the 'deemed consent' provisions, 'legitimate interests' and indeed 'business improvement purposes' (which appears to be a specification of such a legitimate interest) are provided as alternatives to consent in the First and Second Schedules to that Act.

The wider legal implications of consent as a basis for data processing also remain uncertain. Is it consent to data processing in accordance with the information disclosed in the privacy policy as required by statute, or consent to data processing according to the terms provided to the consumer by the data controller? If the latter, then is this a contract? Can a contract be formed and used as a justification for processing even where the more robust standard of consent has not been met? The distinction with contract as a basis for data processing under the GDPR, or as a means of differentiating a form of 'deemed consent' under the Singaporean PDPA, would seem then to be that contract as a basis relies on the contractual standard of valid consent (as that applies in the relevant jurisdiction), but the processing must be *necessary* for the performance of

[15] Personal Data Protection Act 2012 (2020 Rev Ed) (PDPA).
[16] See ibid s 15(1).
[17] See ibid s 15(3).
[18] See ibid s 15A.

that contract.[19] In its guidance on the UK GDPR as tailored by the Data Protection Act 2018, the UK Information Commissioner's Office notes for instance that use of the term *necessary* in this context signifies that the processing 'must be more than just useful, and more than just part of your standard terms'.[20] Consent as a basis for processing therefore may authorise a wider range of data uses, provided it meets the more robust requirements, which will also then be incorporated into any resultant contract.

III. Data Rights, Contract Formation and the Vitiation of Consent

Answers to the question of when the provision of personal data for access to a service will result in the formation of a contract is a matter for the application of the doctrines developed by the courts. Leaving aside deeds, the common law distinguishes between enforceable contracts and unenforceable promises by reference to a series of formal requirements: typically there must be: (1) agreement (traditionally expressed in terms of an offer and acceptance); (2) the objective appearance of an intention to create legal relations between the parties; (3) consideration, or in other words something given in return for the promises made by the other party; and (4) certainty and completeness in the contract. While these requirements certainly play a distinct role, they also overlap significantly in their operation. As we shall see, the overlapping requirements particularly of consideration and intent are by no means clear in their application to agreements about data.

A. Consent and Agreement

To explore the formal requirements for a valid contract about data, it is useful to consider a specific context in order to draw out the complexity in application. For instance, imagine a supermarket that has implemented a series of technical means for tracking customer movements throughout the store for security, but also commercial, purposes – let us assume that part of these commercial purposes is to track consumer behaviour to capitalise on customer footfall, by optimising store layout and product placement. The terms of this tracking are included at the entrance visible to customers before they enter. While visible however, it is clear that the requirements for valid consent such as under the GDPR will not have been met in such circumstances. As explained above, according to the GDPR, for consent to be valid it must be 'freely given, specific, informed and unambiguous'.[21]

[19] The GDPR operates alongside national contract law. It recognises that personal data processing may be *necessary* for the formation or performance of a contract. *Necessary* processing will be lawful. Processing will not be *necessary* for an invalid contract, but the validity of the underlying contract is a matter for national contract law.

[20] Information Commissioner's Office, 'Guide to the General Data Protection Regulation (GDPR)' (Regulatory Guidance, 14 October 2022) 92, ico.org.uk/media/for-organisations/guide-to-data-protection/guide-to-the-general-data-protection-regulation-gdpr-1-1.pdf.

[21] GDPR, Art 4(11).

Is this the end of the story then? It seems very likely that a robust standard of consent as a condition for lawful personal data processing would be impractical as a means of legitimising the activities in question. Indeed, in other similar contexts, both scholars and data protection authorities agree that consent as defined in the GDPR is inappropriate for such forms of data processing.[22] In jurisdictions such as Australia, where consent, if even required at all under the current regime,[23] may be implied in the circumstances from the conduct of the consumers.[24] In jurisdictions such as the United Kingdom (UK) (ie with the UK GDPR) and Ireland (ie with the EU GDPR), consent will be bypassed in favour of legitimate interest, as a distinct condition for lawful processing. Legitimate interest as provided in Article 6(1)(f) of the GDPR is often seen by businesses as an alternative to consent legitimising personal data processing, alongside contract. In contrast to consent, and indeed similar to the other conditions for lawful processing, in EU law the application of legitimate interest requires that the processing in question be 'necessary'.

Legitimate interests as a condition for lawful processing essentially mandates the balancing of interests to determine if the processing itself is necessary, with the provision differentiating between the interests of three distinct entities: the controller (ie the one responsible for the processing), the data subject and third parties, with all being relevant in the operation of the provision. A multitude of elements may need to be considered and these factors are often difficult to identify and quantify.[25] This reflects the point that Article 6(1)(f) acts as a context-dependent, fair balancing mechanism that is deliberately constructed in an open-ended manner.[26] In keeping with the analysis of the necessity test in contract as a grounds for processing discussed above, EU courts, guidance documents and scholarly interpretations for the most part have also viewed the 'necessity test' at the centre of the legitimate interest ground as very narrowly requiring the processing to be *strictly* necessary.

The necessity test is not a universal feature of legitimate interests as a condition for lawful processing in other jurisdictions. Here we can again refer to the Singaporean PDPA which provides specific examples of legitimate interests in Part 3 of the First Schedule, while also providing a broad catch-all exception which can be relied upon if 'the legitimate interests of the organisation or other person outweigh any adverse effect on the individual'. Even in the arguably more open PDPA, therefore, it would appear that there are limits to the scope of these grounds for processing. Accordingly, to repeat, in circumstances where there is intensive data processing for marketing purposes, consent may be the only appropriate condition, but this may not always be practically possible to obtain.

[22] See, eg, Article 29 Working Party, 'Guidelines on Consent under Regulation 2016/679' (2017) WP259 23. For an academic analysis related to this point, see generally, D Clifford, 'Citizen-Consumers in a Personalised Galaxy: Emotion Influenced Decision-Making, A True Path to the Dark Side?' in L Edwards, B Schafer and E Harbinja (eds), *Future Law: Emerging Technology, Regulation and Ethics* (Edinburgh, Edinburgh University Press 2020).

[23] Privacy Act 1988 (Cth) Sch 1 Australian Privacy Principle 5.

[24] ibid s 6: '*consent* means express consent or implied consent'.

[25] See, eg, Article 29 Working Party, 'Opinion 06/2014 on the "Notion of Legitimate Interests of the Data Controller under Article 7 of Directive 95/46/EC"' (Advisory Body Opinion, European Commission, 2014), ec.europa.eu/justice/article-29/documentation/opinion-recommendation/files/2014/wp217_en.pdf.

[26] Case C-582/14 *Patrick Breyer v Bundesrepublik Deutschland* ECLI:EU:C:2016:779.

In the example provided of a supermarket tracking the movements of its customers throughout the store for security and also commercial purposes, relevant considerations under EU law might be, on the one hand, that the store has, in law, the right to determine who enters its premises and on what condition, and, on the other hand, the undoubted interest of consumers in privacy and their likely lack of awareness of the tracking that might occur. Also relevant to the inquiry would be the technology used to effect the tracking – facial recognition for instance is difficult to justify for mere commercial purposes, and also even for security given its far reaching effects.[27] But even less intrusive technologies – such as Bluetooth tracking or beacons – may be difficult to justify as necessary, at least for commercial purposes.

Similarly, in the interpretation of contract as a condition for lawful processing, the dominant approach appears to require that any such processing be necessary for the performance of a contract as opposed to being the object of the contract itself. To clarify, although it is necessary to process payment details including personal data so that the customer in our hypothetical may purchase their items in the store, it is less clear whether the gathering of the personal data can be the focus of the agreement itself and be legitimised under Article 6(1)(b). This appears to reflect the idea that under the GDPR you cannot 'contract out' of the protections afforded in the Regulation – although admittedly this is not made explicit it nevertheless seems an uncontroversial point. The question then becomes what these outcomes mean for the common law contract. Might legitimate interests as a condition for lawful processing, left purely in an *ex ante* sense in the hands of the entity processing the data, also result in the formation of a valid contract with consumers?

These issues are again very much to the fore in the EU law and policy debates in the discussions of the overlaps between consumer and data protection law. For instance, the EU's Digital Content Directive,[28] which lays down protections dealing with contracts for the supply of digital content or digital services, essentially provides in Article 3(1) that where the 'consumer provides or undertakes to provide personal data to the trader' the consumer will be protected. This Directive, inter alia, appears to state that a consumer's decision to provide or undertake to provide personal data in exchange for access to a service, results in the formation of a consumer contract, but that processing necessary for the provision of such a service or to comply with a legal obligation does not. However, despite referring to consent in the recitals, the Directive fails to appropriately clarify if legitimate interest may also result in a consumer contract. Due to the use of rather open language therefore, the Directive appears to implicitly leave this matter to national contract law.

In the example provided, it seems unlikely that there is any contract between the parties around the data collection and processing. The store will in most cases not have presented an offer and nor will consumers have manifest an intention to be bound. Certainly, an offer can be made to the world at large, if that objectively can be deemed to

[27] See, eg, 'Retailers Must Ensure Compliance with Privacy Laws' (Media Release, Office of the Australian Information Commissioner, 16 June 2022), www.oaic.gov.au/updates/news-and-media/retailers-must-ensure-compliance-with-privacy-laws.

[28] Directive (EU) 2019/770 of the European Parliament and of the Council of 20 May 2019 on certain aspects concerning contracts for the supply of digital content and digital services [2019] OJ L136/1.

consumer contract in the context of 'active' collection – perhaps ultimately resulting in its deletion in the adopted Directive.[35]

The separation is perhaps less artificial in jurisdictions that do not have specific cookie rules. For instance, in Australia there is currently uncertainty as to whether the Privacy Act 1988 (Cth) actually applies to device-related information, notwithstanding the absence of any similar protections regarding the collection of cookie-like information. Indeed, the definition of personal information in the current Act has been a point of contention for several years and a key point in reform discussions.[36] But what could this mean practically for common law contract? Could, for instance, the consent to the accessing of information already placed on the machine (ie their 'terminal equipment' in the EU law parlance) of a user that is required under EU law be deemed to automatically result in the formation of a consumer contract, given that such consent must be 'informed' 'unambiguous', 'specific' and 'freely given' as defined cumulatively in the GDPR? In the absence of the requirement for such a consent in jurisdictions without cookie-specific rules could there still be a valid contract? And what is the role of the information (personal or otherwise) that is being provided?

It seems unlikely that an objective intention to enter a consumer contract could be established in jurisdictions without these or similar cookie rules – thereby mirroring the debates, discussed above, relating to the gathering of information in a supermarket. Can we really say that an objective intention to enter into a legal relationship can be construed from conduct amounting to mere browsing of a publicly accessible website? And, even in the EU with its robust standard of consent, can we really say that consent to a cookie usage policy manifests the intention to enter into legal relations especially when such a policy may be one amongst many other documents (ie terms and conditions including an IP policy)? It is certainly arguable that such documents may again be understood more as mere licences to use the website.

Whether the basis for the transaction is contract, notice or licence, the analysis does not end there. Contractual consent, and presumably consent provided by a notice, may be vitiated by various legal doctrines, an issue to which we now turn.

C. Vitiating Factors as a Response to Misconduct Tainting Consent

Contract law contains a number of doctrines which give relief from a validly formed contract where consent is tainted by a vitiating factor that makes it insecure as a basis for a contract. Similar but broader doctrines are found in consumer protection regimes

[35] See R Robert and L Smit, 'The Proposal for a Directive on Digital Content: A Complex Relationship with Data Protection Law' (2018) 19 *ERA Forum* 159; G Malgieri, '"User-Provided Personal Content" in the EU: Digital Currency between Data Protection and Intellectual Property' (2018) 32 *International Review of Law, Computers & Technology* 118; D Clifford, I Graef and P Valcke, 'Preformulated Declarations of Data Subject Consent' (2019) 20 *German Law Journal* 679; V Mak, 'Contract and Consumer Law' in V Mak, E Tjong Tjin Tai and A Berlee (eds), *Research Handbook in Data Science and Law* (Cheltenham, Edward Elgar Publishing, 2018).

[36] See Attorney General's Department, 'Privacy Act Review' (Report, 2022) 23–24.

such as the EU Unfair Commercial Practices Directive.[37] Vitiating factors and their statutory analogues may be used to respond to misconduct in the transacting process that occurs regardless of compliance with the robust consent requirements of data protection regimes. These doctrines do not ensure that parties read or understand contract terms, or that parties who are experiencing vulnerability are able to navigate those terms. Nonetheless, they provide limits to the use by business of contracts to exploit consumers' weaker bargaining power or experience, and therefore should not be dismissed when understanding the regime governing data collection from consumers.

Statutory prohibitions on misleading and unfair conduct have been used by regulators to penalise companies that depart from their representations about the term of their privacy policies.[38] They may also be effective in responding to manipulative contracting practice, including the use of dark patterns, as demonstrated by some nascent EU case law and policy statements[39] and the stance of the US Federal Trade Commission.[40] Even accepting the role for bans on specific kinds of problematic conduct,[41] vitiating factors act as a safety net for sanctioning conduct that cannot be captured by particular rules in either consumer protection or data regimes. At the same time, at some point, we meet the limits of conduct obligations in addressing issues of substantive unfairness in data contracts.

IV. Data Contract Terms

A. Incorporation of Cookie and Privacy Policies

Data collection and processing is typically governed by pre-formulated terms in notices and standard form contracts. The use of privacy policies and cookies policies reflects a practical reality. Pre-formulation is necessary given the scale and characteristics of the provision of online services. For example, data protection and privacy legislation

[37] Directive 2005/29/EC of the European Parliament and of the Council of 11 May 2005 concerning unfair business-to-consumer commercial practices in the internal market and amending Council Directive 84/450/EEC, Directives 97/7/EC, 98/27/EC and 2002/65/EC of the European Parliament and of the Council and Regulation (EC) No 2006/2004 of the European Parliament and of the Council (Unfair Commercial Practices Directive) [2005] OJ L149/22.

[38] For a fuller discussion, see JM Paterson, E Bant and H Cooney, 'Australian Competition and Consumer Commission v Google: Deterring Misleading Conduct in Digital Privacy Policies' (2021) 26 *Communications Law* 136.

[39] See European Data Protection Board, 'Guidelines 3/2022 on Dark Patterns in Social Media Platform Interfaces: How to Recognise and Avoid Them' (Regulatory Guidelines, 3/2022, 14 March 2022). The European Consumer Organisation, '"Dark Patterns" and the EU Consumer Law Acquis – Recommendations for Better Enforcement and Reform' (Policy Paper, 7 February 2022).

[40] See Federal Trade Commission/Bureau of Consumer Protection, 'Bringing Dark Patterns to Light' (Report, September 2022), www.ftc.gov/reports/bringing-dark-patterns-light; Federal Trade Commission, 'FTC Takes Action Against Amazon for Enrolling Consumers in Amazon Prime without Consent and Sabotaging their Attempts to Cancel' (Press Release, 21 June 2023), www.ftc.gov/news-events/news/press-releases/2023/06/ftc-takes-action-against-amazon-enrolling-consumers-amazon-prime-without-consent-sabotaging-their.

[41] For an example from the EU, see Regulation (EU) 2022/2065 of the European Parliament and of the Council of 19 October 2022 on a single market for digital services and amending Directive 2000/31/EC (Digital Services Act) [2022] OJ L277/1.

typically require entities processing personal data to inform data subjects about the nature and extent of this conduct, this model of transparency being a key component of accountability-based frameworks. Given the scale of these operations, pre-formulation is therefore necessary – we can think here of the arguments in favour of standard form contracts as being of comparative value.[42] But how should we understand these policies in contract law? Although it is clear that when signing up to a social media account for example, a consumer contract will form, what does this mean in relation to the incorporation of these policies in the agreement?

The rules relating to the incorporation of terms in common law contracts are straightforward. Prior notice is required, albeit in certain circumstances where there is a course of dealings between the parties, terms may be objectively interpreted to come within the scope. The consequence of signing a document known to contain obligations is also clear – signing objectively manifests the intention to enter into legal relations and those who do so are bound to the specified terms,[43] although this is subject to certain statutory requirements, such as those stipulating protections against the use of unfair terms, but also more generally protections provided in legislation such as data protection and privacy law. The law of contract has continually adapted to new technologies, and contracts made online are no exception. Browse-wrap (the contract made by using a website) and click-wrap contracts (the contract made through an online sign-up) have been subject to repeated contractual analysis. The conclusion is that the ordinary rules of contract formation apply – and in particular as to the incorporation of terms. Notice must be given to incorporate terms in a browse-wrap contract, while a click-wrap contract will usually be the equivalent of a signed contract with the onus on the consumer to familiarise themselves with the terms.[44] Presumably these rules apply to contracts for data in exchange for services, and the more awkward case of attempts to collect data from the mere use of a website, for which greater notice and presumably more robust manifestations of consent might be required, as discussed earlier.[45]

However, when dealing with click-wrap or browse-wrap contracts a question arises over precisely which terms are in fact part of the so-called agreement. Online, terms relating to the variety of matters affecting the interaction between the parties are provided through hyperlinked content. For example, imagine a social networking site where, when you visit the website, you are required to set-up an account and agree to terms and conditions in order to access the services. The contract is then akin to a signed contract in law. During this process, consumers will be provided with notice of the standard terms but there may also be hyperlinks to specific policies relating to privacy, cookies usage, intellectual property protection, and also broader community-based policies for the safety/security of the service and its users. Are all of these to be understood as part of one overarching agreement or are some of these policies merely

[42] See RA Hillman and JJ Rachlinski, 'Standard-Form Contracting in the Electronic Age' (2002) 77 *New York University Law Review* 429.

[43] *L'Estrange v F Graucob Ltd* [1934] 2 KB 394.

[44] See E Macdonald, 'Incorporation of Standard Terms in Website Contracting: Clicking "I Agree"' (2011) 27 *Journal of Contract Law* 198; JM Paterson, 'Consumer Contracting in the Age of the Digital Natives' (2011) 27 *Journal of Contract Law* 152.

[45] Reference here can again be made to legislation such as the EU Digital Content Directive (n 28).

licences, or not relevant at all failing adequate notice of the terms? The issue is important insofar as data processers seek to rely on contract, rather than consent (in the way defined by data protection regimes) as a basis for processing.

It should be noted that regulatory requirements might add further complexity to this question. For instance, as explained above, to comply with cookie-rules such as those provided for in Article 5(3) of the EU's ePrivacy Directive, consumer consent may be required. Such an obligation often manifests itself as a separate box to be ticked and consented to distinct from the acceptance of the terms of service. Moreover, other legislative requirements stemming again from data protection and privacy law may mean that the service provider (ie as the entity processing the personal data) may be basing its various processing operations on lawful grounds other than consent such as contract and/or legitimate interests. What are the consequences of this separation between different conditions for lawful processing? Again, there appears to be a potential practical separation between processing requiring consent (such as relating to the use of cookies) and processing more generally – ie which may be interpreted as being 'necessary' for the performance of the service contract accepted by the consumer.

B. Substantive Fairness and Unfair Terms in Data Contracts

Legislative protections against unfair terms provide substantive fairness tests and raise interesting questions regarding their application to data gathering practices. More specifically, one must consider the extent to which unfair terms protections apply to data collection notices. This is particularly significant as, outside of jurisdictions such as the UK where the unfair contract terms regime applies to mere notices,[46] these legislative protections generally require a contract to be in existence to apply.

More broadly, unfair terms regimes raise an interesting tension with data protection law. Data protection laws typically assume that provided the justification for data collection is satisfied – consent, contract, or legitimate interests – the underlying contract is valid as it stands. Yet the unfair terms regime may in principle render void overreaching or one-sided terms that are not in good faith, and go beyond even requirements of fair and reasonable processing. This is an important check on the often-raised concern that consumers, even when informed, etc, may consent to terms not in their best interests because they do not understand the impact of such consent. We suspect, for example, that the privacy impacts of facial recognition technology are not well understood. Terms justifying the use and long retention of this kind of biometric data may well be unfair, in addition to any concerns that may be raised in data protection concerning principles such as purpose limitation and data minimisation. Therefore, there are important overlaps.

Reference can also be made here, for instance, to Recital 42 of the GDPR which states that pre-formulated declarations of consent to personal data processing must comply with the EU Unfair Terms in Consumer Contracts Directive[47] and, more specifically,

[46] Consumer Rights Act 2015, s 61(4).
[47] Council Directive 93/13/EEC of 5 April 1993 on unfair terms in consumer contracts [1993] OJ L95/29.

that such statements 'should be provided in an intelligible and easily accessible form, using clear and plain language and … should not contain unfair terms'. Together the regimes provide important safeguards to consumers, precluding overreaching or one-sided terms. The application of an unfair terms regime also potentially resolves practical challenges that might arise if the focus is purely one of data protection. For example, consider attempts by the data processer to change the terms of privacy and/or cookies policies, often pursuant to a power reserved to the provider in the terms of service. Consumer protection authorities have explored these issues – typically arriving at the view that unilateral variation provisions are unfair unless highly transparent,[48] and at least without some kind of fetter or right to exit that would protect the interests of consumers.[49]

C. Perpetuating the Ideal of the 'Rational' Data Subject

One criticism of a reliance on consent, notice and even consumer protection in regulating the collection of personal data is that it reinforces a focus on the individual, and their rights and responsibilities. This distracts attention from the fundamental harms of data processing or profiling on groups and populations.[50] Additionally, the focus on how individuals should be regarded as manifesting consent might be an aid to gloss over the disparities of market power that justify the 'trade' in data. From this perspective, the qualifications of consumer protection might be seen as reinforcing the dominant ideal of the rational consumer who exercises considered informed choice in entering the data exchange, whereas in reality most consumers do nothing of the kind, while failing to address structural and social issues surrounding the trade in data.[51] On this approach, consumer protection regimes merely tinker around the edges while confirming the dominant paradigm as being the rational contracting data subject. The regimes do little to combat the reality that consumers have very little choice in arriving at this position.

While recognising these concerns, we consider that data and consumer protection regimes perform a valuable role in the overall regulatory network of data protection. The goal of demanding a more robust standard of consent is valuable as a way of recognising the value of individual autonomy, including over data, in the market place. There is also value in continuing to scrutinise and reform the circumstances in which consumer protection law goes beyond merely monitoring consent to exercising some substantive control over the substance of bargains. Indeed, the conclusion of critics of the current frameworks and the role of individual decision-makers is a call for more

[48] See, eg, Case C-472/10 *Nemzeti Fogyastóvédelmi Hatóság v Invitel Távközlési Zrt* ECLI:EU:C:2012:242 and Case C-583/18 *Vertrieb v Verbraucherzentrale Nordrhei-Westfalen eV* ECLIR:EU:C:2020:199.

[49] See further JM Paterson and R Smith, 'Why Unilateral Variation Clauses are Unfair' (2016) 23 *Competition and Consumer Law Journal* 201.

[50] S Viljoen, 'Democratic Data: A Relational Theory for Data Governance' (2021) 131 *Yale Law Journal* 573, 578.

[51] See, eg, D Hoffman, 'Defeating the Empire of Forms' (2023) *Virginia Law Review* (forthcoming); Hartzog, 'Opinions · The Case Against Idealising Control' (n 1); E Bietti, 'Consent as a Free Pass: Platform Power and the Limits of the Informational Turn' (2020) 40 *Pace Law Review* 310.

tests share similarities with innovations in the Internet of Things, such as mobile health and wearable fitness monitors.[80] They also can be viewed as contributing to the generation of 'biometric big data'.[81] This reality reinforces the view that DTC test results should be considered 'personal data' that individuals provide to data controllers. Such personal data is subject to the right to data portability under the GDPR.

Furthermore, genetic information constitutes sensitive information that is subject to specific protections under the GDPR.[82] Article 9 of the GDPR prohibits processing of genetic data, with a few exceptions, the most relevant of which is explicit consent.

Implementing stronger protections to users and empowering them to control their data in the DTC genetics context would allow consumers to receive and move their data from one company (such as a healthcare entity) to another. Recall that the GDPR also provides consumers with the right to erasure, increasing the control that data subjects have over their personal data.[83] The literature suggests that the right to delete could be vital in protecting consumers of DTC genetic services.[84]

While we do not have space herein to address this in detail, we also note the proposal in 2022 for a Regulation on a European Health Data Space.[85] This proposed Regulation aims to enhance the right to data portability for European citizens in their health data and we hope to explore this in future work.

Other countries, including Australia and New Zealand, also treat genetic information as sensitive, although currently New Zealand's Privacy Act 2020 does not afford special protection for genetic information in the same manner as the GDPR.[86] However, proposals for CDRs outside the EU are often more limited in scope than the rights set out in the GDPR. Frequently, they take the form of sectoral rights. This is true of the Australian CDR regime, to which we now turn.

The Australian CDR was introduced in 2019 through Part IVD of the Competition and Consumer Act 2010.[87] The Australian Competition & Consumer Commission (ACCC) developed this CDR in consultation with industry players.[88] The objective of this CDR is to allow 'consumers greater access to and control over their data and […] improve consumers' ability to compare and switch between products and services'.[89] The Australian Federal Treasury is responsible for the overall enforcement of the CDR

[80] ibid.

[81] E Vayena and A Blasimme, 'Biomedical Big Data: New Models of Control Over Access, Use and Governance' (2017) 14 *Journal of Bioethical Inquiry* 501.

[82] GDPR.

[83] Vayena and Blasimme, 'Biomedical Big Data' (n 81) 508.

[84] Gassner, 'The Right to Delete' (n 78).

[85] Commission, 'Proposal for a Regulation of the European Parliament and of the Council on the European Health Data Space' COM (2022) 197 final.

[86] In Australia, there are guidelines for health practitioners in the private sector that apply to the use and disclosure of genetic information. Australian Information Commissioner (OAIC), 'Genetic Information', www.oaic.gov.au/privacy/privacy-legislation/the-privacy-act/rules-and-guidelines.

[87] Australian Competition & Consumer Commission (ACCC), 'Consumer Data Right (CDR)', accc.gov.au/focus-areas/consumer-data-right-cdr-0.

[88] ACCC, 'ACCC Consultation on Rules Framework', accc.gov.au/focus-areas/consumer-data-right-cdr-0/accc-consultation-on-rules-framework; ACCC, 'CDR in the Energy Sector', accc.gov.au/focus-areas/consumer-data-right-cdr/cdr-in-the-energy-sector; and ACCC, 'Energy Rules Framework Consultation', accc.gov.au/focus-areas/consumer-data-right-cdr/cdr-in-the-energy-sector/energy-rules-framework-consultation.

[89] ACCC, 'Consumer Data Right (CDR)' (n 87).

regime.[90] This responsibility includes the development of implementation rules and advising the Government on the expansion of CDRs to other sectors.[91]

As part of the Australian implementation, CDRs are subject to 13 privacy safeguards[92] set out in the Privacy Safeguard Guidelines for the CDR,[93] which were developed by the Australian Information Commissioner (OAIC). These Guidelines, subject to regular review,[94] aim to help businesses implement CDRs and avoid breaching the privacy safeguards.[95]

The Australian CDRs are framed as sectoral rights, first deployed in the banking sector.[96] There are plans to introduce the CDRs into the energy and telecommunications sectors.[97] However, there is no indication that the Australian Federal Treasury intends to recommend CDRs tailored to DTC genetic testing or healthcare services.

In New Zealand, the Privacy Commissioner has the power to issue codes of practice for specific industries and they have recently revised the Health Information Privacy Code, which applies to the healthcare sector.[98] Nonetheless, much of the DTC industry is located outside New Zealand and is characterised as a consumer service. Consequently, the Code does not directly apply to these services. Furthermore, New Zealand's Privacy Act 2020 has extraterritorial effect.[99] As such, DTC companies targeting their services to New Zealanders should comply with it. However, some researchers suggest that more collaboration and partnerships with Indigenous communities are needed.[100] To date, we are not aware of any of the market leaders in this space engaging directly with Indigenous communities. Given that the DTC industry is commercial, government and regulatory support may be necessary to advance such partnerships.

In July 2021, the New Zealand Government announced its intention to create CDRs in New Zealand.[101] The Ministry of Business, Innovation, and Employment (MBIE) has played an essential role in developing CDRs in New Zealand.[102] As in Australia, the proposed CDR in New Zealand will also be developed on a sectoral basis 'with the Government designating individual markets, industries and sectors to which it

[90] ibid.
[91] ibid.
[92] OAIC, 'Consumer Data Right Privacy Safeguards', oaic.gov.au/consumer-data-right/cdr-privacy-safeguards.
[93] ibid; see also M Burdon and T Mackie, 'Australia's Consumer Data Right and the Uncertain Role of Information Privacy Law' (2020) 10 *International Data Privacy Law* 222.
[94] This is the most recent version: OAIC, 'Consumer Data Right Privacy Safeguard Guidelines' Version 3.0 (Regulatory Guidelines, June 2021), oaic.gov.au/__data/assets/pdf_file/0012/8013/privacy-safeguard-combined-chapters.pdf.
[95] ibid para A2.
[96] ACCC, 'Consumer Data Right (CDR)' (n 87); OAIC, 'What is the Consumer Data Right?', oaic.gov.au/consumer-data-right/what-is-the-consumer-data-right.
[97] ACCC, 'Consumer Data Right (CDR)' (n 87); ACCC, 'CDR in the Energy Sector', www.cdr.gov.au/rollout/cdr-energy-sector.
[98] Office of the New Zealand Privacy Commissioner, 'Health Information Privacy Code 2020', privacy.org.nz/privacy-act-2020/codes-of-practice/hipc2020/.
[99] Privacy Act 2020 (NZ), s 4.
[100] Garrison et al, 'Genomic Research Through an Indigenous Lens' (n 64).
[101] Ministry of Business, Innovation, and Employment (MBIE), 'Consumer Data Right', mbie.govt.nz/business-and-employment/business/competition-regulation-and-policy/consumer-data-right/.
[102] Amongst other things, it engaged in a public consultation on CDRs in 2019 and 2020. See ibid.

7

Private Law Rights Mechanisms for Consumer Data – Filling the Gaps

CHRIS REED*

I. Introduction

Data is the lifeblood of online commerce, especially e-commerce. It is now standard for almost every online business to collect data about its customers, not only about their current transactions but even about previous websites they visited and their destinations upon leaving.

In addition to this direct collection of data, it is also common for third parties to track the activities of online actors. Research by Koop et al has identified that user activity is almost always tracked by one or more third parties.[1]

A third source of data is a user's social media activity. This is analysed by social media companies to identify the things that the user is interested in and to predict their future attitudes and intentions, especially towards purchasing decisions.

Finally, much of this data is shared by its collectors on commercial terms with e-commerce sellers and with aggregation enterprises. Aggregated data can be used to analyse the collective actions, sentiments and plans of users, suggesting new products, new marketing methods and so on. Data on individual users can be used by sellers to tailor products and services more precisely to them, offer differential pricing based on the user's calculated worth and their willingness to pay, market products and services to them in ways which are more likely to persuade them to buy, amongst many other purposes. Market pressures drive e-commerce sellers to use this data in order to maintain competitiveness with other sellers.[2]

* Professor of Electronic Commerce Law, Queen Mary University of London. My thanks are due to Professor Samuel Becher for his helpful comments on an early draft of this chapter.

[1] M Koop, E Tews and S Katzenbeisser, 'In-Depth Evaluation of Redirect Tracking and Link Usage' (2020) 2020(4) *Proceedings on Privacy Enhancing Technologies* 394, 401. Their analysis of commonly visited websites finds that on 42% of them the user is tracked by doubleclick.net, on 26% by facebook.com, and to a lesser degree by more than 25 other third party data collectors.

[2] See J Krämer and D Schnurr, 'Big Data and Digital Markets Contestability: Theory of Harm and Data Access Remedies' (2022) 18 *Journal of Competition Law & Economics* 255: 'independent websites can end up in a dilemma, whereby competitive pressure forces them to adopt such ancillary services in an effort to gain a

II. Restricting Collection and Use

Although this vast quantity of data sharing has clear benefits for online sellers to consumers, and of course for those who collect, aggregate and analyse consumer data, the benefits for consumers or society more widely are contested, particularly by those concerned with consumer privacy. For this reason, there is growing pressure to restrict collection and use.

Consumers have concerns about such data collection and use because it has the potential to undermine their autonomy to make a free purchasing choice. It takes their already weak position vis-à-vis the e-commerce seller and weakens it further. '[E]very personalized ad signals that the retailer has tracked and analysed detailed information about the consumer's browsing activities and is willing to exploit this knowledge'.[3] Regulators and lawmakers have concerns because collection and use of consumer data presents obvious threats to their fundamental rights of privacy and data protection, and also opens the way to commercial practices[4] which might disadvantage the consumer to such an extent that legal intervention is required.

For this reason, many legal systems already impose controls and restrictions on data collection and data sharing. Controls and restrictions based on data protection and privacy law focus mainly on the justifications for collecting and sharing data, and on the fairness of the uses made of it. Consumer protection law has generally been more concerned with the consequences of how data is used to market and sell to consumers, and on the fairness of seller conduct which results in those consequences, though it may also have relevance to contractual terms and non-contractual notices which legitimate data collection by sellers and service suppliers.[5]

Privacy law and data protection law examine different aspects of the consumer data lifecycle. Privacy law is mainly concerned with disclosure of information. For example, data about my purchase from Amazon is not private, as between Amazon and myself, but if Amazon discloses that data to others then privacy law may be engaged. Data protection law concentrates on the fairness of all elements of the data lifecycle – collection, storage, processing and disclosure. Any of these might contravene the law, even if they present no risk to privacy. Thus, in my Amazon transaction, Amazon is subject to data protection law for all that it does with my data, including some obligations to ensure its subsequent fair use if it is disclosed to others (irrespective of whether that disclosure has any effect on my privacy).

In most countries, privacy law provides a remedy for actual or anticipated breaches via court action. Whether a disclosure of information amounts to a breach of privacy rights usually depends on a combination of the claimant's expectations about

competitive advantage over other independent websites with whom they compete immediately for users in a given market'.

[3] A Bleier and M Eisenbeiss, 'The Importance of Trust for Personalized Online Advertising' (2015) 91 *Journal of Retailing* 390, 390. Empirical research in this paper also finds that highly personalised advertisements generate lower responses from consumers than less targeted advertisements, unless the seller is already trusted by the consumer, in which case they increase response rates.

[4] Practices which manipulate the consumer's free choice, such as 'dark patterns' and other potentially manipulative ways of influencing consumers – see text to n 17 ff.

[5] See Samuel Becher and Andelka Phillips in chapter 6 of this volume.

disclosure, and the deleterious effects of disclosure on the claimant.[6] Typical remedies include damages and injunctions. The cost of seeking such remedies is high, and so privacy law is likely to have little effect in shaping the actions of those who collect and use consumer data. If Amazon were wrongfully to disclose data about my purchase of, say, a USB cable, the cost of seeking redress would be out of all proportion to the damages I might receive.

In some countries privacy law is enforced by a regulator, such as Canada's Privacy Commissioner,[7] and data protection law is always enforced by a regulator, in the United Kingdom the Information Commissioner's Office. These regulators will have enough resources to take enforcement action against at least some breaches of the law, though only a minority. In theory this might be enough to incentivise compliance by others because penalties for breach can be high.[8] Although data protection law tends to be highly detailed and complex, its core aims are quite simple. To take the European Union (EU) General Data Protection Regulation (GDPR) as our example, the fundamental requirement of the law is that a person who controls or processes personal data (data relating to a living individual) must do so fairly.[9] Of course, defining fairness is far from simple, and has been left to the courts to decide in individual cases.

Under data protection laws, all forms of data processing, including collection and sharing, require a justification which complies with the law. The primary justifications for consumer data are, in broad summary:

- That the consumer has consented to processing for specified purposes;
- That processing is necessary for entering into or performing a contract with the data subject; or
- That the processing is in the legitimate interest of the data controller, and is not overridden by the interest of the data subject.[10]

Consumer consent is notoriously easy to obtain, usually via a pop-up menu which is impatiently clicked away by agreeing. This form of consent is almost certainly inadequate to comply with the GDPR, which demands free and informed consent,[11] and

[6] See, eg, *Campbell v MGN Ltd* [2004] UKHL 22, [2004] 2 AC 457.

[7] Office of the Privacy Commissioner of Canada, priv.gc.ca/en/.

[8] Under the EU General Data Protection Regulation (GDPR) (Regulation (EU) 2016/679 of the European Parliament and of the Council of 27 April 2016 on the protection of natural persons with regard to the processing of personal data and on the free movement of such data, and repealing Directive 95/46/EC (General Data Protection Regulation) [2016] OJ L119/1), the maximum penalty which the regulator can impose is set at €20 million or 4% of annual global turnover, whichever is the greater. Heavy penalties for serious breaches are becoming more common – in October 2022 the UK Information Commissioner fined Interserve £4.4m for a breach which led to the disclosure of the data of 113,000 employees.

[9] Art 5(1) of the GDPR sets out the principles of data protection, and principle (a) reads that personal data shall be:

(a) processed lawfully, fairly and in a transparent manner in relation to the data subject.

The remaining principles, (b)–(f) can be seen as more detailed examples of the general obligation of fairness – for example, limiting processing to data which is adequate, relevant and necessary for the purpose (principle (c)).

[10] ibid Art 6(1)(a) and (f).

[11] ibid Art 7. See also 'Guidelines 05/2020 on Consent under Regulation 2016/679' (Regulatory Guidelines, European Data Protection Board (EDPB), 4 May 2020), edpb.europa.eu/sites/default/files/files/file1/edpb_guidelines_202005_consent_en.pdf.

Merchants also use the language and presentation of contractual materials to influence consumer behaviour to the merchant's advantage.[21]

Dark patterns were initially developed to take advantage of the psychology of consumers generally, but the ability of online merchants to use their access to individual consumer data to identify biases or weaknesses in *that particular consumer*, enables them to reconfigure their offering to exploit that consumer even more effectively by securing their consent to extensive data collection and, of course, influencing their purchasing decisions.[22]

The ability to sell to individual consumers in individual ways undermines some of the protections of consumer law. For example, the EU Unfair Commercial Practices Directive assesses the unfairness of trading practices by reference to the 'average consumer'.[23] In the online world, increasingly there is no longer any such person as the average consumer.

Mik argues persuasively that consumer protection law needs reform to recognise this move to individualisation. She points out that 'All online consumers can be vulnerable, *each* in its own way',[24] and that even temporary vulnerabilities, such as low mood or intoxication, can be recognised and exploited through data analysis. She argues that the law should recognise that vulnerability 'can be a "dynamic state" which affects consumers at different times and in different circumstances',[25] and thus that the law should define and control 'the legally permissible levels of transactional exploitation'.[26]

How this might be implemented via legislation is more difficult though. The existing controls on trading practices focus on misleading and aggressive trading practices, assessed by reference to the average consumer. Using psychological techniques to persuade a consumer to buy is rarely misleading unless it takes advantage of individual vulnerabilities. Heavy persuasion can eventually shade into aggressive selling, and again individual vulnerabilities would need to be assessed. In effect, the law would need to be personalised for each particular consumer in those particular circumstances. And of course, the seller would need to be aware of the consumer's vulnerabilities at the time. Reshaping consumer protection law on the basis of intention, motivation and understanding is a very fundamental change, and a substantial challenge for courts which are asked to assess whether breaches have occurred.

Indeed, even if the law *were* changed in these ways, consumer protection would still face the same enforcement problems as data protection law. The resources to bring enforcement actions are disproportionately low in relation to the problem. In many cases cross-border enforcement would be needed, which brings in questions of public

[21] S Becher and U Benoliel, 'Dark Contracts' (2023) 64 *Boston College Law Review* (forthcoming), papers.ssrn.com/sol3/papers.cfm?abstract_id=3911528.

[22] ibid 27. See also N de Marcellis-Warin, F Marty, E Thelisson and T Warin, 'Artificial Intelligence and Consumer Manipulations: From Consumer's Counter Algorithms to Firm's Self-Regulation Tools' (2020) 2 *AI Ethics* 259.

[23] EU Unfair Commercial Practices Directive, Art 5(2)(b).

[24] Mik 'The Erosion of Autonomy in Online Consumer Transactions' (n 20) 14. See also N Helberger, F Zuiderveen Borgesius and A Reyna, 'The Perfect Match? A Closer Look at the Relationship between EU Consumer Law and Data Protection Law' (2017) 54 *CMLR* 1427.

[25] Mik, ibid 34.

[26] ibid 11. See also JM Paterson and E Bant, 'Should Australia Introduce a Prohibition on Unfair Trading? Responding to Exploitative Business Systems in Person and Online' (2021) 44 *Journal of Consumer Policy* 1.

and private international law as well as increased costs. Furthermore, technology evolves at a far swifter pace than law can manage, so that new commercial practices based on data might well fall outside the scope of such reforms.

The outcome in practice is thus that the law does little to constrain the data collection and sharing activities of online actors, or to mitigate the ways they use that data to influence their consumers. The law has *some* normative force, bolstered a little by the risk that enforcement action might be taken, but compliance plays only lip service to the aims of the law because the commercial benefits are so great.

III. Could Private Law Mechanisms Fill the Gaps?

Readers might be surprised to hear that state law is no longer the primary consumer protection mechanism for online sales transactions. It has been ousted, though not usurped, by private law mechanisms devised by online platforms.[27]

State law is supremely ill-adapted for online consumer disputes, particularly those where seller and buyer are in different countries. Even within the same country, using state law mechanisms can be far more costly than the dispute is worth. For example, the average online spend in the United Kingdom (UK) from a mobile phone in late 2020 was US$66.80[28] (just under £50), whilst the small claims court fee to issue a claim for a consumer dispute is currently £35, with an additional £27 payable for a hearing, and further fees if the judgment needs to be enforced. Add in the cost of the consumer's time in making the claim, and it becomes clear that only a minority of online purchase disputes are valuable enough to use state law. The costs of cross-border litigation are many multiples of these amounts and will inevitably require the engagement of foreign lawyers.

Online platforms which host seller sites, such as eBay, Amazon Marketplace and Alibaba, recognised this problem early on. The role of these platforms is to attract buyers and facilitate sales, and unresolved disputes reduce the attractiveness of the platform and make buyers reluctant to risk purchasing.

This led eBay, first in the field, to develop its own rule system for consumer protection, which has been copied with some additional elements by other online trading platforms such as Alibaba. eBay users had already developed a set of trading norms which achieved a high level of voluntary compliance because the eBay community was so small that participants felt they knew each other. Continued growth produced the need for a formal way of resolving disputes, and so the community's trading norms were entrenched in the eBay user terms, to which buyers and seller must sign up

[27] By 'private law mechanisms' I mean governance and regulatory structures established by the platforms themselves, applying rules which are not identical to state law and, to the extent that external assistance in enforcement is needed, achieving this enforcement through the private law of contract. This is part of a wider trend for online platforms to act as (self-) regulatory gatekeepers – see E Laidlaw, *Regulating Speech in Cyberspace: Gatekeepers, Human Rights and Corporate Responsibility* (Cambridge, Cambridge University Press, 2017); R Van Loo, 'The New Gatekeepers' (2020) 106 *Virginia Law Review* 467.

[28] S Chevalier, 'Average Value of Online Shopping Orders in Great Britain from 2nd quarter 2021 to 2nd Quarter 2022, by Device' (Webpage, *Statista*, 31 October 2022), statista.com/statistics/960448/great-britain-online-shopping-order-values-by-device/.

to become members.[29] The resulting rule system is known (in English) as the 'eBay Money Back Guarantee', and is included in substantially identical wording, allowing for language differences, in the terms of the eBay sites for the United States (US), UK, France, Germany, Ireland and Australia. It appears probable that it is drafted to achieve the same effect in almost all of eBay's other sites. eBay claims that its sites attract buyers from 208 countries,[30] so there is no doubt that this system is a global one. Sellers agree to comply with the procedures which underpin the Money Back Guarantee, and buyers are promised that eBay will operate those procedures to give redress.

The eBay seller's obligations under the scheme are simple:

a) sellers must deliver the products they sell; and
b) the products must be substantially as described by the seller.

If sellers fail to meet these obligations, eBay runs an online mechanism for mediating and determining disputes. It begins by requiring buyer and seller to communicate in an attempt to reach a mutually acceptable settlement. If a settlement cannot be agreed, eBay staff review the claims of each side and decide whether the seller was in breach. If the buyer is successful eBay arranges for a refund. Most disputes are resolved within 14 days without any fee being charged.[31]

The eBay dispute resolution scheme goes beyond national contract law in a number of important respects:

1. It imposes its rules on sellers, and on those buyers who choose to use it. It is thus very different from a seller's contractual promises to provide redress, because the seller does not make the decision about whether redress is appropriate. The scheme only applies to disputes between buyers and sellers – any claim against eBay is a claim under the applicable national law.
2. The rules are set by eBay for the entire community of buyers and sellers, irrespective of their nationality or location. Thus, there is a uniform, global rule system for the entire eBay seller/buyer ecosystem, with no need for conflicts of law rules.
3. eBay's decisions under this rule system are enforceable entirely within the eBay system, without the need to refer to external legal systems for assistance. eBay has sole decision-making power once a buyer has referred a dispute to the process and, because the only remedy available is a refund, can enforce that remedy autonomously through its relationships with payment providers.

In practice, the eBay rule-system operates like an autonomous transnational law system and is the primary source of regulation for the trading activities of its participants. High-value claims, or claims which fall outside the very limited eBay rules, will still need resolution in national courts, but the vast majority of consumer claims are for

[29] For ebay.com: 'User Agreement' (Webpage, *eBay*), pages.ebay.com/help/policies/user-agreement.html, and for ebay.co.uk: 'User Agreement' (Webpage, *eBay UK*), pages.ebay.co.uk/help/policies/user-agreement.html. All the eBay User Agreements, so far as is possible under the national laws which apply, impose the same trading obligations on sellers and buyers.

[30] 'Where to Sell Internationally' (Archived webpage, *eBay UK*, as at 25 April 2016), web.archive.org/web/20160425033304/http://sellercentre.ebay.co.uk/where-to-sell-internationally.

[31] Though this, of course, means that the cost of the system is covered from the seller fees collectively and thus, ultimately, shared between all buyers.

refunds for products which do not work properly or have not been delivered, and for these the eBay system provides the main forum for dispute resolution.

Schultz suggests that this system is so much superior to national law in practice that it could be seen as a community legal system, operating outside national law.[32] It is clear that the system is used extensively in preference to national law, even though national law in theory provides buyers with far more extensive rights than the eBay rules in many countries.[33] In 2010, the last year for which statistics appear to have been released, eBay handled in excess of 60 million disputes worldwide, averaging US$70–100 in value.[34] To put this number in context, in 2011 the *total* number of small claims handled by the UK courts (under £5,000 at that time) was in the region of 30,000, and the vast majority of these did not relate to complaints by buyers of products.[35] If any eBay buyer is dissatisfied with a decision there is nothing in the rules to prevent bringing a national law claim against the seller, but there appear to have been few if any such cases. There is insufficient data to identify whether the availability of the eBay system has reduced the number of consumer claims in national courts, but it is clear that millions of consumer disputes which would never have come before a national court, because of their low value, have received some form of resolution.

Amazon Marketplace and AliExpress (the business-to-consumer arm of Alibaba) have adopted similar systems with modifications. Amazon Marketplace is particularly interesting because it goes well beyond the simple dispute resolution of eBay. In addition, Amazon controls the information disclosures which its Marketplace sellers must make, and requires them to offer refunds for non-defective goods for a period which exceeds the right of withdrawal in the EU Consumer Rights Directive.[36] Because Amazon Marketplace is a global trading platform, these protections are offered to consumers world-wide. In effect, Amazon has taken most of the transactional protections from EU consumer protection law, integrated them into its terms and conditions and added to them.[37] Disputes are resolved by Amazon itself, equally as quickly as eBay does and with no fees payable by consumer claimants.

Winn points out that Amazon's development of a global consumer protection system has had interesting consequences. In particular, it has imported some elements of EU consumer protection law into the US,[38] specifically the EU right of withdrawal from distance contracts, but not the broader regulation of unfair or deceptive trade practices.

[32] T Schultz, 'Private Legal Systems: What Cyberspace Might Teach Legal Theorists' (2007) 10 *Yale Journal of Law & Technology* 151.

[33] For example, the EU Consumer Rights Directive gives EU consumers the rights, inter alia, to prior information about the seller and charges, a right to withdraw from the contract, and rights to receive goods of appropriate quality. None of these are provided for in the eBay rules.

[34] L Del Duca, C Rule and B Cressman, 'Lessons and Best Practices for Designers of Fast Track, Low Value, High Volume Global E-Commerce ODR Systems' (2015) 4 *Penn State Journal of Law & International Affairs* 243, 248, citing eBay Corporate Factsheet Q4 2010.

[35] 'Court Statistics Quarterly October to December 2012' (Report, UK Ministry of Justice, 28 March 2012) 12, figure 1.3.

[36] EU Consumer Rights Directive.

[37] J Winn, 'The Secession of the Successful: The rise of Amazon as Private Global Consumer Protection Regulator' (2016) 58 *Arizona Law Review* 193.

[38] ibid 207–208.

which cannot be explained by economic theories.[49] This sense of ownership applies to information as well as to physical property.[50] Apple's move to tell consumers that they are giving away something that they 'own', information about their online activities, will help produce this endowment effect.

This psychological aspect of property produces strong emotional feelings in information 'owners'. If they perceive the information in question as 'mine', then this influences how far they are prepared to allow others to make use of it. A likely reason for this strong desire for control is that legal ownership of physical property confers control over use by others, and this might explain the strength of our emotional need to control the information which we think we own. Psychologists certainly find that a key psychological element of ownership is the right, or at least the perceived right, to control the thing which is owned.[51]

A third driver for change might be competition between sellers. If a major e-commerce platform operator were to decide that there would be a competitive advantage in offering its customers some reassurance about how their data would be used and shared, others might feel pressured into following suit. This is exactly what seems to be happening with consumer rights, with Amazon leading the way.[52] If this is coupled with a feeling of ownership, so that consumers begin to demand more control over the collection, sharing and use of their data, online companies would inevitably begin to compete on the basis of the controls they offer.

The final incentive is law and regulation. Two examples which have been referred to earlier, data protection law and EU consumer protection law, have clearly influenced the normative landscape for online sellers, even foreign laws which do not apply to them directly or laws which are unlikely to be enforced in practice. The EU Digital Services Act 2020[53] in effect requires online service providers to establish and publicise internal systems for detecting and removing illegal content, products and services, incorporating complaints and dispute resolution mechanisms. The Act sets out the principles for these systems, leaving the detail to each provider. It is possible to envisage legislation along the same lines, designed to limit the ways in which online sellers use consumer data.

[49] J Beggan, 'On the Social Nature of Nonsocial Perception: The Mere Ownership Effect' (1992) 62 *Journal of Personality and Social Psychology* 229, suggesting that this is explained by the role which property ownership plays in one's self-image.

[50] Spiekermann, Korunovska and Bauer, 'Psychology of Ownership and Asset Defense' (n 46) conducted experiments on personal information stored in Facebook accounts which found that the more strongly an individual believed they owned that information, the more they would be willing to pay to preserve it from deletion. They also found that knowledge that a third party was interested in acquiring the information led individuals to value it even more highly. Interestingly, and perhaps counter to what lawyers have thought in this field, a belief in information ownership was demonstrated experimentally to be far more influential in valuing personal information highly than whether the information was considered private or not.

[51] F Rudmin and J Berry, 'Semantics of Ownership: A Free-Recall Study of Property' (1987) 37 *The Psychological Record* 257. See also L Furby, 'Possession in Humans: An Exploratory Study of Its Meaning and Motivation' (1978) 6 *Social Behavior and Personality* 49, 60: 'Possessions have an instrumental function – they make possible certain activities and pleasures. In other words, they enable one to effect desired outcomes in one's environment … a central feature of possession is the ability to affect and control the object in whatever way one wishes.'

[52] See text to n 36.

[53] Regulation (EU) 2022/2065 of the European Parliament and of the Council of 19 October 2022 on a single market for digital services and amending Directive 2000/31/EC [2022] OJ L277/1 (Digital Services Act).

The threat or prospect of such a law might be enough to persuade the major gatekeepers,[54] which include Apple, Microsoft, Facebook, Google and Amazon, to pre-empt or shape legislation by establishing their own consumer data governance systems. Each has different commercial drivers, and so their private law systems would initially take very different approaches to this issue.[55] In time, competition or legislation might force convergence of those systems.

Some readers might at this point be thinking that state law is so obviously superior that the emergence of private law systems should, if possible, be pre-empted by legislation. It is worth summarising here some of the advantages of private law systems which have emerged from the previous discussion:

- Simplicity and focus. Private law systems must be paid for from merchant and platform revenues, and so aim to solve a high proportion of common issues at the lowest possible costs. This means that their rules will concentrate on the most frequently complained of issues and be designed to resolve them quickly. We saw that the dispute resolution systems of the major e-commerce platforms focus on easily understood subsets of consumer rights, and as sole remedy offer the consumer a refund.
- Enforceability. Platforms have a range of enforcement levers under their control, such as refunds, limiting seller activities on the platform and expulsion. By limiting the remedies available to those which the platform can enforce directly itself, a private law system can provide highly effective enforcement of its rules. Enforceability also drives the simplicity and focus of the rules – for example, eBay will not entertain a consumer's claim for personal injury because it is unlikely to hold sufficient funds from the seller to satisfy that claim.
- Speed. Disputes and complaints can be resolved quickly if the rules are simple and enforced directly. Even complex private law systems like ICANN's UDRP dispute policy for domain names[56] provide resolution within months, rather than the years which state law litigation can take, and simple consumer disputes are resolved by eBay within days or weeks.
- Cost. Simplicity, enforceability and speed mean that disputes can be decided fast, and in most cases by staff with much less experience and training, and thus pay, than a judge or arbitrator would need.
- Universality. Private law systems apply the same rules to all participants, irrespective of their location or residence. Difficult and expensive questions about applicable law and jurisdiction are avoided, and there are no extra costs to enforce decisions where the parties are located in different countries.

[54] See E Laidlaw, *Regulating Speech in Cyberspace: Gatekeepers, Human Rights and Corporate Responsibility* (Cambridge, Cambridge University Press, 2015).

[55] For example, Facebook has a long history of changing its terms of service to allow it to capture ever more information about its users – see C Reed and A Murray, *Rethinking the Jurisprudence of Cyberspace* (Cheltenham, Edward Elgar, 2018) 97–99 – and as this is the fundamental basis of the Facebook business model we might expect it to do no more than modify its terms of service to the minimum extent acceptable to its users.

[56] 'Uniform Domain-Name Dispute-Resolution Policy' (Webpage, *ICANN*), www.icann.org/resources/pages/help/dndr/udrp-en.

- Flexibility. Changing laws takes years, decades in most cases. If the nature of online transactions changes and new problems arise, a private law dispute resolution system can modify its rules almost immediately.

State law will always lag behind private law systems, but it can help to shape them nonetheless. We have already seen how law has influenced consumer rights, as one example, and the prospect or threat of future legislation if private law systems fail to provide satisfactory solutions will always be influential in their development.

IV. What Would Private Law Systems Look Like?

Much of the recent work on private law systems to regulate data collection, use and sharing has been undertaken in relation to data trusts. A data trust is a legal governance mechanism for controlling data sharing activities so that the rights and interest of stakeholders, such as data 'owners' and data subjects, are respected. A wide range of legal structures is possible, from equitable trusts through public sector or corporate organisations to purely contractual mechanisms.

The initial impetus towards data trusts comes from a perception by Edwards in 2004[57] that if personal data could be conceptualised as trust property, then those who held and processed that data would owe fiduciary duties as trustees which could provide some protection for the privacy and other interests of data subjects. This idea was seized on by Hall and Pessenti[58] in their 2017 report which began the current wave of interest in data trusts. Because Hall and Pessenti began their analysis from a trust law perspective, the legal structure they had in mind was of course a common-law trust. More recent analysis in the Open Data Institute report[59] tells us that trust law might not offer the most suitable structure for a functional data trust, for reasons too technical to require discussion here. The important point is that a choice of suitable structures is available.

The main characteristic of a data trust is that it has a legal structure which is separate from those who are sharing data with each other. This separation allows control of data to be transferred from the current data 'owner' to the trust. It should thus be obvious that data trusts are unlikely to be seen as appropriate by the gatekeepers discussed above, such as Google and Amazon, because they will not wish to relinquish control of the data they possess.

But gatekeepers will share a common aim with data trusts. They will want their private law mechanisms to reassure stakeholders, in this case consumers, that data is being collected, used and shared appropriately, in ways which preserve the interests of those stakeholders. Data trusts achieve this by two means.

[57] L Edwards, 'The Problem with Privacy: A Modest Proposal' (2004) 18 *International Review of Law, Computer, and Technology* 309.

[58] W Hall and J Pesenti, 'Growing the Artificial Intelligence Industry in the UK' (Independent Review, UK Government Department for Digital, Culture, Media & Sport and Department for Business, Energy & Industrial Strategy, October 2017), www.gov.uk/government/publications/growing-the-artificial-intelligence-industry-in-the-uk.

[59] C Reed, BPE Solicitors, Pinsent Masons, *Data Trusts: Legal and Governance Considerations* (Report, Open Data Institute, 2019) 14–19, theodi.org/article/data-trusts-legal-report/.

First, they have published rules about what purposes data is collected and used for, how it will be shared, restrictions upon its use, and so on. It is worth thinking of these as the constitution of the system, even if they are not presented in this way – a gatekeeper is likely to promulgate them as 'policies' or as part of the terms of service. This constitution might also include statements about the processes which will be used to decide about matters like data sharing, and to deal with concerns raised by stakeholders such as consumers or their representatives. It will need to bind all those who are subject to the private law system; in other words all those who make use of the consumer data concerned.

The aim of these rules and processes is to engender trust among consumers, so that they are prepared to allow their data to be used subject to those rules. Trust is a complex phenomenon, though.[60] In close relationships, such as those with family, friends and work colleagues, trust is emotionally based. We believe that the other will do what they ought to do because of the nature of the relationship, and because of our past dealings with them in the relationship. No consumer is likely to have that kind of relationship with an information gatekeeper. So here we need a different kind of trust, based on some kind of regulation, which gives us confidence that the other will do what they ought to do. In a business dealing the law of contract gives us confidence that the other party will perform their promises (or more accurately, that either they will perform, or the law will provide us with a remedy if they do not). If we visit a new dentist, we trust the dentist to some degree because their training has been certified and their performance is overseen by a regulatory body. Of course, repeated dealings can lead to the kind of relationship which engenders the first kind of trust, so that long-term business partners will often rely on each other's promises even in the absence of a contract.

Our constitution therefore needs to engender this second type of trust, in order to persuade consumers to allow their data to be processed and shared. The rules, as drafted and published, amount to promises by the gatekeeper and others who make use of consumer data, but merely promising is not enough. Consumers also need assurance that these promises will be kept.

Governance of a rule system aims to ensure that the published rules are complied with. Thus, a gatekeeper who wishes to enhance consumer trust in its data use will need to establish a governance system which provides consumers with that assurance. The precise design of such a system would be driven by the types of data which are collected and shared, but at a minimum it should be expected to exhibit two fundamental elements: transparency and external oversight.

Transparency about operational decision-making is what can convince consumers that their data is being treated properly, respecting what they conceive as their interests. One mechanism for doing this is to publish all policy and data sharing decisions to stakeholders, but this risks overwhelming them and also gives them only a fragmentary review of how their interests are being safeguarded. It also risks disclosing confidential information about the business activities of those involved in the data sharing and use.

[60] For detailed discussion of the trust concepts explained here, see E Khalil (ed), *Trust* (Cheltenham, Edward Elgar, 2003). Social scientists have investigated trust and trustworthiness extensively, producing numerous competing theories and sets of terminology. For a helpful overview, see P Nannestad, 'What Have We Learned about Generalized Trust, if Anything?' (2008) 11 *Annual Review of Political Science* 413.

Decisions made under Google's rule system are unpublished, in part at least because doing so would risk infringing the rights of the data subjects concerned under data protection law. It is clearly concerning that decisions already made were not even made available to the Advisory Council as part of its work.[74] Data subjects therefore have little information with which to assess the fairness, justice and consistency of de-listing decisions, which are rightly described as 'a jurisprudence built in the dark'.[75]

Google has, though, made some attempt at transparency by publishing brief summaries of decisions which it believes raise important points of principle, as part of its Transparency Report.[76] However, as at November 2021 only 159 summaries were disclosed from nearly 1.2 million de-listing requests, although aggregated data analysis of the reasons for refusals to de-list is also published.[77] This information is interesting, but it is hardly an adequate basis on which to assess whether the decisions Google makes are fair and just.

Whether this rule system might evolve into a wider system is far too early to be predicted, but a route for such evolution is already apparent. It seems clear that at some point Google will need to address the independence of this decision-making system because there is a conflict between Google's judicial role and its commercial interest in disseminating as much information as possible as widely as possible.[78] Other search providers such as Bing and Yahoo! have the same legal obligation to develop their own systems for de-listing, and at some point they could decide to pool their experiences and produce a consolidated set of guidelines for making de-listing decisions. These might in turn evolve into a quasi-independent decision-making system, funded by search providers but not directly controlled by them, which would help legitimate the system by demonstrating a degree of independence. Once the system was independent, pressure from individuals such as consumers, and from external lawmakers, could easily lead to it expanding its regulatory role beyond simple de-listing.

V. Conclusions

This chapter has, I hope, demonstrated that the widespread collection, use and sharing of consumer data by online actors has created problems, by increasing the persuasive power of online merchants to such an extent that consumer autonomy to make purchasing decisions has been reduced to an unacceptable degree. It also shows that

[74] ibid.

[75] E Goodman, 'Open Letter to Google from 80 Internet Scholars: Release RTBF Compliance Data' (Open letter, 13 May 2015), ellgood.medium.com/open-letter-to-google-from-80-internet-scholars-release-rtbf-compliance-data-cbfc6d59f1bd.

[76] 'Transparency Report (n 65).

[77] 'Google EU Privacy Data November 2015' (Report, November 2015), storage.googleapis.com/transparencyreport/faqs/eu-privacy/Google_EU_privacy_data_nov2015.pdf.

[78] See Chenou and Radou, 'The "Right to be Forgotten"' (n 72) 20: 'The power delegation from the public to the private sector transforms the latter not only by adding new responsibilities (from indexing information to assessing the content of the links) but also by entrusting the corporation to adopt a public interest approach that would be typical of an independent agency. In principle, the public interest logic would encourage the deindexing of content, yet the corporate strategy would advise in favor of minimizing risks.'

these are activities which existing laws, in particular data protection and consumer protection, aim to control by reference to their fairness, but that these laws are not adequately effective to achieve the desired controls.

In the absence of law reform, which would need to be on a global scale and not merely national, might solutions develop from within the online trading community? My answer is a qualified yes, or perhaps just a tentative perhaps. Online gatekeepers have a clear interest in maintaining the trust of the consumers on whose data they rely, and thus in developing their own controls which bolster and maintain that trust. E-commerce intermediaries such as eBay and Amazon already operate private law systems which deal with the basic consumer law issues of delivering goods which meet their description and are of adequate quality, and these systems are more effective globally than any national consumer law. There is no conceptual reason why they should not develop similar systems to control data collection, use and sharing, and Google has already been forced to go some way towards doing so.

At present, restricting the collection, use and sharing of consumer data would be a cost to gatekeepers, both in terms of the costs of a rule system and, more importantly, the opportunity cost of reduced ability to use data. Only if the cost-benefit calculus alters will such systems develop. Apple's recent privacy initiative has already changed that calculus, though it is still an open question whether the change is enough to bring private law into play.

8

Access to Platform Data and the Right to Research under US Law

NIVA ELKIN-KOREN,* MAAYAN PEREL** AND OHAD SOMECH***

I. Introduction

Social media platforms like Meta, Twitter and YouTube host and mediate online interactions, while collecting, aggregating and processing vast amounts of data.[1] Often, they entertain a unique access point to types of data which cannot be replicated or accessed elsewhere.[2] During the COVID-19 pandemic, people have become even more dependent on digital platforms for work, education, finance, social interaction, news and media consumption, thus increasing the hold of platforms over troves of personal data.[3] Social media platforms have thus become a living lab of real-time data and a critical source for extracting data and training machine learning (ML) models.[4] While individual preferences may vary on how and when data is shared, and for which purposes, this chapter focuses on the practices of platforms as controllers of data. Such data includes both personal data about individual users and their preferences, as well as non-personal data that is unrelated to an identified or identifiable person, such as aggregated and anonymised datasets. While some data is publicly accessible (eg LinkedIn profiles[5]), other types may only be extracted via Application Programming Interfaces (APIs). Moreover, some of the data is generated by users (User Generated Content, such as

* Professor of Law, Tel Aviv University.
** Assistant Professor, Netanya Academic College School of Law.
*** Post-doctoral Fellow, BIU LawData lab.

[1] T Poell et al, 'Platformisation' (2019) 8 *Internet Policy Review* 1.

[2] D Rubinfeld and M Gal, 'Access Barriers to Big Data' (2017) 59 *Arizona Law Review* 339, 351; C Nebeker et al, 'A Retrospective Analysis of NIH-funded Digital Health Research Using Social Media Platforms' (2020) 6 *Digital Health* 1.

[3] N Lomas, 'Privacy Not a Blocker for "Meaningful" Research Access to Platform Data, Says Report' (2020) (*Techcrunch*, 25 June 25), techcrunch.com/2020/06/25/privacy-not-a-blocker-for-meaningful-research-access-to-platform-data-says-report/.

[4] Data extraction via the Application Programming Interfaces (APIs) of platforms, for example, enables the analysis of large volumes of data. See, eg, J Perriam et al, 'Digital Methods in a Post-API Environment' (2019) 23 *International Journal of Social Science Methodology* 1.

[5] See below, nn 44–45 and accompanying text.

Especially, copyright does not apply to the underlying facts.[17] So, from a copyright law perspective, researchers should be allowed to use the raw data on platforms, such as data about the number or frequency of 'likes', 'tweets' or 'followers' related to a specific content or content provider.

A database or compilation of facts, however, could be subject to copyright, if there is a minimum degree of originality in the manner in which the underlying facts were selected or arranged.[18] This means that original data listings, reports, archives or aggregations of data created by the platforms could be protected by copyright.

Nevertheless, access and use of copyrighted works could be allowed to the extent permitted under exceptions and limitations provided by law.[19] Specifically, the Fair Use doctrine permits certain uses of copyrighted works for socially valuable objectives, such as research.[20] The legitimacy of each use depends on the particular circumstances of the case involved and on the way they implicate the application of the statutory factors of fair use.[21] Special weight is given to the 'transformative' nature of the use, that is 'the more the appropriator is using the copied material for new, transformative purposes, the more it serves the copyright's goals of enriching public knowledge …'.[22]

Accordingly, US courts have held that the automatic reading (or 'crawling') and indexing of data is fair use.[23] Recently, following a long legal battle between Oracle America and Google, the Court found that the copying of 37 packages of Oracle's application programming interface was fair use.[24] Specifically, the Court emphasised the transformative nature of Google's use of the Sun Java API, which 'seeks to create new products'[25] while promoting progress and innovation. Less certainty exists regarding the legality of ML techniques of Text and Data Mining (TDM).[26] In the context of training ML systems, it has been argued that the use of databases of copyrighted content should generally be permitted under fair use.[27]

In addition to copyright law, trade secret law may also protect platform data and restrict researchers' access to data which brings economic value to the platform.[28] Trade secret law may give plaintiffs redress against those who appropriate their secret information.[29] Recently, however, in *Compulife Software, Inc v Newman*, the Court found

[17] ibid § 102(b) (excluding from copyright protection 'any idea, procedure, process system, method of operation, concept, principle, or discovery'); *Feist Publications Inc v Rural Tel Serv Co* [1991] 499 US 340, 340.
[18] ibid 340.
[19] 17 USC § 107 (1994).
[20] *Campbell v Acuff-Rose Music* [1994] 510 US 569, 575–78.
[21] ibid.
[22] *Authors Guild v Google Inc* 804 F 3d 202 (2d Cir 2015).
[23] N Elkin-Koren, 'Let the Crawlers Crawl: On Virtual Gatekeepers and the Right to Exclude Indexing' (2001) 26 *University of Dayton Law Review* 179; M Sag, 'Copyright and Copy-Reliant Technology' (2009) 103 *Northwestern University Law Review* 1607, 1608; J Grimmelmann, 'Copyright for Literate Robots' (2016) 101 *Iowa Law Review* 657, 659.
[24] *Google LLC v Oracle Am, Inc*, No 18-956, 523 US __, 141 S Ct 1183 (2021).
[25] ibid 25.
[26] S Flynn et al, 'Implementing User Rights for Research in the Field of Artificial Intelligence: A Call for International Action' (2020) 7 *European Intellectual Property Review* 1; Lemley and Casey, 'Fair Learning' (n 10) 763.
[27] ibid.
[28] 18 USC § 1836(b) (2021).
[29] *DHI Grp, Inc v Kent* 397 F Supp 3d 904, 921 (SD Tex 2019).

trade secret law applicable also to non-secret information. In that case, the Eleventh Circuit Court of Appeals found that using data scraping to reproduce a portion of an insurance quotes database constitutes unlawful misappropriation.[30] Nevertheless, the data obtained by the defendants – 43 million insurance quotes – would have been available to a human user, thus negating its 'secretive' status. Moreover, the scrapers didn't bypass any passwords to reproduce the database, but rather submitted individual insurance queries. Yet, according to the Court, even though each of the individual quotes obtained in the scraping attack was not entitled to protection, the database as a whole may be protectable.[31] This could possibly discourage researchers seeking to engage in automatic data collection or apply reverse engineering techniques which are critical for oversight and accountability.

Besides intellectual property, data access may be restricted by neighbouring rights. In the US, laws on misappropriation grant limited rights in collections of information that were made with significant investment.[32] Framed as torts, these rights aim to ensure business integrity and fair competition.[33] Accordingly, platforms may rely on this protection to prevent researchers from accessing and using data collections they have created intentionally and which are valuable for their business.

Privacy laws may further restrict data access. While the US lacks a comprehensive set of privacy protections vis-à-vis companies and users, it protects reasonable privacy expectations under tort laws and sector specific regulations, such as the Health Insurance Portability and Accountability Act (HIPAA), or the California Consumer Privacy Act (CCPA) that is particularly relevant to digital platforms which reside in California.[34] The Federal Trade Commission (FTC) is tasked with protecting consumers' privacy, however it operates from a narrow, competition perspective.[35] The FTC's enforcement practices primarily focus on ensuring that platforms comply with their privacy policies and follow the notice-and-choice approach to online privacy.[36] Privacy policies should therefore inform users about what information platforms collect, how and for what purpose they collect it, and with whom they share it (notice). Users should then have the opportunity to opt-out (choice).[37] Accordingly, platforms risk violating the privacy rights of their users, if they afford third parties access to their data, without first notifying their users about the potential uses of their data for research purposes.[38]

[30] *Compulife Software Inc v Newman* No 18-12004, 2020 WL 2549505 (11th Cir 2020).

[31] ibid 1314.

[32] L Determann, 'No One Owns Data' (2019) 70 *Hastings Law Journal* 1, 21.

[33] ibid. In the EU, database makers are entitled to prevent the extraction or re-utilisation of a substantial part of their database (Directive 96/9/EC of the European Parliament and of the Council of 11 March 1996 on the legal protection of databases [1996] OJ L77/20, art 7(1) (Database Directive)).

[34] PM Napoli, 'User Data as a Public Resource: Implications for Social Media Regulation' (2019) 11 *Policy & Internet* 439. In Europe, Regulation 2016/679 of the European Parliament and of the Council of 27 April 2016 on the protection of natural persons with regard to the processing of personal data and on the free movement of such data, and repealing Directive 95/46/EC [2016] OJ L119/1 (General Data Protection Regulation) gives EU citizens control over their personal data, requiring explicit consent for the very collection and processing, subject to limited statutory exceptions.

[35] 15 USC § 45(a)(1) (2012) (prohibiting unfair or deceptive acts or practices in or affecting commerce).

[36] A Waldman, 'Privacy, Notice, and Design' (2018) 21 *Stanford Technology Law Review* 129.

[37] ibid 131.

[38] Note, that because platforms unilaterally decide on their privacy policy they retain (some) control on whether access to data conforms to users' privacy rights.

Finally, in the US, unauthorised access to platforms' data could trigger criminal liability under the CFAA.[39] Recently, in *Sandvig v Barr*,[40] the Court considered whether researchers, who sought to study race and gender discrimination in employment websites would violate the CFAA. The researchers sought to create multiple fake accounts in violation of the websites' Terms-of-Service (ToS), which prohibits misrepresentation. The District Court ruled that the plaintiffs' specific research plans do not violate the access provision of the CFAA, explaining that this law does not criminalise mere Terms-of-Use violations on consumer websites.[41]

Outside the context of academic research, the Supreme Court has recently limited the applicability of the CFAA, holding that it does not criminalise access made for an improper purpose, when access itself was not unauthorised.[42] In that case, a police officer was convicted under the CFAA for looking up licence plates for improper monetary purposes using a law enforcement database he was authorised to access. The Court held, that an individual 'exceeds authorized access' when 'he accesses a computer with authorization but then obtains information located in particular areas of the computer – such as files, folders, or databases – that are off limits to him'.[43] Accordingly, since the police officer was authorised to use the database to retrieve licence plate information, he didn't exceed authorised access.

Following *Van Buren*, in *LinkedIn v hiQ*, the Ninth Circuit found the CFAA inapplicable to the defendants' unauthorised use of plaintiff's data because the data was accessible to the general public.[44] According to the Ninth Circuit, accessing publicly available profile information cannot be 'unauthorised', as opposed to accessing sites that are restricted to users who sign-in to the platform with their username and password.[45]

B. Contractual Rights

Platforms may also use contract law to restrict researchers' access to data via their ToS, privacy policies and community guidelines. Some contractual terms are straightforward prohibitions on the collection of data. For instance, under LinkedIn's user agreement, users are not allowed to '[d]evelop, support or use software, devices, scripts, robots or any other means or processes … to scrape the Services or otherwise copy

[39] See 18 USC § 1030(a)(2)(c) ('Whoever … intentionally access a computer without authorization or exceeds authorized access and thereby obtains … information from any protected computer … shall be punished …'). A Sellars, 'Twenty Years of Web Scraping and the Computer Fraud and Abuse Act' (2018) 24 *Boston University Journal of Science & Technology Law* 372, 390.

[40] *Sandvig v Barr* 451 F Supp 3d 73 (DDC 2020).

[41] ibid.

[42] *Van Buren v United States* No. 19-783, 593 US __, 141 S Ct 1648, 210 L Ed 2d 26 (2021).

[43] *Van Buren v United States* No 19-783, 593 US __, 141 S Ct 1648, 1662 (2021).

[44] *hiQ Labs, Inc v LinkedIn Corp*, No 17-16783 (9th Cir Apr 18, 2022).

[45] *hiQ Labs, Inc v LinkedIn Corp* 938 F 3d 985, 1001-1002 (2019).

profiles and other data from the Services',[46] with many social platforms adopting similar prohibitions.[47] Other contractual terms impede access to data less directly. For example, the contractual requirement that users use their real name and open only one account may (even if unintendedly) impose an access barrier on researchers seeking to study discrimination.[48] The same holds for contractual terms that prohibit users from overriding the platform's security measures or overburdening the platform, which may limit the ability of researchers to implement different methodologies[49]

Platforms may further use their ToS to shield the technological barriers they embed in their systems for the purpose of limiting data access. On the technological side, platforms typically use username and user-created password authentication gates to prevent non-users access to platform data.[50] But platforms also use more sophisticated technological tools to prevent others from accessing their data, leading to what the Ninth Circuit Court aptly called: 'technological gamesmanship'.[51]

Craigslist and Facebook, for example, use internet protocol (IP) address blockers to prevent third parties from scraping the data on their servers.[52] Recently, in *hiQ Labs Inc v LinkedIn Corp*,[53] the Court provided a detailed overview of the technological measures used to prevent third party access to the platform's data. LinkedIn, the Court states, revised its robots.txt file to 'prohibit access to LinkedIn servers via automated bots'. It also uses 'several technological systems to detect suspicious activity and restrict automated scraping', including 'LinkedIn's Quicksand system' which detect 'non-human activity indicative of scraping'. Moreover, LinkedIn 'Sentinel system throttles (slows or limits) or even blocks activity from suspicious IP addresses; and its Org Block system generates a list of known "bad" IP addresses serving as large-scale scrapers'. 'In total', the Court concludes, 'LinkedIn blocks approximately 95 million automated attempts to scrape data every day.'[54]

Naturally, the above is but a partial list of the technological measures deployed by platforms to prevent access to their data, and platforms may be reluctant to reveal such measures to prevent others from circumventing them. What is clear is that social media platforms heavily invest in developing systems that maintain their control over user-generated data, as well as the high volume of attempts to access that data. Next, we turn to explain why.

[46] LinkedIn, 'User Agreement' (Webpage, 1 February 2022) s 8.2(2), www.linkedin.com/legal/user-agreement.

[47] See C Fiesler et al, 'No Robots, Spiders, or Scrapers: Legal and Ethical Regulation of Data Collection Methods in Social Media Terms of Service' (2020) 14 *Proceedings of the International AAAI Conference on Web and Social Media* 187.

[48] See, eg, *Sandvig v Sessions* 315 F Supp 3d 1, 9–10 (DDC. 2018).

[49] See, eg, Facebook, 'Terms of Service' (Webpage, 26 July 2022) ss 3(2)(2), www.facebook.com/legal/terms; LinkedIn, 'User Agreement' (n 46) s 8.2(3).

[50] See O Kerr, 'Cybercrime's Scope: Interpreting "Access" and "Authorization" in Computer Misuse Statutes' (2003) 78 *New York University Law Review* 1596, 1664.

[51] *Facebook, Inc v Power Ventures, Inc.* 844 F 3d 1058, 1067 (9th Cir 2016).

[52] ibid; *Craigslist Inc. v. 3Taps Inc.* 942 F. Supp. 2d 962, 966, 967 (N.D. Cal. 2013).

[53] *hiQ Labs Inc v LinkedIn Corp* 31 F.4th 1180 (9th Cir. 2022).

[54] ibid, 1186.

III. Why do Digital Platforms Lock their Data?

Social media platforms are private businesses operating in a concentrated, multi-sided, data-driven market.[55] Catering to users and advertisers, as well as their own stakeholders, platforms collect vast amounts of personal and non-personal information for diverse purposes, from tailoring content to users' preferences, to targeted advertising, and the selling of data.[56] Their market environment explains the interests, pressures and concerns that informs platforms' access-to-data policies in general and in the context of research in particular. In this section, we explore these interests and concerns.

A. Business Interests

Platforms' revenues rarely come directly from users. Instead, platforms rely on advertisers, business users, and the sale of data itself to generate their income. In all of these, data plays a crucial role.

It is well recognised that non-business users pay platforms with data rather than money. Platforms use this data for multiple revenue-generating purposes. Data is needed for targeted advertisement, allowing platforms to reap greater revenues from advertisers by identifying personal traits and predicting trends, desires and needs, insights which may be sold to third parties or employed by the platform to more accurately tailor its own goods and services to users.[57] Access to platform data is also a 'bargaining chip'. Facebook, for example, used access to its data to reward its partners while denying similar access to firms it identified as potential competitors.[58] Finally, as the 'new oil', data is a commodity sold to third parties, ranging from data-brokers to prospective employers.[59] In this respect, platforms also compile, process and analyse data to improve customers' experience. Thus, to protect their competitive advantage in the data economy, platforms use a host of legal and non-legal measures, including prolonged and expensive litigation,[60] to maintain their control of the data on their servers.

Platforms' use of data to anticipate and meet users' desires and improve their experience also relates to the digital platform market concentrated structure, in particular, the relatively high switching costs and the network and lock-in effects that characterise it.

The network effect means that any additional user exponentially increases the benefits each user derives from the platform. Lock-in and switching costs suggest that, once users have become accustomed to the platform, they will be less willing to switch to a competitor.[61] Thus, the ability to sustain their user-base is crucial for platforms' survival.

[55] See, eg, N Elkin-Koren et al, 'Social Media as Contractual Networks: A Bottom Up Check on Content Moderation' (2022) 107 *Iowa Law Review* 987.

[56] See R Calo and A Rosenblat, 'The Taking Economy: Uber, Information, and Power' (2017) 117 *Columbia Law Review* 1623.

[57] ibid.

[58] T Kadri, 'Digital Gatekeepers' (2021) 99 *Texas Law Review* 951.

[59] ibid.

[60] See, eg, *hiQ Labs, Inc v LinkedIn Corp*, No 17-16783 (9th Cir Apr 18, 2022); *Facebook, Inc v Power Ventures, Inc* 844 F 3d 1058, 1067 (9th Cir 2016).

[61] See N Guggenberger, 'Essential Platforms' (2021) 24 *Stanford Technology Law Review* 237.

Because dominant platforms enjoy a larger, more comprehensive and diverse user-base than their competitors', and since the quality of the output often depends on the quality of the input ('garbage in garbage out'), controlling superior datasets provides dominant platforms with a competitive advantage.[62] Here, too, then, control of user-generated data plays a crucial role in allowing dominant platforms to innovate and improve their products, lure new users, and maintain their dominant position.[63]

In its various shapes, forms and uses, data is at the centre of digital platforms' business model.[64] Whether this business model is necessary or a mere contingency depicting the platform market as it happened to evolve is a question beyond the scope of this chapter. As things stand, data control forms an essential part of platforms' ability to generate revenue and to increase and maintain their market share. Platforms, therefore, have a profound business interest in controlling who is given access to the data, for which purposes, and under what terms.

B. Legal, Reputational and Regulatory Concerns

Alongside their direct business interests, digital platforms limit data access to minimise potential legal risks and avoid liability for violating users' privacy, data protection laws, mainly the General Data Protection Regulation, or security regulations.[65] The aftermath of the Facebook/Cambridge Analytica scandal,[66] which involved the misuse of personal data of millions of Facebook users acquired by researchers through Facebooks' API, is a prominent example. After the scandal was revealed, platforms moved to restrict access to their APIs by *any* third parties in order to prevent abusive treatment of sensitive data by bad actors.[67]

Digital platforms further limit data access to protect their reputation. Indeed, while Facebook was the only social network directly involved in the Cambridge Analytica scandal, the immediate aftermath included intense public criticism against all major social media platforms for failing to sufficiently safeguard users' privacy, and for exposing them to manipulative and false information.[68] Highlighting the potential real-world effects of social media, the Cambridge Analytica scandal also drew noticeable regulatory attention. For example, the FTC urged Facebook to limit third party access to user-generated data.[69]

[62] ibid (n 61).
[63] Calo and Rosenblat, 'The Taking Economy' (n 56).
[64] I Stepanov, 'Introducing a Property Right over Data in the EU: The Data Producer's Right – an Evaluation' (2020) 34 *Intentional Review of Law Computers and Technology* 65.
[65] See J Carrero, 'Access Granted: A First Amendment Theory of Reform Of The CFAA Access Provision' (2020) 120 *Columbia Law Review* 131.
[66] M Townsend, 'Facebook-Cambridge Analytica Data Breach Lawsuit Ends in 11th Hour Settlement' (2022) *The Guardian* (28 August 2022), www.theguardian.com/technology/2022/aug/27/facebook-cambridge-analytica-data-breach-lawsuit-ends-in-11th-hour-settlement.
[67] D Freelon, 'Computational Research in the Post-API Age' (2018) 35 *Political Communication* 665.
[68] See A Bruns, 'After the "APIcalypse": Social Media Platforms and their Fight against Critical Scholarly Research' (2019) 22 *Information, Communication & Society* 1544.
[69] ibid.

Another reputational concern in granting access to data comes from the use of such data in scholarly and journalistic work critical of platforms.[70] In the past, scholars and journalists used their access to platform data to expose the ills of social media, from discrimination to eating disorders and body image problems, to unfair competition practices.[71] In this context, platforms found the silver-lining of the Cambridge Analytica scandal to be the pretext to severely limit third parties' access to data, including researchers and journalists, in the name of preserving users' privacy and protecting them from manipulation.[72]

Notwithstanding the significant reputational and regulatory disadvantages for social media platforms which allow access to their data for research purposes, many large platforms don't ban access altogether. Facebook, for instance, in partnership with researchers from Harvard and Stanford and the Social Science Research Council, has created *Social Science One*, which shares Facebook's users-generated data with researchers who, in Facebook's words, 'align with our mission of building community and bringing the world closer together'.[73] Standing behind such limited research collaborations is a reputational upside from presumably supporting research. From their beginning, many social media platforms presented themselves as a force for the good, seeking to build communities and bring the world together. Allowing researchers access to data is a way for platforms to substantiate these claims.[74] But, since providing researchers with unlimited access to comprehensive, rich and unique data may expose platforms to criticism, limiting these projects to those pre-selected by the platform enable platforms to enjoy the publicity without the risk of it backfiring. As Axel Bruns notes:

> [W]hile Twitter offered elevated API access to researchers and developers in the early days of the platform, in order to build its ecosystem and generate publicity, such access was eventually rescinded as the platform began to exploit the value of its data through commercial access … [This] was summed up by one developer as 'thanks for getting so many people interested in Twitter. Now get lost'.[75]

IV. Using Private Law to Establish a Right to Research

In section II, we showed that beyond the legal protections of data, platforms gain de facto control over the data on their servers through private ordering mechanisms – contractual

[70] See, eg, J Horwitz, 'Facebook Seeks Shutdown of NYU Research Project into Political Ad Targeting' *Wall Street Journal* (New York, 23 October 2020), www.wsj.com/articles/facebook-seeks-shutdown-of-nyu-research-project-into-political-ad-targeting-11603488533.

[71] See, eg, J Cohen, '*Law for the Platform Economy*' (2017) 51 *UC Davis Law Review* 133, 190; Kadri, 'Digital Gatekeepers'(n 58) 978–79; P Suciu, 'Is Social Media Increasing Eating Disorders in Teens?' (*Forbes*, 17 December 2019), www.forbes.com/sites/petersuciu/2019/12/17/is-social-media-increasing-eating-disorders-in-teens/?sh=6e30b39df246.

[72] See Bruns, 'After the "APIcalypse"' (n 68).

[73] Facebook 'Research Awards' (Website), research.fb.com/research-awards, perma.cc/4WXT-VJ2W. See also G King and N Persily, 'A New Model for Industry-Academic Partnerships' (2020) 53 *Political Science and Politics* 703.

[74] Bruns, 'After the "APIcalypse"' (n 68).

[75] ibid (citations omitted).

restrictions that limit access to data and safeguard the technological barriers to access to data. In section III, we explained why platforms have strong incentives to develop and maintain such private ordering mechanisms. In this final normative section, we explain two ways in which private law may narrow the scope of contractual restrictions on data access for research and support a right to research. First, US copyright law may deter contractual claims that effectively expand the scope of proprietary claims in platform data based on copyright pre-emption doctrine. Second, contract law may narrowly interpret and even refuse to enforce contractual restrictions on data access, in accordance with the interests of the parties and of the public interest in facilitating academic research and critical public debate.

A. External Limits to Contractual Barriers to Data

As summarised in section II, platforms deploy multiple contractual limitations to restrict access and use of platforms' data by third parties. For instance, many platforms generally prohibit the automatic collection of data, irrespective of whether the data is raw or aggregated, public or private.[76] These limitations effectively expand the legal protections accorded to data, thereby disrupting the balance between competing rights, interests and values defined by law.

A critical way in which US copyright law may facilitate platform-based research is by pre-empting contractual claims that override copyright law.[77]

Copyright law should be perceived as a comprehensive, mandatory arrangement that restricts the freedom of the parties to contract around it.[78] In the US, copyright protection arises exclusively under federal law as the Copyright Act broadly pre-empts state law claims involving rights that are 'equivalent to any of the exclusive rights within the general scope of copyright' and that 'come within the subject matter of copyright'.[79] To pre-empt a contractual claim, courts apply a two-prong test: First, they inquire whether the right being claimed is equivalent to an exclusive right within the general scope of copyright. Then, they examine whether the contractual claim comes within the subject matter of copyright.[80] The application of this two-prong test, however, is currently subject to a major circuit split.[81]

The use of data for scientific purposes is often non-expressive use, which aims to extract unprotected ideas. Arguably, such data is explicitly excluded from copyright protection and therefore may not be covered by pre-emption doctrine. Also, unlike

[76] See, eg, Fiesler et al, 'No Robots, Spiders, or Scrapers' (n 47).

[77] 1976 US Copyright Act, § 301. See generally M Lemley, 'Beyond Preemption: The Law and Policy of Intellectual Property Licensing' (1999) 87 *California Law Review* 111.

[78] N Elkin-Koren, 'Copyright in The Digital Ecosystem: A User Rights Approach' in RL Okediji (ed), *Copyright Law in an Age of Limitations and Exceptions* (Cambridge, Cambridge University Press, 2017) 132, 98.

[79] 17 USC § 301.

[80] See *ML Genius Holdings LLC v Google LLC* No 20-3113, 2022 US App LEXIS 6206 (2d Cir Mar 10 2022).

[81] See ML Genius LLC v Google LLC, Petition for a Writ of Certiorari (5 August 2022); DA Miro et al, 'Appeal of the Second Circuit's ML Genius Holdings LLC v. Google LLC Decision May Resolve a Circuit Split on Copyright Act Preemption Tests' (2022) 31 *NYSBA Bright Ideas* 30, www.arelaw.com/images/file/BrightIdeas-2022-vol-31-no-2_8_5X11_WEB.pdf.

copyright, a contract requires consent, and is enforceable only against a party who has assented to its terms.[82] Nevertheless, the Second Circuit has recently confirmed that pre-emption doctrine 'prevents States from protecting a work even if it fails to achieve Federal statutory copyright because it is too minimal or lacking in originality to qualify'.[83] Specifically in relation to data, the Seventh Circuit Court of Appeals struck down an attempt to restrict access to data that was not copyrighted to prevent 'copyright holders from leveraging their limited monopoly to allow them control of areas outside the monopoly'.[84] Moreover, as suggested before, courts should not limit themselves to the express pre-emption doctrine. Rather, they should apply the principles of implied pre-emption whenever state law seems to directly conflict or to stand as an obstacle to federal copyright policy.[85]

Intellectual property reflects the public interest in encouraging innovation by providing property rights in innovative and creative works. Because data often provides the building blocks for innovation, intellectual property explicitly excludes data from its protection. To allow actors to create de facto rights in data, therefore, would be to undermine intellectual property's raison d'être. That is, if each individual researcher would be bound by such restrictions, the general public interest in promoting research and innovation would be hampered. Creating de facto property rights in data based on an actor's ability to effectively control access to data would determine the allocation of rights based on contingent and legally irrelevant grounds and may distort actors' decisions by incentivising them to control access to data even when doing so would otherwise be inefficient from a social welfare perspective. Moreover, the use of copyrighted material for research purposes is often exempted under the fair use doctrine.[86] Thus, such use should be allowed notwithstanding any contractual restriction to the contrary.[87]

Accordingly, a contractual provision that prohibits any automatic collection of platforms' data should not be enforced against researchers who scrape any processed or aggregated data because such use should be permissible under the fair use doctrine. Similarly, a contractual restriction on automatic data collection should not be enforced against researchers who reverse engineer a platform's trade secret using automatic methods of the type used in the *Compulife Software* case discussed earlier. This is because reverse engineering that does not involve improper means is allowed under trade secret law. Additionally, data access restrictions should not be enforced against researchers using copyrighted information shared by users on their public profiles, and made available for viewing by anyone with a web browser, such as public LinkedIn profiles.[88]

[82] MW Carroll, 'Intellectual Property and Related Rights in Climate Data' in JD Sarnoff (ed), *Research Handbook on Intellectual Property and Climate Change* (Cheltenham, Edward Elgar, 2016).

[83] *ML Genius Holdings LLC v Google LLC* (n 80).

[84] *Assessment Technologies of Wi, LLC v Wiredata*, 350 F 3d 640 (2003).

[85] G Rob, 'A Less Formalistic Copyright Preemption' (2017), 24 *Journal of Intellectual Property Law* 329.

[86] 1976 US Copyright Act, § 107 ('Notwithstanding the provisions of sections 106 and 106A, the fair use of a copyrighted work … for purposes such as criticism, comment … scholarship, or research, is not an infringement of copyright. …').

[87] Elkin-Koren, *Copyright in The Digital Ecosystem* (n 78); P Samuelson and K Opsahl, 'Licensing Information in the Global Information Market: Freedom of Contract Meets Public Policy' (1999) 21 *European Intellectual Property Review* 386.

[88] See, above, nn 45–46 and accompanying text.

The consent granted by non-drafting parties to boilerplate contracts that define such restrictions should not allow platforms to change the underlining proprietary regime, even if it is sufficient for the formation of contracts. A different approach would tilt the delicate balance between the platforms' exclusionary rights and users' access rights.[89]

B. Internal Limits to Contractual Barriers

In subsection A we suggested that social media platforms should be prevented from using contractual terms to create de facto rights on grounds external to contract law, namely: the internal logic of intellectual property law.[90] Though the limits of contract law are often set by other legal fields,[91] US courts may be reluctant to strike down contractual terms based on non-contractual grounds, that arguably undermine the intentions of the parties.[92] Thus, we end this chapter by showing that the inner working of the common law of contracts can create and sustain a right to research.

First, platforms' ToS are a form of so-called 'standard form contracts', 'boilerplate contracts', or 'contracts of adhesion', characterised by the use of standardised language not based on negotiations between the contractual parties.[93] Decided unilaterally by the platform, ToS become the rule for all users under a take-it-or-leave-it basis. Given the concentrated market structure of digital platforms, and considering the network effects surrounding this market,[94] platforms' users practically have not much of a choice but to agree to these terms. Yet, despite the imbalanced bargaining powers of users and platforms, US courts have generally upheld the binding force of platforms' ToS, provided that a notice of the terms was provided to the prospective user.[95] Even the 'unconscionability doctrine'[96] mostly fails to assure fairness in contracts of adhesion.[97]

The academic literature, however, has raised considerable challenges to the enforceability of platforms' ToS, particularly when they are severely unfair or otherwise contradict public welfare.[98] In particular, though Freedom of Contract generally

[89] See RA Kreiss, 'Accessibility and Commercialization in Copyright Theory' (1995) 43 *UCLA Law Review* 1, 2–4.

[90] Though beyond the scope of our discussion, similar external restriction may be grounded in competition law, see, eg, Guggenberger, 'Essential Platforms' (n 61).

[91] See D Hoffman and C Hwang, 'The Social Cost of Contract' (2021) 121 *Columbia Law Review* 979, 994.

[92] For discussion see ibid; A Bagchi, 'Other People's Contracts' (2015) 32 *Yale Journal of Regulation* 211.

[93] See T Rakoff, 'Contracts of Adhesion: An Essay in Reconstruction' (1983) 96 *Harvard Law Review* 1173.

[94] Rubinfeld and Gal, 'Access Barriers' (n 2) 355.

[95] See *Hancock v AT&T Co* 701 F 3d 1248, 1256 (10th Cir 2012); *Specht v Netscape Commc'ns Corp.* 306 F 3d 17, 32–35 (2d Cir 2002); *Serrano v Cablevision Sys Corp* 863 F Supp 2d 157, 164 (EDNY 2012). M Radin, *Boilerplate: The Fine Print, Vanishing Rights, and the Rule of Law*(New Jersey, Princeton University Press, 2013).

[96] *Hume v United States* 132 U.S. 406, 411 (1889) (holding that unconscionable contracts, defined as contracts that no man would enter into, are void).

[97] Elkin-Koren et al, 'Social Media as Contractual Networks' (n 55) 1023; but see discussion below in nn 92–93 and accompanying text.

[98] N Suzor, *Lawless: The Secret Rules that Govern Our Digital Lives* (Cambridge, Cambridge University Press, 2019); H Micklitz et al, 'The Empire Strikes Back: Digital Control of Unfair Terms of Online Services' (2017) 40 *Journal of Consumer Policy* 367; M Loos and J Luzak, 'Wanted: a Bigger Stick. On Unfair Terms in Consumer Contracts with Online Service Providers' (2016) 39 *Journal of Consumer Policy* 63, doi.org/10.1007/s10603-015-9303-7.

suggests that parties should be allowed to freely bargain over their rights, this proposition cannot hold given the deep power discrepancies between academic researchers seeking to access the rich, unique and authentic data on platforms' servers for non-commercial purposes, and the platforms which control the data.[99] The imbalance of power between researchers and platforms and its outcome of a de facto appropriation of resources explicitly placed in the public domain suggest that the practice is unconscionable. In particular, platforms' use of their excessive bargaining power to create for themselves rights which the law explicitly denied them implies that both the procedural and substantive requirements of the unconscionability doctrine are met.[100]

Second, and relatedly, when platforms contractually restrict access to data, it may be questionable whether researchers *qua* researchers gain any benefit from the bargain. Unlike typical users, researchers do not seek to contract with platforms for the prospect of using the features, applications or other functions that induce others to join the platform. Instead, researchers' sole interest in engaging with platforms is to gain access to the data stored on their computers. Yet, if engaging with the platforms requires researchers to enter into a contract whose terms restrict the ability to collect and use data, it may be doubted whether the agreement is supported by consideration and therefore enforceable.[101] This requires courts to consider the specific purpose for which academic researchers contract with platforms, as opposed to treating them as 'generic' users. But, platforms already distinguish between different types of users (eg, business-users and consumers) and among users from different countries (eg the European Union and California) in their agreements.[102] The same, we suggest, can and should be done for scientific-users and in the context of access to data terms.[103] Courts, that is, should not reward platforms' unwillingness to offer different (boilerplate) terms for different types of users, and should instead incentivise platforms to make such distinction by recognising researchers' scientific purposes in using the platform.[104]

Even assuming the agreement is enforceable, the legal implications of its terms can only be known after they were interpreted and construed by the courts.[105] In the US, courts are often reluctant to interpret agreements against their unambiguous meaning. Whether a term is said to be ambiguous, however, is very much an open question. A foundational insight of contemporary contract theory is that the plain meaning of a promise to perform is not necessarily interpreted as a promise to perform in all

[99] Elkin-Koren, *Copyright in The Digital Ecosystem* (n 78) 108.

[100] For the distinction see AA Leff, 'Unconscionability and the Code – The Emperor's New Clause' (1967) 115 *University of Pennsylvania Law Review* 485; A Fleming, 'The Rise and Fall of Unconscionability as the "Law of the Poor"' (2014) 102 *Georgetown Law Journal* 1383.

[101] See *Restatement (Second) of Contracts* (Philadelphia, American Law Institute, 1981) s 71, 81.

[102] Choice of law clauses, for example, are often only applicable to business users, not consumers, see eg, Facebook, 'Terms of Service' (Webpage, 26 July 2022) s 4(4) ('If you are a consumer, the laws of the country in which you reside will apply … In all other cases … claim must be resolved exclusively in the U.S. District Court for the Northern District of California.').

[103] Following the example in n 102, clauses that restrict the collection and use of data can exclude scientific users, and state that 'if you are a scientific-user, you may collect data for scientific, non-commercial purposes'.

[104] On the normative foundation for a requirement to offer diverse contract types, see H Dagan and M Heller, *The Choice Theory of Contracts* (Cambridge UK, Cambridge University Press 2017).

[105] G Klass, 'Interpretation and Construction in Contract Law' (2018), *SSRN* ssrn.com/abstract=2913228.

circumstances.[106] Indeed, contract law recognises multiple circumstances, such as a failure of the parties' basic assumption, that limit the scope of the promise as well as the promisor's obligation to perform.[107] The courts, we argue, should apply a similar logic to determine the reasonable interpretation of contractual restrictions on the collection and use of data.

When it comes to accessing data for the purpose of academic research, the interpretation of terms limiting access to data should not be understood as limiting such access for any purpose. Instead, the reasonable interpretation of the terms suggests its scope should be confined to uses that undermine the legitimate interests of the platform.[108] Accordingly, *even if* we accept platforms' legitimate interest in profiting from data, such interest is not undermined by the use of data for academic purposes which do not conflict with legitimate business interests. Similarly, while platforms have a legitimate interest in protecting the privacy of their users, the ethical requirements placed on academic researchers suggest that allowing them access to data would not undermine this interest. Finally, contract law should not recognise platforms' bare interest in avoiding critique and regulatory scrutiny as legitimate and, therefore, even if such interests are undermined by academic research, they should not inform the reasonable interpretation and construction of the parties' agreement or provide grounds to prevent access to data for research purposes.

Thus far, we implicitly assumed that researchers are a party to the agreement with digital platforms, and offered three arguments for why and how the common law of contracts can (and should) preserve researchers' access to data notwithstanding contractual terms to the contrary. We end this chapter by arguing that researchers' ability to access data may also be thought of from the perspective of a non-party interest. Access to data could be considered a non-party interest, either because to assume otherwise is already to assume that platforms' effective control of the data legitimately allows them to impose their terms and conditions on anyone who seeks access to it; or because the right to research is a public interest, and the public is the non-party whose interests are undermined.

In practice, third party interests are an integral part of the common law of contracts. Famously, courts will not enforce illegal agreements, such as agreement for the killing of another, or agreements contrary to public policy. Courts will also not enforce contracts to pursue anti-competitive purposes or to circumvent consumer or employment regulation, with some courts determining non-compete clauses to be ambiguous and narrowly interpreting them.[109] Indeed, as David Hoffman and Cathy

[106] C Fried, *Contract as Promise: A Theory of Contractual Obligation* (Cambridge MA, Harvard University Press, 1981).

[107] See, eg, H Dagan and O Somech, 'When Contract's Basic Assumptions Fail' (2021) 34 *Canadian Journal of Law & Jurisprudence* 297.

[108] See, eg, *Sutton v East River Say Bank* 55 NY 2d 550, 555 (1982) ('Our goal must be to accord the words of the contract their "fair and reasonable meaning"'); *Glenn Distribution Corp v Carlisle Plastics Inc* 297 F 3d 294, 301 (3d Cir 2002); *Tessmar v Grosner* 23 NJ 193, 201 (1957).

[109] See 18 USC § 1958 (2018); Federal Trade Commission, 'Price Fixing' (Website), www.ftc.gov/advice-guidance/competition-guidance/guide-antitrust-laws/dealings-competitors/price-fixing. See also Bagchi, 'Other People Contracts' (n 92); O Ben-Shahar et al, 'Nonparty Interests in Contract Law' (forthcoming) *University of Pennsylvania Law Review*, dx.doi.org/10.2139/ssrn.4038584.

Hwang note, it is through courts' interpretation and enforcement of agreement that 'the general public always has the last say in a contract',[110] one explicitly recognised in the Restatement (Second) of Contracts.[111]

For example, in *IBP S'holders Litig v Tyson Foods*, the Delaware Court issued an order for the specific enforcement of a merger agreement, noting that the 'impact of a forced merger on constituencies beyond the stockholders and top managers of IBP and Tyson weighs heavily' on his decision.[112] Similarly, in *State Farm Mut Auto Ins Co v Est of Carey*, the Court expanded the coverage of liability insurance on grounds that such rule 'implements an underlying legislative policy that, for the protection of the public, liability insurance should follow the automobile under nearly all circumstances'.[113]

In these and other cases,[114] contract law restricts the parties from using contracts to impose negative externalities on non-parties. Of course, contract law does not (and should not) always prevent negative externalities.[115] Courts will enforce agreements to lease a property for the purpose of opening a business, even if it would create negative externalities to nearby competing businesses. Still, courts often use contract law rules of enforcement and interpretation to protect non-party (including public) interests, especially when these are already legally recognised and well established.[116]

Access to data, as a constitutive part of the right to research, qualifies as such an interest. A right to conduct research and obtain access to the finding of scientific research is instrumental to an informed citizenry in a democratic society and to economic growth arising from entrepreneurship and innovation, and could also be grounded in fundamental rights, including freedom of information and the public's right to information.[117] Moreover, access to science and scientific knowledge has long been pursued by the Open Access and Access to Knowledge movements,[118] and scholars have argued that research, the 'capacity to make disciplined inquiries into those things we need to know, but do not know yet', should be recognised as a right necessary to exercise informed citizenship.[119]

As part of the right to research, then, access to data for scientific purposes (pursuant to adequate privacy protections) is a recognised and established interest of both researchers as a group within society and of the public in general. Accordingly, when access to data is sought for research purposes, contract law's internal principles and doctrines suggest that courts can and should narrowly interpret terms restricting access to data, to the exclusion of access made for scientific purposes, to prevent the negative externalities generated by such limitations.

[110] Hoffman and Hwang, 'The Social Cost of Contract' (n 91) 994.

[111] *Restatement (Second) of Contracts*, s 207.

[112] *IBP S'holders Litig v Tyson Foods* 789 A 2d 14, 83 (Del Ch. 2001).

[113] *State Farm Mut Auto Ins Co v Est of Carey* 68 A 3d 1242 (Me 2012).

[114] See, eg, *Proprietors of Charles River Bridge v Proprietors of Warren Bridge* 36 US 420 (1837) (interpreting an agreement to advance public interest); *Larson v South Dakota* 278 US 429 (1929) (an interpretation against the public interest requires explicit in the contract); *Atlanta Ctr Ltd v Hilton Hotels Corp* 848 F 2d 146 (11th Cir 1988).

[115] For discussion see Bagchi, 'Other People Contracts' (n 92).

[116] See ibid; Ben-Shahar et al, 'Nonparty Interests in Contract Law' (n 109).

[117] Flynn et al, 'Implementing User Rights for Research' (n 26).

[118] A Kapczynski, 'Access to Knowledge: A Conceptual Genealogy' in G Krikorian (ed), *Access to Knowledge in the Age of Intellectual Property* (New York, Zones Press Publisher, 2010).

[119] A Appadurai, 'The Right to Research' (2006) 4 *Globalization, Societies & Education* 167.

V. Conclusion

Social media platforms are a 'living lab' holding a trove of real-time data essential to basic scientific research as well research into platform governance. Researchers' access to platform data therefore promotes the public interest in scientific research and forms an integral part of the 'right to research'. Platforms, however, use multiple technological barriers and contractual terms to prevent researchers from accessing data. This chapter offered a private law perspective on such practices. It argued that, in the context of access to data for scientific purposes, contractual terms that restrict access should be narrowly interpreted and limited in application. We based this argument on two claims. *First*, that because access restricting terms may provide platforms with de facto property rights in data, thereby hampering the explicit objectives of intellectual property law, they should be pre-empted by copyright laws. Courts, that is, should reject such attempts, especially when made via boilerplate contracts and in circumstances of deep power discrepancies between parties. *Second*, from a contractual perspective, we claimed that terms restricting access to data for scientific purposes may be unenforceable and that, even if enforceable, the reasonable interpretation of terms restricting access to platform data would make them inapplicable to cases in which access is sought for scientific purposes, as such access does not undermine any of the platforms' *legitimate* interests, while harmful to researchers' and the public's recognised interests in research and innovation.

PART IV

Uses of Data – Rights and Obligations

9

Tort-Based Protections for Data Privacy

JELENA GLIGORIJEVIC*

I. Introduction

Data privacy rights have conventionally been protected by behemoth-like statutory regimes, particularly in the European Union (EU). The value of tort law to deal with and protect data privacy has been underexplored in that regulatory context. This chapter will discuss how tort law, particularly as developed in common law jurisdictions, may have the capacity to provide clearer, more internally coherent, and better protection for individuals' informational privacy, than data protection regulation, where tort law is also intended to safeguard data privacy. At the very least tort law is a valuable route to take for data privacy protection, in addition to, or aside from, existing or available regulatory routes that are aimed, at least in part, at protecting privacy. Informational privacy torts have been developed in most common law jurisdictions, and the common formula of a 'reasonable expectation' threshold and a general defence can offer an alternative, if not superior, way of recognising and addressing interferences with data privacy otherwise covered by fine-grained data protection regulation of sweeping application.[1] The central arguments developed in this chapter are that tort law can offer better doctrinal coherence and greater normative force in the pursuit of protecting individuals' data privacy than more detailed and prescriptive regulatory regimes necessarily do.

Section II outlines briefly the structure and operation of informational privacy torts currently recognised in the relevant jurisdictions, and notes the common, defining features of a cross-section of data protection regulation, with particular emphasis on the EU's influential General Data Protection Regulation (GDPR).[2] Section III discusses how tort law can provide more normative and doctrinal coherence and clarity in the way in which individuals' right to data privacy is protected in law, than can

* Senior Lecturer in Law, Australian National University.

[1] See Roger Brownsword in chapter 2 of this volume for a contrasting position on the value of statutory regimes relative to private law actions.

[2] Regulation (EU) 2016/679 of the European Parliament and of the Council of 27 April 2016 on the protection of natural persons with regard to the processing of personal data and on the free movement of such data, and repealing Directive 95/46/EC (General Data Protection Regulation or GDPR) [2016] OJ L119/1.

data protection regulation insofar as it too is orientated towards protecting privacy. There is, through the evolution of a tort tailored to protecting informational privacy, significant capacity for analytic precision and principled reasoning in both the scope of legal protection and the direct connection with the normative underpinnings of that legal protection. Section IV explains how tort law can also provide better protection for individuals seeking protection of their data privacy. Both the 'reasonable expectation of privacy' threshold and the general defence allow courts to assess each case, in all of its circumstances, in a more nuanced and principled way than may be possible under data protection regulation.

II. Informational Privacy Torts and Data Protection

To what extent is tort law able to deal with and protect data privacy, given its experience in some jurisdictions with informational privacy, misuse of private information, or wrongful publication of private facts? The gist of this question is what sort of (legal) heuristic is best suited to dealing with the acknowledged need to protect data privacy and informational privacy, given the availability of regulation, insofar as it is directed towards privacy-protection, as well as tort law. Would a tortious duty not to interfere with data privacy, fashioned in a particular way, be of more or at least equal value than current (or any future) regulatory schemes which purport to be orientated towards privacy protection?[3] Now that several decades have passed since the first iteration of trans-border data protection scheme (at least in Europe),[4] might tort law (as developed at common law) offer a better, more principled, way of analysing the problem, and incorporating the normative demand, than these regulatory schemes: to the benefit not only of plaintiffs (privacy-seeking individuals) but also defendants (firms, public bodies, health providers, media operators, etc) in terms of analytical purity, doctrinal clarity, accessibility and normative consistency?

Given the ever-growing demand for legal, and principled, protection of data rights, it is legitimate to ask this question, not only because of the inherent potential availability of tort law to deal with civil wrongs and provide redress for wrongs recognised as such in law, but also because of the nature and origins of these data protection regulatory schemes, which are today ostensibly aimed at protecting individual privacy rights. Data protection legislation was born in the late twentieth century, with Europe's first iterations of infotech regulation, not out of a sensibility necessarily orientated exclusively towards the protection of individual privacy[5] as a strong, dignitary fundamental right to be protected by law, taking centre-stage and per se the primary driver of such regulation. Rather it was born out of a parallel, if not superior, need to put some controls on how new information technology was being used

[3] Again, see Roger Brownsword in chapter 2 of this volume, who makes the case for statutory schemes, as opposed to private law actions.

[4] Convention for the Protection of Individuals with regard to Automatic Processing of Personal Data (Strasbourg, 28 January 1981).

[5] Albeit today it is clear that the EU's regime expresses a commitment to human rights protection, in particular, the right to privacy.

and could be used.[6] Significantly, the trans-border regulatory schemes were fashioned primarily to enable the free flow of data through these ever-evolving new means, and to enable and legitimise large-scale, computerised[7] collection and storage of personal data by public institutions.[8] The fundamental right to privacy, and the concept of data *privacy* rights, were not as strongly present at the genesis of data regulatory regimes, as they were and continue to be at the evolution of common law tortious protection of informational privacy (and as they are now claimed to be in present iterations of data protection regulation).[9]

This common law protection of privacy has evolved over the past two to three decades, with courts in several common law jurisdictions recognising tortious liability for interference with informational privacy.[10] These courts have recognised that misuse, or wrongful use, of an individual's private information amounts to a civil wrong, giving rise to legal remedies for the aggrieved party.[11]

The shared formula, or common denominator, of these privacy torts includes a requirement that the plaintiff prove he or she had a reasonable expectation of privacy in the circumstances and covering the information (or activity) in issue, and an opportunity for the defendant to prove his or her use or publication of the information in question was legitimate or justified in the public interest, in accordance with the principle of freedom of expression. The torts are comprehensive in their application, in that they do not have wholesale exceptions or exclusions, for example, for journalists or state security services.

How the courts reason within each of the two broad elements of the generic privacy tort may vary across jurisdictions, including whether the defence involves an 'ultimate balancing test' as between two fundamental rights, as in England and Wales,[12] or an outright assessment of whether publication was of legitimate public concern, as in New Zealand.[13] Further, some jurisdictions may recognise additional elements, including a requirement that the plaintiff prove publication of the information was highly

[6] See the Council of Europe Resolution on this issue vis-à-vis the private sector in 1973 (Resolution (73) 22), a similar resolution vis-à-vis the public sector in 1974 (Resolution (74) 29), and a legally binding Data Protection Convention (ETS No 108). Note, however, the 1981 Convention did start emphasising more than the previous materials the need to protect individual rights and liberties.

[7] UK Home Office, *Computers: Safeguards for Privacy* (London, HMSO, 1975) 36–37.

[8] See Convention for the Protection of Individuals with regard to Automatic Processing of Personal Data above. See also L Bygrave, *Data Privacy Law: An International Perspective* (Oxford, Oxford University Press, 2014) 3–30.

[9] Eg, General Data Protection Regulation.

[10] See Eoin O'Dell in chapter 10 of this volume, for an excellent exposition of this evolution.

[11] United Kingdom: *Vidal-Hall v Google Inc* [2015] EWCA Civ 311, [2016] QB 1003, and *PJS v News Group Newspapers Ltd* [2016] UKSC 26, [2016] AC 1081; New Zealand: *Hosking v Runting* [2005] 1 NZLR 1; some Canadian jurisdictions, including Ontario: *Doe 464533 v D* (2016) 394 DLR (4th) 169; in the United States, it is open to common law courts to recognise informational privacy wrongs in tort law: American Law Institute, *Restatement (Second) of Torts* (St Paul MN, American Law Institute Publishers, 1977) §652D; in Australia, no appellate court has yet recognised an outright standalone tort of misuse of private information, but, where courts have awarded compensation for serious interferences with informational privacy, remedies have been in equity and confidentiality: *Giller v Procopets (No 2)* [2008] VSCA 236, (2008) 24 VR 1, and *Wilson v Ferguson* [2015] WASC 15.

[12] *Re S (A Child)* [2004] UKHL 47, [2005] 1 AC 593, 603, para 17: privacy and freedom of expression.

[13] *Hosking v Runting* (n 11) para 129.

reflect more directly the *quality* of privacy in question, and provide greater clarity at the earliest stage of the claim exactly what may count as an interference giving rise to remedies. A reasonable expectation of privacy test gives rise to a more constrained, coherent and normatively tethered remedy for breach of data privacy. It may be, as a result, that in some cases the interests of search engine or other online platform users are better protected by consumer protection laws or contract law, especially in circumstances where a reasonable expectation of privacy may be lost or may never have arisen in the first place, for example, where a user has given proper, informed consent for the use of their personal information, in exchange for choosing to use certain services. A well-defined and normatively tethered tort would not prevent the use of all personal data by digital platforms, always and everywhere. The circumstances of the activity and the user's actions and situation would be centrally relevant. Where these digital services can be interpreted to be necessary services, and are offered by only one provider with an effective monopoly, then, in those circumstances, and adverting to the norms of autonomy and liberty as they underpin the right to privacy,[29] an individual may well retain a reasonable expectation of privacy vis-à-vis the use of some of their information, even after a form of consent has been elicited from him or her. This doctrinal possibility will be discussed further in section IV.

Evolving common law torts of interference with privacy, based upon a reasonable expectation threshold, better capture and disambiguate the normative importance of privacy, and the nature and scope of legal protection, including what a plaintiff must prove, and what loss a plaintiff may expect to be remedied. For example, common law principles have evolved, and continue to evolve as it is in their nature to do so, to provide clear and coherent doctrines of when certain plaintiffs, certain information, or certain activities might be covered by a reasonable expectation of privacy: there are (albeit still crystallising) rebuttable presumptions of an expectation of privacy, for example, where the plaintiff is a child,[30] or where the plaintiff is the subject of a police investigation.[31] A common law tort, with a threshold of reasonableness, allows the courts to interpret, apply and develop informational or data privacy law in a way that is fastened to the reasons why informational privacy is protected in the first place. There is far less capacity, in a data protection regulatory scheme, to find a coherent and clear link between the purpose and scope of the protection offered (by reference to the catch-all category of 'personal information'), and the reason for that protection (specifically, the value of privacy to individuals as recognised in law).[32]

[29] For a more fulsome discussion of the normative underpinnings of the right to individual privacy, see Gligorijevic, 'A Common Law Tort of Interference with Privacy in Australia' (n 26), 683–93.

[30] *Re S (A Child)* (n 12). See generally J Gligorijevic, 'Children's Privacy: The Role of Parental Control and Consent' (2019) 19 *Human Rights Law Review* 201.

[31] *Richard v BBC* (n 22); and *Bloomberg LP v ZXC* [2022] UKSC 5, [2022] 3 All ER 1.

[32] It is noted that data protection regimes may have other protective purposes, distinct from the protection of individual privacy, including the right of an individual to access information about himself or herself, and the right to have inaccurate information about himself or herself corrected. These regulatory protections sit quite separately from the purpose to protect individual privacy per se, and are therefore in this chapter not compared with privacy torts, as are other aspects of the regulatory regime which are clearly orientated to protecting individual privacy.

Therefore, the reasonable expectation of privacy element common in privacy torts provides a clearer and more coherent link with the normative demand to be answered, than does a low-threshold regulatory approach catching all 'personal information', defined liberally as it is in many such schemes. The reasonable expectation of privacy test involves a holistic but principled analysis of all of the circumstances, both allowing and obligating a court to *link* its assessment of all the facts to the recognised, distinct reasons why this interest is protected, as such: that is not possible under the regulatory regimes, even where today nominally, 'privacy' appears to be prioritised (even as a fundamental right) in the purposes of those regimes.

Where there is a clearer link to normative underpinnings, where an objective standard confines judges to precedent and principle,[33] rather than leaving them to roam in the realms of policy, there should then be a clearer way of scoping out the boundaries of the interest protected, of liability, of how different facts (data uses) will be dealt with by the law. And the courts have had the opportunity at common law to develop (and they continue to develop) principles that inform how they do the scoping exercise: is this activity, is this information, covered by a reasonable expectation of privacy? Such an analytical approach offers more by way of normative consistency and clarity, than an approach asking the court to accept effectively all manner of data, and then to decide whether a controller or processor's actions were in line with highly specific rules, which might or might not account for the reasonableness of the plaintiff's claim, or whether the quality of privacy is indeed implicated in the activity in question. There may be other interests implicated, quite separate from privacy, including contractual or consumer interests following the provision of services. Tort law would go some way to disambiguate the privacy interest and tidy up the various data privacy related claims that can be brought under such regulation, insofar as that regulation is at least nominally intended to safeguard 'privacy'.

Another way in which tort law disambiguates the value of privacy central to the claim, and offers clearer and more principled boundaries of liability than does data protection regulation, is through its ability to highlight the wrongdoing that is in issue. Tort law provides discipline in how acts or omissions are classified as civil wrongs, to the extent that they can lead to compensation. The tort of *misuse* of private information, or of *wrongful use* of private information, is an intentional tort, as has been accepted in England and Wales, and in New Zealand.[34] Wrongdoing here, the affront to an individual's privacy, his or her dignity, autonomy, liberty, psychological sanctity,[35] entails intentional or reckless behaviour in respect of a reasonable expectation of privacy. That standard of fault is commensurate with the nature of the interest protected. Negligence, and negligent omission, does not suffice. This element of the privacy tort therefore limits the liability of controllers or processors, in a principled, clear, and normatively anchored way, whose systems are compromised by third-party wrongdoers, at no fault

[33] For an elucidation of the common law's evolutionary nature and its strengths, see T Allan, 'Principle, Practice, and Precedent' (2018) 77 *CLJ* 269.

[34] See generally D Butler, 'A Tort of Invasion of Privacy in Australia?' (2005) 29 *Melbourne University Law Review* 339, 360.

[35] On the normative underpinnings of the value of privacy, see again: Gligorijevic, 'A Common Law Tort of Interference with Privacy in Australia' (n 26) 683–93.

of their own.[36] A remedy against a controller or processor in such circumstances may lie in the tort of negligence,[37] but, as matter of principle, that controller or processor has not committed a privacy wrong: it is the hacker who has committed the wrong. The liability of the controller or processor here turns not on an interference with privacy, but on a breach of duty of care (if it at all arises) related to the conditions on which it holds or uses data. In this context, tort law offers the principled distinction between intentional wrongdoing and negligent or accidental omission, and a principled limitation of liability for controllers and processers.

Internal coherence, anchoring to normative underpinnings, and a strongly principled form of liability, as offered by a privacy tort, culminates in a heuristically attractive cause of action, with clear boundaries of protection (of privacy) and liability (of controllers and processors): it is clear what can and cannot be admitted under a tortious cause of action based specifically on the right to *individual privacy*. The circumstances in which data subjects may seek a remedy, the persons whom data subjects may pursue for compensation, and the exact nature of controllers' and processors' (moral and legal) responsibility for others' data and privacy, can be delineated in a clearer and more principled, privacy-connected way under tort law than under an all-encompassing and fine-grained regulatory regime, which aims at least in part to protect individual privacy.

IV. Protection of the Privacy-Seeking Individual

In addition to offering greater clarity and internal coherence, in respect of both scope of protection and the purposes of that protection, a common law tort may offer better protection for a privacy-seeking individual, than can a data protection regulatory regime. This is in spite of the principled limitations discussed in the preceding section (including limitations on controller or processor liability in the context of third-party data compromise). The proposition here is not that tort law can or should or would offer unlimited or biased protection to plaintiffs, but, rather, that the principled and normatively tethered nature of a privacy tort can better protect an individual's *privacy*, than can a regulatory regime whose exclusions may appear to be less principled and less connected with an underlying privacy-protection rationale. By virtue of the defining characteristics of either regime (tort or regulation), there is greater overall opportunity for a court to apply nuanced and fact-specific, principled reasoning under a common law tort than under a fine-grained body of rules of broad application. It is precisely because a common law tort is not tied to such arbitrarily codified, fine-grained regulation, and because it more clearly and directly embodies a sensibility for the protection of privacy *per se*, that a plaintiff may be able to make a legitimate

[36] *Various Claimants v WM Morrison Supermarkets Plc* [2017] EWHC 3113 (QB), [2019] QB 772; *Warren v DSG Retail* (n 24); *Stadler v Currys Group Limited* [2022] EWHC 160 (QB); *Underwood v Bounty UK Ltd and Hampshire NHS* [2022] EWHC 888 (QB); *Smith v TalkTalk Telecom Group* (n 24); *Sterritt v Telegraph Media Group Ltd* [2022] NIQB 43.

[37] Albeit at least in England and Wales the courts have not received such claims very favourably; see Eoin O'Dell in chapter 10 of this volume.

claim in data privacy under the tort where he or she would not be able to do so under an arbitrarily limited data protection regulation – that is, where that limitation is *not* normatively justified.

Privacy torts embody a sensibility for privacy protection that is not limited to regulation characterised by highly prescriptive provisions, not restricted in scope by the defendant's activity or character rather than the value of privacy itself, and not based upon multiple conflicting purposes, some of which are normatively distinct from the protection of individual privacy, such as regulatory uniformity, or digital economy growth – as legitimate as these purposes might well be. Instead, the tort offers protection for a privacy-seeking individual that is conditional on a normatively informed, holistically assessed reasonable expectation of privacy, and not conditional on a broad definition of personal information paired with the absence of consent for its use (or otherwise 'fair processing'). Further, the tort does not exclude, at the outset, certain uses of information (whether or not they may be covered by a reasonable expectation of privacy), for example, journalism, research, and state securitisation: it has a general defence, tethered to the principle of freedom of expression. These points of contrast between a tort regime and a data protection regulatory regime illuminate why there may be more capacity in the former than there is in the latter for each data privacy case to be assessed through nuanced and fact-specific, principled reasoning, and in that way permits some claims to be tested that might not be entertained at all in a more arbitrary, rigid and highly specific codified regulatory regime.[38]

For example, a claim in the tort would not be defeated by rules concerning consent, in circumstances where there still may be a reasonable expectation of privacy. There may still be such a reasonable expectation, for example, even when a plaintiff has 'agreed' online to long and complex terms and conditions, in order to access a digital service which is necessary for his or her work, or necessary for him or her to access other services or exercise certain freedoms, and in circumstances where this digital service is offered by only one provider in the market. A normatively anchored, holistically assessed reasonable expectation of privacy would induce the court to consider how all of the circumstances might remove the plaintiff's control over his or her personal information, contrary to the demands of autonomy-based privacy,[39] and how they might place the plaintiff and his or her private life at the behest of a digital service provider, an employer, or a governmental department, contrary to the demands of dignity-based privacy.[40] A common law tort hinging on a reasonable expectation of privacy provides greater opportunity to make out a case for privacy protection taking

[38] For example, the use of personal information by news media companies or journalists.

[39] For an autonomy-based rationale for the legal protection of privacy, see K Hughes, 'A Behavioural Understanding of Privacy and Its Implications for Privacy Law' (2012) 75 *MLR* 806; F Schauer, 'Free Speech and the Social Construction of Privacy' (2001) 68 *Social Research* 221, 223; J Rachels, 'Why Privacy Is Important' (1975) 4 *Philosophy and Public Affairs* 323, 323–26; T Scanlon, 'Thomson on Privacy' (1975) 4 *Philosophy and Public Affairs* 315, 315–22.

[40] For a dignity-based rationale for the legal protection of privacy, see E Bloustein, 'Privacy as an Aspect of Human Dignity: An Answer to Dean Prosser' (1964) 39 *New York University Law Review* 962; B Rössler 'Should Personal Data Be a Tradable Good? On the Moral Limits of Markets in Privacy' in Rössler and Mokrosinska, *Social Dimensions of Privacy* (n 26) 141; E Bloustein, 'Privacy Is Dear at Any Price: A Response to Professor Posner's Economic Theory' (1978) 12 *Georgia Law Review* 429.

in question is of sufficient public interest, of sufficient legitimate public concern, or sufficiently embodied in the demands of freedom of expression, to be publicised, in spite of a legitimate privacy claim.[56] Contrastingly, data protection regulatory regimes force courts to determine issues of who counts as a news media journalist, what material counts as 'news',[57] whether accreditation matters, and the extent to which social media users can be news publishers. Such issues are remote from the core, underlying value of privacy, and they deflect the inquiry away from whether a reasonable expectation of privacy should legitimately be set aside in the circumstances, towards whether a particular defendant is covered by the regulatory regime in the first place.

In developing nuanced principles relating to journalistic activities under a general justificatory defence to a privacy tort, the courts have also had the opportunity to consider justifications based upon the defendant's commercial objectives and business model.[58] This developing area of privacy tort law is particularly pertinent for the context of digital service providers, whose own commercial objectives and business models currently depend in large part upon advertising and the commodification of user data. Under evolving tort doctrine, the courts have rejected arguments that a media defendant's commercial objectives, and even its purported ability to survive in the marketplace, can in and of themselves defeat a recognised privacy claim.[59] In the same way, a plaintiff in a digital services context may be well equipped to argue, in response to a general defence, that the commercial incentive or need to commodify his or her private data is not a justification for such a privacy interference, and that more is needed to set aside any recognised privacy claim, for instance by adducing evidence of how the use or non-use of certain private data is necessary for the provision of the service sought.

Just as they do not exclude journalists or news media from liability, privacy torts do not automatically exclude other actors, such as state security services, or researchers, on an arbitrary footing that data processing by those actors is always legitimate or desirable and should not be scrutinised for privacy interference.[60] Data protection regulations characteristically provide for such exclusions (whether qualified or unqualified),[61] and this may be a result of such regulations being both fine-grained in their provisions and sweeping in their application: a wholesale exclusion from such a regime is the most efficient way to protect certain actors from being thwarted by data protection claims. A privacy tort, not encumbered either by such fine-grained rules or by such a low (almost non-existent) threshold, orientates the inquiry to whether there is, in all of the circumstances, a reasonable expectation of privacy covering the information in question. Following a principled and normatively anchored inquiry,

[56] See, eg, *Ali v Channel 5 Broadcasting Ltd* [2019] EWCA Civ 677.

[57] *Dotcom v Attorney-General* [2014] NZHC 1343.

[58] U Cheer, 'Recognition of Business and Economic Interests of Media in Defamation and Privacy Law' (2016) 23 *Torts Law Journal* 193.

[59] *McKennitt v Ash* (n 44) para 66.

[60] Though there may be other general legal immunities in operation that bar any legal action being taken against officials working for some of those entities. In that case, no claim, including under tort law, would stand against such users of personal data in the context of their work for those entities.

[61] See n 20.

a court may conclude, in the particular circumstances of a case, that there is no reasonable expectation of privacy in respect of information that needs to be used for purposes of state securitisation, or information that is being used for research purposes. A subliminal doctrine of necessity may influence how the law draws limits on the normative right to privacy, and the entitlements to autonomy, dignity and liberty which underpin it, in circumstances where it would be unjustified or disproportionate for an individual's rights to hinder the securitisation of their society, or to deny the collective benefit that accrues from scientific or academic research. Alternatively, a reasonable expectation of privacy may persist in such circumstances, and a general defence of legitimate public concern may be interpreted as embodying not only the principle of freedom of expression, but also this principle of necessity.[62] At the very least, a common law tort would in principle permit arguments to be made by a plaintiff against a defendant, who may be otherwise excluded wholesale from a data protection regulatory regime.

It is precisely because a common law tort is not tied to such arbitrarily set out, fine-grained regulation, and because it more clearly and directly embodies a sensibility for the protection of privacy per se, that a plaintiff may be able to make a legitimate claim in data privacy under the tort where he or she would not be able to do so under data protection regulation. The lens shifts under tort law, away from a catch-all threshold definition, fine-grained rules largely about consent and fair use, and several arbitrary, wholesale exceptions, towards a universally applicable, normatively anchored reasonableness threshold, with a general defence that is intended to account for the legitimate, conflicting interests that might arise. So far, recognised informational privacy torts have focused upon freedom of expression, but there is scope for expansion towards acknowledging something akin to necessity for the sake of securitisation, or the like – most importantly, tort law should, and characteristically does, fashion its justificatory or excusatory defences on interests that sit at the same level of normative importance as the interest protected in the first place. Tort law has decided that the privacy interest is weighty enough for protection, and that it is to be prioritised over the positive enabling of data flows and infotech development, and it allows that protected interest to be set aside when equally important interests, not just collateral damage, can be shown to be more weighty on the facts of a particular case.

A privacy tort applied to the data privacy context would exclude trivial claims, which are nothing to do with privacy and which impede unreasonably the free use of information technology, at the threshold stage (reasonable expectation of privacy). Where that threshold is passed, the tort would account for more weighty, conflicting interests at the defence stage, to ensure that each plaintiff has a sensible and normatively tethered opportunity to seek protection against any processor, for interferences with that scoped-out reasonable expectation of privacy. That same tort would then allow such a processor to answer back, on the facts, under a general defence, instead of trying to prove that it, or its activity, fits within a defined exception or derogation from the scheme in the first place.

[62] Something which is already built into the qualification, in Article 8(2) of the ECHR.

Finally, a privacy tort may offer better protection for plaintiffs than a data protection regulation regime, by offering a greater opportunity for substantial compensation for non-material harm. At least in the EU, and England and Wales, data protection regimes are not being interpreted as permissive or well-adapted to recovery of (non-trivial) damages for pure dignitary or psychological harm.[63] Courts appear to be ill-equipped under data protection regimes, even with their references to fundamental rights and privacy, to deal with non-economic loss, which runs the risk of being classed as 'mere upset',[64] or a 'modest degree of distress', even where a plaintiff has had to seek medical support for stress resulting from the data privacy interference.[65] In jurisdictions where a standalone privacy tort has a developed jurisprudence, such as England and Wales, the courts have had no issues with recognising and compensating serious dignitary, non-pecuniary harm, occasioned by or inherent in the wrongful interference: the misuse of private information.[66] Although damages for non-economic loss is not a characteristic or paradigmatic aspect of causes of action in tort, tort law is sufficiently capacious to provide for them, even beyond privacy torts,[67] where they are merited on the facts.

V. Conclusion

When compared with arguably the most prominent legal means to date of dealing with and protecting data privacy (data protection regulation), tort law has much to offer in the pursuit of well-defined, alternative – if not better – data privacy protection. This chapter has sought to argue that there are core, common aspects of torts of interference with informational privacy, which, when applied to a data privacy context (most commonly a digital services context), can offer both greater clarity and internal coherence in how issues of data privacy are dealt with in law, and better, more principled, protection of an individual's data privacy. A universally applicable tort, composed of a reasonable expectation of privacy threshold and a general justificatory defence, may be able to provide more normative and doctrinal coherence and clarity to how data privacy is measured and protected, particularly in terms of ensuring that the principles applied to determine the scope and nature of protection are directly and explicitly connected with the core reasons for that protection.

[63] Case C-300/12 *UI v Österreichische Post AG* ECLI:EU:C:2022:756 (ECJ, 6 October 2022), Opinion of AG Campos Sánchez-Bordona; *Driver v Crown Prosecution Service* [2022] EWHC 2500 (KB). This is in spite of the regulation or statute in question making some provision for remedies for non-pecuniary damage. Note, however, the Singaporean Court of Appeal's recent judgment permitting individuals to commence a private action for loss or damage due to a privacy interference under the Personal Data Protection Act 2012, where the 'loss or damage' may be emotional distress, as long as that distress is suffered directly as a result of a contravention of the statute's provisions and it is not trivial: *Reed v Bellingham* [2022] SGCA 60.

[64] *UI v Österreichische Post*, ibid.

[65] *Driver v Crown Prosecution Service* (n 63).

[66] See, eg, *Gulati v MGN Ltd* [2015] EWHC 1482 (Ch), paras 108–127, where Mann J held privacy damages should be awarded to reflect infringement of claimant privacy rights, as well as compensate claimants for injury to their feelings, resulting from phone-hacking.

[67] Eg, in the tort of defamation, and the tort of intentional infliction of emotional distress.

Such a tort, which is normatively anchored in its application and evolution, and whose scope is determined by reference to the value of privacy to individuals over and above any other considerations, may provide greater clarity for controllers and processors, particularly where their liability begins and ends. It may also provide better protection for privacy-seeking individuals in a digital services or digital economy context, precisely because the strong links to those normative underpinnings of privacy necessitate a more nuanced, fact-specific, and principled assessment of data privacy claims, than can be expected of a highly complex, fine-grained, and broadly applicable regulatory regime that also aims to protect individual privacy.

10

Closing Off the *Warren* of Negligence Claims for Data Breaches

EOIN O'DELL*

I. Introduction: Claims for Data Breaches

Like bees to a honey pot, large troves of personal data attract the malevolent attentions of criminal hackers. In the United Kingdom (UK),[1] to protect the personal data of data subjects, data controllers must implement 'appropriate technical or organisational measures' against breaches,[2] but they regularly fail to do so. For example, between 24 July 2017 and 25 April 2018, hackers installed malware on 5,930 point-of-sale terminals at DSG Retail's Currys PC World and Dixons Travel retail stores, exposing the personal data of at least 14 million of their customers. This was the biggest online

* Fellow and Associate Professor of Law, Trinity College Dublin. All weblinks in these notes were last accessed on 1 April 2023.

[1] The terms 'data controller', 'data subject', and 'personal data' include – but are not necessarily limited to – their definitions in Article 4(1) & (7) of Regulation (EU) 2016/679 of the European Parliament and of the Council of 27 April 2016 on the protection of natural persons with regard to the processing of personal data and on the free movement of such data, and repealing Directive 95/46/EC (General Data Protection Regulation) [2016] OJ L119/1 (GDPR).

[2] From 1 March 2000, this obligation flowed from Article 17(1) of Directive 95/46/EC of the European Parliament and of the Council of 24 October 1995 on the protection of individuals with regard to the processing of personal data and on the free movement of such data [1995] OJ L281/31 (DPD), as implemented in UK law by section 4 of, and Principle 7 in Schedule 1 to, the Data Protection Act 1998 (DPA 1998) (for the date, see the Data Protection Act 1998 (Commencement) Order 2000, SI No 2000/183).

From 25 May 2018, this obligation flowed from Article 5(1)(f) GDPR, as implemented in UK law by section 432(5)(a) of Schedule 19 to the Data Protection Act 2018 (DPA 2018) (for the date, see Article 99(2) GDPR and Regulation 2 of the DPA 2018 (Commencement No 1 and Transitional and Saving Provisions) Regulations 2018, SI 2018/625).

When the UK left the EU on 31 January 2020, the GDPR was retained and renamed the UK GDPR, and the obligation in the text now flows from Article 5(1)(f) UK GDPR.

The GDPR was retained pursuant to section 3 of the European Union (Withdrawal) Act 2018 [the Withdrawal Act] and sections 3(10) and 205(4) DPA 2018 (as inserted by Regulations 4(4) and 85(7) of Schedule 2 to the Data Protection, Privacy and Electronic Communications (Amendments etc) (EU Exit) Regulations 2019, SI No 2019/419 (2019 Regulations); see also Regulation 5(2) of the Data Protection, Privacy and Electronic Communications (Amendments etc) (EU Exit) Regulations 2020, SI No 2020/1568 (2020 Regulations)). Having been retained, it was (pursuant to section 2 of Schedule 1 to the 2019 Regulations) renamed for the purposes of UK law as the Regulation (EU) 2016/679 of the European Parliament and of data breach in UK history;[3] DSG's share price immediately plummeted;[4] and, in January 2020, the Information Commissioner's Office (ICO) imposed a fine of £500,000 on DSG.[5] This fine came almost exactly two years to the day after the ICO had imposed a fine of £400,000 on Carphone Warehouse, another DSG company, for a breach caused by a similar failure to implement appropriate measures against breaches.[6]

Where regulation and public enforcement leave off, litigation and private enforcement often pick up.[7] In the context of the DSG point-of-sale malware, data subjects whose personal data was compromised have at least three possible claims. First, there is a statutory claim; it was initially derived from European Union (EU) law; but it now has an exclusively domestic basis. At EU law, Article 23(1) DPD provided that any person who suffered damage from unlawful processing was 'entitled to receive compensation from the controller for the damage suffered'. This was implemented into UK law by section 13(1) DPA 1998, which provided that any individual who suffered damage by reason of any breach of the Act was 'entitled to compensation from the data controller for that damage'.[8] The Directive was repealed and replaced by the GDPR, Article 82(1) of which provides that: 'Any person who has suffered material or non-material damage as a result of an infringement of this Regulation shall have the right to receive compensation from the controller or processor for the damage suffered'.

Section 168 DPA 2018 assumed that this Article 82 GDPR right to compensation was directly applicable in UK law, and this gave rise to some potential analytical wrinkles.[9]

the Council of 27 April 2016 on the protection of natural persons with regard to the processing of personal data and on the free movement of such data (United Kingdom General Data Protection Regulation) or, for short (pursuant to Regulation 2 of 2019 Regulations) the UK GDPR. For the date, see section 21(1) of the Withdrawal Act, as amended by Regulation 2 of the European Union (Withdrawal) Act 2018 (Exit Day) (Amendment) (No 3) Regulations 2019, SI No 2019/1423).

If enacted, pending Data Protection and Digital Information (No 2) Bill 2023 will not change anything in this footnote.

[3] M Vincent, 'Institutional Complacency Exposes Dixons Carphone Customers Again' *Financial Times* (London, 13 June 2018).

[4] 'Dixons Carphone Fined for Systemic Failures that Led to Cyber Attack: ICO' (*Reuters*, London, 9 January 2020), www.reuters.com/article/us-dixons-carphone-cybercrime-idUSKBN1Z82AZ.

[5] 'Monetary Penalty Notice' (Notice of Regulatory Penalty, Information Commissioner's Office, 7 January 2020), ico.org.uk/media/action-weve-taken/mpns/2616891/dsg-mpn-20200107.pdf. This was the highest fine available to the ICO at the time, pursuant to section 55A DPA 1998 (as inserted by section 144 of the Criminal Justice and Immigration Act 2008). From 25 May 2018 (for this date, see n 2 above), the ceiling is now €20m or 4% of an undertaking's total worldwide annual turnover, whichever is higher (see Article 83 GDPR and UK GDPR); since then, the highest fines have been £20m, imposed on British Airways (see 'Penalty Notice' (Notice of Regulatory Penalty, Information Commissioner's Office, 16 October 2020), ico.org.uk/media/action-weve-taken/mpns/2618421/ba-penalty-20201016.pdf) and £18.4m imposed on Marriott Hotels (see 'Penalty Notice' (Notice of Regulatory Penalty, Information Commissioner's Office, 30 October 2020), ico.org.uk/media/action-weve-taken/mpns/2618524/marriott-international-inc-mpn-20201030.pdf). DSG can count themselves lucky that the breach was discovered and terminated a month before the higher fines could have kicked in.

[6] 'Monetary Penalty Notice' (Notice of Regulatory Penalty, Information Commissioner's Office, 8 January 2018), ico.org.uk/media/action-weve-taken/mpns/2172972/carphone-warehouse-mpn-20180110.pdf.

[7] LH Scholz, 'Private Rights of Action in Privacy Law' (2022) 63 *William & Mary Law Review* 1639.

[8] In *Google Inc v Vidal-Hall* [2015] EWCA Civ 311, [2016] QB 1003, 'damage' under Article 23 DPD was given a broad interpretation, and limitations in section 13(2) on claims for distress were disapplied for EU law reasons. In *Lloyd v Google LLC* [2021] UKSC 50, paras 93–96, 123, [2022] AC 1217, 1252, 1260 (Lord Leggatt; Lord Reed, Lady Arden, Lord Sales and Lord Burrows concurring) *Vidal-Hall* was approved but not expanded.

[9] E O'Dell, 'Compensation for Breach of the General Data Protection Regulation' (2017) 40 *Dublin University Law Journal (ns)* 97, ss 2.4, 2.6.

However, when the UK left the EU, the GDPR was retained by the UK GDPR,[10] the current version of which does not amend Article 82(1).[11] Moreover, since the UK GDPR is now a piece of domestic legislation, potential EU wrinkles fall away. These statutory provisions provide private causes of action for data breaches. But each has its limitations. Section 13 of the 1998 Act required significant judicial surgery,[12] and potential infirmities with section 168 of the 2018 Act only fell away as a fortunate by-product of Brexit.[13] But section 13 was a secure private cause of action for data breaches after its surgery, and section 168 is now similarly secure after its outrageous slice of good fortune.

Second, at common law, whilst there is no tort of invasion of privacy,[14] a tort of misuse of private information[15] has recently spun out[16] of the equitable doctrine of breach of confidence,[17] and it is now routinely pleaded in data breach cases in parallel with statutory data protection claims.[18]

Third, from DSG's perspective, to be hacked once may be regarded as a misfortune, to be hacked twice looks like carelessness.[19] Indeed, a failure to implement measures against breaches certainly sounds like it could be a failure to take reasonable care. Hence, a claim in the tort of negligence seems entirely plausible. In principle, there can be no objection to the protection of privacy interests by means of the general law of torts, even if it is indirect and piecemeal.[20] For example, in *Fearn v Tate Gallery*,[21] the UK Supreme Court protected the claimants' privacy interests by means of the tort of private nuisance.

[10] See n 2 above. K McCullagh, 'Post-Brexit Data Protection in the UK – Leaving the EU but not EU Data Protection Law Behind' in GG Fuster, R van Brakel and P de Hert (eds), *Research Handbook on Privacy and Data Protection Law* (Cheltenham, Edward Elgar, 2022) 36.

[11] Nothing in the 2019 or 2020 Regulations amends Article 82.

[12] See n 8 above.

[13] On Brexit, see n 2 above. On such claims for damages, see Normann Witzleb and Kwan Ho Lau in chapters 14 and 15 of this volume respectively.

[14] *Wainwright v Home Office* [2003] UKHL 53, paras 23–30, [2004] 2 AC 406, 421–423 (Lord Hoffmann; Lords Bingham, Hope and Hutton concurring; Lord Scott concurring in a short speech).

[15] *PJS v News Group Newspapers Ltd* [2016] UKSC 26, [2016] 1 AC 1081; *Bloomberg LP v ZXC* [2022] UKSC 5, para 45, [2022] AC 1158, 1190 (Lords Hamblen and Stephens; Lords Reed, Lloyd-Jone and Sales concurring).

[16] *Google Inc v Vidal-Hall* (n 8) paras 43, 51, [2016] QB 1003, 1028, 1031 (Lord Dyson MR and Sharpe LJ in a joint judgment; McFarlane LJ concurring); on 23 July 2015, the Supreme Court declined leave to appeal against this conclusion because it did 'not raise an arguable point of law' (see 'Permission to Appeal results – June 2015/July 2015' (UK Supreme Court, July 2015) 5, www.supremecourt.uk/docs/permission-to-appeal-2015-0607.pdf); leave was granted on other grounds (*ibid*) but the case subsequently settled (see C Knight, '*Vidal-Hall* Appeal Withdrawn; Section 13(2) DPA Still Dead' (*Panopticon*, 12 July 2016), panopticonblog.com/2016/07/12/vidal-hall-appeal-withdrawn-section-132-dpa-still-dead/).

[17] *Campbell v MGN Ltd* [2004] UKHL 22, paras 13–17, [2004] 2 AC 457, 464–465 (Lord Nicholls); *Douglas v Hello! Ltd (No 3)* [2007] UKHL 21, para 255, [2008] AC 1, 72 (Lord Nicholls).

[18] F Brimblecombe and H Fenwick, 'Protecting Private Information in the Digital Era: Making the Most Effective Use of the Availability of the Actions under the GDPR/DPA and the Tort of Misuse of Private Information' (2022) 73 *Northern Ireland Legal Quarterly* 26.

[19] With apologies to Lady Bracknell in Oscar Wilde's *The Importance of Being Earnest* (first performed 1895; first published 1899) (R Jackson ed) (London, Bloomsbury Publishing, 2014) 70, Act 1, lines 539–40.

[20] A Wolanski and V Shore, 'Context and Background' in NA Moreham, M Warby, M Tugendhat and I Christie (eds), *Tugendhat and Christie: The Law of Privacy and The Media*, 3rd edn, (Oxford, Oxford University Press, 2016) para 1.01; E O'Dell, 'When Two Tribes Go to War. Privacy Interests and Media Speech' in M McGonagle (ed), *Law and the Media: Views of Journalists and Lawyers* (Dublin, Round Hall Sweet & Maxwell, 1997) 181, 184ff.

[21] *Fearn v Board of Trustees of the Tate Gallery* [2023] UKSC 4, paras 111–113 (Lord Leggatt; Lords Reed and Lloyd-Jones concurring) paras 176, 180, 204 (Lord Sales; Lord Kitchen concurring) (dissenting, but not

And, in Ireland, the High Court has twice found that leaks of personal data breached duties of care in negligence.[22] A warren of negligence claims for data breaches might therefore in principle arise.

In *Warren v DSG Retail Ltd*,[23] all three claims featured. The claimant had purchased goods from Currys PC World; he claimed that his personal data was compromised in the hack; and he sought £5,000 in damages for distress pursuant to section 13(1) DPA 1998, for misuse of private information, and in common law negligence. Saini J struck out the common law claims, and transferred the statutory claim to the County Court.[24] In the claim for misuse of private information, he held that those who had misused the claimant data subject's personal data were the criminal third party hackers, and not the defendant data controller which had been hacked.[25] Hence, he dismissed the claim for damages for misuse of private information[26] because there was no *misuse by the defendant* of the private information.[27]

Saini J also rejected the claim in negligence in terms that forcibly slammed shut the door to such claims, at least insofar as the law in England and Wales is concerned, holding that:

> … there is neither need nor warrant to impose such a duty of care where the statutory duties under the DPA 1998 operate … there is no room (nor indeed any need identified) to construct a concurrent duty in negligence when there exists a bespoke statutory regime for determining the liability of data controllers. That regime provides for relief of precisely the same nature as is claimed in negligence in this claim.[28]

on this point); *cf Victoria Park Racing and Recreation Grounds Co Ltd v Taylor* [1937] HCA 45, (1937) 58 CLR 479; Wolanski and Shore, 'Context and Background' (n 20) paras 1.15–1.16, 10.60ff.

[22] *Hanahoe v Hussey* [1997] IEHC 173, [1998] 3 IR 69 (Kinlen J); *Gray v Minister for Justice* [2007] IEHC 52, [2007] 2 IR 654 (Dunne J).

[23] *Warren v DSG Retail Ltd* [2021] EWHC 2168 (QB).

[24] After The Event (ATE) insurance premia paid by the claimant may be recovered by way of costs in claims for breach of confidence and misuse of private information (section 1(2)(c)-(d) of the Legal Aid, Sentencing and Punishment of Offenders Act 2012 (Commencement No 13) Order 2018, SI 2018/1287) but not in the statutory claims (R Hopkins, 'Important New High Court Judgment on Data Breach Litigation' (*Panopticon*, 30 July 2021), panopticonblog.com/2021/07/30/important-new-high-court-judgment-on-data-breach-litigation/; A Vakil and R Canbilen, 'Striking Out of Privacy and Confidence Actions in the Dixons Data Breach Case' (2022) 33 *Entertainment Law Review* 34). Worse, Warren's solicitors subsequently went into administration (N Rose, 'Hundreds of Staff Lose Jobs as Parts of PURE Legal Group Enter Administration' (*Legal Futures*, 3 November 2021), www.legalfutures.co.uk/latest-news/hundreds-of-staff-lose-jobs-as-parts-of-pure-legal-group-enter-administration), which probably brought the County Court proceedings to an end.

[25] *Warren v DSG Retail Ltd* (n 23) para 31 following *WM Morrison Supermarkets Plc v Various Claimants* [2017] EWHC 3113 (QB), para 64, [2018] 3 WLR 691, 711–12 (Langstaff J). The matter was not pursued on appeal [2018] EWCA Civ 2339, [2019] QB 772, and [2020] UKSC 12, [2020] AC 989. See also *Collins v Ticketmaster UK Ltd* [2022] Costs LR 123 (HHJ Pearce); *Stadler v Currys Group Limited* [2022] EWHC 160 (QB), paras 47–59 (HHJ Lewis); *Underwood v Bounty UK Ltd* [2022] EWHC 888 (QB) para 52 (Nicklin J); *Smith v TalkTalk Telecom Group Plc* [2022] EWHC 1311 (QB), para 46 (Saini J); *Prismall v Google UK Ltd* [2023] EWHC 1169 (KB), para 79 (Williams J).

[26] A separate claim in breach of confidence was not maintained (*Warren v DSG Retail Ltd, ibid* para 18); nevertheless, Saini J considered it and held that it failed for the same reason (paras 25–26); see Y Chua, 'Claiming for Breach of Confidence after a Cyberattack' (2022) 34 *Singapore Academy of Law Journal* 672. See Megan Richardson in chapter 11 of this volume.

[27] In Canada, following similar data breaches, claims in the privacy tort of intrusion upon seclusion failed for the same reason in *Owsianik v Equifax Canada Co 2021* 2022 ONCA 813; *Obodo v Trans Union of Canada Inc* 2022 ONCA 814; *Winder v Marriott International Inc* 2022 ONCA 815. See Jelena Gligorijevic in chapter 9 of this volume.

[28] *Warren v DSG Retail Ltd* (n 23) paras 34, 35(iii).

This policy applies with greater force now that an even stronger statutory claim is available to data subjects pursuant to Article 82 UK GDPR and section 168 DPA 2018.

The failure of the negligence claim in *Warren* is the focus of this piece. Saini J derived his approach to the statutory policy bar from the decision of the Court of Appeal in *Smeaton v Equifax Plc*.[29] That decision discussed liability in the tort of negligence in data breach cases in terms of voluntary assumption of responsibility, and it is discussed in section II. Saini J's application of *Smeaton* in *Warren* is discussed in section III. Finally, section IV concludes that some voluntary assumption claims should not be precluded by the policy bar.

II. *Smeaton v Equifax* and Voluntary Assumption of Responsibility in the Tort of Negligence

In *Smeaton*, the Court of Appeal relied on the earlier case of *Swinney v Chief Constable of Northumbria Police Force*.[30] Here, the first claimant saw a car hit and kill a police officer, and provided that information to the police. Her personal details were in a file stolen from a police car and they eventually made their way to the alleged driver. She was subject to threats of violence and arson. The Court of Appeal held that there was an arguable case that there was a special relationship giving rise to a duty of care owed by the police to the claimant.[31] However, absent such a special relationship, there would have been no grounds for such a duty of care between the defendant police as data controllers and the claimant as data subject. In *White v Jones*,[32] Lord Browne-Wilkinson held that:

> Although the categories of cases in which such special relationship can be held to exist are not closed, as yet only two categories have been identified, *viz.* (1) where there is a fiduciary relationship and (2) where the defendant has voluntarily answered a question or tenders skilled advice or services in circumstances where he knows or ought to know that an identified claimant will rely on his answers or advice. *In both these categories the special relationship is created by the defendant voluntarily assuming to act in the matter by involving himself in the plaintiff's affairs* or by choosing to speak. If he does so assume to act or speak he is said to have assumed responsibility for carrying through the matter he has entered upon (emphasis added).[33]

Given that a special relationship may be created by a voluntary assumption of responsibility, it is unsurprising that, in *Chief Constable of the Hertfordshire Police v Van Colle*, Lord Browne described *Swinney* as a case in which the facts suggested that 'the police had assumed responsibility for the complainant informer's safety'.[34]

[29] *Smeaton v Equifax Plc* [2013] EWCA Civ 108.
[30] *Swinney v Chief Constable of Northumbria Police Force* [1996] EWCA Civ 1322, [1997] QB 464.
[31] *ibid* 479 (Hirst LJ).
[32] *White v Jones* [1995] UKHL 5, [1995] 2 AC 207.
[33] *ibid* 274; see also *Customs & Excise Commissioners v Barclays Bank* [2006] UKHL 28, para 92, [2007] 1 AC 181, 216 (Lord Mance).
[34] *Hertfordshire Police v Van Colle* [2008] UKHL 50, para 120, [2009] 1 AC 225, 282 (Lord Browne).

The leading case on such a voluntary assumption of responsibility in the context of a data breach is *Smeaton v Equifax Plc*.[35] The defendant, Equifax, had registered the claimant's bankruptcy on their credit reference service, but had not registered that it had been discharged. After the discharge, the claimant had been denied a bank loan on foot of the defendant's inaccurate information. The claimant data subject's claim that the defendant data controller was negligent and in breach of a duty of care owed him failed. Tomlinson LJ held that, although data protection legislation imposed duties upon data controllers, that was insufficient of itself to give rise to a statutory duty for the purposes of the tort of breach of statutory duty: 'you cannot derive a common law duty of care directly from a statutory duty'.[36] Nor had Equifax voluntarily assumed responsibility towards every member of the public simply by choosing to operate as a credit reference agency: such an approach would 'assign to the concept of voluntary assumption of responsibility so wide a meaning as to deprive it of effective utility'.[37]

In *Caparo Industries Plc v Dickman*,[38] Lord Bridge explained that the necessary ingredients giving rise to a duty of care are threefold. First, damage to the defendant should have been foreseeable by the claimant. Second, there should exist between the parties a relationship of 'proximity' or 'neighbourhood'. And, third, it should be 'fair, just and reasonable' in all the circumstances to impose a duty of care upon the defendant.[39] The *Caparo* threefold framework is particularly applicable where a claimant seeks to establish a novel category of liability in negligence at common law,[40] and it is therefore a convenient starting point for analysing whether, in data breach cases, a data controller owes a duty of care in negligence to data subjects whose personal data has been compromised by third parties, such as criminal hackers.

On the first leg of *Caparo*, it will often be foreseeable that damage, or harm, or distress, or financial loss, is likely to befall a data subject whose personal data is compromised by third parties. On the second leg of *Caparo*, one means of establishing proximity is the criterion at issue in *Smeaton* that the defendant had voluntarily assumed responsibility towards the claimant.[41] As Lord Goff held in *Henderson v Merrett Syndicates*,[42] a party who has assumed a responsibility towards another party in respect of certain services, can be liable in damages to that other party in respect of economic loss which flows from the negligent performance of those services.[43]

[35] *Smeaton v Equifax* (n 29); on the limits of a statutory claim in such circumstances, compare *Transunion LCC v Ramirez* 594 US __ (2021).

[36] *ibid* para 73 citing *Barclays Bank* (n 33) para 39, [2007] 1 AC 181, 200 (Lord Hoffmann).

[37] *ibid* para 74 citing *Barclays Bank, ibid* para 94, 217 (Lord Mance).

[38] *Caparo v Dickman* [1990] UKHL 2, [1990] 2 AC 605.

[39] *ibid* para 12, [1990] 2 AC 605, 617–18 (Lord Bridge); on the three-stage test, see J Morgan *Great Debates in Tort Law* (Oxford, Hart Publishing, 2022) ch 2.

[40] *Barclays Bank* (n 33) para [53], [2007] 1 AC 181, 204 (Lord Rodger); *Okpabi v Royal Dutch Shell Plc* [2021] UKSC 3, para 151, [2021] 1 WLR 1294, 1324 (Lord Hamblen; Lord Hodge, Lady Black and Lord Briggs concurring).

[41] *Barclays Bank* (n 33) para [52], [2007] 1 AC 181, 204 (Lord Rodger), para 73, 209–10 (Lord Walker); see, generally, A Robertson and J Wang, 'The Assumption of Responsibility' in K Barker, R Grantham and W Swain (eds), *The Law of Misstatements: 50 Years on from Hedley Byrne v Heller* (Oxford, Hart Publishing, 2015) ch 3; D Nolan, 'Assumption of Responsibility: Four Questions' (2019) 72 *Current Legal Problems* 123.

[42] *Henderson v Merrett* [1994] UKHL 5, [1995] 2 AC 145.

[43] *ibid* 13–14, [1995] 2 AC 145, 181 (Lord Goff; Lords Keith, Browne-Wilkinson, Mustill and Nolan concurring) discussing *Hedley Byrne & Co Ltd v Heller & Partners Ltd* [1963] UKHL 4, [1964] AC 465; see also

And, whilst this is directed to economic loss, if *Swinney* is best understood as an example of that principle,[44] then that case illustrates that Lord Goff's principle can, in principle, reach claims for damages for distress and pain and suffering as well.

Moreover, in *Henderson*, Lord Goff emphasised that an assumption of responsibility by a professional 'may give rise to liability in respect of *negligent omissions* as much as negligent acts of commission' (emphasis added).[45] This consideration is particularly important in data breach cases, where it is often the case that third party hackers have exploited security failures that the data controllers have omitted to remedy.

On the third leg of *Caparo*, in *Smeaton*, Tomlinson LJ also held that, as a matter of policy, it would not be fair, just and reasonable to impose a duty of care, because to impose a duty owed to members of the public generally would potentially give rise to an indeterminate liability to an indeterminate class.[46] However, as Lord Sumption explained in *Banca Nazionale del Lavoro SPA v Playboy Club London Ltd*,[47] it

> is fundamental to this way of analysing the duty that the defendant is assuming a responsibility to an identifiable (although not necessarily identified) person or group of persons, and not to the world at large or to a wholly indeterminate group.[48]

Hence, where responsibility is assumed towards an identifiable, if not necessarily identified, person or group, a duty of care should not be excluded.

Tomlinson LJ also held that a common law claim in negligence would be 'otiose' given that the Data Protection Act 1998 provided a detailed code for determining the liability of data controllers.[49] As Davis LJ put it, there was 'simply no room for – as well as no need for – the construct of some concurrent duty in tort. The statute itself exhaustively provides for the applicable obligations and remedies in a case such as this'.[50]

The availability of alternative effective redress can provide an important policy consideration, independent of the parties' relationship, that means that it is not just, fair and reasonable to impose a duty of care in negligence at common law. *Customs &*

White v Jones [1995] UKHL 5, 19–20, [1995] 2 AC 207, 268–69 (Lord Goff; Lord Browne-Wilkinson and Nolan concurring). The principle is older than *Hedley Byrne* and of wider significance (*Poole Borough Council v GN* [2019] UKSC 25 para 67, [2020] AC 780, 836 (Lord Reed; Lady Hale, Lord Wilson, Lord Hodge and Lady Black concurring)); on *Hedley Byrne*, see P Mitchell, '*Hedley Byrne & Co Ltd v Heller & Partners Ltd*' in Charles Mitchell and Paul Mitchell (eds), *Landmark Cases in the Law of Tort* (Oxford, Hart Publishing, 2010) 171, and, generally, Barker, Grantham and Swain, (eds) *The Law of Misstatements* (n 41).

[44] See n 34 above.

[45] *Henderson v Merrett* (n 42) 14, [1995] 2 AC 145, 181; *White v Jones* [1995] UKHL 5, 19–20, [1995] 2 AC 207, 269 (Lord Goff).

[46] *Smeaton v Equifax* (n 29) para 75(2).

[47] *Banca Nazionale del Lavoro SPA v Playboy Club London Ltd* [2018] UKSC 43, [2018] 1 WLR 4041.

[48] *ibid* para 7, 4046 (Lord Sumption; Lady Hale, Lord Reed and Lord Briggs concurring).

[49] *Smeaton v Equifax* (n 29) para 75(3).

[50] *ibid* para 81. Equifax subsequently suffered a major hack, for which the ICO imposed the then maximum fine of £500,000 (see 'Monetary Penalty Notice' (Notice of Regulatory Penalty, Information Commissioner's Office, 19 September 2018), ico.org.uk/media/2259808/equifax-ltd-mpn-20180919.pdf), but a representative action was withdrawn after the Supreme Court decision in *Lloyd v Google* (A Proops, '*Atkinson v Equifax*: Representative Action Withdrawn' (*Panopticon*, 1 April 2020), panopticonblog.com/2020/04/01/atkinson-v-equifax-representative-action-withdrawn/). However, negligence claims arising out of the same breach have been allowed to proceed in Canada (*Owsianik v Equifax* 2022 ONCA 813) and the United States (*In re Equifax Inc Customer Data Security Breach Litigation* 362 F Supp 3d 1295 (ND Ga, 2019) (Thrash J)).

Excise Commissioners v Barclays Bank[51] is a good illustration. The House of Lords held that the defendant bank did not owe a duty of care to the claimant Commissioners to prevent payments out of frozen bank accounts. The bank had not assumed responsibility to the Commissioners because its compliance was not voluntary but compelled by a freezing order.[52] Furthermore, it was not fair, just and reasonable to impose such a duty of care. The bank should not, on being notified of an order which it had no opportunity to resist, become exposed to a liability for which it had not been in any way rewarded.[53] Indeed, if that duty of care were to be imposed on a bank, then it would also have to be imposed on any other person with notice of the freezing order, and this would produce unfair, unjust and unreasonable results.[54] Nor would it be just, fair and reasonable to disturb the fair and normally effective balance between the respective interests involved.[55] Moreover, if the bank had intentionally breached the freezing order, it would have been in contempt of court, and this would have provided sufficient protection for the Commissioners. If so, then the availability of alternative effective redress for contempt would have provided a further policy reason why it would not have been just, fair and reasonable to impose a duty upon the bank.[56] Similarly, then, *Smeaton* illustrates that, in data breach cases, the availability of alternative effective redress pursuant to a detailed and exhaustive statutory claim provides an important policy reason why it would not be just, fair and reasonable to impose upon the data controller a duty of care in negligence to data subjects whose personal data has been compromised by third parties, such as criminal hackers.

III. *Warren v DSG Retail* and Claims in Negligence for Data Breaches

Smeaton was followed by Saini J in *Warren v DSG Retail Ltd*,[57] rejecting the claim that the defendant data controller had breached a duty of care to the claimant data subject. On the question of the existence of a duty of care, Saini J held that proximity was not created simply by the customer relationship.[58] However, there is rather more to be said about proximity than he allowed. In the canonical formulation, a relationship of neighbourhood or proximity between a claimant and a defendant arises where the claimant is so closely and directly affected by the defendant's act that the defendant ought reasonably to have the claimant in contemplation as being so affected when the defendant

[51] *Barclays Bank* (n 33).

[52] *ibid* para 14, 194 (Lord Bingham), para 39, 200 (Lord Hoffmann), para 65, 208 (Lord Rodger), para 74, 210 (Lord Walker), paras 94, 109, 216–17, 221 (Lord Mance).

[53] *ibid* para 23, 196–97 (Lord Bingham), paras 65–66, 205 (Lord Rodger).

[54] *ibid* para 77, 211 (Lord Walker), para 111, 222–23 (Lord Mance).

[55] *ibid* para 113, 223 (Lord Mance).

[56] *ibid* paras 16–17, 195 (Lord Bingham), para 29, 197–98 (Lord Hoffmann), para 59–64, 206–208 (Lord Rodger), para 74, 210 (Lord Walker), para 101, 219 (Lord Mance). However, the bank had not intentionally breached the freezing order, and so had not committed contempt.

[57] *Warren v DSG Retail Ltd* (n 23).

[58] *ibid* [36].

is considering the acts or omissions which are called in question.[59] Since a customer can be closely and directly affected by a vendor's act, the vendor ought reasonably to have the customer in contemplation as being so affected when the vendor is considering whether and how to act. Liability in *Swinney* and *Smeaton* was posited on the basis of the defendants' voluntary assumption of responsibility in respect of the claimants; and, as Lord Goff pointed out in *Henderson v Merrett Syndicates*, this principle of liability 'is capable of application not only where the services are rendered gratuitously, but also where they are rendered under a contract'.[60] Hence, as Lord Leggatt put it in *Triple Point Technology, Inc v PTT Public Company Ltd*, 'someone who provides services to another person generally owes that person a duty of care in tort whether or not the relationship between them is contractual …'.[61] So, the issue of proximity is not as straightforward as Saini J suggested in *Warren*.

He gave two further reasons for rejecting duty of care claimed by the claimant. He held that it would not be fair, just and reasonable to impose such a duty.[62] And, following *Smeaton*, he said that it is not necessary 'to construct a concurrent duty in negligence when there exists a bespoke statutory regime for determining the liability of data controllers'.[63] In truth, these two reasons amount to the same thing. Section 13(1) DPA 1998 provided that any individual who suffered damage by reason of any breach of the Act was 'entitled to compensation from the data controller for that damage'.[64] The availability of alternative effective redress pursuant to this detailed and exhaustive cause of action meant that, in *Warren*, it was not fair, just and reasonable to impose a duty of care in the circumstances. It is decidedly odd, though, that this policy should doom a common law claim in negligence but leave untouched the common law claim in misuse of private information that is now routinely pleaded in data breach cases in parallel with statutory data protection claims. Indeed, the misuse of private information claim failed in *Warren*, not for policy reasons, but because the element of misuse by the defendant was absent.[65]

Even if there had been a duty of care, the claim in *Warren* would have failed because Saini J held that the claimant had suffered no loss. He had claimed damages for distress, but Saini J held that 'a state of anxiety produced by some negligent act or omission but falling short of a clinically recognisable psychiatric illness does not constitute damage sufficient to complete a tortious cause of action'.[66] If *Swinney* illustrates that claims in

[59] *Donoghue v Stevenson* [1932] UKHL 100, para 4, [1932] AC 562, 580 (Lord Atkin).

[60] *Henderson v Merrett* (n 42) 5, 20, [1995] 2 AC 145, 187 (Lord Goff); 26, 192 ('no reason in principle why a tortious duty should not co-exist with a contractual duty') 29, 195 (same).

[61] *Triple Point Technology, Inc v PTT Public Company Ltd* [2021] UKSC 29, para 103, [2021] AC 1148, 1186–1187 (Lord Leggatt; Lord Burrows concurring) (concurring in judgment).

[62] *Warren v DSG Retail Ltd* (n 23) para 36.

[63] See *Smeaton v Equifax* (n 29).

[64] See n 8 above.

[65] See nn 23–27 above.

[66] *Warren v DSG Retail Ltd* (n 23) para 40; *Rolfe v Veale Wasbrough Vizards LLP* [2021] EWHC 2809 (QB), paras 11–13 (Master McCloud) (no distress above a *de minimis* level); *cf Ashley v Amplifon Ltd* [2021] EWHC 2921 (QB) (remitted to County Court); *Johnson v Eastlight Community Homes Ltd* [2021] EWHC 3069 (QB) (same); *Cleary v Marston (Holdings) Ltd* [2021] EWHC 3809 (QB) (same); F McCombie, 'Damages & Distress: Data Protection Leaks in Court' (2022) 172 *New Law Journal* 13; D Citron and D Solove, 'Risk and Anxiety: A Theory of Data Breach Harms' (2018) 96 *Texas Law Review* 737; JP Kesan and CM Hayes, 'Liability for

voluntary assumption of responsibility can, in principle, reach claims for damages for distress and pain and suffering, then *Warren* illustrates that, in many data breach cases the general rules of liability for psychiatric harm are unlikely to be satisfied.

The statutory bar at issue in *Smeaton* and *Warren* also arose in *Stadler v Currys Group Ltd*.[67] The claimant traded in a smart television to the defendant retailer, Currys, which sold it to a third party. Currys did not delete the data from the TV before selling it on, and the third party used the customer's account on one of the applications on the TV to purchase a movie; Currys refunded this cost. The claimant's statutory claim pursuant to Article 82 UK GDPR and section 168 DPA 2018 was allowed to proceed, but his claim in negligence failed. HHJ Lewis also that, in *Warren*, Saini J had held that there was no room for the Court to construct a concurrent duty in negligence where there existed a bespoke statutory regime for determining the liability of data controllers.[68] He also held that the claimant had suffered no loss, harm or injury: the cost of the movie had been refunded, and he had suffered no cognisable distress; so he had not pleaded a complete cause of action in common law negligence.[69]

The statutory bar also arose in *Smith v TalkTalk Telecom Group Plc*.[70] In September 2014, TalkTalk customers began to receive scam calls purporting to be from TalkTalk, which were ultimately traced to data obtained by users of Wipro, a third party providing network services to TalkTalk. However, neither TalkTalk nor Wipro had put adequate controls in place to prevent unauthorised access by Wipro's users to the data supplied by TalkTalk. In August 2017, the ICO imposed a fine of £100,000 on TalkTalk for their failure to implement appropriate security measures.[71] Saini J dismissed an action for damages for misuse of private information for the same reason that he had in *Warren*: those who had misused the claimant data subject's personal data were the third parties, Wipro's unauthorised users, and not the defendant data controller, TalkTalk. Again, there had been no *misuse by the defendant* of the private information.[72]

Moreover, Saini J characterised the claim as an impermissible negligence action 'masquerading' as a claim for misuse of private information.[73] He explained that, in *Swinney*, 'a duty to take care to protect information from disclosure to another person will arise only if there is a special relationship between the parties giving rise to a duty of care under the law of negligence'.[74] In *White v Jones*, Lord Browne-Wilkinson said that such a special relationship may be created by a voluntary assumption of responsibility; and in *Van Colle*, Lord Browne said that the facts in *Swinney* suggested that the police

Data Injuries' (2019) 2019 *University of Illinois Law Review* 295; I Kilovaty, 'Psychological Data Breach Harms' (2021) 23 *North Carolina Journal of Law & Technology* 1.

[67] *Stadler v Currys Group Ltd* [2022] EWHC 160 (QB).

[68] *ibid* para 61.

[69] *ibid* paras 63–64; *Ashley v Amplifon* (n 66) para 54 (Kerr J).

[70] *Smith v TalkTalk Telecom* (n 25); a claim in negligence also failed in *Sterritt v Telegraph Media Group Ltd* [2022] NIQB 43.

[71] 'Monetary Penalty Notice' (Notice of Regulatory Penalty, Information Commissioner's Office, 7 August 2017), ico.org.uk/media/action-weve-taken/mpns/2014626/mpn-talktalk-20170807.pdf.

[72] *Smith v TalkTalk Telecom* (n 25) para [46]; see nn 23–27 above.

[73] *ibid* para 48; see also para 4.

[74] *ibid* paras 58–61 discussing C Phipps, W Harman and S Teasdale, *Toulson and Phipps on Confidentiality*, 4th edn (London, Sweet & Maxwell, 2020) para 5.009ff.

had assumed responsibility for the claimant's safety.[75] *Smeaton* and *Smith* illustrate that there is unlikely to be such a voluntary assumption in data breach cases, though *Swinney* and Lord Sumption's comments in *Banca Nazionale* illustrate that the possibility cannot be ruled out if the facts so align.

Hence, in England and Wales, at least at the level of the High Court after *Warren*, and perhaps even at the level of the Court of Appeal after *Smeaton*, there is little if any scope for a claim that a data controller owes a duty of care in negligence to data subjects whose personal data has been compromised by third parties, such as criminal hackers. In *Smith*, there was no proximity because there was no special relationship between the parties. In *Smeaton*, there was no proximity because the defendant had not voluntarily assumed responsibility towards the claimant. In *Warren*, proximity was not created simply by the customer relationship. In *Smeaton* and *Warren*, it was not just, fair and reasonable to impose a duty of care. Conversely, it might be thought to follow that if, on an appropriate set of data breach facts, damage to the claimant data subject is foreseeable, there is sufficient proximity between the claimant data subject and the defendant data controller (either by a special relationship, or by a voluntary assumption of responsibility, or for some other reason), and if it is just, fair and reasonable to impose a duty of care, then the defendant data controller may very well owe a duty of care in negligence to a claimant data subject whose personal data has been compromised by third parties, such as criminal hackers. But if so, *Smeaton*, *Warren* and *Stadler* demonstrate that the availability of alternative effective redress pursuant to detailed and exhaustive data protection legislation would mean that it would not be fair, just and reasonable to impose such a duty of care. Finally, as if all of this weren't enough, even if all of these hurdles are jumped, *Stadler* and *Sterritt* demonstrate that it will be exceedingly difficult to establish the claim on the facts. It is unsurprising, therefore, that a pleaded claim in negligence was not pursued in *Driver v Crown Prosecution Service*,[76] where a statutory claim barely succeeded.

However, there is a serious flaw at the heart of these cases. *Swinney*, *Smeaton* and *Smith* all demonstrate that the most plausible basis for a claim in negligence in data breach cases is that the defendant data controller had voluntarily assumed responsibility towards the claimant data subject. And *Smeaton*, *Warren* and *Stadler* all hold that, as a matter of policy, the availability of alternative effective redress pursuant to the detailed and exhaustive data protection legislation means that it is not fair, just and reasonable to impose a duty of care. However, as Lord Goff explained in *Henderson v Merrett*, once a voluntary assumption of responsibility is established, 'there should be no need to embark upon any further enquiry whether it is "fair, just and reasonable" to impose liability'.[77] As a consequence, it should not have been necessary in data breach cases like *Smeaton*, *Warren* and *Stadler* to determine whether, as a matter of policy, the availability of alternative effective redress pursuant to the detailed and exhaustive data protection legislation means that it is not fair, just and reasonable to impose a duty of care.

[75] See nn 32–34 above.

[76] *Driver v Crown Prosecution Service* [2022] EWHC 2500 (KB) para 1 (Knowles J).

[77] *Henderson v Merrett* (n 42) 14, [1995] 2 AC 145, 181; see also *Barclays Bank* (n 33) para 4, [2007] 1 AC 181, 189–90, (Lord Bingham), para 35, 198–199 (Lord Hoffmann), para 50, 203 (Lord Rodger).

Swinney almost illustrates the point. Although policy considerations limit the range of claims in negligence against the police,[78] they did not preclude the claim in *Swinney*.[79] The police are not normally under a duty of care to protect against a danger of injury which they have not themselves created, unless there are special circumstances such as an assumption of responsibility.[80] *Swinney* illustrates that, where there is such an assumption of responsibility, policy reasons need not prevent a duty of care arising. Indeed, applying *Henderson v Merrett*, it is possible to go further and say that, if *Swinney* is best understood as a case in which the police had assumed responsibility for the claimant's safety,[81] then it was not necessary to embark upon any further enquiry as to policy. Nor should it be necessary in any other voluntary assumption case, including the data breach cases at issue here, to embark on any such enquiry. As a consequence, in voluntary assumption cases, there is no basis for considering whether, as a matter of policy, the availability of alternative effective redress pursuant to the detailed and exhaustive data protection legislation means that it is not fair, just and reasonable to impose a duty of care.

More generally, it is an incoherent policy, inconsistently applied. For example, in cases like *Warren* and *Smith*, where it barred the common law claim in negligence, it was not applied to bar the common law claim in misuse of private information. This provokes various questions: why should that policy bar some common law claims but not others? What is so special about the tort of misuse of private information that it should be allowed to be pleaded in parallel with the statutory data protection claims? What is so different about the tort of negligence that it cannot? The obvious answers to these questions damn the policy: there is no good reason to distinguish between common law claims, to permit some (such as misuse of private information) but to bar others (such as negligence); if the tort of misuse of private information can be pleaded in parallel with the statutory data protection claims, then so should the tort of negligence – there is nothing special about the tort of misuse of private information or different about the tort of negligence to preclude this.

Nor does an alternative claim always bar a negligence claim; in *Spring v Guardian Assurance*,[82] a claim in negligence did not undermine, and, as a matter of policy, was not barred by, an alternative claim in defamation.[83] By analogy, in a data breach situation, a claim in negligence should not undermine, and, as a matter of policy, should not be barred by, an alternative statutory data protection claim, or for that matter, by an alternative common law claim for misuse of private information. The judgments in *Smeaton*, *Warren* and *Stadler* neither engage with *Spring* nor replicate the careful calibration of policy in the speeches.

[78] *Hill v Chief Constable of West Yorkshire* [1987] UKHL 12, [1989] AC 53; *Commissioner of Police of the Metropolis v DSD* [2018] UKSC 11, [2019] AC 196.

[79] *Swinney* (n 30) para 49, [1997] QB 464, 484 (Hirst LJ).

[80] *Robinson v Chief Constable of West Yorkshire Police* [2018] UKSC 4, para 70, [2018] AC 736, 760 (Lord Reed; Lady Hale and Lord Hodge concurring).

[81] See n 34 above.

[82] *Spring v Guardian Assurance Plc* [1994] UKHL 7, [1995] 2 AC 296.

[83] *ibid* 21, [1995] 2 AC 296, 324 (Lord Goff), 23, 326 (Lord Lowry), 33, 335 (Lord Slynn), 52, 352 (Lord Woolf); compare *Young v Bella* 2006 SCC 3, [2006] 1 SCR 108.

Finally, the usual rule is that, where there are concurrent remedies, the claimant may choose which one to claim.[84] The judgments in *Smeaton*, *Warren* and *Stadler* do not explain why that general rule ought to be displaced in the data breach context.

Even though the law does not recognise a general duty of care to prevent others from suffering loss or damage caused by the deliberate wrongdoing of third parties, a defendant may nevertheless be held liable in negligence to a claimant, where the defendant negligently causes or permits to be created a source of danger, and it is reasonably foreseeable that third parties may interfere with it and thereby cause damage to the claimant.[85] Indeed, this is particularly so where the defendant voluntarily assumes responsibility towards the claimant.[86] So, in data breach cases, even though the law may not recognise a general duty of care on data controllers to prevent data subjects from suffering loss or damage caused by the deliberate wrongdoing of third party hackers, a defendant data controller may nevertheless be held liable in negligence to a claimant data subject, not only where the defendant data controller voluntarily assumes responsibility towards the claimant data subject, but also where the defendant data controller negligently causes or permits creation of a source of danger such as a inadequately protected database containing the data subject's personal data, and it is reasonably foreseeable that third parties, such as hackers or rogue employees of agents, may compromise that personal data and thereby cause damage to the claimant data subject. It may be that such cases are rare,[87] but they cannot be excluded in principle.

IV. Conclusion: The *Warren* of Negligence Claims for Data Breaches should not be Closed Off

As a matter of policy in data breach cases, the strong statutory cause of action provided by Article 82 UK GDPR and section 168 DPA 2018 precludes a duty of care in negligence at common law. But that policy bar is much shakier than it seems at first blush in *Smeaton* and *Warren*. In principle, of course, the availability of alternative effective redress can provide an important policy consideration, independent of the parties' relationship, that means that it is not just, fair and reasonable to impose a duty of care in negligence at common law. However, the mere existence of an alternative claim does not always bar a negligence claim. The statutory bar is an incoherent policy, inconsistently applied, illogically barring common law claims in negligence but not other common law claims such as those for misuse of private information.

Moreover, if a cause of action in negligence were to arise on the basis that a defendant data controller had, on a particular set of facts, voluntarily assumed responsibility towards a claimant data subject, that claim can in principle give rise to liability in respect

[84] *Henderson v Merrett* (n 60) (concurrent remedies in contract and tort); see, generally, *United Australia Ltd v Barclays Bank Ltd* [1941] AC 1 (HL) (election between compensatory and restitutionary damages); *Johnson v Agnew* [1980] AC 367 (HL) (election between specific performance and damages); *Tang Man Sit v Capacious Investments Ltd* [1995] UKPC 54, [1996] AC 514 (election between award of damages and account of profits).

[85] *Smith v Littlewoods Organisation Ltd* [1987] UKHL 18, para 8, [1987] AC 241, 272–73 (Lord Goff).

[86] *ibid* para 7, 272.

[87] *Begum v Maran (UK) Ltd* [2021] EWCA Civ 326, para 63 (Coulson LJ; Males and Bean LJJ concurring).

of negligent omissions, and sound in damages for distress and pain and suffering. Furthermore, once such a voluntary assumption of responsibility is established, policy considerations as to whether it is fair, just and reasonable to impose liability simply do not arise. A voluntary assumption of responsibility may not arise in very many data breach cases; but in those in which it does, a policy bar based on the existence of an alternative statutory bar should not damn the claim *in limine*.

Because the *Warren* of negligence claims for data breaches has been closed off, data controllers will not face claims that they failed to take reasonable care to prevent breaches compromising the data subjects' personal data. Hence, data controllers will not have the threat of negligence claims by data subjects to incentivise them to implement appropriate measures against breaches. Bees will still be attracted to honey pots; but after *Warren*, the tort of negligence provides no incentive for the controllers of the honey pots to protect them.

11

Trust, Confidence and Data Rights

MEGAN RICHARDSON*

I. Introduction

As Niklas Luhmann says, '[t]he only thing we can know about the future is that it will be different from the past'.[1] Certainly, there is a basic question to be asked about the future of the traditional equitable doctrine of breach of confidence: namely, can it serve as a source of protection of data rights? On the one hand, this is a doctrine that has largely fallen into decay in many common law jurisdictions. On the other hand, in those jurisdictions including the United Kingdom (UK) and Australia where it continues to thrive, it continues to serve as a source of protection of diverse informational rights.[2] So, more precisely, we perhaps should ask how this doctrine (in these jurisdictions) has become so modern?

In some ways it was modern to start with. A creature largely of nineteenth century English jurisprudence, with its high point the 'royal etchings' case of *Prince Albert v Strange* in 1849,[3] the idea of an obligation of 'trust [and] confidence',[4] akin to an obligation of good 'faith',[5] applying to the collection and disclosure along with other uses of confidential information may seem anachronistic in our digital century so centred on data exploitation. Yet it is worth remembering that the nineteenth century was itself an information century, featuring new information and communications technologies and practices ranging from photography to telegraphy and telephony. These would inevitably have an impact on the nascent breach of confidence doctrine focussed on

* Professor, University of Melbourne. With grateful thanks to Michael Bryan for reading and commenting perceptively on an earlier draft, to the various participants at a data harms workshop hosted by the Centre of Excellence for Automated Decision-Making and Society (ADM+S) for their interest and insights, and to the editors and other authors in this collection for their constructive questions and helpful advice.

[1] N Luhmann, *Observations on Modernity* (translated by W Whobrey) (Stanford, Stanford University Press, 1998) 21.

[2] I might equally say 'interests' because in Australia there is still reluctance to talk about data 'rights': see below section II.

[3] *Prince Albert v Strange* (1849) 1 H & Tw 1, 47 ER 1302.

[4] See, for instance, Lord Eldon LC in *Abernethy v Hutchinson* (1825) 1 H & Tw 33, 38, 47 ER 1315, 1317 ('breach of contract or trust'); Lord Cottenham LC in *Prince Albert v Strange* (n 3) 1 H & Tw 1, 24, 47 ER 1302, 1311 ('breach of trust, confidence or contract').

[5] *Morison v Moat* (1851) 9 Hare 241, 255, 68 ER 492, 498 (Turner VC).

engendering trust and confidence and supporting rights of information subjects and authors.[6] For, even with the Victorian ethos of assumed rationality and limited judicial sympathy for anything less on the part of the public at large,[7] this was still a time when the acknowledged moral as well as economic imperative of law – and most especially of equity – was the protection of 'private rights'.[8] At the same time, the 'rights' themselves were (re)shaped in function of the technological transformations that engulfed and propelled them. They might still be cast as rights (say) of privacy or authorship in the leading cases.[9] But what they amounted to in the face of the deprivations of the technologies and practices of the Victorian age would be different from the way they were imagined and framed in earlier times – even if the doctrine's broad prohibition on 'surreptitious[] and improper[] obtain[ing]', per Lord Cottenham LC in Prince Albert's case,[10] seemed well enough designed to address at least some deprivations.

Contrast the position by the last decades of the century when the doctrine's ability to deal with the phenomenon of the popular portable camera in the hands of the ambient photographer was placed in doubt by a passing comment of a single English judge (North J) that it surely did not extend to photographs taken 'on the sly'.[11] Even if in that case it was well accepted that a photographic subject could claim breach of confidence as against a commissioned photographer breaching the terms of commission, relying on a doctrine shaped in like terms to breach of contract, the same latitude was not extended to surreptitious photography by a timid judge confronted by a marvellous new technology.[12] No wonder that Samuel Warren and Louis Brandeis in the *Harvard Law Review* in 1890[13] argued for a privacy tort in support of the right to privacy developing in the United States (US), in the face of these changes, specifically referencing 'instantaneous photographs' along with 'any other modern device for recording or reproducing scenes or sound'.[14] As to the doctrine's potential protection of literary, artistic and scientific productions, this was barely noted by the US Supreme Court in framing a misappropriation doctrine in the *International News Service* case of 1918, to deal with practices of unfair 'reap[ing] without sowing' of news generated through 'organization and the expenditure of labor, skill, and money' as between intensely competitive news agencies during the First World War.[15]

[6] See generally M Richardson et al, *Breach of Confidence: Social Origins and Modern Developments* (Cheltenham, Edward Elgar, 2012) chs 2 and 3 for a discussion of the cases.

[7] See A Rosenberg, *The Rise of Mass Advertising* (Oxford, Oxford University Press, 2022).

[8] See *Batty v Hill* (1863) 1 H & M 264, 268, 117 ER 115, 117 (Page Wood VC): not for judges to enforce 'the observance of the dictates of morality', in the absence of an infringement on 'some private right'.

[9] See, eg, *Prince Albert v Strange* (n 3) 1 H & Tw 26; 47 ER 1312 (in this case of an unauthorised exhibition complete with catalogue of private etchings of family scenes made by Queen Victoria and Prince Albert, the right to privacy is expressly referenced as 'the right invaded', but the case also effectively protects the rights of Victoria and Albert as authors). See further Richardson et al, *Breach of Confidence* (n 6) ch 3; and M Richardson, *The Right to Privacy: Origins and Influence of a Nineteenth-Century Idea* (Cambridge, Cambridge University Press, 2017) ch 2.

[10] *Prince Albert v Strange* (n 3) 1 H & Tw 26, 47 ER 1312 (Lord Cottenham LC).

[11] *Pollard v Photographic Company* (1888) 40 Ch D 345, 346 (North J).

[12] See M Richardson, '*Pollard v Photographic Company* (1888)' in P Wragg and P Coe (eds), *Landmark Cases in Privacy Law* (Oxford, Hart Publishing, 2023).

[13] S Warren and L Brandeis, 'The Right to Privacy' (1890) 4 *Harvard Law Review* 193.

[14] *ibid* 195, 206.

[15] *International News Service v Associated Press* 248 US 215, 235, 239 (1918).

As detailed elsewhere,[16] breach of confidence even in the UK and Australia fell largely into disuse in the first half of the twentieth century,[17] until it was resurrected by the Court of Appeal in *Saltman Engineering Co Ltd v Campbell Engineering Co Ltd*[18] and put back to work in this case about the deployment of design drawings for the construction of leather punches in rebuilding the post-war industrial economy.[19] However, it took until towards the end of the twentieth century for the broad parameters of the mid-nineteenth century cases to be fully re-established,[20] with Lord Goff in the *Spycatcher* case talking of a 'broad general principle' (albeit not definitive) that 'a duty of confidence arises when confidential information comes to the knowledge of a person', in circumstances where that person 'has notice, or is held to have agreed, that the information is confidential, with the effect that it would be just in all the circumstances that he should be precluded from disclosing the information to others'.[21] Or per Deane J in the Australian case of *Moorgate Tobacco Co Ltd v Philip Morris Ltd* (a case cited by Lord Goff in *Spycatcher*), the obligation is one that '[arises] from the circumstances in or through which the information was communicated or obtained',[22] while other Australian judges revert to the language of 'improper or surreptitious obtaining' from older cases.[23] Yet notwithstanding these modern restatements, there are sometimes suggestions that breach of confidence has limited value compared with modern torts that are more explicitly framed in terms of data rights – for instance, that the UK's misuse of private information tort framed after the Human Rights Act 1998 to give effect to the right to private life in the European Convention on Human Rights has the advantage of being fashioned in terms of the right to privacy which enables it to deal more directly with intrusions on privacy than a doctrine framed in terms of confidentiality.[24] Indeed, the deeper question is whether breach of confidence, whatever its modern form, can add value as a source of rights protection beyond doctrines framed more directly in terms of the vindication and protection of rights.[25]

Nevertheless, I argue below that breach of confidence is well placed to serve as a modern rights-protection doctrine in the present and future, as at certain key points in its past. Luhmann points to an understanding of modernity as requiring not just a

[16] See Richardson et al, *Breach of Confidence* (n 6) ch 5.

[17] Although see (for an unusually broad statement of the doctrine) *Lord Ashburton v Pape* [1913] 2 Ch 469, 475 (Swinfen Eady LJ) reiterating the older 19th-century language of 'improperly or surreptitiously obtained'; and *cf* 473 (Cozens Hardy MR).

[18] *Saltman Engineering Co Ltd v Campbell Engineering Co Ltd* (1948) 65 RPC 203.

[19] *ibid* 213, Lord Greene MR stating the principle as follows: 'If a defendant is proved to have used confidential information, directly or indirectly obtained from a plaintiff, without the consent, express, or implied, of the plaintiff, he will be guilty of an infringement the plaintiff's rights'.

[20] See Richardson et al, *Breach of Confidence* (n 6) ch 7.

[21] *Attorney-General v Guardian Newspapers Ltd* (No 2) [1990] 1 AC 109, 281 (Lord Goff) ('*Spycatcher*'). See Richardson et al, *Breach of Confidence* (n 6) ch 7, 125–30.

[22] *Moorgate Tobacco Co Ltd v Philip Morris Ltd (No 2)* (1984) 156 CLR 414, 438 (Deane J).

[23] See *Australian Broadcasting Corporation (ABC) v Lenah Game Meats Pty Ltd* (2001) 208 CLR 199, para 34 (Gleeson CJ), citing *Commonwealth of Australia v John Fairfax & Sons Ltd* (1980) 147 CLR 39, 50 (Mason J) and *Lord Ashburton v Pape* (n 17) (Swinfen Eady LJ). *cff Glencore International AG v Commissioner of Taxation* (2019) 265 CLR 646, para 35 (Kiefel CJ); *Farm Transparency International Ltd v New South Wales* [2022] HCA 23, para 40 (Kiefel CJ and Keane J). But note that Gleeson CJ in *Lenah*, *ibid*, also cites Lord Goff in *Spycatcher* (n 21) at para 36.

[24] See below section III.

[25] See below section IV.

(conventional) emphasis on 'the tandem of technology and individuality with which we proceed into the fog of the future', but also a recognition that the so-called natural social order is a 'social construct' despite all its reification.[26] And I take this to mean that a modern legal doctrine is one that combines an emphasis on technology and individuality with a recognition of its nature as both socially constructed and capable of adaptation. Breach of confidence in its most progressive state exhibits both features. First, its ordering principle of trust and confidence offers the prospect of a doctrine that is well attuned to addressing problems of uncertainty and risk associated with new and emerging digital technologies and practices. Second, its character as a social construct without an immutable form allows us to treat this doctrine as capable of further adaptation over time to address the impacts of these technologies and practices for heterogeneous individuals as well as, I would add, heterogeneous groups.[27] On the other hand, as in earlier times, much of its success depends on the creativity of judges – and experience to date is mixed.

II. Keep on Trusting

Already we can see that a hallmark of breach of confidence is its promise of trust and confidence, and allied good faith, helping to explain the doctrine's generation and regeneration in times of heightened uncertainty and risk. It is not for nothing that the most significant moments in the doctrine's history to date were, first, the rapidly industrialising early-to-middle years of the Victorian century and, second, the rapidly re-industrialising post-war decades, both periods that entailed significant opportunities for advancement and flourishing but also significant uncertainty and risk. In the words of Diego Gambetta writing in the 1980s,[28] the ability to 'trust trust' becomes key to prospects of beneficial co-operation in these times. We see this idea of confidence being aligned to trust facilitating beneficial co-operation reflected in the language of the rejuvenating doctrine in the post-war cases – for instance the 1948 case of *Saltman Engineering v Campbell Engineering* where Lord Greene MR talks of the 'honest[y]' of acknowledging the defendants' obligation of 'conscience' not to misuse the plaintiff's design obtained in confidence;[29] the 1969 case of *Coco v AN Clark (Engineers) Ltd*,[30] another case of a failed joint venture to exploit the plaintiff's invention, where Megarry J reminds us that 'confidence is the cousin of trust' in both its history and in the present day;[31] the 1967 case of *Seager v Copydex Ltd*, yet another case of a failed joint venture to exploit an invention,[32] where Lord Denning MR uses the language of 'unfair

[26] Luhmann, *Observations on Modernity* (n 1) 7–8.

[27] See Richardson, *The Right to Privacy* (n 9) ch 5 (rights such as privacy not just for individuals but also for groups).

[28] D Gambetta, 'Can We Trust Trust?' in D Gambetta (ed), *Trust: Making and Breaking Cooperative Relations* (New York, Blackwell, 1988).

[29] *Saltman Engineering v Campbell Engineering* (n 18) 213 (Lord Greene MR).

[30] *Coco v AN Clark (Engineers) Ltd* [1969] RPC 41.

[31] *ibid* 46 (although the claim ultimately failed for lack of confidentiality of the plaintiff's moped design).

[32] *Seager v Copydex Ltd* [1967] RPC 349.

advantage';[33] the 1969 case of *Fraser v Evans*,[34] involving a commissioned government report, where the same judge talks of an obligation of 'good faith' as restraining the ability to publish at the behest of the Government,[35] echoing Ungoed-Thomas J in the scandalous marriage secrets tabloid press case of *Argyll v Argyll* in 1967 (reviewing some of the nineteenth century cases).[36] 'Good faith' is also the language deployed by Australian judge Muirhead J in talking about the defendant's attempt to publish his account of the Pitjantjatjara people's cultural secrets conveyed during visits to the remote community in his book, *Nomads of the Australian Desert*, in the 1976 case of *Foster v Mountford & Rigby Ltd*.[37] Likewise, in the face of contemporary media incursions employing current technologies and techniques such as 'the telephoto lens',[38] 'secret surveillance',[39] and 'a vast system of electronic networks',[40] concepts of trust, confidence and good faith are all invoked in tandem in Gleeson CJ's significant sweeping statement in the 2001 surreptitious filming case of *Australian Broadcasting Corporation v Lenah Game Meats Pty Ltd* that the 'principle of good faith upon which equity acts to protect information imparted in confidence' may also be invoked to 'restrain the publication of confidential information improperly or surreptitiously obtained'.[41]

In such statements there is a rough and ready appreciation that 'trust' and 'confidence', and likewise 'good faith', are somehow related in framing and understanding the obligation of confidence. But query whether there is any specific ordering along the lines signalled by scholars of this period who hold that trust is 'something suspended between faith and confidence', as Diego Gambetta puts it.[42] Or, as Luhmann elaborates, 'if you do not consider alternatives … you are in a situation of confidence'; if you choose between alternatives in spite of the risk that things may not work out as desired, 'you define the situation as one of trust'.[43] Possibly, in a more rigorous version of the judicial analysis, trust can be seen as a prior step before confidence, explaining the common sequence of 'trust and confidence'. And, as in older invocations, 'good faith' might be aligned somewhat to contractual obligations? But in Gleeson CJ's comment, 'trust' and 'confidence' are mixed up in the same idea of a willing suspension of disbelief, and 'the principle of good faith' is simply another way of explaining the nature of the trust obligation as extending beyond the relational scenario – reflecting the point that Gambetta also makes that our ability to reliably trust in the

[33] *ibid* 368.
[34] *Fraser v Evans* [1969] 1 QB 349.
[35] *ibid* 361 (albeit not extending the same protection against unwanted publication to the author of the report).
[36] *Argyll (Duchess) v Argyll (Duke)* [1967] Ch 302, 322 (Ungoed-Thomas J).
[37] *Foster v Mountford and Rigby Ltd* (1976) 14 ALR 71, 75 (Muirhead J).
[38] *Hellewell v Chief Constable of Derbyshire* [1995] 1 WLR 804, 807 (Laws J), cited in *ABC v Lenah Game Meats* (n 23) para 33 (Laws J).
[39] *ABC v Lenah Game Meats*, *ibid*, para 24 (Gleeson CJ) citing the statement of claim in that case.
[40] *Bartnicki v Vopper* (2001) 69 USLW 4323, 4331 (Rehnquist CJ), cited in *ABC v Lenah Game Meats*, *ibid*, para 40 (Gleeson CJ).
[41] See *ABC v Lenah Game Meats*, *ibid*, para 34.
[42] Gambetta, 'Can We Trust Trust?' (n 28) 218, citing HLA Hart and N Luhmann in the same volume.
[43] N Luhmann, 'Familiarity, Confidence, Trust: Problems and Alternatives' in Gambetta (ed), *Trust: Making and Breaking Cooperative Relations* (n 28) 97.

conduct of others around us is important even outside the relational context if we are to function in a risk society.[44] Likewise, Dunn J reasoned in the 1978 Australian stolen budwood case of *Franklin v Giddins*,[45] a 'thief who steals a trade secret' is no different from a traitorous servant when it comes to assessing their 'unconscionability', with both logically subject to the obligation of trust and confidence as framed in *Prince Albert v Strange*.[46]

Note also that in these discussions there is an implicit acceptance of trust and confidence (along with good faith) being not just about a party placing trust and confidence in another party, ie the act of trusting, but of that other party being worthy of that trust – and a failure in this regard being deemed to not only be a breach of confidence but a breach of trust(worthiness). What is it that makes up what might be termed 'rational trust' that makes trust socially worthwhile, ie not just 'damaging or costly'?[47] Onora O'Neill, who writes specifically on this issue, points to a trustworthy party's compliance with 'inter alia norms of honesty, norms of reliability, and norms of competence'.[48] Luhmann goes further in referencing not just what he calls 'technical competence', and continuity with 'the moral order' encompassing a minimum of honesty and integrity, but also the 'duty and motives [of a trustworthy party] to place the interests of others before their own'.[49] And in a leading study of the 1990s, Roger Mayer, James Davis and David Schoorman reference Luhmann to derive similar principles of 'ability', 'integrity' and 'benevolence',[50] arguing that organisations that pay attention to these indicators of trustworthiness in their dealings with others can benefit from opportunities for collaboration that rational trust fosters and facilitates. In my view, these ideas about rational trust and trustworthiness are key to understanding the social value of the doctrine of breach of confidence.

Interestingly, Luhmann, in discussing the duty and motives of a trustworthy party to place the interests of others before their own, draws an analogy to fiduciary liability with its other-centred duty of loyalty as between fiduciary and beneficiary.[51] But I

[44] See Gambetta, 'Can We Trust Trust?' (n 28) 226, giving the example of the co-operation of 'live and let live' between enemy soldiers in the First World War, as discussed by Robert Axelrod (who uses a game theory analysis to explain why even strangers might choose to act effectively in concert) in R Axelrod, *The Evolution of Cooperation* (New York, Basic Books, 1984).

[45] *Franklin v Giddins* [1978] Qd R 72, 79 (Dunn J), citing inter alia *Argyll v Argyll* (n 36).

[46] *ibid* 78–80.

[47] See, for instance, O O'Neill, 'Linking Trust to Trustworthiness' (2018) 26 *International Journal of Philosophical Studies* 293, 295.

[48] *ibid.*

[49] Luhmann, 'Familiarity, Confidence, Trust' (n 43) 94–95, citing B Barber, *The Logic and Limits of Trust* (New Brunswick, Rutgers University Press, 1983). *cf* O'Neill, 'Linking Trust to Trustworthiness' (n 47) 294–95 (the question is 'whether action meets or will meet relevant norms – inter alia norms of honesty, norms of reliability, and norms of competence').

[50] R Mayer, J Davis and F Schoorman, 'An Integrative Model of Organizational Trust' (1995) 20 *Academy of Management Review* 709, 720. *cf* FD Schoorman, R Mayer and J Davis, 'An Integrative Model of Organizational Trust: Past, Present, and Future' (2007) 32 *Academy of Management Review* 344, 345 (the multi-factorial approach is now 'accepted' in management circles).

[51] Luhmann, 'Familiarity, Confidence, Trust' (n 43) 95. *cff* J Balkin, 'The Fiduciary Model of Privacy' (2020) 134 *Harvard Law Review Forum* 11, arguing that digital companies which collect and hold their users' data should inter alia be subject to a duty of loyalty in the way of a fiduciary. But see L Khan and D Pozen, 'A Skeptical View of Information Fiduciaries' (2019) 133 *Harvard Law Review* 497, arguing that full fiduciary liability (which eg is not limited to the protection of confidential information) would impose overly stringent obligations on digital companies placing them in conflict with their duties to shareholders, and more restricted obligations should be looked to instead.

argue that we can equally look to breach of confidence as embodying an other-centred duty of confidence as between trusting and trustworthy parties. For this is a duty that requires not just a non-disclosure of confidential information obtained directly or indirectly from a trusting party,[52] but a refraining from any misuse of the information contrary to that party's purposes.[53] Viewed this way, the doctrine can be seen as not merely offering tangible support to data rights,[54] important as that may continue to be in its modern operation,[55] but more generally as nurturing a moral idea of trust and trustworthiness rooted in equity's 'conscience'.[56] And, as we have seen, there is an element of rationality as well, ie that this is a doctrine geared to rational trust and trustworthiness associated with mutually beneficial co-operation – as with the sharing of a valuable invention with a commercialising partner talked about in cases like *Saltman Engineering* and *Coco v AN Clark*;[57] or a personal relationship developed through sharing of intimacies as in *Argyll v Argyll*;[58] or the readiness of members of a remote Indigenous community to explain their secrets to an anthropologist in the case of *Foster v Mountford*;[59] or a less aggressively self-protective approach adopted to the prospect of data theft as with the plaintiff's unfenced orchard in *Franklin v Giddins*.[60] Indeed, society as a whole can benefit if it means greater access to innovation, more opportunities for friendship and community, and a less guarded approach to the knowledge under one's lawful control.

What precisely then is the role of law (or equity) in fostering these beneficial outcomes? Luhmann takes a rather limited view of law's role, suggesting that, at best,

[52] As per Lord Goff's non-definitive 'broad' statement in *Spycatcher* (n 21) (where disclosure was the issue).

[53] *Saltman Engineering* (n 18) 213 ('use' of plaintiff's confidential information 'without the consent, express or implied of the plaintiff' constitutes an infringement). *cf Coco v AN Clark* (n 30) 51 (Megarry J), suggesting there may need to be detriment as well as misuse, but keeping open the possibility that misuse is sufficient, as 'I can conceive of cases where a plaintiff might have substantial motives for seeking the aid of equity'. And see *Spycatcher* (n 21) 282, Lord Goff also noting that 'detriment' may be very broadly construed in this context. Certainly, in *Moorgate Tobacco v Philip Morris* (n 22) Deane J suggests 'substantial concern' is sufficient for private parties.

[54] 'Interests' is the term preferred by Gleeson CJ in *ABC v Lenah Game Meats* (n 23) para 41, suggesting talk of 'rights', as for instance with a 'right' to privacy, may be 'question-begging' in Australia without a bill of rights.

[55] See *ibid* para 39 ('if the activities filmed were private, then the law of breach of confidence is adequate'), as well as UK cases like *Campbell v MGN Ltd* [2004] UKHL 22, [2004] 2 AC 457, where breach of confidence was relied on to give effect to the right to privacy in Art 8 of the European Convention on Human Rights after the coming into force of the Human Rights Act 1998 but before the fuller development of the UK misuse of private information tort.

[56] See, eg, *Coco v AN Clark* (n 30) 51 (Megarry J) ('an obligation based on good conscience').

[57] See *Saltman Engineering v Campbell Engineering* (n 18) 213 (Lord Greene MR) (initially, at least, this was seen as 'a very good commercial proposition' on all sides). *cf Coco v AN Clark* (n 30) 48 (Megarry J) ('information of commercial or industrial value is given on a business-like basis and with some avowed common object in mind, such as a joint venture or the manufacture of articles by one party for the other').

[58] See *Argyll v Argyll* (n 36) 330 (Ungoed-Thomas J) ('the protection of confidential communications between husband and wife is not designed to intrude into this domain but to protect it, not to break their confidential relationship but to encourage and preserve it').

[59] *Foster v Mountford and Rigby* (n 37) 73 (Muirhead J) (noting that Dr Mountford in his book 'writes with obvious affection and gratitude of the "friendly cooperation and help in gaining a knowledge of [the Pitjantjara community's] life and beliefs' over many years).

[60] See *Franklin v Giddins* (n 45) 80 (Dunn J) (noting that the plaintiff's orchard 'was not guarded by an electric fence or patrolled by guard dogs').

law substitutes for a failure in social norms in a modern society.[61] As he puts it, '[o]ne can afford a higher degree of uncertain confidence or even of mistrust as long as one has confidence in law' with the result that 'one can live in a more complex society, in which personal or interaction mechanisms to secure trust no longer suffice'.[62] By contrast, judges in breach of confidence cases seem to see their role as not only stepping in where called upon to coercively secure trust through the finding of breach and award of remedies but more broadly working to foster desirable social norms in their language of 'trust and confidence', 'good faith' or 'conscionable' behaviour. In short, this doctrine, in its emphasis on the moral and social value of rational trust and trustworthiness engendering co-operation, is geared not just to achieving beneficial outcomes in particular cases, but also to fostering social norms shaping future cooperative behaviour for the benefit of individuals and society. Or, per Lord Goff in *Spycatcher*, what we have here is a 'public interest' in maintaining confidence, both underpinning the doctrine and informing its balance with '[any] countervailing interest favouring disclosure'.[63] Read this way, the doctrine offers an example of what Robert Cooter calls 'expressive law', engendering co-operation and reducing the need for coercive legal intervention in a liberal society.[64] Although mainly concerned with the efficiency, or social value, of expressive law, Cooter is also concerned with morality, adding, 'I believe that law breeds respect by tracking morality' – and 'legal expression must enlist the natural sense of justice among citizens'.[65] And this, I think, is what Deane J in *Moorgate Tobacco v Philip Morris* also means when he refers to the obligation of confidence as a 'rational … obligation of conscience'.[66]

III. Boundary Work

Nevertheless, as Deane J also highlights, this is a rational obligation of conscience that has an inbuilt flexibility and can adapt further, where need be, to meet 'new situations and circumstance',[67] including (I would say) new understandings about data rights as not necessarily confined to narrow conceptions of privacy and authorship but encompassing individuality and identity as conceptions that can develop over time and in light of context. Bearing in mind all the doctrinal adaptations we have seen in the past, we can already anticipate how breach of confidence might be reshaped in the present and future. Already, some possible future adaptations are being debated in some recent

[61] See N Luhmann, *Law as a Social System with an Introduction by R Nobles and D Schiff* (translated by K Ziegert and edited by F Kastner et al) (Oxford, Oxford University Press, 2004).

[62] *ibid* 148.

[63] *Spycatcher* (n 21) 282 (Lord Goff), referencing here the doctrine's 'public interest' defence as a matter of UK law. In Australia the defence may be a narrower iniquity defence but see *ABC v Lenah Game Meats* (n 23) para 35 (Gleeson CJ).

[64] R Cooter, 'Expressive Law and Economics' (1998) 27 *Journal of Legal Studies* 585.

[65] *ibid* 596.

[66] *Moorgate Tobacco v Philip Morris* (n 22) 438.

[67] *ibid* 448 (treating this as a reason not to move to an INS-style doctrine of unfair competition). *cf ABC v Lenah Game Meats* (n 23) paras 110 and 130 (Gummow and Hayne JJ) for equivalent reasoning regarding adaptive breach of confidence versus a US-style privacy tort, citing Deane J in *Moorgate Tobacco v Philip Morris* (n 22).

cases – for instance, that the act of surreptitiously or improperly obtaining information, eg by hacking into a computer, might itself be considered a breach;[68] that the receipt of confidential information should place the burden on the recipient to disprove any breach thus overcoming the evidential problems of proving breach of confidence by a party with greater knowledge of their systems and processes;[69] and that if a platform or company holds itself out as securely looking after customers' data but then finds itself the subject of a hack that this might amount to breach of confidence even in the absence of some more obvious active 'misuse' – although the latter argument has been rejected in the UK case of *Warren v DSG*,[70] it finds some support in the US where the subject of the hack was a bank and identity theft was in issue.[71]

What then of the doctrine's most apparently immutable 'requirement',[72] namely the 'principle of confidentiality that gives its character and rationale as a doctrine about 'trust and confidence'? To begin with, we should note that this principle is framed in extremely flexible terms of 'not … public knowledge' (as Lord Greene put it in *Saltman Engineering*),[73] or 'no more than that the information in question is so generally accessible that, in all the circumstances, it cannot be regarded as confidential' (as Lord Goff put it in *Spycatcher*).[74] Further, it has been held, for instance, that information is not public knowledge merely because tools on the market could be reverse engineered to work out the information,[75] or some aspects have been published but not inventive 'twist',[76] or activities could be observed in a public place that go largely unobserved,[77] or information is briefly published in a fleeting way before the news cycle moves on.[78] On the other hand, there are cases where judges have taken a narrower view, holding for instance that the prospect of reverse engineering a computer-programmed coin-changing machine on the market is enough to undermine confidentiality even if that would require expertise and skill,[79] and that the fact that a plaintiff's online activities are geared to public expression such as journalism or blogging may undermine a claim of confidentiality

[68] See *Imerman v Tchenguiz* [2010] EWCA Civ 908, [2011] 2 WLR 592, para 68 (Lord Neuberger MR).

[69] See *I-Admin (Singapore) Pte Ltd v Hong Ying Ting* [2020] 1 SLR 1130, para 61.

[70] *Warren v DSG Retail Ltd* [2021] EWHC 2168 (QB), paras 21–27 (Saini J) (holding that active misuse is required on existing authority). See further *Smith v Talktalk Telecom Group Plc* [2022] EWHC 1311 (QB), [2022] 1 WLR 5213, another hacking case before the same judge where the breach of confidence claim was discontinued. However, as noted by Saini J in *Smith v Talktalk*, the older case of *Swinney v Chief Constable of Northumbria Police Force* [1997] QB 464, para 61 appears to support the argued possibility of claiming breach of confidence as well as negligence where as a result of a defendant's negligence (in breach of a duty of care) confidential information is stolen by a third party.

[71] See *In re Capital One Consumer Data Security Breach Litigation*, 488 F Supp 3d 374 (ED Va 2020) (noting that the company in breach was a bank which held itself out as secure, and identity theft was a concern).

[72] *Moorgate Tobacco v Philip Morris* (n 22) 438 (Deane J).

[73] *Saltman Engineering v Campbell Engineering* (n 18) 215 (Lord Greene MR).

[74] *Spycatcher* (n 21) 282 (Lord Goff).

[75] See *Saltman Engineering v Campbell Engineering* (n 18) 215 (Lord Greene MR).

[76] See *Talbot v General Television Corporation Pty Ltd* [1980] VR 224, 230–31 (Harris J). See also *Coco v AN Clark* (n 30) 47 (Megarry J) ('[s]omething that has been constructed solely from materials in the public domain may possess the necessary quality of confidentiality: for something new and confidential may have been brought into being by the application of the skill and ingenuity of the human brain') – although in this case declining to find there was sufficient evidence of confidentiality even applying this apparently liberal test.

[77] See *Campbell v MGN Ltd* (n 55) (where the plaintiff celebrity Naomi Campbell was surreptitiously photographed in a street exiting a Narcotics Anonymous meeting).

[78] See *G v Day* [1982] 1 NSWLR 24, 40–41 (Yeldham J).

[79] See *Mars v Teknowledge Ltd* [2000] FSR 138, para 31 (Jacob J).

regarding their personal identity.[80] But it is hard to see such reasoning fitting with the logic of 'confidentiality' as not public knowledge. And, if the goal is fostering rational trust and trustworthiness there is much to be said for a liberal approach to 'confidentiality', treated as a test of whether a party has something worth exchanging for a benefit from co-operation, and setting the parameters on its protection of data rights before one gets to the question of balancing with other rights, freedoms and interests.

Likewise, I would go further to argue that a liberal approach more generally should be adopted to the assessment of confidentiality, including in more borderline cases. Consider, for instance, the question of information that is formally in the 'public domain' yet is not widely accessed or attended to in any significant way – as with information posted in obscure corners of the internet, or made technically available, but with skills needed to access it, or circulated in non-authoritative forms. One feature of the digital environment O'Neill notes, is that:

> [i]t is easy to place information in the public domain, but hard to ensure that it is in practice accessible to those for whom it might be valuable, intelligible to them if they find it, or assessable by them if they find and understand it.[81]

Yet courts may persist in adopting a formalistic approach to the question of when information can be judged as 'public knowledge'. An example is the comment of Lord Neuberger in the UK Supreme Court in PJS v News Group Newspapers,[82] that the plaintiff's identity as the individual at the heart of a scandalous sexual story had been the subject of 'publications of the story on websites, in tweets and other forms of social networks, coupled with consequential oral communications', with some claiming that 'between 20% and 25% of the population know who PJS is'.[83] Despite acknowledging that 'it is fair to say, [this] suggests that at least 75% of the population do not know the identity of PJS, and presumably more than 75% do not know much if anything about the details of the story', Lord Neuberger intimated that a notional 20–25 per cent level of 'knowledge' is 'probably' enough for confidentiality to be lost – making it difficult for the plaintiff to rely on breach of confidence for an injunction against publication in a national newspaper unlike the UK misuse of private information tort which is more focused on intrusion.[84] Contrast Kellam J in *Australian Football League (AFL) v The Age*,[85] finding that information concerning the identity of football players who tested positive for drug use in breach of AFL policy was still confidential and so could not be published in the defendant newspapers, despite internet 'chatter', on the basis that, unlike publications in trusted media outlets, '[o]n the evidence before me the public … have no such expectation' of authenticity, veracity or otherwise of the information posted on … [internet chatroom type] websites'.[86]

[80] See *The Author of a Blog v Times Newspapers Ltd* [2009] EWHC 1358, paras 11 and 33 (Eady J).
[81] O'Neill, 'Linking Trust to Trustworthiness' (n 47) 298–99.
[82] *PJS v News Group Newspapers Ltd* [2016] UKSC 26, [2016] AC 1081.
[83] *ibid* para 57 (Lord Neuberger PSC).
[84] *ibid* para 65 (Lord Neuberger PSC).
[85] *Australian Football League (AFL) v The Age* [2006] VSC 308, (2006) 15 VR 419.
[86] ibid para 56 (Kellam J) (adding that 'speculative gossip, innuendo and assertion by unknown persons … placed on the websites of various discussion fora does not make confidential material lose its confidential nature').

Another borderline case concerns the question of inferred data, that is of how to treat any inferences that may be drawn by those who (to revert to O'Neill's words above) 'understand' the raw information, which may themselves be viewed as forms of information obtained directly or indirectly from a data subject by another party using available technologies and expertise. Again, I would suggest that inferences which fall at the boundary between what is confidential information and what is public knowledge should be assessed in qualitative rather than formalistic terms.[87] For instance, in PJS is the press's anticipated 'wall-to-wall excoriation' of the plaintiff for his claimed lack of sexual mores to be viewed as a matter of intrusion legitimately invoking the privacy tort but not so much within the purview of breach of confidence, as suggested by various judges of the UK Supreme Court in that case?[88] Or might the inference publicly drawn by a national newspaper about the plaintiff's sexual mores at the same time as revealing his identity be viewed as also relevant to breach of confidence? I would think the latter (adopting a liberal approach), and that view seems to be the one adopted by Kellam J in *AFL v The Age*, noting that this case concerned not only breach of confidence involving the proposed publication in newspapers that certain AFL players had twice tested positive for drug use, in breach of the club's drug policy which prescribed internal steps but not publication of one or two positive drug tests, but also an 'infer[ence]' drawn by of the newspapers that these players had engaged in 'seriously wrongful conduct'.[89]

IV. Postscript

In this chapter I have argued that, construed in a flexible way and adapted where necessary to meet new situations and circumstances, breach of confidence can function as a modern doctrine geared to prompting and fostering trust and confidence under conditions of uncertainty and risk, at the same time offering significant support for data rights in the digital age. Thus, this already quite modern doctrine is well placed to reflect two distinct features of modernity: first, a keen focus on individuals and, it might be added, groups; and second, a recognition that the so-called indelible social order is a social construct which is capable of change. But, of course, it might still be that those individuals and groups at the centre of disputes about treatment of their rights may opt for an even more modern approach (where available), ie that, even in its most progressive state, modern breach of confidence cannot match up to a modern privacy or other tort specifically focussed on the protection of privacy or other data rights.[90]

[87] *cf* the Levison inquiry report: Leveson LJ, 'An Inquiry into the Culture, Practices and Ethics of the Press' (Independent Report, Department for Digital, Culture, Media & Sport and Leveson Inquiry, 29 November 2012) (HC 780) 737, para 3.4: newspaper publication (as compared, say, to circulation on social media), 'inflates the [information's] apparent newsworthiness, placing it 'more firmly within the public domain and at the top of the news agenda'.

[88] *PJS v News Group Newspapers* (n 82) paras 25–35 (Lord Mance JSC); paras 57–65 (Lord Neuberger PSC).

[89] *AFL v The Age* (n 85) para 72 (Kellam J).

[90] And see, eg, chapters in this volume by Jelena Gligorijevic and Kimberlee Weatherall in chapters 9 and 12 respectively.

Is this the conclusion drawn from the recent case of *ZXC v Bloomberg LP*?[91] Although the case involved a leaked confidential Letter of Request from a UK law-enforcement body, revealing that the plaintiff (a company executive) was under criminal investigation, which was published on the Bloomberg website, breach of confidence was not pursued. Instead, a claim for misuse of private information was pursued and the claim succeeded in the Supreme Court with confidentiality treated as a factor in assessing a reasonable expectation of privacy applying the 'Murray factors'.[92] Commenting on the case, Gavin Phillipson observes that:

> *ZXC*, like many privacy cases, involved a breach of confidence; that does not stop it being properly brought as an MPI case. Claimants are only confined to pleading breach of confidence where the case involves information that does not relate to private life at all, such as commercial or state secrets.[93]

But does it necessarily mean that there is no value to be gained from bringing a claim for breach of confidence if misuse of private information is available?[94] I would like to wait and see the position adopted by parties in future cases. *ZXC* suggests some difficult strategic decisions which might have gone either way in terms of their success. In particular, the plaintiff's withdrawal of his claim for breach of confidence appears to have been influenced by a doubt raised by the defendant as to whether the subject of the leaked Letter of Request had standing to complain about breach of confidence when the author did not itself wish to pursue a claim.[95] The plaintiff succeeded via the UK privacy tort which was broadly construed to encompass reputational interests enmeshed with privacy interests (and, on the other side, the argument of public interest in publication of details of a criminal investigation prior to charge was dubious).[96] But it could equally be considered an appropriate use of the breach of confidence doctrine, broadly construed, to allow a data subject to bring a claim, even in the face of lack of action on the part of the author. Indeed, the first instance judge made clear his view that 'the LoR had been given to the Journalist in what must have been (and should have been recognised as) a serious breach of confidence by the person who originally supplied it'.[97] This suggests that, had the breach of confidence claim been pursued, the judge may well have been inclined in favour of finding a breach of confidence and moreover, of treating the case as a matter of expressive law directed at fostering social norms of trust and confidence.[98]

[91] *ZXC v Bloomberg LP* [2022] UKSC 5, [2022] AC 1158.

[92] See *Murray v Express Newspapers Plc* [2008] EWCA Civ 446, [2009] Ch 481, para 36 (Sir Anthony Clarke MR) (the seventh referencing 'the circumstances in which and the purposes for which the information came into the hands of the publisher').

[93] G Phillipson, 'Supreme Court Confirms Suspects' Privacy Rights: The Judgment Clarified, Two Criticisms Answered' (2022) 14 *Journal of Media Law* 257.

[94] For debate on this question, plus related questions of the proper scope of the misuse of private information tort versus breach of confidence, in the *Journal of Media Law*, see, eg, Phillipson, 'Supreme Court Confirms Suspects' Privacy Rights', *ibid*; NA Moreham, 'Privacy, Defamation and *ZXC v Bloomberg*' (2022) 14 *Journal of Media Law* 226; and T Bennett, 'Confidence, Privacy, and Incoherence' (2022) 14 *Journal of Media Law* 245.

[95] See *ZXC v Bloomberg LP* [2019] EWHC 970 (QB), para 70 (Nicklin J). *cf Fraser v Evans* (n 34).

[96] According to R Craig and G Phillipson, 'Privacy, Reputation and Anonymity until Charge: *ZXC* Goes to the Supreme Court' (2021) 13 *Journal of Media Law* 153.

[97] *ZXC v Bloomberg LP* (n 95) para 125 (Nicklin J).

[98] Recall Cooter, 'Expressive Law and Economics' (n 64).

In short, while in *ZXC* the plaintiff succeeded under the UK privacy tort geared to the protection of privacy, with confidentiality merely one (albeit an important one) of several 'Murray factors', under breach of confidence a serious breach of trust and confidence must surely be a preeminent concern in the balance with other rights, freedoms and interests. So, to rule out a breach of confidence claim just because there is a viable privacy tort claim seems unnecessarily restrictive.

12

IP *and* Data, IP *in* Data, IP *as* Data

KIMBERLEE WEATHERALL*

I. Introduction

Data has always been intangible; it is becoming increasingly valuable. For well over a century, intellectual property (IP) laws have managed rights and interests in valuable intangibles. What then, of the relationship between data and IP? Could property rights, or more specifically IP-style rights help us ensure that the multiple interests in data are appropriately recognised and managed, and pathologies or undesirable uses prevented?

This chapter explores relationships between IP and data: both IP *in* data, and IP *as* data. It is often noted, correctly, that there is no IP in data or information as such.[1] In fact, IP laws have been drafted, developed and interpreted in ways that reserve to creators, or owners, the exclusive right to exploit the expression of information (copyright) or the invention that embodies an idea (patent), while enabling others to take up and use the information and ideas in other ways. It is frequently asserted that not only *is* there no IP in data: such rights *ought not be.*[2]

When stated so starkly, these assertions hide a much more interesting, complex and nuanced history and jurisprudence. Thinking more deeply about the reasons usually ranged *against* IP in data reveals that not all of them are convincing. Many of the controversies that arise when seeking to control, or allocate rights in, or remediate harm arising out of, the collection and use of data today have equivalents in the history of IP. As a result, there are doctrines and institutions in IP law and scholarship that can help shed light on how to manage these issues. This chapter agrees that IP is too limited a frame for considering the urgent questions of justice arising from data use today, but not because IP rights all have to look a certain way; or because data is 'too hard' a subject matter.

* Professor, University of Sydney; Chief Investigator, ARC Centre of Excellence on Automated Decision-Making and Society (CE200100005).

[1] See, eg, L Bennett Moses, 'Who Owns Information? Law Enforcement Information Sharing as a Case Study in Conceptual Confusion' (2020) 43 *UNSW Law Journal* 615; Law Commission, *Digital Assets: Consultation Paper* (Law Com No 256, 2022) ch 3.

[2] This leaves to one side the question of trade secret/the law of confidence. There is debate over whether trade secrets and/or the law of confidence can even be properly described as 'IP': they may be better characterised as not 'propertising' information *as such* but managing *relationships and obligations around* information, see *OBG Ltd v Allan* [2007] UKHL 21, [2008] AC 1.

IP is not the right frame because – as a brief case study around generative artificial intelligence (AI) at the end of the chapter seeks to show – IP does not effectively address concerns about the distribution of benefits, or power, which are the key questions that new technologies of data use pose for us today.

II. Copyright (or IP) in Data

A. No IP in Data

It is a truth (almost) universally asserted that there is no IP in facts, information or data. Copyright, for example, protects authors' expressions, not facts or ideas: this is formalised in international treaty and regional law,[3] and in cases where courts have refused protection for bare collections of fact with nothing more.[4] Patent law has similar basic doctrines: patents can be obtained for inventions but not discoveries about the world, meaning that no patents will be granted for laws (or facts) of nature; physical phenomena or abstract ideas like mathematical equations.[5]

Not only is (bare) information or facts not protectable subject matter in copyright or patent, but IP rules are structured to allow free use of facts and information contained in works and inventions that are protected. This is an important part of IP law's design, reflecting the foundational goals of encouraging creation or invention, including *follow-on* creation or invention, and allowing the broader society to learn from those creations and inventions. In copyright, protected expressions often contain, express or embody data or information; indeed, the value of some works lies principally in the facts they contain: history texts, for example, maps, or even databases. These are protected where their creation has involved some skill, selectivity or judgement, but courts find various ways to ensure that copyright law does not prevent others using the collected facts or information, even where that extraction takes 'value' or profit from the copyright owner. At its most basic, copyright in a book does not prevent another from 'taking' facts from the book and re-expressing them a different way, no matter how much work went into ascertaining those facts. It is even permissible to recreate the value in a copyright work by copying facts, provided expression is not copied. In *IceTV*, the Australian High Court was pressed by a broadcaster wanting to control re-publication of TV guides to find that a defendant who copied key snippets from a television guide – the title of television programmes, and the time they would be broadcast – infringed copyright.[6] The High Court held, however, that this did not involve copying the human authorship involved

[3] Article 9(2) of the Agreement on Trade-Related Aspects of Intellectual Property Rights (adopted 15 April 1994, entered into force 1 January 1995) 1869 UNTS 299 ('TRIPS Agreement'); Directive 2004/48/EC of the European Parliament and of the Council of 29 April 2004 on the enforcement of intellectual property rights [2004] OJ L157/45.

[4] *Feist Publications Inc v Rural Telephone Service Co Inc*, 499 US 340 (1991).

[5] See, eg, *Diamond v Diehr* 450 US 175, 185 (1981); Article 52(2) of the Convention on the Grant of European Patents ('European Patent Convention') (adopted 5 October 1973, entered into force 7 October 1977) 1065 UNTS 199 (excluding discoveries, scientific theories and mathematical methods; schemes, rules and methods; and presentations of information).

[6] *IceTV Pty Ltd v Nine Network Australia Pty Ltd* (2009) 239 CLR 458.

in the guide. Another example is the United States' (US) merger doctrine, which holds that if an idea can only be expressed in one or a small number of ways, the merged idea and expression are not protected.[7]

Exceptions in copyright law also operate to allow the reuse of data, and underline that copyright only prevents reuse of expression. Many countries recognise exceptions that excuse uses of copyright material that are aimed at extracting the facts, or information, from copyright content: to allow use in research, for example, or to report news.[8] This role played by exceptions is perhaps clearest in the US. There, the open-textured fair use exception,[9] which allows use of copyright material provided it is judged 'fair' by the court, has enabled the development of a sophisticated jurisprudence excusing uses which US courts judge consistent with the nature and goals of copyright law. In this case law, developed over decades, US courts have treated the scope of the copyright owner's rights as confined to the direct human enjoyment of the particular works they create, ie their use for their original purpose: as a book or artwork.[10] US courts have permitted, as fair and consistent with the proper boundaries of copyright owners' rights, a range of uses involving the processing of copyright works as an intermediate step in the pursuit of some *other* 'orthogonal'[11] or 'non-expressive'[12] purpose: indexing content for a search engine,[13] enabling search of book text,[14] or checking submitted essays for plagiarism,[15] have all been held by US courts to be fair and consistent with owners' rights.[16] In so finding, the courts have emphasised the *transformative* nature of these uses, ie the fact that they lead to the creation of something new.[17] To oversimplify somewhat, even mass technological copying has been considered fair where, and because, it is intended to achieve *some other purpose or expression, or to add something new*: where it does not replicate or substitute for the expressive function of the original copyright material. Further support for this reading of the boundaries of copyright may be found in the actions of policymakers beyond the US: Europe,[18] the

[7] See, eg, *Apple Computer, Inc v Franklin Computer Corp* 714 F 2d 1240, 1253 (3d Cir 1983); P Samuelson, 'Reconceptualizing Copyright's Merger Doctrine' (2016) 63 *Journal of the Copyright Society of the USA* 417.

[8] See, eg, Copyright Act 1968 (Cth) ss 40, 42, 103B, 103C (Australia).

[9] Copyright Act of 1976, 17 USC 107 (United States).

[10] M Sag, 'Copyright and Copy-Reliant Technology' (2009) 103 *Northwestern University Law Review* 1607.

[11] P Samuelson, 'Unbundling Fair Uses' (2009) 77 *Fordham Law Review* 2537.

[12] Sag, 'Copyright and Copy-Reliant Technology' (n 10).

[13] *Perfect 10, Inc v Amazon.com*, 508 F 3d 1146 (9th Cir 2007); *Kelly v Arriba Soft Corp*, 336 F 3d 811 (9th Cir 2003).

[14] *Authors Guild v Google, Inc*, 804 F 3d 202 (2d Cir 2015).

[15] *AV ex rel Vanderhye v iParadigms, LLC*, 562 F 3d 630 (4th Cir 2009).

[16] Large scale technological 'processing' or use of copyright material but for the purposes of recommunicating that same material, on the other hand, has been held not to be transformative and not fair use: *Metro-Goldwyn-Mayer Studios, Inc v Grokster, Ltd*, 545 US 913, 945 (2005) (peer-to-peer file-sharing); *Associated Press v Meltwater*, 931 F Supp 2d 537, 554 (SDNY 2013).

[17] *Authors Guild v Google* (n 14) 214. Note that the scope of this concept was, at the time of writing, before the US Supreme Court in *Andy Warhol Foundation for the Visual Arts, Inc v Goldsmith*, a case concerning an Andy Warhol print based on a photograph. On 18 May 2023 the Supreme Court issued a decision which maintained the relevance of 'transformativeness' in determining fair use, but also held that licensing the print to a magazine was not fair use. The broader impact of this decision remains to be seen.

[18] Directive 2019/790 of the European Parliament and of the Council of 17 April 2019 on copyright and related rights in the Digital Single Market and amending Directives 96/9/EC and 2001/29/EC [2019] OJ L130/92, Arts 3 and 4.

United Kingdom,[19] Singapore[20] and Japan[21] (among others) have all drafted exceptions to also allow the use of copyright material in non-expressive analytical processes without permission or payment to owners. These exceptions are not unqualified: the European law allows copyright owners to opt out of text and data mining that is not scientific research; Japan's provision only allows uses that would not 'unreasonably prejudice the interests of the copyright owner'. Still, they continue a path, in copyright law, of allowing the reuse of data and information to promote innovation. I return in section III to these doctrines and developments, in exploring where the relationship between IP and data is under pressure from the rise of data analytics.

In patent law, too, the patent document that sets out the boundaries of the claimed monopoly must, as a matter of law, contain certain important scientific information, such as how to perform the invention.[22] A competitor who can find a way to achieve the same goals as an invention, but in a different way not explicitly covered by the patent claims, does not infringe – even if inspired by the patent document or invention.[23] Exclusion of data or information from IP protection is, in other words, built into the very structure of IP laws.

B. Should We Have IP in Data?

We have a tendency, nevertheless, to turn to the idea of 'property' to manage relationships and interests, rights to profit and rights of access whenever a 'thing' becomes (more) valuable. Data is no exception. Periodically the intrepid thinker, perhaps unfamiliar with past fruitless explorations of the same idea, suggests that the best way to appropriately allocate the increasing benefits that can be extracted from data, and address our unbalanced data economy, is to recognise an IP-like right in data. It is no surprise that this question is arising with some urgency today. We are moving from a capitalism based on resources and/or labour, to one based on information,[24] data,[25]

[19] Copyright, Designs and Patents Act 1988 (UK) s 29A. At the time of writing the UK was considering expanding this exception: Intellectual Property Office, 'Artificial Intelligence and Intellectual Property: Copyright and Patents: Government Response to Consultation' (Webpage, 28 June 2022), www.gov.uk/government/consultations/artificial-intelligence-and-ip-copyright-and-patents/outcome/artificial-intelligence-and-intellectual-property-copyright-and-patents-government-response-to-consultation.

[20] Copyright Act 2021, s 244 (Singapore).

[21] Copyright Act 1970, art 30-4 (Japan).

[22] Patents Act 1990 (Cth) s 40 (Australia); see also TRIPS Agreement (n 3) Art 29.

[23] Whether the defendant's method is 'different' can be controversial: courts may find infringement where there is 'equivalence' between the patent and the defendant's process or machine, under the 'doctrine of equivalents': *Warner-Jenkinson Co Inc v Hilton Davis Chemical Co*, 520 US 17 (1997); in other jurisdictions see W Ralston, 'Foreign Equivalents of the US Doctrine of Equivalents: We're Playing in the Same Key but It's Not Quite Harmony' (2007) 6 *Chicago-Kent Journal of Intellectual Property* 177. The doctrine is controversial, with debate over its rationale and scope: J Allison and M Lemley, 'The (Unnoticed) Demise of the Doctrine of Equivalents' (2007) 59 *Stanford Law Review* 955.

[24] M Castells, *The Rise of the Network Society*, The Information Age: Economy, Society and Culture 1, 2nd edn (Chichester, Wiley-Blackwell, 2009); M Castells, *The Power of Identity*, The Information Age: Economy, Society and Culture 2, 2nd edn (Chichester, Wiley-Blackwell, 2009); M Castells, *End of Millennium*, The Information Age: Economy, Society and Culture 3, 2nd edn (Chichester, Wiley-Blackwell, 2010).

[25] J Sadowski, 'When Data Is Capital: Datafication, Accumulation, and Extraction' (2019) 6 *Big Data & Society*, https://doi.org/10.1177/2053951718820549.

and its gathering and use (surveillance).[26] With data becoming more valuable, and the negative impacts of its untrammelled collection and use becoming more evident daily, property is embraced as a rhetorically and legally powerful mechanism for individuals to exert control over 'their' data.[27] Property rights have a recognised potential to force firms to internalise costs: here the costs 'of the widespread collection and use of personal data now borne by others'.[28] The argument for property in data is motivated by a desire to give data subjects (ie people) the power to stop certain uses of data perceived to be harmful, and/or involve a wider group of stakeholders in the growing data economy, including data subjects.[29]

When people argue for 'ownership' of data, they are not necessarily arguing for property rights that look like conventional IP.[30] Conventional IP law's repertoire lacks some rights which attach to other kinds of legal property that people might want in 'their' data.[31] Owning IP does not grant you rights of access where someone else controls it,[32] nor rights against its destruction, nor to compensation if it happens.[33] This is troubling if, for example, the 'data' in question is irreplaceable family photos, your entire oeuvre of original compositions, the history of your social media feed or your network of connections.[34] Rights modelled on personal property law could arguably be better for providing access and rights against destruction.[35]

Another source of quasi-proprietary models for thinking about data would be in the law relating to the body and body parts.[36] An Australian Discussion Paper on data in professional sport, for example, suggested that athletes could have a kind of property in the highly intimate data on body measurements, health, movements and performance (and how all these change over time) collected and used for a range of purposes, from use in research, performance enhancement and training – and for sports betting.[37]

[26] S Zuboff, *The Age of Surveillance Capitalism: The Fight for a Human Future at the New Frontier of Power* (New York, PublicAffairs, 2019).

[27] L Lessig, 'Privacy as Property' (2002) 69 *Social Research: An International Quarterly* 247.

[28] P Samuelson, 'Privacy as Intellectual Property?' (2000) 52 *Stanford Law Review* 1125, 1129.

[29] This line of thinking is particularly prominent in the Australian Productivity Commission's 2017 report on data: Productivity Commission, *Data Availability and Use* (Productivity Commission Inquiry Report No 82, 31 March 2017).

[30] J Grimmelmann and C Mulligan, 'Data Property' (2023) 72 *American University Law Review* 829.

[31] J Michels, D Kamarinou and C Millard, 'Beyond the Clouds, Part 2: What Happens to the Files You Store in the Clouds When You Die?' (2019) Queen Mary School of Law Legal Studies Research Paper 316/2019, https://papers.ssrn.com/abstract=3387398; J Michels and C Millard, 'Mind the Gap: The Status of Digital Files Under Property Law' (2019) Queen Mary School of Law Legal Studies Research Paper 317/2019, https://papers.ssrn.com/abstract=3387400; N Purtova, 'The Illusion of Personal Data as No One's Property' (2015) 7 *Law, Innovation and Technology* 83.

[32] Michels, Kamarinou and Millard, 'Beyond the Clouds, Part 2' (n 31); NSW Law Reform Commission, *Access to Digital Records upon Death or Incapacity* (NSW Law Reform Commission No 147, December 2019); *Re Dickens* [1935] Ch 267 (CA).

[33] Grimmelmann and Mulligan, 'Data Property' (n 30).

[34] *ibid.*

[35] *ibid.*

[36] *Doodeward v Spence* (1908) 6 CLR 406 (HCA); *Yearworth v North Bristol NHS Trust* [2009] EWCA Civ 37, [2010] QB 1. The question of property in (extracted) body parts is mixed: *Doodeward* suggests that property only arises where 'work and skill' has been applied; *Yearworth* appears to allow for property from the fact of extraction.

[37] Australian Academy of Science, *Getting Ahead of the Game: Athlete Data in Professional Sport* (Report, 13 April 2022).

The Paper noted that granting property could give athletes a stronger say over the extraordinary levels of collection and use of such data that currently occurs.

IP models, nevertheless, are our most common default for thinking about property in valuable intangibles. IP laws allocate *in rem* exclusive rights to use the protected subject matter in certain defined ways, enforceable against the world. In this way, IP rights confer on the holder the power to control the (usually commercial) exploitation of the protected subject matter. Were we to consider seriously the grant of IP rights in data, this simple summary would be only a starting point: developing IP rights entails a whole series of further drafting questions, defining what is protected; who owns it; the scope of rights; what acts infringe and what exceptions apply. But the first, and most fundamental question is whether data should be property at all.

In relation to non-personal data, such as the vast collections of information generated by Internet of Things (IoT) technologies like connected sensors, Europe has seen more than one iteration of the argument for an IP-style right in data. In 1996 the European Union (EU) introduced a *sui generis* database right,[38] with the goal (and perhaps with a slightly jealous eye over the Atlantic) of encouraging investment in the local data and digital economy. The database right confers a 15-year temporary monopoly against unauthorised access to or extraction from a database. It remains law, although it has not been considered a success.[39] It has not been adopted beyond Europe, nor does Europe even try to export the model.[40] European courts have limited its operation significantly by applying it only where a party sets out to collect facts, thus excluding perhaps a majority of cases of non-personal data generation where the data is a by-product of some other commercial process.[41]

The argument for IP in non-personal data cycled around again in Europe in 2017, when European officials mooted a 'data producers' right'. This would grant the data producer the exclusive right to use certain data, including the right to license its usage. The idea was motivated somewhat differently from the database right: in part out of a desire to increase access to and circulation of data. Gangjee has written the obituary for this short-lived thought bubble, setting out the reasons for its failure: worries including transaction costs, a fear about multiplying the stakeholders in data economies, as well as more general queries whether an IP style *exclusionary* right could promote data *access*. Europe has more recently developed new models for the management of interests in data, built around a governance and management model.[42]

[38] Directive 96/9/EC of the European Parliament and of the Council of 11 March 1996 on the legal protection of databases [1996] OJ L77/20 (European Union).

[39] European Commission, *First Evaluation of Directive 96/9/EC on the legal protection of databases* (Report, 2005); European Commission, *Second Evaluation of Directive 96/9/EC on the legal protection of databases* (Commission Staff Working Document 147, 2018); D Gangjee, 'The Data Producer's Right: An Instructive Obituary' in E Lim and P Morgan (eds), *The Cambridge Handbook of Private Law and Artificial Intelligence* (Cambridge, Cambridge University Press, 2022).

[40] The EU omits the database right from its long list of IP demands when negotiating free trade agreements: European Commission, 'Proposal for the EU-Australia Free Trade Agreement: Intellectual Property' (17 June 2018) art X.48.

[41] Case C-46/02 *Fixtures Marketing Ltd v Oy Veikkaus Ab* ECLI:EU:C:2004:694, [2004] ECR I-10365; Case C-338/02 *Fixtures Marketing Ltd v Svenska Spel Ab* ECLI:EU:C:2004:696, [2004] ECR I-10497; Case C-203/02 *British Horseracing Board Ltd v William Hill* ECLI:EU:C:2004:695, [2004] ECR I-10415; Case C-444/02 *Fixtures Marketing Ltd v OPAP* ECLI:EU:C:2004:697, [2004] ECR I-10549.

[42] Gangjee, 'The Data Producer's Right' (n 39).

The idea of IP in data comes up more persistently in relation to personal data. Twenty years ago, Harvard Law Professor Lawrence Lessig suggested protecting privacy through a property right, causing a critical flurry in the scholarly literature.[43] More recent proponents include Trakman et al,[44] and even US Democratic candidate Andrew Yang, who included the idea in his 2019–2020 policy platform.[45] The details of these proposals vary: sometimes imagining empowered individuals, owning and actively controlling and licensing their own data; at other times proposing property rights as a legal foundation for a data governance institution: a data collective, or a data trust, or some other collective mechanism for governing personal data.[46] But the argument boils down to this: if people *owned* their own data, in the IP sense of being able to exclude others from using it, they could make choices: to participate in markets for information, and claim some share of the profits being made, or choose not to participate.[47]

Every time IP in data has been raised, scholars respond not only that there *is no* IP in data, but that there *ought not be* such rights. But not all of the reasons commonly given are convincing. Each of the next three subheadings addresses a high-level argument as to why we ought not grant IP in data, and some potential nuances that emerge from a more thoughtful engagement with the IP law and literature, pointing to the ways that IP systems have had to grapple with some of the same questions that confront us in relation to data today.

C. Data is Too Uncertain, or Too Dynamic

One argument raised against the recognition of IP in data (or in personal data) is that data is too indefinite: that for something to be 'property', it must be possible to identify it in some stable way; to draw boundaries. Data, or information, defies such attempts to pin it down; it can be small (a single, binary piece of information)[48] or it can be large; it could be comprised of facts, or opinions, inferences or predictions; it can be combined to generate new data and insights.

But the idea that a thing must have certain boundaries to be property is a misconception. Uncertainty about subject matter is 'situation normal' in IP regimes.[49] Copyright protection arises automatically and globally on creation, and the scope and boundaries

[43] Lessig, 'Privacy as Property' (n 27).

[44] L Trakman, R Walters and B Zeller, 'Is Privacy and Personal Data Set to Become the New Intellectual Property?' (2019) 50 *IIC – International Review of Intellectual Property and Competition Law* 937.

[45] A Yang, 'Data as a Property Right' (*Yang2020* – Andrew Yang for President, 1 October 2019), 2020. yang2020.com/policies/data-property-right/.

[46] For a discussion of data institutions, including data trusts, see J Hardinges and J Keller, 'What Are Data Institutions and Why Are They Important? – The ODI' (*Open Data Institute*, 29 January 2021), theodi.org/article/what-are-data-institutions-and-why-are-they-important/; Ada Lovelace Institute, *Exploring Legal Mechanisms for Data Stewardship* (Report, Ada Lovelace Institute, 4 March 2021), adalovelaceinstitute.org/report/legal-mechanisms-data-stewardship/.

[47] Productivity Commission, *Data Availability and Use* (n 29).

[48] See, eg, C Shannon, 'A Mathematical Theory of Communication' (1948) 27 *Bell System Technical Journal* 379; Australian Computer Society, *Data Sharing Frameworks: Technical White Paper* (Australian Computer Society, September 2017) ch 3.

[49] J Pila, 'An Intentional View of the Copyright Work' (2008) 71 *MLR* 535; B Sherman, 'What Is a Copyright Work?' (2011) 12 *Theoretical Inquiries in Law* 99.

of the copyright 'work' in general need only be affirmatively identified if, and when, there is a dispute. Even in the event of a dispute it is not uncommon for multiple different potential copyright works to be identified. In *Fairfax v Reed*, the parties disputed whether the protected work was the whole newspaper, the individual article, or even the headline alone.[50] In *Coffey v Warner/Chappell*, they disputed whether copyright subsisted in the riff separately from the song.[51] In *JR Consulting & Drafting v Cummings*, parties disputed different versions of software generated over time.[52] There have even been cases where the protected work was *never* defined, because the parties chose to argue only about infringement.[53] If they seek more certainty, parties may identify copyright subject matter via contract: but even here the language is often vague: the subject matter is identified in terms that mirror legislation ('all IP generated during the course of the project, including any copyrights …') or using highly specific definitions of convenience ('the manuscript titled [x] and dated [y]').

Even systems such as patent and trade mark, which require *ex ante* registration as a prerequisite for protection, do not clearly define their subject matter. In patent, the boundaries of the exclusive right are defined by patent claims, which set out, in a series of nested clauses, different descriptions of the invention at differing degrees of specificity. The actual boundaries of exclusivity are not really known until a dispute, when words in the claims are interpreted as they apply to an alleged infringement, and the validity and scope of claims is tested in court. Even then, in truth the bounds of the patent are settled only as between the litigating parties: it is open to future accused infringers to challenge claims in different ways. The boundaries of a registered trade mark are also porous and can be infringed by adopting a mark that is 'deceptively' (or, in US parlance, 'confusingly') similar.[54] The penumbra of the registered property right depends on consumer perceptions, determined when a dispute arises.

Data is also dynamic; information about people is constantly changing. It is most valuable in flow and in growth (and, for some purposes, such as insurance, when collected over a period of time for longitudinal analysis). In most commercial contexts, data gains value through immediacy and currency, via the ever-shifting classifications of a person that can be used to make predictions or judgements about them. Are they likely to suffer adverse life events such as loss of a job, such that insurance should be denied? What information, advertising or opportunities should be targeted at them? Are they fulfilling their obligations as employees, or welfare recipients? Are they hungry, or sad, *right now*, giving rise to immediate commercial opportunities?

But dynamism is also no barrier to IP protection. Not only does copyright manage rights in frequently updated works,[55] but many countries recognise copyright in

[50] *Fairfax Media Publications Pty Ltd v Reed International Books Australia Pty Ltd* (2010) 189 FCR 109 (FCA).

[51] *Coffey v Warner/Chappell Music Ltd* [2005] EWHC 449 (Ch).

[52] *JR Consulting & Drafting Pty Ltd v Cummings* [2016] FCAFC 20, (2016) 329 ALR 625; *JR Consulting & Drafting Pty Ltd v Cummings* [2016] HCATrans 202.

[53] *Nine Films & Television Pty Ltd v Ninox Television Ltd* [2005] FCA 1404.

[54] Trade Marks Act 1995 (Cth) ss 120(2) and 120(3) (Australia); Trade Marks Act 1994 (UK) ss 10(1) and 10(2); TRIPS Agreement (n 3) Art 16(1); 15 USC 1114, 1125; R Burrell, 'Trade Mark Bureaucracies' in M Janis and G Dinwoodie (eds), *Trademark Law and Theory: A Handbook of Contemporary Research* (Cham, Edward Elgar, 2007).

[55] *JR Consulting & Drafting v Cummings* (n 52) paras 277–278.

'broadcast', which, like much data, is not so much a thing as a stream of images and sound, without beginning or end.[56] Ways have been found to manage this anomalous property right, case by case, by looking at what is important and valuable within the stream and recognising property in extracts.[57]

In short, IP law manages to function without seeking fully to define the boundaries of the *res* – the protected object – in advance. Challenges of definition and dynamism are not, therefore, a strong argument against IP in data. In defining rights in data, IP doctrine shows that we do not need to define the boundaries of data for all purposes and for all time; rather, we can define it as a thing *for particular legal purposes*, at the point where it becomes necessary.

D. Data is Relational and Collective; IP is Individual

A second argument often raised against recognising IP in data is that it risks a 'tragedy of the anti-commons'[58] where property rights held by multiple stakeholders become an insurmountable barrier to beneficial uses of data across the public, private and research sectors.

A related critique focuses on data's inherent relationality. Data about a person reveals things about them, but also about other people like and unlike them, so there are collective, as well as individual interests in data about people.[59] While an individual may have strong personal interests in their health data, there can also be collective interests in understanding, say, the prevalence of a disease in a community and the features of patients which could reveal something about causation, or cure. There can also be collective interests in the *non-use* or non-availability of data. While facial recognition as a mechanism for unlocking doors or gates can be convenient for the individual who forgets their travel or work card, there are collective privacy, associative and other interests in reducing overall capacities for surveillance. Furthermore, individual pieces of data about people often have relatively little value: often it is the *aggregation* of data that holds value, whether for commercial purposes (such as targeting products, prices, services and advertising), or for governmental uses (such as monitoring the outcomes of policy initiatives) and research purposes (including medical research). Much of our current data protection law ignores collective interests by conferring rights of control of data collection into the hands of individuals: my preference for privacy may be frustrated where many others consent to data collection. In the case of the Australian Data Availability and Transparency Act, government data holders requested to share data are asked to decide whether sharing is in the collective or 'public' interest: effectively pitting collective interests against individual interests.[60]

[56] Copyright Act 1968 (Cth) s 10 (Australia) (definition of 'broadcast'); International Convention for the Protection of Performers, Producers of Phonograms and Broadcasting Organisations (Rome, 26 October 1961) 496 UNTS 43, Art 3(f).

[57] *Network Ten Ltd v TCN Channel Nine Pty Ltd* (2004) 218 CLR 273; M Handler, 'The Panel Case and Television Broadcast Copyright' (2003) 25 *Sydney Law Review* 391.

[58] M Heller, *The Gridlock Economy: How Too Much Ownership Wrecks Markets, Stops Innovation, and Costs Lives* (New York, Basic Books, 2008).

[59] S Viljoen, 'A Relational Theory of Data Governance' (2021) 131 *Yale Law Journal* 573.

[60] Data Availability and Transparency Act 2022 (Cth) ss 3(a), 16B(3)(b)(ii), 126(2C)(b)(ii) (Australia).

While IP is often seen as highly individualistic, in fact IP owners face some of the same conundrums. There almost always seems to be more value in aggregating IP rights, than in the individual unit.[61] While it is certainly possible to prefer individual songs or albums, institutional users of music (radio stations, gyms, restaurants) want access to the full repertoire of popular music – *without* negotiating licences with every IP owner. To avoid market failure, IP systems have developed collective management. Copyright collecting societies are privately or publicly established legal entities dedicated to the licensing of large repertoires to users, and distributing the benefits among their members, the rightsholders. The history of collecting societies can tell us much about representation of different interests (and conflicts of interest) in the governance of valuable intangibles; methods for (and challenges in) distributing benefits; and much more.

It might be argued that collecting societies are not a useful model for the management of data. Copyright collecting societies are member-driven entities comprised of professional creators with some common interests; by way of contrast, everyone in a jurisdiction is a data subject: from young to old; from those concerned about privacy to those who think little about it. On the other hand, the need to address a broad membership pool is not necessarily a barrier: some countries have legislated for extended collective licensing: giving collecting societies power to license even content of non-members; and not all materials licensed by collecting societies are created by professionals.

Notably too, collecting societies manage only certain rights, and mostly via blanket licensing, ie licensing large repertoires to a user for a specific use. The Australasian Performing Right Association (APRA), for example, *only* deals with music copyright owned by a composer, and only owns and licenses certain rights (performance and digital communication rights); you must negotiate directly with the copyright owner if you want to use a particular song in your movie, and license recordings of those same musical works from another collecting society dealing with a different set of owners. When one thinks about the multifarious uses for personal data, and its population-wide relevance, perhaps APRA looks like a less relevant model.

It is true that the collecting society model may not make sense as a model or even analogy for governing an undifferentiated mass of personal data. But a frequent problem in our discussion of data is … that we talk about 'data'.[62] This blanket term implies that all data is equal and must be controlled together, when greater clarity can be achieved by talking about *medical* data, or *biometric* data, *financial* data or *geolocation* data. Or rather, more accurately, data of whatever kind has a range of distinct uses and users. All data is health data because even the contents of your shopping cart or the activities revealed in your social media feed say something about your health and fitness;[63] all data is insurance data because, similarly, those same data streams may be

[61] K Bowrey, *Copyright, Creativity, Big Media and Cultural Value: Incorporating the Author* (Abingdon, Routledge, 2020); J Cohen, *Between Truth and Power: The Legal Constructions of Informational Capitalism* (New York, Oxford University Press, 2019).

[62] I thank Julia Powles for this insight.

[63] C Warzel, 'All Your Data Is Health Data' *The New York Times* (New York, 13 August 2019), www.nytimes.com/2019/08/13/opinion/health-data.html.

relevant to underwriters. Rather than thinking about personal data as a unitary thing that would be managed by a single entity for all purposes – an impossible task – we should think about distinct activities to be managed separately.

And if that is right, perhaps the nature of IP and the structure of collecting societies *are* a useful analogy for considering governance and use of data, because we do not manage IP rights in a singular way. A fundamental feature of copyright, for example, is the way that ownership can be divided up; distinct rights can be transferred to different entities. As an author of a book,[64] I can assign the right to print the novel to one entity; the right to make a film version to another entity. Building on this, different collecting societies can own and/or manage different rights, in relation to different uses, even while other rights are often retained by copyright owners. This could have useful analogues for data: say, when dealing with the collected medical data relating to people with a particular condition or genetic trait. Such data, collected, could be useful for both research and commercial purposes, with people feeling differently about those different uses;[65] a collecting society model that managed data only for medical research purposes (even perhaps differentiating among members interested or not interested in commercial research) is not impossible to imagine.[66]

I emphasise that I am not *advocating* for one or more collecting societies for data, whether personal or not. Collecting societies have well-known limitations. Many devote limited effort to collective governance and lack serious avenues for resolving political or policy differences between their members, perhaps reflecting the fact that they were established to manage the narrow question of generating licensing revenue on the assumption that all possible members would desire maximal licensing revenue. To the extent that the reasons for creating property in personal data are not purely commercial, or where decisions about data use may involve challenging political or policy choices, the collecting society model may not provide an apt analogy. Collecting societies also expend a great deal of effort to ensuring that the distribution of benefits to an individual owner from use of copyright material reflects the extent of use of *that owner's* material – which may make less sense in relation to data. And collecting societies are good for managing collective interests, but not for reconciling conflicts between individual and collective interests, so to the extent that individual interests in privacy conflict with other collective interests in convenience or data-sharing, collecting societies and collective management as currently constituted are an incomplete answer to our data challenges. Nevertheless, with all their faults or differences, there could be lessons in the comparison with the emerging discussion around data institutions and data trusts.

[64] Copyright Act 1968 (Cth) s 196(2) (Australia).

[65] J Powles and H Hodson, 'Google DeepMind and Healthcare in an Age of Algorithms' (2017) 7 *Health Technology* 351; M Taylor and T Whitton, 'Public Interest, Health Research and Data Protection Law: Establishing a Legitimate Trade-Off between Individual Control and Research Access to Health Data' (2020) 9 *Laws* 6; European Commission, *Guidance on Sharing Private Sector Data in the European Data Economy* (Commission Staff Working Document 232, 2018).

[66] See E Hafen, 'Personal Data Cooperatives – A New Data Governance Framework for Data Donations and Precision Health' in J Krutzinna and L Floridi (eds), *The Ethics of Medical Data Donation* (Cham, Springer, 2019); T Kariotis et al, 'Emerging Health Data Platforms: From Individual Control to Collective Data Governance' (2020) 2 *Data & Policy* e13.

E. IP Rights in Data will Accelerate Data Exploitation

A third critique of IP rights especially in personal data is that they are the wrong tool to limit the mass commercial use of personal data, because IP's role is to enable, not reduce, exploitation. Property (and especially intellectual property) is more often a mechanism to bring things *into* the market. People currently give away their data in return for services; granting them property rights would not stop that, but legitimate and formalise it. Individuals are unlikely to receive significant commercial benefits, because as discussed above, individual information has relatively low value.[67] A related concern is that propertising data in this way potentially exacerbates inequality: privacy becomes an asset: a privilege of the wealthy.[68]

Arguably there is a certain naivety in positing IP as a model for empowering data subjects, given that IP systems are frequently criticised for *failing* to benefit individual human creators. Some of the most fervent critics opposing IP in data are IP scholars who have seen, up close and ugly, the failures of IP systems to strengthen individual creators' hands as against more powerful intermediaries and aggregators who accumulate rights while passing few benefits on to creators. Lemley reminds us of the alacrity with which authors and inventors sign away any IP rights they might have in their creations and inventions, sometimes for what seems like a fraction of a fair price.[69]

But IP models are more diverse than this implies. Copyright law for example – especially outside the US[70] – incorporates non-assignable moral rights. The Berne Convention (the original global copyright treaty) recognises two core moral rights, which in both purpose and effect protect individual, dignitary interests of human creators. These are the right of attribution, ie to be correctly identified as the author of a work, and the right of integrity, ie the author's right not to have their work treated in a way that will prejudice their honour or reputation.[71] Both rights remain with the author even after they have assigned away their economic rights, meaning that even an author with no general right to control commercial uses of their work can object where an otherwise legitimate use of content harms certain dignitary interests of theirs. The idea of rights that remain with the individual, even after other economic rights have been acquired by someone else, could be useful in the context of current debates over data.

Nor are moral rights the only kind of non-economic or non-assignable right. Others can be found in the less well-known borderlands of copyright law, although not all are recognised in every jurisdiction:

[67] J Cohen, 'Examined Lives: Informational Privacy and the Subject as Object' (2000) 52 *Stanford Law Review* 1373; see also M Lemley, 'Private Property' (2000) 52 *Stanford Law Review* 1545.

[68] Cohen, 'Examined Lives', *ibid*; Lemley, 'Private Property', *ibid*; PM Schwartz, 'Property, Privacy, and Personal Data' (2004) 117 *Harvard Law Review* 2056.

[69] Lemley, 'Private Property', *ibid*.

[70] Beyond the specific case of visual artists, the US does not grant moral rights, instead arguing that it provides for protection of the same rights via other legal systems, such as defamation and passing off.

[71] Article 6bis of the Berne Convention for the Protection of Literary and Artistic Works (Berne, 9 September 1886; Revised Paris, 24 July 1971) 1161 UNTS 30 ('Berne Convention').

- Resale royalty rights: the right of a visual artist to a share of the profit, every time their original artwork is sold.[72]
- Performers' (non-proprietary) anti-bootlegging rights:[73] which grant performers rights against the recording of their performance without their consent, or the use (copying or communication) of recordings made without consent.
- Reversion rights: the non-assignable right of an author to have economic rights in copyright returned to them after a period of time.[74]
- 'Windfall profit' rights: the right to a 'share' if it turns out your invention or work was more valuable than expected, so the windfall doesn't all go to the purchaser (or, in the case of a patent, to the employer).

Outside of copyright, geographical indications provide another model for collective and collectively managed, non-assignable rights of producers, tied indelibly to place and other anchors. There has been a distinct recent growth of interest in these alternatives in policy circles.[75] One reason for this interest is a desire to try to empower human creators and to improve their share of the benefits of IP. These various non-economic, non-transferable rights also reflect the fact that IP rights have long been justified in part by reference to non-economic rationales, including rationales that draw on the fundamental dignity of the human creator or author, or in the case of geographical indications, the value of community, history and authenticity. Like data then, the objects of IP have both economic, and non-economic dimensions, both aspects of which can be accommodated within nuanced legal frameworks which are constantly reconciled and re-reconciled as circumstances change.

In summary, 'IP in personal data' does not have to mean fully assignable economic rights that will inevitably accrue to existing, powerful data collectors and accelerate exploitation. An IP-like right in personal data could couple economic rights with something much more personal, and much more aligned with dignitary and reputational interests; it could reserve certain rights to individuals. Note, however, that the nuances described in this section lie at the margins of IP law: accommodations and special rights bolted on to general IP doctrine to prevent exploitation of human creators or harm to their dignitary interests. Whether this adds much to our existing privacy and data protection laws, themselves fundamentally concerned with dignitary interests, is a genuine and important question. As the next section will show, my own view is that the likely contribution of this analysis lies in lessons and analogues.

[72] Resale Royalty Right for Visual Artists Act 2009 (Cth) (Australia); Article 14ter of the Berne Convention (n 71).

[73] Copyright Act 1968 (Cth) ss 248G–248N (Australia).

[74] Copyright Act, 17 USC § 203 (US); Copyright Act, RSC 1985, c C-42, s 14(1) (Canada); *cf* J Yuvaraj and R Giblin, 'Are Contracts Enough? An Empirical Study of Author Rights in Australian Publishing Agreements' (2020) 44 *Melbourne University Law Review* 380; Copyright Act 1968 (Cth) s 239(4) (Australia).

[75] Yuvaraj and Giblin, 'Are Contracts Enough?', *ibid*; R Giblin and C Doctorow, *Chokepoint Capitalism: How Big Tech and Big Content Captured Creative Labor Markets and How We'll Win Them Back* (Boston, Beacon Press, 2022).

III. IP (or Copyright) as Data

I have so far argued that IP systems are less one-dimensional than is often understood. The borderlands of IP law provide instructive precedents for methods of managing rights in valuable intangibles, which could be relevant in managing data notwithstanding its lack of definition; dynamic nature; collective and individual interests; and personal and dignitary implications when collected and used. The careful reader will however note that I have presented IP law, institutions and history as providing *lessons*. I have not advocated for IP rights in data, whether generally or in specific cases. This is because IP models do not offer useful resolutions for the most pressing data challenges we face. The limitations of the IP model for addressing fundamental questions are writ large in current debates over copyright and generative AI.

We are increasingly faced with technologies which treat copyright material *as data*, on a mass scale, and with new implications for copyright owners.[76] The year 2022 saw the rise of AI systems which ingest copyright-protected content in order to generate new material of the same general kind: processing images to 'learn' how to make further images based on text prompts (as in DALL-E or Stable Diffusion), or text to write new text, such as a news story, marketing blurb, or essay (as in large language models such as GPT-4 and ChatGPT), or code to write new code (as in ChatGPT or GitHub's Copilot). To train such models, technology companies copy copyright-protected content, ie art and text created by people: mostly, to date, without permission or remuneration. Stable Diffusion for example was trained on a subset of LAION-5B, a dataset of 5.85 billion image-text pairs obtained from the Common Crawl dataset, itself an archive of the publicly available internet which includes artworks uploaded by artists for promotional purposes.[77] In 2022–23, several court cases were commenced alleging that training these models involved copyright infringement.[78]

These developments raise a policy question at the intersection between IP and data: does, and/or *should*, copyright law treat data about creative works and creativity, data *contained within* creative works and extracted via machine learning, as part of the property of the artist over which the artist has rights of exclusion? In some ways, this is a small, sub-test case for the larger question: should we grant IP in data, and what considerations are relevant to deciding that question?

[76] Sag, 'Copyright and Copy-Reliant Technology' (n 10).

[77] 'stabilityai/stable-diffusion-2. Hugging Face' (Hugging Face, 2022), huggingface.co/stabilityai/stable-diffusion-2. The subset used to train Stable Diffusion filters out adult, violent and sexual content. On LAION-5B, see R Beaumont, 'LAION-5B: A New Era of Open Large-Scale Multi-Modal Datasets' (*LAION*, 31 March 2022), laion.ai/blog/laion-5b/; C Schuhmann et al, 'LAION-5B: An Open Large-Scale Dataset for Training Next Generation Image-Text Models' (36th Conference on Neural Information Processing, Virtual, November 2022), https://arxiv.org/abs/2210.08402. On Common Crawl, see 'Curious About What We Do? – Common Crawl' (Webpage, 2022), commoncrawl.org/big-picture/what-we-do/.

[78] For example, a class action lawsuit was filed in November 2022 in the US District Court over the GitHub AI software Copilot, which can speed up coding, suggesting multi-line code completions based on user prompts. Copilot was trained on publicly available code in GitHub repositories. A group of visual artists filed a lawsuit on 13 January 2023 in the US District Court in San Francisco against Stability AI, Midjourney and DeviantArt over their respective generative AI products based on Stable Diffusion that creates images based on a user's prompt.

In section II, I noted that conventional IP legislation and jurisprudence positively allows, even promotes, the use and reuse of information or facts contained within IP-protected content. Based on this same reasoning, scholars and advocates have argued that use of copyright content to train AI is fair use, because it aims to extract information and create new works.[79] Within the frame of existing fair use analysis described in section II, generative AI is arguably transformative: it is specifically designed to create new expression. And while it does so by drawing on copyright content, what it extracts from that content is information: about how words are used together; how colours and lines and visual effects combine in ways that make sense to human viewers or readers. This is consistent with at least some goals of copyright (and IP law more generally): supporting and encouraging creation. In pursuit of this end, copyright doctrine does not concern itself with who is doing the creating, or what tools are used.

According to other understandings of what is 'fair', we can argue that use of copyright material to train generative AI is distinctly *un*fair. Value extraction on this scale feels like a wrongful taking from rightsholders. To the extent that it is commercial, it has been called unjust enrichment.[80] A key concern here is *distributive justice:* that it is unfair that artists' own work is used to train their replacement; that artists bear all the costs while someone else profits. The new material created increases the supply of art, text or code in a way that could reduce the market value of human creativity and have a very negative impact on human authors and artists. Generative AI threatens to automate some part of their creative practice, and remove a layer of everyday creative jobs: commercial design and graphics; the writing of basic stories, essays, marketing blurbs for products; unlike other workers who have trained their robot replacement, for the most part these artists and coders are not being paid for the use of their knowledge in training. Finally, it could be argued that generative AI is not an unalloyed social good: that, for example, it is a threat to public discourse, or academic integrity, because of its capacity to instantly create text, or pictures, that lack truth or a responsible human author: further undermining any 'social good' argument in favour of training generative AI at the expense of artists.

All of these may be good reasons to be concerned about the impacts of generative AI as a matter of policy. But none are accommodated readily into existing copyright jurisprudence or theory. At least in Anglophone countries which emphasise the pro-innovation role of copyright as a law dedicated to increasing creative production without any real judgement about its quality, arguing that human creativity is special is challenging. We would need to incorporate a new, and broader set of values into the analysis of copyright, including by making judgements about the social value of text, or images, to judge human creativity more worthy of protection, or to worry about human creators being crowded out. This would require at least some retreat from Anglophone IP law's

[79] M Carroll, 'Copyright and the Progress of Science: Why Text and Data Mining Is Lawful' (2019) 53 *UC Davis Law Review* 893; S Fiil-Flynn et al, 'Legal Reform to Enhance Global Text and Data Mining Research' (2022) 378 *Science* 951. It should be noted that the literature cited here is not concerned with the technologies colloquially known as generative AI, but rather other, earlier forms of AI.

[80] Unjust enrichment was asserted as both a cause of action and a remedy in a class action challenging the lawfulness of the operation of GitHub Copilot, filed in November 2022. Copilot is an AI system, trained on open-source software shared on GitHub, that provides users with a prompt or suggestion as to how they should complete their code. The class action website is githubcopilotlitigation.com; the complaint is available at githubcopilotlitigation.com/pdf/06823/1-0-github_complaint.pdf.

fundamental pro-innovation bias: the impulse that more creation, and more access to text, and code, and art is an unqualified good. Notably too, these reasons for apparent unfairness are not unique to creators: artists are not the only workers to be confronted with the fact that they may be training their robot replacement.[81]

Even if courts and policymakers globally *were* to rethink the scope of copyright rights, to treat some or all use of copyright material in training generative AI as requiring permission and/or payment, it is far from clear that this would help human creators unless we did more to reform the way those rights were allocated. Simply recognising 'AI Training' as falling within copyright would give copyright *owners* the right to license, or not license, use of material for that purpose. But copyright owners are frequently *not* the original human authors and artists. On the contrary, a large proportion of commercially important copyright content is owned by intermediaries, such as record producers and publishers. And although many practising visual artists would own their own copyright, in the 'image industry' there are plenty of intermediaries with rights to process images and develop or license generative AI. Intermediaries across the creative industries are surely likely to see the potential for efficiency and productivity gains in automation. Automatically generated music may not satisfy the live music market, but it could supply music for the background in gyms, restaurants and clubs; automatically generated art is already being used in magazines and newspapers, and for book covers. Automatic generation of text, for the first draft of newspaper stories or textbooks or more – even if deeply substandard – could provide a reason to reduce costs for various parts of the publishing industry, by replacing creators or reducing their time or pay. In short, new forms of AI, legally trained pursuant to a copyright licence on content owned by creative industry intermediaries, could further squeeze the interests of creators, even if current copyright claims against technology companies are successful.[82]

Fundamentally, these are challenges – just as we are seeing in the data economy more broadly – regarding the distribution of economic benefits; how we are to constrain, or make accountable, the power that emerges from the collection and use of data; how we balance individual and collective rights and interests in data and its use; and fundamental questions regarding what kinds of data use are acceptable across a range of contexts. The law and jurisprudence of IP is simply too limited to address these questions; it lacks mechanisms for incorporating a sufficiently broad set of considerations.

IV. Conclusion

Data is a tricky subject matter for rights. But property is a highly malleable concept; so too is IP. My contention in this chapter has been that there is nothing fundamental

[81] For example, Lyft is using data generated by its ride-sharing service in its development towards autonomous vehicles: S Mandal et al, 'Motion Prediction for Autonomous Vehicles from Lyft Dataset using Deep Learning, *2020 IEEE 5th International Conference on Computing Communication and Automation (ICCCA)* (Greater Noida, India, 2020). For a deep discussion of firm collection and use of worker data in a range of ways, see L Kresge, *Data and Algorithms in the Workplace: A Primer on New Technologies* (UC Berkley Labor Centre Working Paper, November 2020).

[82] Giblin and Doctorow, *Chokepoint Capitalism* (n 75).

about even personal data, in flow, that makes it impossible to 'propertise': not its indefinite or dynamic nature; not its relational or collective qualities and not the fundamental human, non-economic interests that it implicates. The history and structure of copyright even points to the possibility that we could have multiple actors with rights to control data for different purposes, just as copyright rights are split between multiple owners. As we move forward in designing our future data governance systems, there are lessons in the history, and institutions of copyright specifically and IP more generally.

Nevertheless, as this chapter has also sought to show, seeking to incorporate rights to control data within an *existing* IP system, namely copyright, runs up against deep-seated pro-innovation principles and the trend of authority. We will not find, within copyright doctrine, the answer to whether AI use of content should be allowed, because copyright has only limited answers to questions of distributive justice; accountability; or authenticity posed by the new technologies. And if *that* is right, then so too should we ignore the siren call of IP in framing how best to manage interests in both personal and non-personal data: there is little reason to think that IP doctrine will provide good answers to problems in the distribution of economic benefits and political power there either. These fundamental questions posed by the new data uses are better confronted directly, challenging though that will be.

13

Duties for Datasets

JERROLD SOH TSIN HOWE*

I. Introduction

A develops and deploys a machine learning (ML) system using a dataset B carelessly compiled. The system harms V in a way clearly attributable to flaws in the dataset. Should, and does, B owe V a duty of care? The growing literature on ML liability has generally focused on ML systems rather than the datasets used to train them.[1] Meanwhile, laws targeting dataset providers are primarily regulatory in nature, establishing for instance obligations to obtain consent for data collection[2] and to ensure the dataset's quality,[3] and breaching these obligations trigger fines rather than compensation.[4] State regulations are no doubt important, but liability performs a well-known complementary role – especially when regulators have limited *ex ante* information on the likelihood and extent of potential harm.[5] Given the complexity and opacity of modern ML systems,[6] courts dealing *post facto* with harm occasioned by an ML system may be better placed to determine the scope and extent of precautions to be expected from ML dataset and system providers.[7]

* Assistant Professor, Singapore Management University. I thank Lau Kwan Ho, Jeannie Marie Paterson and Damian Clifford for helpful comments on earlier presentations of this work, as well as Ashley Chin and Rachael Ang for excellent research assistance. All errors are mine.

[1] P Hacker, 'A Legal Framework for AI Training Data – from First Principles to the Artificial Intelligence Act' (2021) 13 *Law, Innovation and Technology* 257, 259. Notable exceptions are Be Sobel, 'A Taxonomy of Training Data: Disentangling the Mismatched Rights, Remedies, and Rationales for Restricting Machine Learning' in R Hilty et al (eds), *Artificial Intelligence and Intellectual Property* (Oxford, Oxford University Press, 2021); F Pasquale, 'Data-Informed Duties in Al Development' (2019) 119 *Columbia Law Review* 1917.

[2] Regulation (EU) 2016/679 of the European Parliament and of the Council of 27 April 2016 on the protection of natural persons with regard to the processing of personal data and on the free movement of such data, and repealing Directive 95/46/EC (General Data Protection Regulation) [2016] OJ L119/1, Art 7.

[3] Commission, 'Proposal for a Regulation of the European Parliament and of the Council Laying Down Harmonised Rules on Artificial Intelligence (Artificial Intelligence Act) and Amending Certain Union Legislative Acts' COM (2021) 206 final, Art 10 (AI Act).

[4] See below section IV.

[5] S Shavell, 'Liability for Harm versus Regulation of Safety' (1984) 13 *Journal of Legal Studies* 357.

[6] Commission, 'Report on the Safety and Liability Implications of Artificial Intelligence, the Internet of Things and Robotics' COM (2020) 64 final, 15–16; J Burrell 'How the Machine "Thinks": Understanding Opacity in Machine Learning Algorithms' (2016) 3 *Big Data & Society* 1.

[7] See below section III.

Emerging legal instruments thus contemplate and indeed aim to facilitate common law tortious suits against these parties by supplementing common law doctrine with statutory definitions of fault and rebuttable presumptions of causality in the context of artificial intelligence (AI) systems.[8] However, as will be explained, these instruments do not address whether and when duties of care arise over ML datasets. The lack of scrutiny over dataset liability is problematic because ML system outputs are fundamentally shaped by their data inputs.[9] It follows that deficiencies in ML systems can typically (albeit not exclusively) be traced back to deficiencies in their training datasets. Yet in standard ML practice, such datasets may neither be compiled nor published by ML systems developers. The recent trend of levelling obligations primarily against system providers may thus provide limited safeguards against dataset defects. This is despite recent ML scholarship demonstrating that such defects are more widespread than commonly assumed.[10]

This chapter therefore examines when and how duties of care may and should arise in respect of ML datasets specifically.[11] Section II opens with a technical discussion of what datasets are and how they are used in existing ML pipelines. This serves as a factual backdrop against which section III assesses how carelessly compiled datasets may harm. Section IV considers arguments for and against establishing private duties of care against dataset providers, referred hereinafter as dataset liability. Section V examines how dataset liability may be analysed from a tort law perspective.

II. Understanding ML Datasets

As the existence of tortious duties is well-known to be a highly fact-sensitive inquiry, in considering dataset duties we must look closely at how these datasets are compiled and how carelessness in their production may cause harm. Although ML algorithms have come to be well-explored in legal scholarship,[12] datasets have received less attention. This section therefore examines them in detail. Knowledge of standard ML terms like supervised learning and model training is assumed.

[8] Most relevant are the draft AI Act (above n 3) and the accompanying proposed AI Liability Directive. Commission, 'Proposal for a Directive of the European Parliament and of the Council on Adapting Non-Contractual Civil Liability Rules to Artificial Intelligence' COM (2022) 496 final, 16. These are discussed below in section IV.

[9] Pasquale, 'Data-Informed Duties' (n 1) 1927–28; Hacker, 'A Legal Framework for AI Training Data' (n 1) 258–59.

[10] See below section II.B.

[11] This is purely a scoping choice and does not imply that alternative channels to liability such as contract and consumer protection law are unavailable or less important. See also section IV below.

[12] See, eg, A Zuckerman, 'Artificial Intelligence – Implications for the Legal Profession Adversarial Process and Rule of Law' (2020) 136 *LQR* 427, 428–32; B Haney, 'The Optimal Agent: The Future of Autonomous Vehicles & Liability Theory' (2020) 30 *Albany Law Journal of Science & Technology* 1, 9–21; Daniel Seng et al, 'An Introduction to the Relevant Technologies' in Simon Chesterman et al (eds), *Law and Technology in Singapore* (Singapore, Academy Publishing, 2021).

A. Datasets in Theory

'Data' is an electronic representation of real-world information.[13] While often numerical, data exists in many forms. My name at the top of this chapter is text data which records the real-world fact that I wrote it; the names in the acknowledgement footnote record how these persons assisted with this endeavour. Occasionally author portraits feature as image data in the frontmatter. Of course, because computers are binary-switch machines writ large, all electronic data is ultimately reducible to ones and zeros: each letter in the English alphabet has an associated American Standard Code for Information Interchange (ASCII), every pixel in any computerised image maps to a triple of Red-Green-Blue values.

Despite common misuse, data per se is *not* the primary input for training ML systems. Instead, they need 'datasets': data that has been selected, compiled, and arranged in a format amenable to the linear algebraic manipulations that ML algorithms are. This distinction is well-established in copyright law, which has long recognised that though copyright cannot subsist in mere facts, it can attach to original compilations of facts.[14] Thinking seriously about datasets thus requires examining who compiled the data and how.[15] Compilers can choose from many technical formats. Tabular datasets are often exchanged via comma-separated value (.csv) files that are functionally similar to Excel (.xls) tables. Equivalent formats include Javascript Object Notation (.json) as well as specialised formats expected by standard ML code libraries.[16] Data format also turns on the specific data types at hand. Text data may be stored as folders of .txt files, image data as collections of .jpg files, and so on.

To be clear, these are merely different technical ways of arranging data. Converting one format to another is often trivial. But dataset providers are responsible for more. Stripped of context, datasets are nothing more than arrangements of numbers; their meaning derives from human labelling and interpretation. Consider the following dataset:

Table 1 Example Dataset

1	0	3	Braund, Mr. Owen Harris	male	22	1	0	A/5 21171	7.25		S
2	1	1	Cumings, Mrs. John Bradley (Florence Briggs Thayer)	female	38	1	0	PC 17599	71.2833	C85	C
3	1	3	Heikkinen, Miss. Laina	female	26	0	0	STON/O2. 3101282	7.925		S

[13] Cambridge Dictionary Online, 'Data' (Online Dictionary Entry), dictionary.cambridge.org/dictionary/english/data.

[14] *IceTV Pty Ltd v Nine Network Australia Pty Ltd* [2009] HCA 14, (2009) 239 CLR 458, para 28; *Global Yellow Pages v Promedia Directories Pte Ltd* [2017] 2 SLR 185, para 15.

[15] Sobel, 'A Taxonomy of Training Data' (n 1) 14–15.

[16] See generally TensorFlow, 'Writing Custom Datasets' (Webpage, 22 December 2022), www.tensorflow.org/datasets/add_dataset.

These are the first three rows of the 'Titanic' dataset popularly used to teach ML.[17] Here they are presented without column names. We could infer what some of the data values signify, but most would be indecipherable to both humans and computers. Dataset providers (and users) imbue meaning to datasets when they append labels and decide what every row represents. The columns (also known as 'features' or variables) which a dataset includes or excludes shapes how the dataset may be used. The Titanic dataset is canonically used for a (human-defined) prediction task which tries to guess who survived the fateful iceberg crash. Thus column 1 contains identification numbers for unique passengers; the second column which comprises ones and zeros encodes whether that passenger survived. So, we know that Passenger 1, Mr Braund, did not.

The other columns carry information deemed relevant for this grim enterprise. For instance, the third column encodes the passenger's ticket class, the column to the right of gender is age, and the next two columns represent the number of siblings/spouses and parents/children the passenger had aboard the Titanic. Notice again that these numbers only gain meaning at the labeller's hands and in the user's eyes – though labellers and users may not see them the same way.

Additionally, ML developers are never obliged to use every variable in a dataset, particularly if a given column provides zero or misleading information for the defined task. Choosing the right variables is a crucial step in the ML process known as 'feature selection'. Algorithms have been developed to automatically perform feature selection through advanced statistical computations that can lead to certain variables being assigned zero or negligible weight by the trained ML algorithm.[18] Yet even with automated feature selection, ML system developers have oversight over the set of features that the algorithm may choose from. Of course, this is in turn constrained by the superset of variables on offer in the dataset to begin with. Variables already there can be readily excluded, but an ML developer who wishes to use a new one has to collect that additional data themselves.

This leads into another important distinction between *datasets* and *databases*. Databases refer to larger stores of data from which particular datasets may be extracted. In practical terms, databases are typically implemented and maintained using specialised database and server architectures. They contain a wide range of data, not all of which would be relevant to a given ML task. Thus databases represent entire 'streams' and 'lakes'; datasets are buckets of water drawn to grow ML systems.[19] This distinction blurs as a dataset gets larger and a database smaller, but it is meaningful to note that ML developers are often working with specific data *subsets* extracted from larger databases, possibly maintained by others, and typically have to craft specific requests in a structured database query language to obtain the exact columns and

[17] Kaggle, 'Titanic – Machine Learning from Disaster' (Webpage), www.kaggle.com/competitions/titanic/overview.

[18] See generally R Tibshirani, 'Regression Shrinkage and Selection via the Lasso: A Retrospective' (2011) 73 *Journal of the Royal Statistical Society: Series B (Statistical Methodology)* 273.

[19] See generally F Ravat and Y Zhao, 'Data Lakes: Trends and Perspectives' in S Hartmann et al (eds), *Database and Expert Systems Applications*, Lecture Notes in Computers Science 11706 (Cham, Springer, 2019), doi.org/10.1007/978-3-030-27615-7_23.

rows desired. Thus, 'providers' should be understood broadly to include both dataset and database creators.

B. Datasets in Practice

How datasets feature in practical ML pipelines will be illustrated using two case studies. First consider ImageNet, a dataset of labelled images published by Deng et al in 2009.[20] Although ImageNet was not the only open-source ML image dataset at the time, when published it claimed to be the largest, most diverse, and most accurate one in existence. Originally it comprised 3.2 million images illustrating 5,247 concepts;[21] presently it covers 14.2 million images across 21,841 concepts.[22] To compile this large dataset economically, researchers programmed software scripts to search for each concept across various search engines and downloaded the resulting images. These 'candidate images' were then labelled by Amazon Mechanical Turks (AMTs) – unnamed human online workers paid minute amounts for simple menial tasks.[23] Each image was labelled by multiple AMTs. Only images reaching a specified level of label consensus were added to the dataset.

ImageNet's popularity skyrocketed after Krizhevsky et al demonstrated in 2012 that computer vision models trained using a 1.2 million image subset of ImageNet significantly improved the state-of-the-art.[24] Krizhevsky and colleagues used the images without any further pre-processing or checks except for down-sampling them to standard dimensions. Eventually ImageNet became a standard plug-and-play dataset for developing and testing computer vision algorithms.[25] It was recently described as 'the most influential dataset of the modern era of deep learning in computer vision'.[26] Such influence is not confined to academia. While ImageNet's terms technically preclude commercial use, there is evidence that algorithms built with ImageNet and other similar open-source datasets are being distributed commercially.[27]

[20] J Deng et al, 'ImageNet: A Large-Scale Hierarchical Image Database' (2009) *IEEE Conference on Computer Vision and Pattern Recognition* 248, doi.org/10.1109/CVPR.2009.5206848.

[21] ibid 248.

[22] Stanford Vision Lab, 'About ImageNet' (Webpage, 2020), www.image-net.org/about.php.

[23] Sorokin and Forsyth proposed an optimal price of US$3/hour for image labelling: A Sorokin and D Forsyth, 'Utility Data Annotation with Amazon Mechanical Turk' (2008) *IEEE Computer Society Conference on Computer Vision and Pattern Recognition Workshops* 1, 2, https://doi.org/10.1109/CVPRW.2008.4562953.

[24] D Gershgorn, 'The Data that Transformed AI Research – and Possibly the World' (*Quartz*, 26 July 2017), qz.com/1034972/the-data-that-changed-the-direction-of-ai-research-and-possibly-the-world.

[25] The original ImageNet paper has been cited 49,541 times according to Google Scholar. See Deng et al, 'Imagenet: A large-Scale Hierarchical Image Database' (n 20).

[26] K Yang et al, 'Towards Fairer Datasets: Filtering and Balancing the Distribution of the People Subtree in the ImageNet Hierarchy' (2020) *Proceedings of the 2020 Conference on Fairness, Accountability, and Transparency* 547, 547, doi.org/10.1145/3351095.3375709.

[27] K Peng et al, 'Mitigating Dataset Harms Requires Stewardship: Lessons from 1000 Papers' (2021) *Proceedings of the Neural Information Processing Systems Track on Datasets and Benchmarks*, 5–6, doi.org/10.48550/arXiv.2108.02922; G Rajbahadur et al, 'Can I Use this Publicly Available Dataset to Build Commercial AI Software? – A Case Study on Publicly Available Image Datasets' (2022) *ACM Transactions on Software Engineering Methodology*, arxiv.org/abs/2111.02374.

ImageNet exemplifies standard data practices in academic and commercial ML development: a dataset is compiled by one group of academic researchers or commercial developers and published online with varying licence restrictions. Others then re-use the dataset, often though not always without further checks, to train ML algorithms for myriad purposes, including purposes beyond the dataset's intended scope[28] and licensing limitations.[29] The dataset could also be republished as part of a larger 'derivative' dataset.[30] Over time, datasets which are more accessible, useful, or both become standard benchmarks that new work in the field is expected to address.[31]

While this practice efficiently avoids the costs of re-compiling data, ML researchers have questioned the unquestioned re-use of such 'canonical' datasets.[32] This is especially in contexts where, and for purposes which, these datasets were not meant to be used.[33] In 2018, ImageNet's maintainers began a systematic fairness review of the dataset.[34] Access to the ImageNet data was disabled while the study was underway.[35] The study concluded that the dataset contained 1,593 'unsafe' concept labels (out of 2,832), included images for what should have been non-imageable concepts (such as 'philanthropist'), and lacked representativeness across gender, skin colour and age.[36] Perhaps most problematic was how ImageNet had contained images purporting to depict persons who were 'losers', 'failures' and 'perverts' – amongst numerous other slurs and misogynistic terms.[37] Resultantly, 600,040 images were deleted from ImageNet before the dataset was re-published.[38] Around the same time, an 80-million image dataset published by MIT researchers was taken down after anonymous researchers identified multiple offensive images and derogatory labels within it.[39] To be sure, this chapter is not primarily concerned with the (important) issue of algorithmic bias.[40] The point rather is to demonstrate the scope for errors, both factual and ethical, in ML datasets – even those which are widely used in research and commerce.

These issues are pertinent given the recent trend towards 'foundation' or 'general purpose' models: large ML models, often developed by large research labs using huge datasets and vast amounts of compute, which downstream developers can finetune

[28] B Koch et al, 'Reduced, Reused and Recycled: The Life of a Dataset in Machine Learning Research' (2021) 1 *Proceedings of the Neural Information Processing Systems Track on Datasets and Benchmarks* 1.

[29] Rajbahadur, 'Can I use this Publicly Available Dataset to Build Commercial AI Software?' (n 27).

[30] Peng et al, 'Mitigating Dataset Harms Requires Stewardship' (n 27) 2.

[31] It remains customary to benchmark computer vision models on ImageNet. See, eg, recent work by Google researchers: J Yu et al, 'CoCa: Contrastive Captioners Are Image-Text Foundation Models' (2022) 8 *Transactions on Machine Learning Research* 1. See also Papers with Code, 'Image Classification on ImageNet: Leaderboard' (Webpage), paperswithcode.com/sota/image-classification-on-imagenet.

[32] Koch et al, 'Reduced, Reused and Recycled' (n 28).

[33] I Raji et al, 'AI and the Everything in the Whole Wide World Benchmark' (2021) *Proceedings of the Neural Information Processing Systems Track on Datasets and Benchmarks*, arxiv.org/abs/2111.15366.

[34] Yang et al, 'Towards Fairer Datasets' (n 26).

[35] ibid.

[36] ibid 548.

[37] K Crawford and T Paglen, 'Excavating AI: The Politics of Images in Machine Learning Training Sets' (2021) 36 *AI & Society* 1105, 1110.

[38] Yang et al, 'Towards Fairer Datasets' (n 26).

[39] A Torralba et al, '80 Million Tiny Images' (Webpage, 29 June 2020), groups.csail.mit.edu/vision/TinyImages/.

[40] On how anti-discrimination laws may regulate ML datasets see Hacker, 'A Legal Framework for AI Training Data' (n 1) 271–76.

towards a wide range of tasks using the (presumably) smaller datasets available to them.[41] Foundation models are typified by the Generative Pre-trained Transformer (GPT) series of language models first published by OpenAI in 2018. Each successive GPT version significantly pushed the natural language processing state-of-the-art and was received with much fanfare. This was especially true for GPT's latest incarnation – ChatGPT – which has received significant media and academia coverage.[42]

Despite architectural and dataset differences, the GPTs are generally developed through a similar two-stage process. First, a vast amount of text is downloaded from the internet and fed unlabelled into a large neural network calibrated with a standard language modelling objective.[43] This process is called 'pre-training'. For GPT1, OpenAI used a pre-existing dataset of 11,038 freely available e-books compiled by Zhu and colleagues.[44] For GPT2, OpenAI built their own 'WebText' dataset by scraping the text of all pages hyperlinked in Reddit posts with a least three 'karma'.[45] GPT3 was pre-trained on a huge corpus derived from merging five different internet-sourced text datasets and amounting to 500 billion tokens[46] in total. Eighty per cent of the tokens originated from a selected subset of the CommonCrawl (a dataset comprising substantially the entire written internet),[47] filtered based on similarity to the other four datasets – WebText, a corpus of English language Wikipedia, and two corpora of internet-based books corpora.[48]

Second, the 'pre-trained' network is 'finetuned' for specific tasks using a separate dataset of text-answer pairs labelled for that task. To illustrate, if we wanted a GPT model which classifies court judgments by topics,[49] we would take the pre-trained model and finetune it on a dataset of judgment texts and their topics. OpenAI provides

[41] R Bommasani et al, 'On the Opportunities and Risks of Foundation Models' (Report, Centre for Research on Foundation Models & Stanford Institute for Human-Centred Artificial Intelligence, 2021); L Edwards, 'Regulating AI in Europe: Four Problems and Four Solutions' (Policy paper, Ada Lovelace Institute, 2022) 6.

[42] See, eg, C Vallance, 'ChatGPT: New AI Chatbot has Everyone Talking to it' (*BBC*, 22 Dec 2022), www.bbc.com/news/technology-63861322; K Roose, 'How ChatGPT Kicked Off an A.I. Arms Race' *New York Times* (New York, 3 Feb 2023), www.nytimes.com/2023/02/03/technology/chatgpt-openai-artificial-intelligence.html; D Bartz, 'As ChatGPT's Popularity Explodes, U.S. Lawmakers Take an Interest' (*Reuters*, 13 Feb 2023), www.reuters.com/technology/chatgpts-popularity-explodes-us-lawmakers-take-an-interest-2023-02-13/.

[43] That is, the network is optimised to predict the next word in a given sequence of words.

[44] Y Zhu et al, Reuters (2015) *IEEE International Conference on Computer Vision* (ICCV) 19, www.cv-foundation.org/openaccess/content_iccv_2015/papers/Zhu_Aligning_Books_and_ICCV_2015_paper.pdf.

[45] Similar to likes on Facebook or Twitter.

[46] This is a technical term for atomic language units such as (most commonly) words as well as punctuations and numbers.

[47] See generally Common Crawl, 'Common Crawl' (Webpage), commoncrawl.org.

[48] T Brown et al, 'Language Models Are Few-Shot Learners' (2020) *Proceedings of the 34th International Conference on Neural Information Processing Systems* 1877. Brown and colleagues do not specifically identify any Wikipedia dataset, version or date so it is impossible to definitively tell which dataset was used. They may have used an existing dataset such as a 2008 copy of English Wikipedia published by Y Xu and Mirella Lapata, 'Weakly Supervised Domain Detection' (2019) 7 *Transactions of the Association for Computational Linguistics* 581, or they may have downloaded a more recent copy from Wikipedia's own data dumps, available at Wikimedia Foundation, 'Index of /enwiki/' (Webpage) https://dumps.wikimedia.org/enwiki/. As Wikipedia is a living encyclopaedia, these data dumps are updated every few weeks. Problems raised by the lack of precision and care surrounding ML datasets are explored below in sections III and IV.

[49] A task explored in J Soh et al, 'Legal Area Classification: A Comparative Study of Text Classifiers on Singapore Supreme Court Judgments' (2019) *Proceedings of the Natural Legal Language Processing Workshop* 67, doi.org/10.48550/arXiv.1904.06470.

paid Application Programmable Interface access for finetuning GPT[50] and recently concluded talks to widen its commercial offerings.[51] GPT has been finetuned for hundreds of commercial applications[52] including lawyering.[53]

Foundation models like GPT are worth attention not only because they represent the leading edge of AI performance. More importantly, they herald a paradigm shift in how ML systems are commercially developed and supplied. Conventionally, the same party would generally be responsible for preparing the dataset, training the algorithm, and deploying the finished system. For foundation models, different actors could be building the pre-training/finetuning datasets/models. Thus, foundation models are like white-labelled spirits produced by large multinational distilleries for smaller craft distilleries to finish, brand and bottle as they please. Carelessness could seep into the datasets used to brew them at varying points in this process.

The ImageNet and GPT case studies yield three key insights. First, 'AI developers' are not one monolithic entity. Even before foundation models, it was common for datasets developed by one group to be used by another; with foundation models, dataset and model development roles even more sharply delineated. Thus, as Edwards notes in her critique of the original draft AI Act, AI products are generally 'not produced by a single organisation, but involve a complex web of procurement, outsourcing, re-use of data from a variety of sources, etc'.[54]

Distinguishing between dataset and model providers is especially important because those whose involvements are limited to data compilation (eg the AMTs hired to created ImageNet, the Mechanical Turk platform, and ImageNet's maintainers themselves) cannot be labelled 'providers' of ML systems which others develop using their datasets. This is despite the crucial role they play: but for ImageNet, many computer vision models may not exist today, and but for problems in the ImageNet data, these models may not be as biased as they have been shown to be.[55] However, this distinction is not often made.[56] Even Pasquale, whose work rightly spotlights 'the use of inaccurate or inappropriate data in training sets for machine learning',[57] ultimately recommends duties for 'developers of AI' broadly speaking.[58]

Indeed, the notion of 'dataset providers' should itself be unpacked given the differing nature of the parties involved at each stage of the ML dataset lifecycle. Providers of large datasets used for pre-training foundation models range from well-funded tech

[50] For technical process see OpenAI, 'Fine-tuning' (Webpage), beta.openai.com/docs/guides/fine-tuning.

[51] OpenAI, 'OpenAI and Microsoft Extend Partnership' (Blog post, 23 January 2023), openai.com/blog/openai-and-microsoft-extend-partnership/.

[52] A catalogue of examples may be found at Apideck, 'GPT-3 Demo' (Website), gpt3demo.com/.

[53] '"My AI Will Talk to Your AI" as DoNotPay Joins the GPT-3 Fray' (*Artificial Lawyer*, 12 December 2022), www.artificiallawyer.com/2022/12/12/my-ai-will-talk-to-your-ai-as-donotpay-joins-the-gpt-3-fray. Now see also S Sundar, 'DoNotPay's CEO says Threat of "Jail for 6 Months" Means Plan to Debut AI "Robot Lawyer" in Courtroom is on Ice' (*Business Insider*, 26 January 2023).

[54] Edwards, 'Regulating AI in Europe' (n 41) 6.

[55] R Steed and A Caliskan, 'Image Representations Learned With Unsupervised Pre-Training Contain Human-like Biases' (2021) *Proceedings of the 2021 ACM Conference on Fairness, Accountability, and Transparency* 701, doi.org/10.1145/3442188.3445932.

[56] On the original draft AI Act's failure to sufficiently distinguish different types of AI providers, see Edwards, 'Regulating AI in Europe' (n 41) 6–10.

[57] Pasquale, 'Data-Informed Duties' (n 1) 1919.

[58] ibid 1937–39.

companies (in the case of WebText) to large research teams (in the case of ImageNet or the CommonCrawl). Meanwhile, finetuning datasets are more likely to be (albeit not exclusively) compiled by smaller downstream providers that rely heavily on resources provided by the former.[59] Painting them with the same legal brush would be akin to expecting all companies, large or small, private or public, listed or unlisted to adhere to the same corporate reporting and governance obligations. Commercial law treats these entities very differently for good reason. While tort law does not generally discriminate by company size,[60] duties of care are particularly sensitive to the specific role that an organisation plays in the supply chain.[61]

Second, there is real potential for careless datasets to harm.[62] The standard practice of re-using datasets without significant independent verification is likely to persist, despite mounting scrutiny,[63] simply because of economic cost savings. Moreover, ML is advancing rapidly, both in the sense that the technology continues to develop at a remarkable pace, and in the sense that ML systems are encroaching on more and more domains of human activity. This includes domains such as medicine, transport, finance and law where ML systems trained on unrepresentative or otherwise problematic data could rather foreseeably cause physical and economic harm. For example, Pasquale details how clinical decision support systems trained on standard healthcare datasets could produce questionable recommendations, particularly for marginalised and under-represented groups. Because poverty typically correlates with bad treatment outcomes, ML systems trained on historical hospital data may wrongly recommend against treating the poor.[64] Likewise, Caruana et al describe how medical ML systems built in the mid-90s for predicting pneumonia death risks 'incorrectly learn[t] that asthma lowers risk, when in fact asthmatics have much higher risk'.[65] This 'reflected a true pattern in the training data', but only because asthmatic pneumonia patients were treated *more* aggressively and directly admitted to intensive care.[66] This point is worth underscoring: even though the dataset was *factually* correct, it remained unsuitable for training medical prescription systems without more because it omitted a crucial variable (treatment levels) which needed to be controlled for.

[59] Edwards, 'Regulating AI in Europe' (n 41) 6.

[60] Though 'deep pockets' arguments are occasionally (and controversially) made especially in the context of vicarious liability. See, eg, J Bell, 'The Basis of Vicarious Liability' (2013) 72 *Cambridge Law Journal* 17, 18–19.

[61] As demonstrated in *TV Media Pte Ltd v De Cruz Andrea Heidi* [2004] 3 SLR(R) 543, where the victim of a liver injury caused by questionable slimming pills sued the pills' importer, their distributor, as well as the freelance agent who sold her the pills, but not the manufacturer (who was out of jurisdiction). Duty was only established against the former two entities. See also below section IV.

[62] See also Pasquale, 'Data-Informed Duties' (n 1); Hacker, 'A Legal Framework for AI Training Data' (n 1).

[63] See, eg, Raji et al, 'AI and the Everything in the Whole Wide World Benchmark' (n 33); B Hutchinson et al, 'Towards Accountability for Machine Learning Datasets: Practices from Software Engineering and Infrastructure' (2021) *Proceedings of the 2021 ACM Conference on Fairness, Accountability, and Transparency* 560 doi.org/10.1145/3442188.3445918.

[64] Pasquale, 'Data-Informed Duties' (n 1) 1923–25. See also A Selbst, 'Negligence and AI's Human Users' (2020) 100 *Boston University Law Review* 1315, 1334–36.

[65] R Caruana et al, 'Intelligible Models for HealthCare: Predicting Pneumonia Risk and Hospital 30-Day Readmission' (2015) *Proceedings of the 12th ACM SIGKDD International Conference on Knowledge Discovery and Data Mining* 1721, 1721.

[66] ibid.

Likewise, in the financial context, Blattner and Nelson found that ML algorithms developed for credit scoring are less accurate for traditionally under-served groups. They attribute this primarily to how data for low income and/or minority groups are typically sparser, more likely to record instances of past defaults, and less likely to contain information on diverse loan types.[67] False credit scores could easily damage one's financial position as well as social reputation.[68] Meanwhile, Selbst worries that financial robo-advisors (software empowered to suggest or make investment decisions) 'may lose all of someone's money because of bad data, a bug, or a runaway feedback loop'.[69] Thus, Hacker identifies several dataset quality and discrimination risks which are insufficiently covered by existing (EU) law.[70]

III. The Case for Dataset Duties

These observations suggest that tortious duties targeted at dataset *providers* should be seriously considered. This is especially so as the effectiveness of existing data quality and representativeness obligations centred on ML developers, such as those set out in the proposed AI Act and the General Data Protection Regulation, is limited where the ML models and datasets are developed by two unrelated parties. To illustrate, suppose A carelessly publishes a problematic dataset which B uses to train an ML system that resultantly harms V. Even assuming it clear that B owes V a tortious (or statutory) duty of care,[71] B may be able to defeat liability on other grounds. In particular, B might argue that their reliance on A's dataset was reasonable given standard ML industry practices. Assuming this argument succeeds[72] and A does not personally owe V a duty, then B would owe a duty they did not breach while A would breach a duty they technically did not owe.

We might think of precluding B from raising reasonable reliance by holding that B's duty extends to *personally* ensuring dataset quality. This runs into two problems. First, it does not impose duties on the cheapest-cost avoider.[73] A, who compiles and publishes the dataset, is naturally in a better position to find and rectify defects therein. This is especially common in situations where dataset providers are large research/corporate

[67] L Blattner and S Nelson, 'How Costly is Noise? Data and Disparities in Consumer Credit' (*ArXiv*, 16 May 2021) 3–5, 13, arxiv.org/abs/2105.07554.

[68] ibid 3.

[69] Selbst, 'Negligence and AI's Human Users' (n 64) 1337.

[70] See generally Hacker, 'A Legal Framework for AI Training Data' (n 1).

[71] Where B deals as a business and V as a consumer, multiple channels may, depending on jurisdiction, be available for holding B liable. These include actions founded on manufacturer or products liability, consumer protection statutes and contract. Products liability for AI systems is clearly contemplated by the EU's recently proposed Products Liability Directive: Commission, 'Proposal for a Directive of the European Parliament and of the Council on Liability for Defective Products' COM (2022) 495 final.

[72] Nothing is implied here about the likelihood of success as this chapter focuses on duty and not breach. Nonetheless it is worth emphasising that industry standards, while relevant, are not conclusive of tortious standards. See, eg, *JSI Shipping (S) Pte Ltd v Teofoongwonglcloong (a firm)* [2007] 4 SLR(R) 460 at para 34, though *cf Bolam v Friern Hospital Management Committee* [1957] 1 WLR 582.

[73] G Calabresi, *The Costs of Accidents: A Legal and Economic Analysis* (New Haven CT, Yale University Press, 1970).

teams while model developers are small downstream developers. B, who effectively insures V against defects in A's dataset, may not have the bargaining power necessary to demand contractual indemnities, etc, from A in return. Indeed, since ML datasets are often provided for free, A may not have contracted with B to begin with. Therefore, the usual strategy of centralising the formal incidence of liability around one entity (system developers) and expecting them to pass effective incidence downstream to those actually responsible for the harm (dataset developers)[74] may have limited effectiveness. The main effect would be to disincentive the marketing of ML systems by developers not prepared to undertake the costs of verifying the dataset,[75] and dataset providers – the source of the problem – would still have no incentives to take care. Second, a duty to ensure the work quality of others is strict – both in the sense of being onerous to fulfil and of being close to strict liability. It approaches the non-delegable duties that courts have been cautious to extend.[76]

Imposing dataset duties would also be logical from an economic perspective. Textbook law and economics holds that laws need not meddle in markets where transaction costs are low and information complete. In such cases whether courts impose a negligence rule (by finding duties of care) or a no-liability rule (by finding otherwise) the societally optimal outcome would result from private ordering by the parties involved (who would, by definition, have superior cost-benefit information relative to courts and regulators).[77] The market for ML datasets is quite the opposite. The sheer scale of the datasets and models involved mean that ML systems are notoriously opaque even to their own developers.[78] Moreover, the standard Coase formulation involves *victims* negotiating preferable outcomes with injurers. B may already have problems negotiating with A; V's bargaining position and information asymmetries would only be worse.[79]

ML opacity also suggests that imposing *regulatory* dataset standards, while undoubtedly important, would not be optimal if not supplemented with liability rules. As Shavell notes, to properly calibrate regulatory standards, regulators should ideally have *ex ante* information on the extent and risks of potential harm and how these vary with

[74] For instance, the UK's Automated and Electric Vehicles Act 2018 (c 18) makes motor insurers liable in the first instance (section 2) but empowers them to then claim against the person(s) responsible for the accident (section 5). Elish identifies and critiques this typical strategy of establishing what they term 'moral crumple zones' in M Elish, 'Moral Crumple Zones: Cautionary Tales in Human-Robot Interaction' (2019) 5 *Engaging Science, Technology, and Society* 40.

[75] To illustrate why this may not be a good thing: suppose an ML system can be made that delivers five units of benefit to society, but only if the dataset is properly checked. Checking would cost the dataset's developers four units. The system developer may also do this, but it would cost them six units instead. The system would benefit society on aggregate and should be built, but only if the dataset developers bear the effective costs of precaution. A liability regime which effectively requires system developers to bear the costs would (even assuming all five units can be captured by the system developers as revenue) lead to the system not being built at all.

[76] *New South Wales v Lepore* [2003] HCA 4, (2003) 212 CLR 511, para 256–269; *Leichhardt Municipal Council v Montgomery* [2007] HCA 6, (2007) 230 CLR 22, para 104. See also *Management Corporation Strata Title Plan No 3322 v Tiong Aik Construction Pte Ltd* [2016] 4 SLR 521, paras 62–63.

[77] R Coase, 'The Problem of Social Cost' (1960) 3 *Journal of Law and Economics* 1.

[78] See generally J Burrell, 'How the Machine "Thinks": Understanding Opacity in Machine Learning Algorithms' (2016) 3 *Big Data & Society* 1.

[79] Selbst notes that epistemic limitations on knowing when ML predictions will be correct mean users must often decide whether to use the system 'almost as an article of faith': Selbst, 'Negligence and AI's Human Users' (n 64) 1339.

precaution and activity levels.[80] But ML opacity obfuscates assessments of exactly how accurate, relevant, representative, error-free and complete[81] datasets must be to efficiently minimise the harms while maximising the benefits of ML systems. Taken too literally, such standards 'can almost never be entirely fulfilled in any large-scale AI training data set'[82] and would therefore overregulate. Moreover, despite the growing litany of proposed ML performance and fairness metrics, ML systems often behave differently under laboratory test conditions vis-à-vis actual field deployments. State regulations, which typically take the form of prescribed ex ante checks, can therefore only go so far in preventing ML systems from causing real world harm. ML operators and users must be incentivised to take due care even when relying on ML systems and/or datasets which have passed all regulatory checks.

To be sure, this may be achieved either through enacting a statutory cause of private action or by recognising a common law duty; the preceding argument does not prefer one to the other. The narrow point is that regulatory standards should be supplemented by a private right to sue for compensation. Even under a statutory scheme, the courts will generally[83] be required to interpret and thereby substantiate statutory standards. Indeed, given the opacity and uncertainty surrounding ML systems and their likely harms, existing standards for ML systems have typically been framed broadly in terms of, for instance, 'fairness', 'accountability' and 'transparency' requirements.[84] Similarly, the proposed AI Act stipulates that ML datasets should be subject to 'appropriate data governance and management practices' (Art 10(2)) and be 'relevant, representative, free of errors and complete' (Art 10(3)). Open-textured terms like 'appropriate' and 'relevant' are suitably adaptive to the unknowns that ML datasets entail but would evidently need to be given more specific and substantial meaning if they are to be operationalised as legal requirements. Thus, tort (and more broadly speaking private) law and its flexibility would arguably still have a role to play even under a primarily statutory scheme.

One objection to dataset duties that the above implicates is that courts may also find it difficult to optimally set negligence standards when faced with opaque ML systems. Even assuming breach was not at issue, proving causation between dataset errors and the ultimate harm may be extremely difficult given the difficulty with pinning any errant ML system behaviour to specific defects in the system's development process. These difficulties are well known and well acknowledged here. Nonetheless, difficulties with proving breach and causation in fact should not preclude the imposition of duties in law. The duty of care which doctors owe to patients is unassailable even though it is notoriously difficult to establish either medical breach (especially where the conventional

[80] Shavell, 'Liability for Harm versus Regulation of Safety' (n 5) 359–61.

[81] Borrowing words from Art 10(3)(1) of the AI Act.

[82] Hacker, 'A Legal Framework for AI Training Data' (n 1) 298.

[83] Unless a no-fault liability regime is created. Some commentators have argued for the superiority of no-fault liability for automated vehicles, but a full consideration of this radical shift away from the tort system is beyond this chapter's scope. See KS Abraham and RL Rabin, 'Automated Vehicles and Manufacturer Responsibility for Accidents: A New Legal Regime for a New Era' (2019) 105 *Virginia Law Review* 127; S Shavell, 'On the Redesign of Accident Liability for the World of Autonomous Vehicles' (2020) 49 *Journal of Legal Studies* 243.

[84] For an international review of AI governance principles, see J Fjeld et al, 'Principled Artificial Intelligence: Mapping Consensus in Ethical and Rights-based Approaches to Principles for AI' (Berkman Klein Center Research Publication No 2020–1, 15 Jan 2020).

Bolam[85] approach applies)[86] or causation (especially for diseases with low survival rates).[87]

Any argument for imposing new obligations on technology developers is also bound to run into the standard objection that the additional compliance and quality assurance costs involved would dampen innovation. The straight counter-objection is that imposing additional costs for those who create (and profit from introducing) risks to society is precisely the point. Chilling effects on innovation cannot preclude all legal obligations – the real question is how the costs of harm should be balanced against the benefits of innovation. More concretely, it is not clear that subjecting dataset providers to duties of reasonable care should be onerous enough to price them out from innovation, especially if these duties are carefully scoped and calibrated.[88] Any excuse that ML-scale datasets are 'too big to inspect' should be scrutinised. It is true that manually verifying and removing errors from datasets with millions of datapoints would be prohibitively tedious. But we have also seen (recall ImageNet) how relatively simple and automated investigations could surface glaring errors which could, in turn, be not too difficult to rectify (recall how ImageNet simply deleted the affected images). After all, negligence does not require duty-bearers to take every possible precaution, only those which are reasonable given the relevant costs and benefits.

IV. Dataset Duties in Existing Law

The legal instruments closest to considering dataset duties are the EU's proposed AI Act and AI Liability Directive. However, as alluded to above, the Act's data quality obligations are regulatory in nature – breaches trigger fines, not compensation[89] – and are primarily targeted at (high-risk) ML *system*, not dataset, providers.[90] Although the Directive clearly contemplates civil suits for ML-related damages, its main effect is to allow causal links between an ML system provider's non-compliance with the AI Act and outputs produced by the system to be rebuttably presumed.[91] This goes towards causality, not the existence of a duty to begin with, and victims are still expected to prove that the system's output caused the harm.[92] Further, because 'fault' under the Directive is defined exhaustively in terms of AI Act breaches,[93] it cannot be equated with fault in

[85] *Bolam v Friern Hospital Management Committee* (n 72).

[86] *Rogers v Whitaker* (1992) 175 CLR 479, paras 11–12. A critical history of *Bolam* is provided in K Amirthalingam, 'Medical Negligence and Patient Autonomy: Bolam Rules in Malaysia and Singapore – Revisited' (2015) 27 *Singapore Academy of Law Journal* 666, 668–71.

[87] Famously, *Gregg v Scott* [2005] 2 AC 176.

[88] See below section IV on how the extent of such duties could be properly limited.

[89] AI Act, Art 71.

[90] On the AI Act scope, see Art 2.

[91] AI Liability Directive (n 8) Art 4.

[92] ibid Art 4(1)(c).

[93] ibid Art 4(2) which governs claims against high risk AI providers states that the requirements to presume causality shall be met 'only' where the AI Act has been demonstrably breached. The word 'only' is strangely absent from Art 4(3) which governs claims against high risk AI users. It is unclear if this omission is intentional. Preamble [26] to the Directive clarifies that for 'the potential fault of providers or persons subject to the obligations of a provider pursuant to [the AI Act] is established **only** through a noncompliance with such requirements' (emphasis added).

general tort law. The Directive therefore 'does not create or harmonise the duties of care or the liability' of entities regulated under the AI Act and other applicable law.[94]

To be sure, the AI Act and AI Liability Directive would likely shape how national courts within the EU analyse tortious duties for ML systems and datasets. A Brussels effect may also arise. Nonetheless, in Australia and Singapore there do not appear to be any statutory, policy, or case law instruments discussing dataset duties.[95] Australia's AI Ethics Framework[96] and Singapore's Model AI Governance Framework[97] are voluntary regimes. While both encourage organisations to take data quality and governance seriously,[98] the very fact that they are voluntary suggests that organisations are thought of as being under no strict legal obligation to do so. It is thus useful to consider how far dataset duties may arise under each jurisdiction's doctrinal approach to duty of care.

Let us begin with the basic case where A carelessly compiles a dataset which A themselves uses to train an ML system that physically harms V. To concretise ideas, suppose A is an automated vehicle (AV) developer whose vehicles use computer vision systems to avoid pedestrians. A deploys a fleet of human-driven vehicles equipped with cameras programmed to capture road junctions. AMTs are then employed to 'label all pedestrians in the footage'. Given these instructions, the AMTs only flag people crossing the road on foot – those on bicycles, wheelchairs, strollers, etc are ignored. A does not check their dataset before using it to build production software. One of its AVs crashes into V while V was cycling across the road.[99]

Because A developed the dataset, algorithm and vehicle, this case should lead to a straightforward duty finding. A manufactures a product (vehicle) known to be dangerous,[100] and V, while not a direct consumer of that product, falls within a class of persons (pedestrians) likely to be in contact with it. Negligence duties are well established in such contexts. In the classic case of *Escola v Coca Cola*, where a defective bottle exploded in a waitress' hand, duty was uncontested even though the plaintiff was not the product's intended consumer. In deciding for the plaintiff based on *res ipsa loquitur*, Gibson CJ held that the manufacturer 'had exclusive control over both the charging and inspection of the bottles'[101] and that 'sound and properly prepared bottles … do not ordinarily explode when carefully handled'.[102] The case for duty in our hypothetical should indeed

[94] AI Liability Directive (n 8) 10.

[95] Based on standard legal database searches conducted by the author and two senior law student assistants.

[96] Department of Industry, Science and Resources, 'Australia's AI Ethics Principles' (Policy Framework, 7 November 2019), www.industry.gov.au/publications/australias-artificial-intelligence-ethics-framework.

[97] Info-communications Media Development Authority and Personal Data Protection Commission Singapore, 'Model Artificial Intelligence Governance Framework: Second Edition' (Policy Framework, 21 January 2020), www.pdpc.gov.sg/-/media/files/pdpc/pdf-files/resource-for-organisation/ai/sgmodelaigovframework2.pdf.

[98] ibid 38; Department of Industry, Science and Resources, 'Australia's AI Ethics Principles' (n 96).

[99] This hypothetical is inspired by but not identical to the facts surrounding the world's first AV fatality. See S Levin and J Wong, 'Self-driving Uber Kills Arizona Woman in First Fatal Crash Involving Pedestrian' *The Guardian* (19 March 2018), www.theguardian.com/technology/2018/mar/19/uber-self-driving-car-kills-woman-arizona-tempe.

[100] Vehicles may be the most dangerous product known to tort law. See generally R Nader, *Unsafe at Any Speed: The Designed-In Dangers of the American Automobile* (New York, Grossman Publishers, 1965). A review of recent AV fatalities is provided in J Soh, 'Towards a Control-Centric Account of Tort Liability for Automated Vehicles' (2021) 26 *Torts Law Journal* 221, 238–40.

[101] *Escola v Coca-Cola Bottling Co* 150 P 2d 436 (1944), para 9.

[102] ibid para 5.

be stronger as A's product does not even go through V's hands. A alone controls where and how its AVs are developed and deployed[103] while V has little knowledge or control over the same. Thus, it is eminently foreseeable that carelessness in developing AVs would harm other road users.[104] Further, liability can be determinately limited to road users, and a duty which promotes traffic safety and victim compensation is consistent with the goals of motor accident law.[105] Sound and properly developed AVs should not ordinarily crash into cyclists; if the use of ML systems means this sort of catastrophic failure cannot be ruled out, then it is even more pressing for AVs manufacturers to take care. Therefore, a duty of care should arise whether analysed under the salient features approach[106] or Singapore's *Spandeck*[107] framework.

The more complex (and interesting) case arises where A relies on a dataset B had created and published freely. Suppose B is, as usual, a reputed research organisation (eg the ML department of a technology giant or a top university). The reasoning above would likely still support a duty for A as the manufacturer. The case for B is less clear. It is still arguable that B has published a potentially dangerous thing, given the increasingly documented concerns around defective ML datasets, and that V, while not a direct, intended consumer of the dataset, was ultimately harmed by it. However, V may not fall clearly within a class of persons foreseeably harmed. The crux is whether B should reasonably have foreseen the dataset being used for training, and thereby influencing the risks of harm posed to society by, AVs. To illustrate, Berkeley's 'DeepDrive' and Oxford's 'RobotCar' datasets are both targeted at AV developers. Indeed, specialised workshops are conducted to encourage AV developers to use the datasets for developing and benchmarking their algorithms.[108] Given the standard practice of dataset re-use, including by commercial parties, it is certainly arguable that carelessly compiling such datasets could foreseeably harm pedestrians. The case would be weaker for general datasets like ImageNet, though it could hold if the dataset becomes canonical for developing algorithms in the AV context.

Even if foreseeability could be established, however, B's relationship with V is intermediated by A. Indeed, in ML pipelines 'A' could represent a long chain of downstream developers: A uses the dataset to build a foundation model which C finetunes for D to include in an app installed in E's hardware. Apart from the lack of causal proximity, B can argue that they do not control the risks of harm. Although they determine the contents and availability of the dataset, they do not control how it is used and by whom. Each downstream developer can (and perhaps should) be expected to independently mitigate the risks of harm through checking if the dataset is fit for purpose or other

[103] The possible objection that AV manufacturers do not control their vehicles is debunked in Soh, 'Towards a Control-Centric Account of Tort Liability for Automated Vehicles' (n 100) 230–37.

[104] ibid 240.

[105] On the interaction between tort law and motor accident statutes, see ibid 224–28.

[106] *Caltex Oil (Australia) Pty Ltd v Dredge 'Willemstad'* [1976] HCA 65, (1976) 136 CLR 529; recently reviewed in *Minister for the Environment v Sharma* [2022] FCAFC 35, (2022) 291 FCR 311.

[107] *Spandeck Engineering (S) Pte Ltd v Defence Science & Technology Agency* [2007] 4 SLR(R) 100. Parallels between the two are explored in D Tan, 'The Salient Features of Proximity: Examining the Spandeck Formulation for Establishing a Duty of Care' [2010] *Singapore Journal of Legal Studies* 459.

[108] 'A Diverse Driving Dataset for Heterogeneous Multitask Learning: Challenges' (Dataset, BDD100K, 2022), www.bdd100k.com/#blog; G Pascoe, 'RobotCar Long-Term Autonomy Benchmark' (Webpage, Oxford Robotcar Dataset, 2 June 2017), robotcar-dataset.robots.ox.ac.uk/news/long-term-autonomy-benchmark/.

precautionary measures. As Allsop CJ recently held in the context of the Environment Minister's control over climate change-related harms potentially caused by the approval of the construction of a coal plant, the extent to which risk may be mitigated by intermediaries militates against the defendant having relevant control.[109]

Nonetheless, dataset publishers are not entirely powerless when others put their datasets to dangerous use. As Beach J held in the same case, other entities also having control over the harm does not mean the defendant has none – especially if the causal chain resulting in harm was set in motion by the defendant's positive act.[110] There the Minister's 'positive act of approval' for the coal mines sufficed for Beach J to find control.[111] Here B creates and publishes, not just approves, datasets which are the starting point for any ML endeavour. As mentioned above, dataset publishers can, and often do, stipulate use restrictions for their datasets. Access can be conditional on the user committing to certain (safe) uses. DeepDrive, for instance, may only be downloaded by those who register accounts and accept a click-wrapped licence agreement (that expressly allows commercial use).[112] Conversely, RobotCar datasets are freely downloadable.[113]

To be sure, B cannot realistically preclude users from ignoring these restrictions. However, they can fairly be expected to include standard 'safety information' surrounding their datasets.[114] Further, as with ImageNet and TinyImages, they can always delete and publicly disclaim dangerous datasets. If B puts up a general-purpose dataset not meant for AV development but receives reasonable notice of the dataset being misused for AVs, leaving the dataset accessible as it is without further checks or requiring users to do the same is a choice on B's part.

Another important question is whether dataset duties would be indeterminate. The determinacy of the class of persons likely to be harmed by a dataset turns on its foreseeable uses. The more generally useful a dataset is, and thus the more likely it will be used in unpredicted contexts, the more difficult it would be to envisage who might be harmed by carelessness in its preparation. This difficulty is significantly reduced for datasets targeted at specific contexts, especially those mentioned above. Defective driving datasets could foreseeably harm other road users, defective medical datasets could harm patients, and defective credit scoring datasets could harm loan applicants. The scalability of ML applications might mean the affected class could be very large, but size must be distinguished from determinacy.[115] Indeed, the idea that many could be affected supports finding a duty.

To be sure, holding B liable for harms caused by a system A developed may seem to result in liability of an amount disproportionate to B's contribution to the risks of harm. This may however be mitigated by careful, case-by-case analysis of the factors above so

[109] *Minister for the Environment v Sharma* (n 106) para 335.
[110] ibid paras 634–68.
[111] ibid para 644.
[112] Berkeley DeepDrive, 'Download the Datasets' (Webpage, BDD100K), bdd-data.berkeley.edu/. The licence terms are available at doc.bdd100k.com/license.html.
[113] 'Datasets' (Webpage, Oxford Robotcar Dataset), robotcar-dataset.robots.ox.ac.uk/datasets/.
[114] This accords with growing calls within the ML community for better dataset accountability and documentation. See, eg, Hutchinson, 'Towards Accountability for Machine Learning Datasets' (n 63); A Rogers et al, '"Just What Do You Think You're Doing, Dave?" A Checklist for Responsible Data Use in NLP' (2021) *Findings of the Association for Computational Linguistics* 4821, doi.org/10.48550/arXiv.2109.06598.
[115] *Minister for the Environment v Sharma* (n 106) [713].

that duties only arise where warranted. That is, where B has effective control over the dataset's risks and the resultant harms are of a foreseeable nature and affect a foreseeable class. Other salient features may also be useful control devices. For instance, since datasets are ultimately arrangements of *information*, one who provides data to the world at large without qualification can arguably be said to have assumed responsibility for its quality.[116] This helpfully provides scope for dataset providers to determinately limit their scope of duty by publishing appropriate disclaimers alongside their datasets. Of course, conventional misstatement doctrine limits duties to instances where the *victim* foreseeably relies on the information. Nonetheless, ML dataset publishers should know, and indeed often intend, that downstream developers rely on their datasets for building ML systems. Extending proximity to persons foreseeably harmed by those systems is not a major stretch.

V. Conclusion

As ML systems continue to advance in society, so too would the scope for carelessly compiled datasets to harm. This chapter argued that imposing duties of care on ML dataset providers plugs a liability gap which could arise when ML system providers reasonably rely on datasets provided by another. Such duties would thereby incentivise greater precaution in the preparation of a crucial ML input. Further, after reviewing two practical case studies of ML datasets and pipelines, the chapter sought to demonstrate that existing tort doctrine could encompass such dataset duties. The argument, to be clear, is *not* that all dataset providers should owe all ML victims duties of care. Rather, its goal has been to show that dataset duties are desirable and arguable under existing tort law in certain contexts. Relevant factors include: (a) whether the dataset is meant for general foundational use or targeted at specific contexts; (b) the complexity of the relevant ML supply chain and the data provider's role within it (particularly if they also developed the ML system themselves); and (c) whether the dataset is and could be accompanied by information and limitations on its safe usage. Depending on the specific types of providers, victims, and harms involved, other standard features and factors used by the courts for finding tortious duties may also become relevant.

[116] *Hedley Byrne & Co Ltd v Heller & Partners Ltd* [1964] AC 465; *L Shaddock & Associates Pty Ltd v Parramatta City Council (No 1)* [1981] HCA 59, (1981) 160 CLR 225.

PART V

Remedies for Breaches of Data Rights

14

Private Enforcement of Data Rights Through Direct Rights of Action: A Comparative Review

NORMANN WITZLEB*

I. Introduction

Most data protection statutes establish complaints-based regimes that empower data protection authorities to investigate alleged breaches of data rights and to recommend, or impose, remedial action where a breach has been established. However, an increasing number of privacy or data protection statutes also give a complainant or their representative standing to seek a personal remedy, such as compensation, in court. A provision granting a 'direct right of action' (DRA) is an important additional enforcement mechanism for statutory data rights. It opens an avenue of redress for data subjects where enforcement authorities are unable or unwilling to investigate, or accept, a privacy complaint in administrative proceedings. It turns regulatory requirements under a data protection statute into civil obligations that become enforceable by judicial order. While a DRA is commonly concerned with monetary relief for interferences with data rights, it can also be directed at obtaining other forms of relief, such as injunctions, orders for rectification or erasure of data, or a declaration.

This chapter will provide a comparative review of direct rights of action under major data protection regimes, such as the European Union (EU), the United States (US), China, Canada and Singapore. It will also consider some of the leading cases that have arisen from litigation under such legislation. Important issues to be addressed are the relationship between direct rights of action and administrative enforcement, between direct rights of action and general torts actions (including but not limited to actions for invasion of privacy), the availability of class action mechanisms, and the range and effectiveness of remedies available to claimants. This analysis will provide insights not only for the further developments of direct rights in the jurisdictions under consideration but also inform law reform debate in other countries, such as Australia, that are currently investigating whether, and if so how, to legislate for a direct right of action.

* Associate Professor, The Chinese University of Hong Kong.

II. Direct Rights of Action in Selected Privacy Regimes

A. The European Union and the United Kingdom

The data protection rules in the EU are widely regarded as the international benchmark. This applies increasingly also to the DRA given the burgeoning jurisprudence on damages claims for breaches of its data protection rules. The Data Protection Directive ('the Directive'),[1] the predecessor of the General Data Protection Regulation (GDPR),[2] contained two relevant provisions dealing with individual access to the courts. Article 22 of the Directive guaranteed a 'right of every person to a judicial remedy for any breach of their domestic data rights'. This general protection was supplemented by Art 23(1) of the Directive, which created more specifically a right to compensation by data controllers for damage suffered as a result of unlawful data processing. As the Directive did not create directly applicable law, these claim rights needed to be created in each Member State's domestic laws.[3] This transposition and the interpretation of these provisions resulted in significant divergence between Member States with regard to the availability, scope and functioning of this private right of action.[4] Civil liability was intended to ensure that harm arising from breaches of data protection obligations is compensated and that adequate measures are available to correct any mistakes or wrongdoing.[5] However, a 2013 review put in doubt that this objective was achieved because it identified only 'very few'[6] judicial proceedings for compensation under the Directive.

i. Direct Rights of Action under s 23 of the (Former) Directive: The UK Example

The difficulties with data protection claims in some European jurisdictions can be illustrated by the example of the United Kingdom (UK), where s 13 of the Data Protection Act 1998 (UK) (DPA) purported to transpose Art 23 of the Directive into domestic law. In the UK, it is not uncommon that claimants proceed concurrently under the tort of

[1] Directive 95/46/EC of the European Parliament and of the Council of 24 October 1995 on the protection of individuals with regard to the processing of personal data and on the free movement of such data [1995] OJ L281/31.

[2] Regulation (EU) 2016/679 of the European Parliament and of the Council of 27 April 2016 on the protection of natural persons with regard to the processing of personal data and on the free movement of such data, and repealing Directive 95/46/EC (General Data Protection Regulation or GDPR) [2016] OJ L119/4.

[3] Some Member States also established similar claim rights under domestic law transposing the ePrivacy Directive (Directive 2002/58/EC of the European Parliament and of the Council of 12 July 2022 concerning the processing of personal data and the protection of privacy in the electronic communications sector (Directive on Privacy and Electronic Communications) [2002] OJ L201/37): see, eg, Privacy and Electronic Communications (EC Directive) Regulations (UK) reg 30.

[4] E O'Dell, 'Compensation for Breach of the General Data Protection Regulation' (2017) 40 *Dublin University Law Journal* 97, 127–36; E Truli, 'The General Data Protection Regulation and Civil Liability' in M Bakhoum et al (eds), *Personal Data in Competition, Consumer Protection and Intellectual Property Law* (Berlin, Springer, 2018) 303, 309–14.

[5] See Article 29 Data Protection Working Party, *Opinion 1/2010 on the Concepts of 'Controller' and 'Processor'* (WP169, 16 February 2010) 5.

[6] European Union Agency for Fundamental Rights (FRA), *Access to Data Protection Remedies in EU Member States* (Luxembourg, Publications Office of the European Union, 2013).

misuse of private information, a breach of confidence as well as a violation of a data protection statute.[7] In many cases,[8] the focus is on the private law claim, primarily the tort of misuse of private information,[9] while the data protection claim tends to be a secondary concern to the claimant as well as to the court.[10]

Problematically, DPA s 13 expressly provided that an individual who suffered distress (that is, emotional harm) by reason of a data controller's contravention of any of the requirements of the DPA was entitled to compensation only if they also suffered pecuniary or material loss thereby or if the contravention related to the processing of personal data for special purposes. In *Vidal-Hall v Google Inc*, the Court of Appeal rejected these restrictions and gave Art 23 of the Directive its 'natural and wide meaning so as to include both material and non-material damage'.[11] Consequently, and in light of the special protection of personal data in Art 8 of the European Charter of Fundamental Rights of the European Union, the Court held that the narrower domestic provision was to be disapplied so that '*any* damage suffered as a result of a data controller's contravention of any of the 1998 Act's requirements' (emphasis in original)[12] was compensable.

ii. Direct Rights of Action under the GDPR

When the GDPR was enacted, the EU legislature sought to strengthen the efficiency of both public and private enforcement. While the penalty provisions with their maximum fines for corporations based on global turnover grabbed the headlines,[13] the private law enforcement mechanisms have also been overhauled. Article 79 of the GDPR, the successor to Art 22 of the Directive, creates a general right to an effective judicial remedy against a controller or processor for non-compliance with the GDPR, notwithstanding the availability of administrative relief. Article 82 of the GDPR, dealing with compensation and liability clarifies and expands upon Art 23 of the Directive. It provides that 'any person who has suffered material or non-material damage as a result of an infringement of this Regulation shall have the right to receive compensation from the controller or processor for the damage suffered'.[14]

[7] For the Data Protection Act 1998 (UK), see, eg: *Campbell v MGN Ltd* [2002] EWHC 499 (QB), [2002] EMLR 617; *Murray v Express Newspapers Plc* [2008] EWCA Civ 446, [2009] Ch 481; *Weller v Associated Newspapers Ltd* [2014] EWHC 1163 (QB), [2014] EMLR 24; *Vidal-Hall v Google Inc* [2015] EWCA Civ 311, [2016] QB 1003; *ZXC v Bloomberg LP* [2020] EWCA Civ 611, [2021] QB 28. On the interplay between tort and data protection law, see also: F Brimblecombe and H Fenwick, 'Keeping Control of Personal Information in the Digital Age: Efficacy and Equivalence of tortious and GDPR/DPA Relief' (2022) 138 *LQR* 456.

[8] *Vidal-Hall v Google*, ibid and *WM Morrison Supermarkets Plc v Various Claimants* [2020] UKSC 12, [2020] AC 989 are exceptions to this.

[9] The pre-*Campbell* decision of *Douglas v Hello! Ltd* [2003] EWHC 786 (Ch), [2003] 3 All ER 996 was argued on the basis of extended breach of confidence; the data protection aspect of the decision was not challenged on appeal: *Douglas v Hello! Ltd* [2005] EWCA Civ 595, [2006] QB 125.

[10] The data protection claim then may not be pursued at trial, particularly if it is regarded as not more advantageous to the claimant than the tort claim: see, eg, *ZXC v Bloomberg* (n 7) para 3; *Richard v The British Broadcasting Corporation* [2018] EWHC 1837 (Ch), [2019] Ch 169, para 226.

[11] *Vidal-Hall v Google* (n 7) para 76 (Lord Dyson MR and Sharp LJ, McFarlane LJ agreeing).

[12] ibid para 105.

[13] See GDPR (n 2) Art 83; M Hill, 'European Data Protection Authorities Issue Record €2.92 billion in GDPR fines' (*CSO Asean*, 17 January 2023), www.csoonline.com/article/3685789/european-data-protection-authorities-issue-record-2-92-billion-in-gdpr-fines.html.

[14] The repealed Art 23 of the Directive was directed only at data controllers.

The UK GDPR, adopted in 2020 to maintain materially identical data protection rules following the UK's departure from the EU, also provides a private right of action for violations in its Art 82(1).[15] While most of the EU jurisprudence on direct claims still relates to the Directive, there is now also an emerging body of case law on the GDPR. While the GDPR as a directly applicable legal instrument creates legislative uniformity in all 27 EU Member States, there remains much disparity between national courts on how to apply Art 82.[16] Many important questions on the interpretation of Art 82 still need to be resolved, as demonstrated by a considerable number of requests for preliminary rulings,[17] in which national courts refer issues relating to interpretation to the Court of Justice of the European Union (CJEU). However, the contours of the remedy are becoming clearer. In a recent decision, the CJEU held that, while the mere infringement of the GDPR does not sound in damages, the non-material damage suffered does not need to reach a threshold of seriousness in order to confer a right to compensation.[18] Pending referrals concern, for example, the scope of the exculpatory provision in Art 82(3),[19] and the relationship between compensation and administrative fines in Art 83.[20] The CJEU decisions on these matters will provide important guidance for future cases, which in turn will determine how robust the judicial protections of data rights in the EU will become.

B. USA

i. Current Regimes

Privacy breach litigation has the longest history, and is most prevalent, in the US. This results from fragmented data privacy regulation, weak public enforcement of data rights, coupled with a permissive class action regime. Privacy class actions are most common for data security breaches or other consumer privacy interferences, especially where they are occurring on a mass scale. The federal Fair Credit Reporting Act (FCRA),[21] the Illinois Biometric Information Privacy Act[22] (BIPA) and now also

[15] See also Data Protection Act 2018 (UK) s 162.

[16] Judicial proceedings to enforce the right to compensation shall be brought before the competent Member State courts: GDPR. (n 2) Art 82(6).

[17] Consolidated Version of the Treaty on the Functioning of the European Union [2012] OJ C326/47, Art 267. See discussion in J Knetsch, 'The Compensation of Non-Pecuniary Loss in GDPR Infringement Cases' (2022) 13 *Journal of European Tort Law* 132, https://doi.org/10.1515/jetl-2022-0008.

[18] *UI v Österreichische Post AG* (C-300/12) ECLI:EU:C:2023:370. *Cf Rolfe v Veale Wasbrough Vizards LLP* [2021] EWHC 2809 (QB), which held that, despite the claimant-friendly approach to the establishment of damage in *Vidal-Hall*, no action is available if the damage claimed does not exceed a *de minimis* threshold.

[19] This provision applies where a controller was not in any way responsible for the harm.

[20] See J Gerritsen, 'Pending CJEU Data Protection Cases', app.digibeetle.eu/pending-cases/.

[21] The civil liability provisions of the FCRA distinguish between wilful or negligent failures to comply with its requirements (15 USC §§ 1681n, 1681o). Wilful failure may be compensated with statutory damages of $100 to $1,000 or actual damages (15 USC § 1681n(a)(1)(A)), including damages for emotional distress; or sanctioned with punitive damages (15 USC § 1681n(a)(2)). Negligent non-compliance with FCRA requirements entitles to actual damages (15 USC § 1681o(a)(1)–(2)), including damages for emotional distress.

[22] Under section 20 (740 Ill Comp Stat 14/20 (2008)), successful claimants can recover statutory damages of $1,000 for each negligent violation (and $5,000 for each intention or reckless violation) or actual damages, whichever is greater, as well as reasonable attorneys' fees and costs.

the California Consumer Privacy Act of 2018 (CCPA)[23] are among the statutes that allow for private actions in cases of alleged violation.[24] In particular, the Illinois BIPA has generated a 'torrent' of litigation relating to the unlawful handling of biometric data,[25] often with very significant settlement figures. The best-known example is the $650 million settlement of a BIPA class action against Facebook, which concerned the social media giant's use of face tagging features without consent.[26] This action, which was described by the judge approving the settlement as a 'landmark result', affected approximately 1.6 million Facebook users, awarding at least $345 to each class member.[27]

The potential of class actions is that they can 'stop business practices that harm consumers, compensate individuals for injuries suffered and deter future misconduct'.[28] More fundamentally, private rights of action have been described as an 'extension of democratic participation',[29] allowing individuals to make their voices heard in court. Class actions seem to provide an attractive procedural mechanism for cases in which breaches cause only limited harm to each affected consumer, who therefore have insufficient incentive for individual action. Class actions are facilitated through legislative provisions that allow for claims of a set amount of statutory damages, irrespective of proof of actual financial or emotional harm. In *Rosenbach v Six Flags*, the Illinois Supreme Court confirmed an expansive interpretation of the BIPA, when it held that 'an individual need not allege some actual injury or adverse effect, beyond violation of his or her rights under the Act'[30] in order to qualify for liquidated damages and injunctive relief. Similarly, the CCPA does not require actual damage in class actions for negligent data breach, although its potential for cases of other data mishandling is yet to be tested in court.[31] In the absence of such provisions, providing evidence of the alleged harm can cause difficulty for class action claimants. Particularly in data breach cases, claimants may struggle to establish actual and concrete harm when it is unknown who obtained access to the improperly disclosed information and how, if at all, it was used by third parties.

[23] Under the Californian Consumer Privacy Act of 2018, Cal Civ Code § 1798.150(a)(1) (CCPA), consumers have a private right of action for specified data breaches. If successful, claimants can recover statutory damages between $100 and $750 per incident, or actual damages.

[24] Other statutes allowing individual suits include Privacy Act of 1974 (see, eg, 5 USC § 552a(g)), Right to Financial Privacy Act of 1978 (see, eg, 12 USC § 3417), Cable Communications Policy Act, Electronic Communications Privacy Act of 1984, Video Privacy Protection Act of 1988, Telephone Consumer Protection Act of 1991 and their progeny at state levels.

[25] D Shifrin and M Tobin, 'Past, Present and Future: What's Happening with Illinois' and Other Biometric Privacy Laws' (28 May 2021) *The National Law Review* vol XI, no 148.

[26] *In Re Facebook Biometric Info Privacy Litig*, 185 F Supp 3d 1155 (ND Cal 2016).

[27] Ibid; *Order Re Final Approval, Attorneys' Fees and Costs, and Incentive Awards*, Case No 14-cv-00582-JD, 1.

[28] M Rotenberg and D Jacobs, 'Enforcing Privacy Rights: Class Action Litigation and the Challenge of *cy pres*' in D Wright and P De Hert (eds), *Enforcing Privacy* (Switzerland, Springer, 2016) 307, 308.

[29] B Chao, E Null and C Park, *Enforcing a New Privacy Law* (Report, Open Technology Institute, 20 November 2019) 16.

[30] *Rosenbach v Six Flags Entertainment Corporation*, 2019 IL 123186, 129 NE 3d 1197, para 4 (Ill 2019).

[31] An important limitation to a consumer's ability to bring a private lawsuit in California is that a business will only be held to be in violation of the CCPA if it fails to cure an alleged violation within 30 days 'after being notified': Cal Civ Code § 1798.155 (West 2018).

ii. Reform Agenda

Despite these advantages, the reliance in the US on class actions as a regulatory mechanism is also subject to considerable criticism. The US Chamber Institute of Legal Reform describes statutory private rights of action as 'inefficient and ineffective for addressing privacy concerns'.[32] Industry opposes expansive consumer class action regimes because they expose companies to 'rampant litigation',[33] including the risk of nation-wide class actions with multi-million-dollar claims. Permissive regimes may encourage frivolous lawsuits in situations when class members have not experienced any tangible harm. Plaintiff attorneys have been accused of engaging in aggressive tactics that are not primarily concerned with protecting the interests of their clients, but with seeking settlement terms that include large attorney fees.[34] Another concern are 'cy-pres' arrangements under which uncollected settlement fees are put to the next best available use.[35] It has been commented that the 'rights of the actual consumers are often sacrificed in these settlements',[36] and courts have been called upon to exercise greater judicial oversight of privacy class action settlements.

A more fundamental criticism is that private rights of action supposedly hinder innovation because they 'allow plaintiffs' lawyers to set policy nationwide' and undermine appropriate agency enforcement that is 'guided by experts in the field who can be expected to understand the complexities of encouraging compliance and innovation while preventing and remediating harms'.[37] The nature and design of class action regimes have therefore emerged as a key battle ground over consumer privacy laws in the US. Strongly divided opinion on their usefulness stymies the development of more effective privacy regulation. However, there is increasing recognition that privacy class action regimes do not raise an all-or-nothing question.[38] More balanced approaches recognise the value of class actions for redressing individual harm or enforcing privacy standards in some circumstances, but aim to curb unmeritorious claims. For example, in a 2020 report, researchers at the Brookings Institution recommended a tiered approach to enforcement of privacy provisions that would take into account the extent to which a statutory provision protected an individual's substantive privacy rights or was of an administrative nature and concerned with accountability.[39] Indeed, there are some recent signs that narrow private rights of action may enjoy bipartisan and industry support in any future federal privacy regulation.[40]

[32] US Chamber Institute of Legal Reform, 'Ill-Suited – Private Rights of Action and Privacy Claims' (Policy Paper, July 2019) 5.

[33] Ibid.

[34] ibid.

[35] Rotenberg and Jacobs, 'Enforcing Privacy Rights' (n 28) 307; for a less sceptical perspective: T Kadri and I Cofone, '*Cy près* Settlements in Privacy Class Actions' in I Cofone (ed), *Class Actions in Privacy Law* (Abingdon, Routledge, 2021) 99.

[36] Kadri and Cofone, '*Cy près* Settlements', ibid.

[37] US Chamber Institute of Legal Reform, 'Private Rights of Action and Privacy Claims' (n 32) 14.

[38] C Kerry and J Morris Jr, 'In Privacy Legislation, a Private Right of Action is not an All-or-Nothing Proposition' (Blog Post, *Brookings*, 7 July 2020), www.brookings.edu/blog/techtank/2020/07/07/in-privacy-legislation-a-private-right-of-action-is-not-an-all-or-nothing-proposition/.

[39] Ibid.

[40] American Data Privacy and Protection Act HR 8152 117th Cong (2021–2022), a bipartisan Bill, includes a limited private right of action for certain privacy violations, but requires individuals first to notify a regulator of their intent to sue, and allows an action only where the regulator decides not to pursue a civil action themselves.

C. Other Jurisdictions

i. Canada

Canada's privacy regulation at federal and provincial levels is currently in a period of transition. The Personal Information Protection and Electronic Documents Act (PIPEDA),[41] dealing with data handling in commercial contexts, is slated to be replaced by a suite of newer legislation. PIPEDA empowers the Federal Court to 'award damages to a complainant, including damages for any humiliation' suffered, as well as make orders for a company to correct its practices.[42] However, court actions become available only after a complaint has been made to the Office of the Privacy Commissioner (OPC) and the Commissioner has either made a report, or discontinued the complaint.[43] In addition, remedies under PIPEDA are discretionary. The Federal Court has held that an award for damages should only be made in the 'most egregious of circumstances',[44] such as where the 'breach has been one of a very serious and violating nature' or the 'result of any sort of malicious behaviour'.[45]

Proposed new federal laws, contained in Bill C-27: Digital Charter Implementation Act 2022, will bolster the substance and enforcement of privacy obligations owed by private entities. The OPC will be given stronger investigative and enforcement powers, and maximum penalties will significantly increase. The Bill also creates a new Personal Information and Data Protection Tribunal that will hear appeals against the Commissioner's findings, orders or decisions, and can make determinations on whether any penalties recommended by the Commissioner are appropriate. In 2019, the OPC advocated for more discretion under PIPEDA to choose which complaints to investigate.[46] Referring to its 'finite resources and a multitude of roles and responsibilities', the OPC also proposed that individuals should have an independent right of action for violation of their privacy rights, including in cases where an OPC complaint was not decided upon within six months.[47]

However, cl 106 of the (expired) Bill C-11 for the introduction of a Consumer Privacy Protection Act, limited the right by requiring a prior finding of a contravention by either the Commissioner or the Tribunal.[48] The new Bill C-27 retains the restrictive position:

[41] SC 2000 c 5 (PIPEDA).

[42] Ibid s 16.

[43] Ibid s 14. For further discussion, see J Walker, '*Douez v Facebook* and Privacy Class Actions' in I Cofone (ed), *Class Actions in Privacy Law* (Abingdon, Routledge, 2021) 56.

[44] *Miglialo v Royal Band of Canada* 2018 FC 525, paras 41 and 48 (Roy J); *Townsend v Sun Life Financial* 2012 FC 550, paras 30–34 (de Montigny J); *Nammo v TransUnion of Canada Inc* 2010 FC 1284, para 71 (Zinn J); *Biron v Royal Bank of Canada* 2012 FC 1095, paras 37–43 (Scott J).

[45] *Randall v Nubodys Fitness Centres*, 2010 FC 681, paras 55–56 (Mosley J).

[46] Office of the Privacy Commissioner (OPC), 'Privacy Law Reform: A Pathway to Respecting Rights and Restoring Trust in Government and the Digital Economy' (Annual Report, 2018/2019) 2.

[47] ibid 13, 19. The OPC has maintained this position in a submission to the new Bill C-27: Submission of the Office of the Privacy Commissioner of Canada on Bill C-27, the Digital Charter Implementation Act 2022, Appendix, para 17.

[48] While the Government suggested that such a tribunal might improve access to quick and effective remedies for consumers, the Commissioner considered the creation of an additional layer before a complainant could seek judicial redress to be 'counterproductive': Office of the Privacy Commissioner of Canada, 'Submission of the Office of the Privacy Commissioner of Canada on Bill C-11, the Digital Charter Implementation Act, 2020' (Regulatory Submission, May 2021), text acc rec 36. While PIPEDA limits the standing for compensation in

a private right of action under cl 107 arises only if either the Commissioner or the Tribunal made a finding of a contravention of the new Act. If the finding is made by the Commissioner, it is further required that either the Tribunal has dismissed an appeal or that the time limit of 30 days for an appeal has expired. The requirement of a Commissioner or Tribunal finding turns the right of action into an annex to the complaints process, rather than create an independent alternative to it. Installing a gatekeeper has therefore been criticised as erecting unnecessary hurdles to ready and timely judicial redress.[49]

ii. China

The new Personal Information Protection Law (PIPL), which came into force on 1 November 2021, is China's first comprehensive law in the field of personal data protection. Among its many innovations, it creates civil liability for personal information processors 'where the handling of personal information infringes upon the rights and interests of the individuals' and causes harm (Art 69).[50] Similar to the GDPR, processors can avoid liability if they prove that they were not at fault. The compensation payable shall be determined on the basis of the resulting loss suffered by the individual or the resulting benefits gained by the processor.[51] If the loss and profit are difficult to ascertain, the amount of the damages shall be decided 'according to practical conditions'.[52] Representative actions are available under PIPL Art 70 if processors of personal information violate the requirements of PIPL and infringe on the rights and interests of many individuals. They can be brought by the People's Procuratorates (law enforcement agencies), organisations endorsed by the state cyberspace authorities, designated consumer organisations and other designated organisations in the People's Court. Given the statute has only recently entered into force, the impact of these new enforcement mechanisms remains to be seen. This will depend in part on how readily affected individuals will seek to protect their privacy rights in this manner, which in turn will depend at least in part on the attractiveness of other enforcement options.

iii. Hong Kong

In Hong Kong, section 66 of the Personal Data (Privacy) Ordinance[53] creates a right of compensation, including for injury to feelings,[54] for breach of the statutory requirements.

court to a 'complainant', the Consumer Privacy Protection Act appears to broaden this to 'an individual who is affected' (cl 107(1)) by a contravention.

[49] See Centre for Digital Rights, 'Not Fit For Purpose: Canada Deserves Much Better, Centre for Digital Rights Statement on Bill C-22' (Statement, 28 October 2022) para 7.6 ('will deny access to justice to most individuals').

[50] «中华人民共和国个人信息保护法» [Personal Information Protection Law] (People's Republic of China) National People's Congress Standing Committee, Order No 91, 20 August 2021 (Translation by Digichina (Stanford University), digichina.stanford.edu/work/translation-personal-information-protection-law-of-the-peoples-republic-of-china-effective-nov-1-2021/) (PIPL).

[51] PIPL Art 69(2).

[52] ibid Art 69(3), as translated by Digichina (Stanford University).

[53] Personal Data (Privacy) Ordinance (Hong Kong) (Cap.486).

[54] The Administrative Appeals Board held that a claim for reputational loss must be pursued in separate proceedings: *何添錦 and 李小雲 v The Privacy Commissioner for Personal Data*, AAB 40/2006.

Similar to the GDPR and the PIPL, the defendant can escape liability upon proof that they were not at fault.[55] Since the direct right of action was introduced in 2012, only a small number of cases have agitated this provision.[56] To date, there is only one decision in which damages have actually been awarded, in a case that concerned the misuse of data collected from a private CCTV system.[57] In another case, the Court refused to hear a claim for damages under the Ordinance, because a complaint to the Commissioner had been rejected and an appeal against that decision to the Administrative Board had been unsuccessful.[58]

iv. New Zealand

The Privacy Act 2020 (NZ) ('Privacy Act') continues the established complaints-based privacy regime. If the Commissioner determines after investigating upon complaint that there has been an interference with privacy, they will seek to facilitate a resolution between the parties. If the Commissioner is unable to resolve the matter, they can refer the complaint to the Director of Human Rights Proceedings, who can in turn take the case to the Human Rights Review Tribunal. The Tribunal can also be accessed by the individual if the Commissioner is not satisfied that there has been a privacy breach or if a substantiated complaint is not resolved. While a direct right to go to court is thus not part of the Privacy Act, the Tribunal has the power to award compensation for breaches of the Privacy Act. Depending on the circumstances, it may decide not to award damages at all, a nominal amount to mark a privacy breach, or an amount that reflects the actual harm suffered by the complainants. The case law establishes that awards at the less serious end of the spectrum will be up to NZ$10,000, whereas more serious cases can range from NZ$10,000 to around NZ$50,000, and the most serious cases will exceed NZ$50,000.[59]

v. Singapore

In Singapore, the Personal Data Protection Act 2012 ('PDPA') provides that any person who suffers loss or damage directly as a result of contravention of specified provisions of the Act by an organisation has a right of action for relief in civil proceedings in a court.[60] This relief can take the form of an injunction or declaration, damages or other relief as the court thinks fit.[61] The PDPA is silent on whether emotional distress or loss of control over personal data is compensable. In the recent decision of *Reed, Michael v Bellingham, Alex*, the Singapore Court of Appeal engaged in a detailed contextual, historical and purposive

[55] Personal Data (Privacy) Ordinance (Hong Kong) (Cap.486), s 66(5) provides that proceedings can be brought in the District Court, but this jurisdiction is not exclusive: *Lee Kwok Tung Albert v Chiyu Banking Corporation Ltd* [2018] HKCA 123.

[56] See, eg, *Yung Mei Chun, Jessie v Merrill Lynch (Asia Pacific) Ltd* [2015] HKDC 112.

[57] *Tsang Po Mann v Tsang Ka Kit* [2021] HKDC 208, [2021] 1 HKLRD 1301.

[58] *X v Melissa Mowbray D'Arbela* [2018] HKDC 215.

[59] *Hammond v Credit Union Baywide* [2015] NZHRRT 6, para 176; *Director of Human Rights Proceedings v Slater* [2019] NZHRRT 13, para 165.

[60] Personal Data Protection Act (Singapore) s 48O(1), re-enacting s 32(1) in February 2021 (PDPA).

[61] PDPA, s 48O(3).

interpretation of the remedial scheme in the PDPA.[62] Overturning a High Court decision, the Court held that it would further the specific purposes of sub-s 32(1) of the PDPA as a statutory tort if the expression 'loss or damage' was interpreted as including emotional distress. Although the Court did not consider consistency with overseas laws as a critical objective, this expansive interpretation ensures that the private action in Singapore is aligned with the law in other jurisdictions such as Canada, New Zealand, Hong Kong, the EU and the UK. The *Reed* litigation, like *Vidal-Hall v Google Inc* before it, exemplifies the importance of specifying clearly in the statutory provision setting out the DRA, what is meant by 'loss or damage'. Although, strictly speaking, this interpretation relates to the former s 32 of the PDPA, it is likely to be applied also to its successor, s 48O of the PDPA, given that there are no textual differences between both provisions.

III. Comparative Discussion

Notwithstanding the variations in the design of the private enforcement regimes explored above, some commonalities in the rationales and features of DRAs are evident. This section will explore the main themes arising from the comparative review. Awareness of the available approaches and their relative strengths has particular significance for countries, such as Australia, that are currently considering the introduction of a DRA. These lessons will be explored in the subsequent section.

A. The Various Functions of a Direct Right of Action

i. Empowering Complainants and Enhancing Compliance

One key reason for enacting DRA provisions is to provide individuals who have suffered a privacy invasion with access to judicial remedies. This purpose is particularly important in data protection regimes with flawed public enforcement, such as where regulatory agencies are weak or underfunded. Deficient complaint regimes may lead to outcomes that do not satisfy the complainant, both substantively in the form of insufficient redress and, procedurally, in the form of delay and uncertainty. Where private enforcement is utilised as a supplementary enforcement mechanism, it not only protects the rights of the parties, but also creates an 'additional incentive' for compliance.[63] Although compensation, even in class action proceedings, may be less substantial than a fine, a judgment will have declaratory force and often guide future privacy practice. In the Final Report of its Digital Platforms Inquiry, the Australian Competition and Consumer Commission (ACCC) recognised that a DRA gives consumers 'greater control over their data and privacy by having the ability [to] bring action against parties that have misused their personal data or breached their privacy'.[64]

[62] *Reed, Michael v Bellingham, Alex* [2022] SGCA 60, [2022] 2 SLR 1156.
[63] Australian Competition and Consumer Commission (ACCC), 'Digital Platforms Inquiry – Final Report' (Report, June 2019) 473.
[64] ibid 442.

B. Clarifying and Developing the Law

Many data protection statutes adopt a principles-based approach to regulation.[65] Under this approach, the statute defines the intended goals and outcomes of regulation but allows the regulated entity to determine how these objectives can be best achieved in their individual circumstances.[66] While principles-based regulation increases adaptability to different industry contexts and maintains flexibility in response to technological or social change, ill-defined data processing obligations can create considerable uncertainty.

Data protection authorities often issue guidance on their interpretation of indeterminate terms such as 'fair processing', 'legitimate interests', 'proportionate' or 'reasonable uses', or 'valid' consent,[67] yet such guidance does generally not have the force of law. Court decisions arising from private action can then authoritatively define and explain the applicable data processing standards. More liberal access to private enforcement through legal proceedings has the potential to generate a greater number of judicial pronouncements on the correct interpretation of privacy obligations. This case law not only decides the dispute in question, but also clarifies and develops the law for future cases. There is a particular need for judicial interpretation in systems where regulatory agencies have a weak mandate, rely extensively on conciliated outcomes[68] or have limited resources for judicial proceedings. In these circumstances, agencies need to direct their enforcement activities to those proceedings which are likely to have the greatest impact. This may sometimes be a strategic litigation which seeks to establish a particular interpretation of the law or approach to enforcement, yet in other cases it may simply be a wide-scale or high-profile breach of privacy that does not raise any fundamental issues of general importance.

C. The Relationship between Direct Rights of Action and Administrative Enforcement

A key regulatory choice is to define the relationship between administrative enforcement and a DRA. The more liberal DRA regimes, such as those in the EU, the UK, Singapore and Hong Kong, do not make the right to bring an action dependent on a prior complaint to the data protection authority. This gives individuals the choice between a complaint to the regulator or the judicial process, which maximises individual empowerment and agency.[69]

[65] For an overview, see W Maxwell, 'Principles-Based Regulation of Personal Data: I Case of "Fair Processing"' (2015) 5 *International Data Privacy Law* 205.

[66] Australian Law Reform Commission (ALRC), 'For Your Information: Australian Privacy Law and Practice' (ALRC Report 108, 2008) para 4.5.

[67] See, eg, the *Guidelines* of the European Data Protection Supervisor, or the PIPEDA Interpretation Bulletins of the OPC.

[68] N Howell, 'Shutting the Courts Out: Developing Consumer Credit Law in the Shadow of Alternative Dispute Resolution and the New Australian Financial Complaints Authority' (2019) 30(2) *Journal of Banking and Finance Law and Practice* 57–78.

[69] In the EU, a duality of public and private enforcement is common also for competition and capital market laws, although it has been commented that the GDPR regime is unique in its severity: A Hellgardt,

In many cases, complainants will opt for a complaints-based mechanism as their first choice if that process promises to achieve a straightforward, cost-effective and timely resolution of a dispute with a data processor. Data processors are likely to prefer administrative processes, especially if this gives them greater influence on the conduct of the proceedings and their outcomes, or if the regulatory sanctions for wrongdoing are less potent than judicial orders. However, a requirement to seek an administrative decision first can be problematic because it diminishes remedial choice. A gatekeeper function is not even necessarily preferred by regulators, as can be illustrated with the Canadian example. The OPC anticipated that making the proposed right of action dependent on the conclusion of the administrative process would not only add to its caseload but also hinder timely justice for complainants.[70]

The concern expressed in the US, that ready access to judicial proceedings has the potential to diminish the ability of regulators to develop policy, is occasionally echoed in other jurisdictions. For example, contrary to the OPC position, the Office of the Australian Information Commissioner (OAIC) favours access to the court being conditional on a prior regulatory complaint.[71] The OAIC considered that this would provide it 'with national oversight of privacy issues and the ability to identify potential systemic issues in the system that may warrant further regulatory or enforcement action'.[72] However, this concern could be addressed with a requirement to inform the OAIC of proceedings brought so as to give it the opportunity to participate in them.[73] A notification requirement would allow the regulator to identify any systemic issues, without requiring an individual who prefers to seek an adjudicated outcome to go through a complaints-based process first. Under the European regimes, national data protection authorities can likewise intervene or appear as amici curiae, if the claim was filed within its jurisdiction or has the potential to affect its jurisdiction.

Another intermediate option is that adopted by the PDPA in Singapore, which bars the direct right of action only temporarily. Once the Personal Data Protection Commission has made a decision under this Act in respect of a contravention, no action can be brought until after that decision has become final.[74] This preserves a data subject's choice between a complaint or judicial proceedings but also ensures in cases where a complaint has been made that a decision of the Commission is not bypassed.[75]

'Die Schadensersatzhaftung für Datenschutzverstöße im System des unionalen Haftungsrechts' [2022] *Zeitschrift für Europäisches Privatrecht* 7, 41.

[70] Seeking a middle ground between unrestricted direct rights found in other jurisdictions, notably the EU, and the highly restricted right proposed in Bill C-11, the OPC proposed that the right ought to be available after a complaint had been made and the OPC has variously decided on the complaint, exercised its discretion not to investigate or not finalised the complaint within six months: OPC (above n 47) rec 41.

[71] Office of the Australian Information Commissioner (OAIC), 'Privacy Act Review – Issues Paper: Submission by the Office of the Australian Information Commissioner' (Regulatory Submission, 11 December 2020) rec 52.

[72] ibid para 10.17.

[73] Similar notification requirements currently exist under the Privacy and Personal Information Protection Act 1998 (NSW), which creates an avenue to seek direct redress from the NSW Civil and Administrative Tribunal.

[74] PDPA, s 48O(2).

[75] See *Reed, Michael v Bellingham, Alex* (n 62) para 83 ('procedural safeguard against parallel proceedings').

D. Class Actions and Representative Actions

Given that legal proceedings are potentially costly for individual consumers, class action mechanisms can improve access to justice for data subjects. Representative proceedings allow consumers to exercise their rights as a group, which creates efficiencies particularly in cases in which the harm suffered by each individual is small in comparison to the cost and risk of litigation.

In the US, privacy litigation is booming because permissive class action regimes in some sectoral and state legislation allow for statutory damages without proof of actual harm. Discussions about possible federal general privacy legislation suggest that a limited right to sue will be maintained, although restricted in scope to repeat or serious violations or with greater procedural hurdles. In the EU, there is also increasing interest in data privacy class actions or representative actions, although the exact potential of such actions depends on national law[76] and is yet to be worked out. In 2020, the EU adopted the Representative Actions Directive,[77] which seeks to harmonise Member States law on collective redress in consumer actions. Under this Directive, Member States need to create mechanisms that allow representative actions by so-called qualified entities, such as consumer organisations and other not-for-profit entities or public authorities. The GDPR is expressly identified as one of the legal instruments for which representative actions must be made available.[78]

In the UK, the recently resolved *Lloyd v Google LLC* litigation[79] tested the potential and limits of representative actions. The claimant, Mr Lloyd, was a consumer advocate, who brought a claim on behalf of more than four million Apple iPhone users for unlawful tracking by Google Inc between 2011 and 2012 in breach of the DPA. As the UK allows class actions only in competition law cases, the action was brought as a representative proceeding. In *Lloyd*, unlike *Vidal-Hall*,[80] the claimant did not argue that members of the class suffered emotional harm from the alleged interference with their data rights. Instead, Mr Lloyd submitted, with the support of the Information Commissioner, that compensation could be awarded for the 'loss of control' of personal data constituted by any non-trivial contravention by a data controller of any of the requirements of the Act. Building on its earlier decision in *Gulati v MGN Ltd*[81] that, in claims for the tort of misuse of private information, damages could be awarded for the loss or diminution of the right to control the use of that private information, the Court of Appeal held that claimants were not required to show pecuniary loss or distress.[82] However, the Supreme Court unanimously rejected this relaxation of the damage requirement and did not allow the representative claim to proceed. In particular, the Supreme Court held

[76] However, the Commission adopted a Recommendation of 11 June 2013 on common principles for injunctive and compensatory collective redress mechanisms in the Member States concerning violations of rights granted under Union law [2013] OJ L201/60.

[77] Directive (EU) 2020/1828 of the European Parliament and of the Council of 25 November 2020 on representative actions for the protection of the collective interests of consumers and repealing Directive 2009/22/EC [2020] OJ L409/1.

[78] ibid Annex I; GDPR (n 2) Art 80.

[79] *Lloyd v Google LLC* [2021] UKSC 50, [2022] AC 1217.

[80] *Vidal-Hall v Google* (n 7).

[81] *Gulati v MGN Ltd* [2015] EWCA Civ 1291, [2017] QB 149.

[82] *Lloyd v Google LLC* [2019] EWCA Civ 1599, [2020] QB 747.

that, properly interpreted, the term 'damage' in DPA 1998, s 13 meant material damage or mental distress resulting from unlawful data processing. The unlawful processing of personal data in contravention of the Act, ie the 'loss of control' over personal data, is not of itself a compensable damage. The Court also held that it was necessary, in order to recover compensation under s 13, to prove what unlawful processing of personal data relating to a given individual was undertaken by Google. While the exact implications of the Supreme Court decision are yet to be worked out, it is safe to say that the prospect of representative proceedings for privacy breaches in the UK is now dampened. This diminishes the availability of an important procedural mechanism that can assist with the effective enforcement of data rights.

E. Direct Rights Need to be Clearly Formulated

i. Damage Requirements and Remedies

The preceding discussion has illustrated the need to formulate the elements of a direct right as clearly as possible. In the UK, the 'damage' element generated significant litigation, initially regarding the questions of whether non-pecuniary loss was independently actionable and more recently on the issue of whether a 'loss of control', or a contravention of privacy obligations as such, can amount to compensable non-pecuniary loss. This compensability of emotional distress has also been the subject of litigation in Ireland[83] and Singapore.[84] Against this background, it is preferable that legislators state unequivocally that distress, which is often the main form of harm, is actionable. Recently, the more contentious issue has become whether a 'naked' breach of a privacy obligation, ie one that does not generate any provable material or non-material loss, should also be actionable. The CJEU, as well as case law from the UK and Singapore, have all recently denied compensability without proof of loss. Requirements to prove loss erect hurdles to claimants who seek vindication of their data rights. In the US, this issue is bypassed in those enactments that give claimants the choice either to seek the statutory damages in a set amount or prove their actual loss. This pragmatic approach obviates doctrinal hurdles associated with vindicatory relief and strengthens the hand of privacy claimants.

A further question relates to the availability of aggravated and exemplary damages, as well as the non-monetary remedies, including injunctions, declarations and apology orders. Additional forms of damages originate from common law principles, and there is little justification to introduce them into statutory damages schemes. Aggravated damages are damages awarded to enhance compensatory damages where the manner of committing the wrong caused additional hurt to the victim. As such damages are understood to be compensatory, the more straightforward approach is simply to increase the quantum of damages in line with the heightened injury to feelings, rather than to

[83] *Collins v FBD Insurance plc* [2013] IEHC 137; *Murphy v Callinan* [2018] IESC 59. But see now the clarification in Data Protection Act 2018 (Ireland) s 128(9) that damage 'includes material and non-material damage'.

[84] *Reed, Michael v Bellingham, Alex* (n 62).

order two awards in the form of compensatory damages and aggravated damages as a top-up. There is also only limited justification for allowing exemplary damages. In Australia, the ACCC proposed that exemplary damages should be made available in exceptional circumstances.[85] However, punitive relief is generally not envisaged in the DRAs overseas, including in other common law jurisdictions. There also does not seem a compelling reason to make exemplary damages available when the regulator is empowered to award fines or other pecuniary penalties for that conduct.

F. Applicability of General Law Doctrines

Section 128(2) of the Irish Data Protection Act 2018 explicitly provides that a data protection action 'shall be deemed … to be an action in tort'. In other jurisdictions, such as Singapore, the courts have identified the action as a statutory tort.[86] Although uncommon, it is clearly desirable that the statute creating a direct right also clarify to what extent general law on tort or, in civil law jurisdictions, delictual liability should be applicable. Such clarification assists all parties because it minimises the potential for disputes on the applicability of general law doctrines, including on issues related to causality, remoteness, defences including consent, contributory fault and time bars, as well as vicarious and other forms of joint liability.

IV. Case Study: Introducing a Direct Right of Action in Australia

A. Judicial Redress under Current Law

The Australian Government is currently considering the introduction of a general right of action for interferences with privacy. The Privacy Act 1988 (Cth) ('Privacy Act') presently contains very limited scope for individuals to bring court proceedings to seek redress for a breach of the Act.[87] In the absence of a DRA, complainants seeking compensation for interferences with statutory privacy rights need to make a complaint to the federal Information Commissioner. The Information Commissioner[88] has the power to make determinations under s 52(1) that include an obligation to pay compensation to a complainant for loss or damage suffered as a result of a privacy interference.[89]

[85] ACCC, 'Digital Platforms Inquiry – Final Report' (n 63) 473.

[86] *Reed, Michael v Bellingham, Alex* (n 62).

[87] Privacy Act 1988 (Cth), s 80W contains a broad power to seek an injunction for contraventions of the Act. Privacy Act 1988 (Cth), ss 25, 25A contain a power to seek a compensation order for breaches of credit reporting provisions.

[88] Privacy Act 1988 (Cth), s 52. See discussion by N Witzleb, 'Determinations under the Privacy Act 1988 (Cth) as a Privacy Remedy' in J Varuhas and N Moreham (eds), *Remedies for Privacy Breaches* (Oxford, Hart Publishing, 2018) 377.

[89] Determinations with compensation awards include: *'EQ' and Great Barrier Reef Marine Authority* [2015] AICmr 11; *'D' and Wentworthville Leagues Club* [2011] AICmr 9; and *'DK' and Telstra Corporation Ltd* [2014] AICmr 118.

If the respondent does not comply with a determination, a complainant may apply to the Federal Court of Australia or the Federal Circuit and Family Court of Australia to enforce it. The Court will engage in a *de novo* hearing and has the power to make any orders it sees fit, including orders relating to compensation.[90] However, to date no such order has been made. This is due not least to the fact that determinations are rare, as the Information Commissioner has traditionally preferred to resolve complaints through a non-public conciliation process.[91]

In *Evans v Health Administration Corporation*,[92] Ward CJ in Eq approved the first Australian settlement of a class action relating to an alleged privacy breach.[93] The action concerned the limited disclosure of health and other personal information relating to NSW Ambulance Workers that was contained in workers' compensation claim files. Without admission of liability, the parties agreed on a settlement of alternative claims for breach of confidence; a breach of the employment contract; a contravention of ss 18 or 29 of the Australian Consumer Law; and under the tort of invasion of privacy. The settlement amount of $275,000 saw each group member receive $2,400, whereas the lead plaintiff received $10,000 in compensation for her distress and the burden of the proceedings. A direct right of action under the Privacy Act would have obviated the need to rely on these alternative claims.[94]

B. Rationale for Reform

Following a comprehensive review of Australian privacy laws, the Attorney-General's Department recently proposed the introduction of a DRA for privacy interferences.[95] The various rationales provided in support of this proposal are all, to a larger or lesser degree, associated with the perceived weaknesses of the current complaints-based enforcement model.[96] This model has been subject to sustained criticism by stakeholders and academic observers, as the Information Commissioner has limited enforcement powers and has long been under-resourced for its multiple functions.[97] The Review Report expected that introducing a right of action would not only empower consumers but also enhance compliance with the Privacy Act.[98] The Report also adopted the

[90] Privacy Act 1988 (Cth), s 55A(2).

[91] Australian Privacy Foundation, 'Bringing Australia's Privacy Act up to International Standards: Submission in Response to the Privacy Act Review – Issues Paper' (Regulatory Submission, 18 December 2020) 33, papers.ssrn.com/sol3/papers.cfm?abstract_id=3752152.

[92] *Evans v Health Administration Corporation* [2019] NSWSC 1781.

[93] In other consumer contexts, class actions are increasingly common in Australia: Allens, 'Class Action Risk 2022' (Webpage, 2022), www.allens.com.au/insights-news/explore/2022/class-action-risk-2022/.

[94] As these claims were in part novel and untested, the resulting uncertainty affected the settlement amount.

[95] Australian Government, Attorney-General's Department, 'Privacy Act Review' (Report, 2022) Proposal 26.1; adopting recommendations by the Australian Consumer and Competition Commission, 'Digital Platforms Inquiry – Final Report' (n 63) rec 16(e).

[96] This bears out the observations made above in section III.A.

[97] See K Kemp, 'Strengthening Enforcement and Redress Under the Australian Privacy Act' (2022) 3 *Global Privacy Law Review* 150.

[98] Attorney-General's Department, 'Privacy Act Review' (n 95) 273; see earlier ACCC, 'Digital Platforms Inquiry – Final Report' (n 63) 473.

view expressed in submissions to the Review that individual actions would increase opportunities for the courts to interpret the Privacy Act.[99]

The introduction of a direct right of action would bring Australia in line with other major jurisdictions. It would also align with Australian community attitudes[100] and create internal coherence with other recent Australian data regimes, such as the Consumer Data Rights regime,[101] which recognises compensation claims for contraventions of privacy safeguards or other privacy-related consumer data rules.[102]

C. Evaluation of the Design

In line with the preponderance of submissions to the Review, the Attorney-General recommends giving individuals and representative classes of individuals the right to seek judicial relief from an interference with privacy. The Review Report identified the Federal Court, or the Federal Circuit and Family Court, as the appropriate forum, given that these courts have experience with managing class actions and with consumer protection matters.[103] In line with the predominant overseas approaches, the Report proposed that a DRA would only be available to claimants who can establish loss or damage, including injury to feelings or humiliation. This approach rejects both calls for the introduction of a seriousness threshold and submissions that advocated DRAs for mere breaches of the Act, ie those that have not resulted in provable loss or damage. The proposal is further that the Information Commissioner would be closely involved in DRAs, acting both as a gatekeeper and, like other regulators, being able to appear as amicus curiae or intervenor. Finally, the Review Report adopted a liberal approach to remedies under which the court would be empowered to make any order it sees fit, including uncapped amounts of damages.

If the Attorney-General Department's proposals were enacted, they would put Australia's DRA comfortably within the international mainstream. It is commendable that representative proceedings would be permitted because they are an important aspect of making a direct right of action accessible to individuals who may otherwise not be able to stem the cost of proceedings. Appropriately, no threshold of seriousness was proposed because procedural and practical hurdles provide sufficient disincentives to proceedings that are not intended to address real grievances. While the gatekeeper role assigned to the Information Commissioner has the potential to add complexity and delay to proceedings, it remains to be seen how this will operate in practice. The remedial powers of the court are in the widest possible terms. While theoretically, a court may even see fit to award exemplary damages, punitive remedies are unlikely to

[99] Attorney-General's Department, 'Privacy Act Review', ibid.

[100] In the latest Australian Community Attitudes Survey, 78% of respondents stated that they should have the right to seek compensation: Lonergan Research, 'Australian Community Attitudes to Privacy Survey 2020' (Report, Office of the Australian Information Commissioner, September 2020) 67.

[101] This is contained in the Competition and Consumer Act 2010 (Cth), Pt IVD div 5 – Consumer Data Rules.

[102] Section 56EY makes specific reference to the definition of loss or damages in sub-s 25(1) of the Privacy Act 1988.

[103] Attorney-General's Department, 'Privacy Act Review' (n 95) 274.

be appropriate in many cases. Cases of flagrant and serious breaches of privacy would seem more suitably pursued by regulatory action.

V. Conclusions

Direct rights of action are increasingly seen as an integral component of data protection enforcement. They allow data subjects to seek judicial remedies for interference with their statutory data rights – in some regimes alongside, in others following, a complaint to a data protection authority. DRAs have long been part of the data protection regime in the EU, Singapore, Hong Kong and in some US laws. More recently, jurisdictions as diverse as China and California have introduced such rights in new data protection statutes. Australia and Canada are also currently debating new or expanded DRAs. There are signs that a future US general privacy law may likewise allow private lawsuits, although probably only in a more limited set of circumstances than under current sectoral or state legislation.

This chapter has identified the main features of these rights in leading privacy jurisdictions. DRAs are introduced for the purpose of empowering data rights holders and encouraging compliance. Private enforcement mechanisms are an important supplement to public enforcement by data protection authorities, particularly where these regulators lack the resources or powers to investigate or prosecute privacy breaches efficiently. However, DRAs need to be carefully designed to achieve the intended regulatory outcomes. The comparative review in this chapter shows that rights that are not fully formed can cause interpretative uncertainty. The legislation needs to be clear on the elements that need to be established by claimants, and the relief that is available. At a minimum, claimants should have access to compensation as well as injunctive relief for ongoing contraventions. One of the most important issues to be addressed is the requirement for loss. Recognising that data rights contraventions often do not cause pecuniary loss, most regimes now appropriately clarify that emotional harm is compensable. An emerging issue in the case law is whether mere 'loss of control' of personal data can, or should, be sufficient to found an action. Statutory minimum damages or damages for loss of control can provide important vindication of data rights if claimants are unable to prove material or non-material loss.

Procedural requirements are another important lever for boosting or throttling the efficacy of DRAs. Some regimes erect hurdles before courts can be accessed, such as through requirements that complaints processes with regulators need to be completed first. The more effective regimes do not interpose data protection authorities as gatekeepers and allow class actions. The availability of class actions or representative proceedings enables consumers to protect their data rights in circumstances where individual harm is too small to incentivise judicial action, but many consumers are affected by a data malpractice. Another issue of practical importance is determining which forum should hear privacy actions. While the general civil courts are the norm, some jurisdictions prefer a tribunal-based approach, as currently operates in New Zealand and is proposed in Canada. This allows for a swift and cost-effective resolution of most matters, without depriving claimants of access to the courts where important questions of interpretation call for judicial resolution.

The ongoing law reform process in Australia provides a case study of the potential of DRAs and the difficult policy choices in formulating the conditions of the action. On the basis of the comparative review, and in light of the specific conditions in Australia, this chapter advocates an expansive approach. To achieve its greatest impact, the direct right should not depend on a prior complaint to the Information Commissioner. It should not be limited to serious invasions of privacy, and the power to award compensation should not be capped. However, in Australia and elsewhere, the introduction of a DRA should not detract from the need to improve the regulatory enforcement mechanisms. Effective enforcement requires adequate regulatory powers and sufficient resources to deal with complaints in a timely and effective manner. Even if a DRA is well-designed, there will be many victims of privacy invasions who do not have sufficient resources, or are unable or unwilling to invest the time and effort needed, to seek redress through judicial proceedings. These individuals continue to depend on an accessible and effective complaints-based process to ensure that their privacy rights are sufficiently protected, that alleged interferences are appropriately investigated and wrongs properly redressed by an administrative process.

15

Data Rights Incursions: Two Hurdles in the Pursuit of Damages

KWAN HO LAU*

I. Introduction

The world we inhabit today generates digital information. A lot of it. By 2025, it is said that an estimated 463 exabytes of new data (equivalent to over 212 million DVDs' worth) will be created daily.[1] With significant portions of that data being of a personal or commercial nature, the rights thereto (as with other rights of value) are likely to be subject to frequent, even deliberate, incursion. The potential severity of the consequences requires little imagination.

This chapter is concerned primarily with the monetary remedies a claimant might seek to recover for an incursion of her rights to data, or what will be called a data rights incursion for brevity.[2] Others have already explored the normative bases for awarding damages following a breach of privacy.[3] The need for the law to provide its subjects with principled guidance on the award and assessment of damages in this domain of growing importance is clear.[4] It will be contended here that the content of such guidance must also take into account relevant policy considerations. This contention is advanced by looking at two main hurdles that a prospective claimant may encounter when pursuing a claim for damages at common law, namely, having to show that the loss or damage

* Assistant Professor, Singapore Management University. I received helpful feedback on ideas contained in this chapter from Goh Yihan to whom a significant debt is owed. I am grateful also to Jeannie Marie Paterson, Damian Chalmers and fellow participants at the Data Rights and Private Law Workshops, and to John Murphy, for their comments. Any errors are mine.

[1] J Desjardins, 'How Much Data Is Generated Each Day?' (*World Economic Forum*, 17 April 2019), www.weforum.org/agenda/2019/04/how-much-data-is-generated-each-day-cf4bddf29f.

[2] Nothing in this chapter should be taken as supporting the primacy of damages over injunctive relief if available (or *vice versa*). On injunctive relief, see generally N Witzleb, 'Interim Injunctions for Invasions of Privacy: Challenging the Rule in *Bonnard* v. *Perryman*?' in N Witzleb et al (eds), *Emerging Challenges in Privacy Law: Comparative Perspectives* (Cambridge, Cambridge University Press, 2014) 438–40.

[3] See, eg, E Chamberlain, 'Snooping: How Should Damages be Assessed for Harmless Breaches of Privacy?' in K Barker, K Fairweather and R Grantham (eds), *Private Law in the 21st Century* (Oxford, Hart Publishing, 2017); J Varuhas and N Moreham (eds), *Remedies for Breach of Privacy* (Oxford, Hart Publishing, 2018).

[4] Chamberlain, 'Snooping', ibid, 390.

suffered is a legally cognisable one, and to prove the content of that loss or damage to a legally satisfactory standard.

II. Policy and Damages in Private Law

The compensatory principle generally reigns supreme in the field of private law damages. As the United Kingdom (UK) Supreme Court recently reminded, damages for a civil wrong are awarded with the object of putting the claimant in the same position, as best as money can do it, as if the wrong had not occurred.[5] What makes the operation of the principle challenging in the case of data rights incursions is the presence of unusual, and occasionally novel, characteristics. Applying the existing rules on damages may lead to an inadequate legal response following the incursion.

The starting point is of course the causes of action recognised at common law and in equity. Depending on the precise facts, the claims that are likely to be relevant are those for breach of contract, breach of a tortious duty, and breach of confidence. Under each of these claims, only some types of loss or damage but not others are cognisable as justifying an award of damages. In English law, for instance, a claim in contract generally acknowledges as actionable monetary loss and personal injury, but not mental suffering unless an important object of the contract was to provide pleasure, relaxation, peace of mind or freedom from molestation and that object was not fulfilled, or unless the mental suffering directly relates to physical inconvenience or discomfort caused by the breach.[6] A tortious claim recognises actionable loss and damage to include pecuniary loss, damage to property and personal and psychiatric injury;[7] in general, however, emotional distress is not recoverable. The equitable claim for breach of confidence requires detriment to be shown by the affected party, usually in monetary terms or some other quantifiable loss.

For someone seeking damages following a data rights incursion, the potential stumbling block is that the substantial loss or damage she suffers may not be pecuniary or quantifiable. The realisation that one's data has been compromised often leads to inconvenience, discomfort and frustration, with the resulting impact ranging from the relatively trivial (eg where anonymised data is lost) to the patently severe (such as where location, medical or financial records are implicated). Yet, as we have seen, the recovery of damages for these types of loss has traditionally been restricted in the common law.[8]

An obvious approach is for the courts to organically update the standards for recovery in data rights incursions, whether in the guise of revising the elements which substantiate an existing cause of action or devising a new cause of action altogether.[9]

[5] *Lloyd v Google LLC* [2021] UKSC 50, [2021] 3 WLR 1268, para 80.

[6] *Farley v Skinner* [2001] UKHL 49, [2002] 2 AC 732.

[7] *Pickering v Liverpool Daily Post and Echo Newspapers Plc* [1991] 2 AC 370 (HL).

[8] See, eg, D Solove and D Citron, 'Risk and Anxiety: A Theory of Data-Breach Harms' (2018) 96 *Texas Law Review* 737, and the response in R Calo, 'A Long-Standing Debate: Reflections on *Risk and Anxiety: A Theory of Data Breach Harms* by Daniel Solove and Danielle Keats Citron' (2018) 96 *Texas Law Review Online* 59. Having said that, there do exist specific common law torts that may permit recovery for distress in identified circumstances, such as deceit and injurious falsehood (see the discussion in J Murphy, 'The Vitality of Injurious Falsehood' (2021) 137 *LQR* 658, 671–72).

[9] By way of mere illustration, as this chapter was being finalised, the UK Supreme Court released its decision in *Fearn v Board of Trustees of the Tate Gallery* [2023] UKSC 4, [2023] 2 WLR 339 concerning whether

That is of course the stage on which we see the common law primarily at work, but in the backdrop – of which scholars are the usual inhabitants – there persists a lengthy debate over the place and legitimacy of 'policy' considerations in the processes of adjudication and of development of legal rules. Such considerations typically refer to communitarian interests over and above the interests of the immediate parties to the dispute. The debate pits those who see a (or the) goal of private law as advancing social imperatives – and who therefore accept judicial acknowledgment of, and reliance on, communitarian-based interests – against those who view private law as a hermetic system for regulating rights and interests amongst (only) the relevant individuals.[10]

Much of this academic debate has historically taken place away from the action zone, because in practice the judicial development of rules (particularly ones fashioned to deal with novel scenarios) *already* frequently involves some consideration of 'policy' as is patent from the judgments. It is therefore understandable that effort has lately been expended on rationalising what goes on in the courts with a more nuanced understanding of private law theory and adjudication. Studying these attempts, James Plunkett concluded that arguments against the use of policy in private law were not as unproblematic as they were often made out to be.[11] An examination Andrew Robertson separately undertook of several seminal private law cases led him to articulate an account of decision-making in which courts might routinely take a 'policy' – enumerated or implicit – into consideration when developing private law principles and rules, or even ground their application of legal rules or standards directly on policy considerations. However, this was applied in a constrained way that variously recognised the countervailing forces of institutional restraints (in the form of precedent-based conventions or commonly held expectations of the judicial role) and imperatives to further legal consistency and coherence as well as to deliver interpersonal justice.[12]

To see how the remedial rules in data rights incursions might develop in future, it is instructive to consider the approaches taken in one notoriously difficult area in private law damages. That pertains to the appropriate remedies in the 'wrongful birth' cases, the facts of which commonly see a claimant conceive, or cause to be conceived, a child that would not have been conceived in circumstances where a defendant has been negligent in undertaking a prior medical procedure (such as sterilisation) relating to the claimant. Are the costs of raising that child recoverable as damages? Such a scenario had to be contemplated in *Rees v Darlington Memorial Hospital NHS Trust*, where Lord Bingham of Cornhill, with whom a majority of the Law Lords agreed, referred to three policy considerations in his speech: (i) an unwillingness to regard a child (even if unwanted) as a financial liability and nothing else; (ii) a recognition that the rewards which parenthood (even if involuntary) may or may not bring cannot be quantified; and (iii) a sense that

nuisance was made out in a unique situation where a viewing gallery had been constructed thereby allowing the public to see into adjacent living apartments that had glass walls. By a narrow 3–2 majority the Court concluded that the tort was established.

[10] See also chapter 2 of this volume, where Roger Brownsword develops some of these themes as well.

[11] J Plunkett, 'Principle and Policy in Private Law Reasoning' [2016] *CLJ* 366. For another view, see R Grantham and D Jensen, 'The Proper Role of Policy in Private Law Adjudication' (2018) 68 *University of Toronto Law Journal* 187.

[12] A Robertson, 'Constraints on Policy-Based Reasoning in Private Law' in A Robertson and H Tang (eds), *The Goals of Private Law* (Oxford, Hart Publishing, 2009).

to award potentially very large sums of damages to the parents of a normal and healthy child against a National Health Service always in need of funds to meet pressing demands would offend the community's sense of how public resources should be allocated.[13]

Some of the judges in *Rees* were adamant that the question of recoverability of upkeep costs involved *legal* policy – where the responsibility lay with the judges to answer it and, in that process, make choices about the development of an area of law – and not *public* policy.[14] The difference between the two, as Lord Millett explained in *McFarlane v Tayside Health Board* (a case preceding *Rees*), was this:

> The admission of a novel head of damages is not solely a question of principle. Limitations on the scope of legal liability arise from legal policy, which is to say 'our more or less inadequately expressed ideas of what justice demands' … This is the case whether the question concerns the admission of a new head of damages or the admission of a duty of care in a new situation. *Legal policy in this sense is not the same as public policy, even though moral considerations may play a part in both. The court is engaged in a search for justice, and this demands that the dispute be resolved in a way which is fair and reasonable and accords with ordinary notions of what is fit and proper. It is also concerned to maintain the coherence of the law and the avoidance of inappropriate distinctions if injustice is to be avoided in other cases* (emphasis added).[15]

In *Rees*, Lord Nicholls of Birkenhead put it this way:

> [T]he law's evaluation of the damages recoverable for a legal wrong is not an automatic, mechanical exercise. *Recoverability of damages is always bounded by considerations of fairness and reasonableness* … Judges of course do not have, and do not claim to have, any special insight into what contemporary society regards as fair and reasonable, although their legal expertise enables them to promote a desirable degree of consistency from one case or type of case to the next, and to avoid other pitfalls. But, however controversial and difficult the subject matter, judges are required to decide the cases brought before the courts. *Where necessary, therefore, they must form a view on what are the requirements of fairness and reasonableness in a novel type of case* (emphasis added).[16]

While this language of legal policy has been assiduously followed in the lower courts when deciding whether a new head of loss should be recognised at law,[17] it is notable that Baroness Hale of Richmond viewed the same issue as implicating public policy considerations.[18] That the underpinnings of the approach itself have been understood in a mixed way is unsurprising; Robertson has argued eloquently that the policy considerations at play in the 'wrongful birth' cases, although appearing to be concerned with intrinsic notions of right and wrong, can be justified also on the basis of a concern to produce socially desirable and community-oriented outcomes.[19]

[13] *Rees v Darlington Memorial Hospital NHS Trust* [2003] UKHL 52, [2004] 1 AC 309, para 6.
[14] ibid paras 6, 29, 33, 52 and 105.
[15] *McFarlane v Tayside Health Board* [2000] 2 AC 59 (HL) 108.
[16] *Rees v Darlington* (n 13) paras 13–14.
[17] *B v IVF Hammersmith Ltd* [2018] EWCA Civ 2803, [2020] QB 93.
[18] *R (Lumba) v Secretary of State for the Home Department* [2011] UKSC 12, [2012] 1 AC 245, para 216. Whether policy considerations would be considered in a similar manner (or at all) following the majority judgments in *Manchester Building Society v Grant Thornton UK LLP* [2021] UKSC 20, [2022] AC 783 and *Meadows v Khan* [2021] UKSC 21, [2022] AC 852 (to the extent that emphasis on policy considerations is reduced when determining liability for negligence) is beyond the scope of the present study.
[19] Robertson, 'Constraints on Policy-Based Reasoning in Private Law' (n 12) 263–64.

One is therefore entitled to wonder whether a more broadly acceptable prism can be located through which to view and apply policy factors, at least in the field of private law damages. Such a search necessarily takes us to the outer realms of the law's reach and, in this instance, to Singapore where new ground is being broken. A variation of the 'wrongful birth' situation occurred in the case of *ACB v Thomson Medical Pte Ltd*.[20] There, a married couple had undergone in-vitro fertilisation treatment at a private medical services provider. Unfortunately, the latter's negligence resulted in fertilisation of the claimant's ovum by sperm from an unknown person, instead of that of her husband. Following the birth of a healthy baby (who had a different skin tone from her parents), the claimant issued a claim for damages including upkeep costs. That claim for the costs of raising the child failed before the Court of Appeal, because in its view the obligation to maintain one's child was an obligation at the heart of parenthood and could not be a legally cognisable head of loss; moreover, recognition of the upkeep claim would require the parent to prove that the child represented a net loss, which was in conflict with the parental duty and fundamentally inconsistent with the nature of the parent-child relationship.[21] Instead, the Court recognised loss of 'genetic affinity' as actionable loss in Singapore. That was the deprivation of the claimant's chance to have a child with whom both she and her husband would be genetically related and, consequently, to have a family structure which comported with her aspirations.

In arriving at its decision – no less than to admit of an entirely new head of loss – the Court of Appeal stated that the decisional autonomy of the claimant to raise the type of family *she* wanted should not be frustrated, but it was also cautious not to lay out a prescriptive definition of what a family unit should be or to denigrate adoption as a means of raising a family.[22] Had matters stopped there, the decision would have been remarkable[23] but its reasoning orthodox, given the Court's self-imposed restraint in not pronouncing on social values relating to the familial unit. That was *not*, however, the end of the Court's reasoning. It also sought to identify the claimant's loss by reference to the 'deep socio-cultural significance' of the consanguineous bond between parent and child, including the sense of common ancestry and recognition of commonalities (in appearance, temperament and physical appearance), religious and cultural belonging, and even the 'social reality' that one could possibly face discrimination in Singapore on the basis of race and physical appearance.[24] In a significant passage, the Court said that

> the loss suffered … is the result of a complex amalgam of biological, social, ethical, and historical factors … [W]hat is clear is that the [claimant] would be ill-served by a judicial refusal to fully engage with these issues in order to recognise the true loss which has been suffered.[25]

[20] *ACB v Thomson Medical Pte Ltd* [2017] SGCA 20, [2017] 1 SLR 918.

[21] ibid paras 86–100. See also A Phang, 'Pure Economic Loss and Reproductive Negligence: The Singapore Experience' (2017) 24 *Torts Law Journal* 95, 114–16; A Phang, 'The Importance of Comparative Common Law – A View from Singapore' [2023] *Journal of Business Law* 538.

[22] *ACB v Thomson*, ibid, paras 129–130.

[23] See, eg, critical commentary in J English and M Hafeez-Baig, 'Recovery of Upkeep Costs, Claims for Loss of Autonomy and Loss of Genetic Affinity: Fertile Ground for Development?' (2018) 41 *Melbourne University Law Review* 1360; T Foxton, 'Inaccurate Conception' (2018) 81 *MLR* 337; C Purshouse, 'Autonomy, Affinity, and the Assessment of Damages' (2018) 26 *Medical Law Review* 675.

[24] *ACB v Thomson* (n 20) paras 128 and 134.

[25] ibid para 135.

Substantial damages were therefore awarded for the claimant's anguish, stigma, disconcertment and embarrassment.[26]

There is no doubt that the claim for upkeep costs in *ACB* was rejected on the basis of arguments that were 'explicitly about the common good in socio-economic terms'.[27] As seen from the discussion above, the same could be said of the Court's recognition of the loss of 'genetic affinity' claim.[28] Public policy considerations are often already taken into account where the recoverability of private law damages is being delimited, although the Singapore courts have travelled further than many in enunciating the precise impact of those considerations. In a later case, which concerned an application by a homosexual man in Singapore to adopt his biological son birthed through surrogacy in the United States, Sundaresh Menon CJ (giving the judgment of the High Court) laid out some guiding principles:

- Public policy may justify either the existence and scope of a claimed right or the curtailment of a claimed right which would otherwise be established under the law. In the former, the analysis proceeds theoretically on a blank canvas, and the goal is to find the solution which is best supported by the relevant public policy considerations. In the latter, the analysis tends to take the form of an attempt to balance: (i) the need to give effect to the default regime, whether that be statutory or judge-made; and (ii) the need to protect the common good from injury if that default regime were to apply.[29]
- Two limitations exist in relation to the role of public policy in judicial decisions: (i) the protection of the democratic process and respect for the democratic legitimacy of elected institutions necessitates deference by the courts to the Legislature on matters of public policy, especially socio-economic policy and especially in areas where legislation already exists; and (ii) institutional competence and whether a court (or some other branch of government) is best placed to make the decisions in issue due to its expertise and experience and its role and function in the constitutional framework of powers.[30]
- The courts should consider the body of law in question against the type of public policy considerations relied on. In some areas of law (judge-made law) the courts have been given the power to develop the bulk of substantive rules, such as contract and torts; while in other areas (statutory law) Parliament has retained the principal rule-making role, such as land law. As to policy, legal policy involves arguments for the common good that relate to the conduct and consequences of legal practice, whereas socio-economic policy is shorthand for arguments for the common good that relate more broadly to what would be good for society in general, especially from a social, economic, cultural and political perspective.[31]
- That juxtaposition of law and policy can be represented as set out in Table 1:

[26] ibid para 150. The award was pegged at 30% of the financial costs of raising the child.
[27] *UKM v Attorney-General* [2018] SGHCF 18, [2019] 3 SLR 874.
[28] See also *Reed v Bellingham* [2022] SGCA 60, [2022] 2 SLR 1156, para 74.
[29] *UKM v Attorney-General* (n 27) paras 117–118.
[30] ibid paras 125–126.
[31] ibid para 111.

Table 1 Type of Public Policy

		Type of public policy	
		Socio-economic	Legal
Type of law	Judge-made law	Category 1A	Category 1B
	Statutory law	Category 2A	Category 2B

> In a case falling within Category 1A or 1B, a court may generally rest its decision on public policy, as it has principal responsibility for making and changing the law, doing so not only with the individual case in view, but also with the common good in sight. In a case falling within Category 2A or 2B, the court should be very cautious to rest its decision on public policy, because its task is not to decide the merits of any implicated policy, but to faithfully interpret and apply the statutory regime embedding the public policies which the Legislature regards as relevant, and which have been subject to democratic debate.[32]

These principles cannot be exhaustive given the myriad of situations that arise for judicial determination, and each jurisdiction must forge its own path in light of its particular constitutional, social and historical milieu. Nevertheless, the abstracted statements in Singapore on the explicit recognition of policy factors, with an emphasis on treating such factors with appropriate sensitivity and restraint, may be thought to capture the zeitgeist of an era where courts now more readily take into account the relevant policy considerations. More than that, the concomitant development of guiding principles will give judges the assurance of a proper discharge of their function if they place reliance on such considerations in a transparent and responsible manner.

III. The Nature of Loss in Data Rights Incursions

In relation to the specific inquiry of how policy considerations may influence the recognition of a new head of injury, it has been said that:

> The list of legally cognisable injuries has evolved with time because the world has changed, and the law must, as Lord Macmillan said in *Donoghue v Stevenson*, 'adapt itself to the changing circumstances of life' (at 619). This is perhaps clearest in the area of medical science, where scientific advancement has made it possible for us to do things today which would previously have been unimaginable a few decades ago. This has brought untold prosperity to many, and hope to those who previously had none; but it has also given us greater capacity for harm.[33]

Today, much the same story could be told of advancements in information technology which have allowed the mass collection and processing of data.

The common law rules surrounding the recognition and proof of losses in the field of privacy and confidence have certainly adapted in some ways to the 'changing

[32] ibid paras 111, 112 and 115.

[33] *ACB v Thomson* (n 20) para 2. The modern construction of glass walls, for instance, has given rise to vulnerabilities that may be protected in certain circumstances by the tort of nuisance, as vividly shown in the case of *Fearn v Board of Trustees of the Tate Gallery* (n 9).

circumstances of life'. For instance, English tort law has reaffirmed that the tort of misuse of private information does not require the claimant to have to demonstrate material damage and distress as a necessary ingredient; general damages are available where the misuse of private information has resulted in a loss or diminution of a right to control the use of the information.[34] Another notable development pertains to the breach of confidence action: after reviewing the position in other jurisdictions, the Court of Appeal in Singapore removed the requirement for unauthorised use or detriment so that a claimant only needs to show that information of a confidential nature has been imparted to the defendant in circumstances of confidence, whereupon a presumption of breach of confidence arises (and which the defendant can displace by showing that its conscience was unaffected).[35]

In the case of the privacy tort, it has been explained that English common law does not require material damage and distress to substantiate the tort because the freedom to choose, and the right to control, whether and when others have access to one's private affairs is a fundamental aspect of personal autonomy which if deprived of can attract compensation.[36]

Over in Singapore, change was justified on more prosaic grounds:

> [T]he dissipation of the confidential character of the information … does not always immediately translate into monetary terms or quantifiable detriment. The owner of the compromised information may know he has suffered loss but may only be able to speculate as to how, for example, this will negatively affect his business or future operations. This means that even a simple claim for damages will not necessarily succeed … A shift in the burden of proof [] addresses the practical difficulties faced by owners of confidential information in bringing a claim in confidence. [Claimants] may often be unaware of the fact that someone has done an act inconsistent with their right of confidentiality. A potential breach could be discovered years after, placing them on an evidential back-foot. Defendants are comparatively better positioned to account for their suspected wrongdoing.[37]

Although its merits can be debated,[38] the reasoning timeously identifies the practical challenges faced by claimants when seeking redress in respect of their protected information. In the court's view these challenges require an urgent intervention – to jettison the requirement for unauthorised use and reverse the burden of proof – the significance of which is further underscored in how it was then able to make an order for equitable damages under the domestic equivalent of section 2 of Lord Cairns' Act,[39] whereas it is at least doubtful that a similar order could have been issued in other common law jurisdictions in the absence of wrongful use of the information.

[34] *Vidal-Hall v Google Inc* [2015] EWCA Civ 311, [2016] QB 1003; *Gulati v MGN Ltd* [2015] EWCA Civ 1291, [2017] QB 149.

[35] *I-Admin (Singapore) Pte Ltd v Hong Ying Ting* [2020] SGCA 32, [2020] 1 SLR 1130.

[36] *Lloyd v Google* (n 5) para 104.

[37] *I-Admin v Hong* (n 35) paras 57 and 62.

[38] See the commentary in C Saw, S Chan and W Chai, 'Revisiting the Law of Confidence in Singapore and a Proposal for a New Tort of Misuse of Private Information' (2020) 32 *Singapore Academy of Law Journal* 891; B Wong and D Tan, 'A Modern Approach to Breach of Confidence Based on an Obligation of Conscience' (2020) 136 *LQR* 548.

[39] Chancery Amendment Act 1858. In this case the Court of Appeal remitted the matter to the first instance judge to assess the quantum of damages, but in doing so also stating its view that the value of the confidential

Some accustomed to the unhurried method of the common law will find these rapid developments surprising. The motivation for change is not identical in each case – fuller recognition of personal autonomy in England and Wales, and a keen appreciation of commercial practicalities in Singapore – not to mention the tortious and equitable actions being different in scope and emphasis.[40] Take a broader perspective, however, and something else may be going on. We are being reminded of the intrinsic value of data and information, the fluid and intangible nature of which renders its loss particularly difficult for claimants to pinpoint in precise economic or monetary terms. There is also a public policy concern which is especially acute in international financial centres, pertaining to how they witness and thrive on heavy data flows such that data rights incursions may frequently arise and pose significant challenges of substantiation for claimants there. On this view, the courts in both jurisdictions have been responding in decisive terms – even attenuating constituent elements of a cause of action – to issues which are themselves pieces of a larger problem transcending national borders.

It would be a mistake, however, to think that the hard part is done. Consider the principle that substantial damages are awarded to a claimant who is able to prove that it has suffered loss.[41] Even with a low threshold to surmount – such as the English position that material damage or distress is unnecessary for proving the tort of misuse of private information – an individual claimant still has to show on a balance of probabilities that its control of private information was in fact adversely impacted, as well as the extent of that impact. The burden rests on the claimant in the ordinary course. In many contexts that will be unobjectionable, but when it comes to data rights incursions, particularly those undertaken deliberately and surreptitiously, individual claimants are likely to face a severe uphill task in demonstrating a non-trivial, adverse impact (and its extent) upon their right to control of information, much less material damage. Such incursions occur, by definition, in the virtual medium and (we can be increasingly confident of this) tend to involve multiple actors in the improper collection, use or disposal of data. Those harbouring an insalubrious motive will not announce their operations, which are already disguisable within an anonymised and intermediated network. The legal rules devised for compensation of data subjects – including those pertaining to causation and proof – ought to reflect and accommodate this reality and it is an understatement to say that they currently do not.

Somewhat perversely, defendants may even be motivated to use existing legal rules on loss and damage to avoid what would otherwise be clear grounds for finding liability. Take the case of *Reed v Bellingham*.[42] Mr Michael Reed had invested some money with a fund investment company. The investment was managed by Mr Alex Bellingham, who later left the company to join a competitor. In the course of his new employment, Mr Bellingham reached out to Mr Reed saying that the competitor could offer 'opportunities'

information taken was the cost saved by the erstwhile employees in taking that information, such as in not having to compile the information themselves or to hire additional staff. The judge was therefore to consider the savings in financial expense and time spent when determining the quantum of damages: *I-Admin v Hong* (n 35) paras 77–79.

[40] *ZXC v Bloomberg LP* [2022] UKSC 5, [2022] AC 1158, para 150.

[41] For instance, in the case of privacy claims, see generally Varuhas and Moreham (eds), *Remedies for Breach of Privacy* (n 3).

[42] *Reed v Bellingham* (n 28).

following Mr Reed's impending exit from the investment. Surprised that the competitor was aware of his private investment with the company, Mr Reed initiated proceedings in Singapore under the Personal Data Protection Act 2012 ('PDPA 2012') to restrain Mr Bellingham from using Mr Reed's personal data.

Mr Reed relied on section 32 (since renumbered as section 48O) of the PDPA 2012 which afforded a person a direct right of action for relief in civil proceedings if that person had suffered 'loss or damage directly as a result of a contravention' of the relevant statutory provisions. Of relevance here is how the phrase 'loss or damage' was interpreted. Mr Bellingham submitted – as did the Attorney-General who intervened in the case – that that phrase was to be interpreted by reference to actionable heads of tortious loss or damage under common law, namely, pecuniary loss, damage to property and personal injury.[43] Note the essence of the argument, which was that the common law (and its strictures) ought to limit the pathway of recovery under statute. The defence would have been all too aware that emotional distress, which was the only damage Mr Reed could show in the circumstances, was generally not actionable at common law.

That argument was roundly rejected by the Singapore Court of Appeal. Examining the nature of the statutory action, the Court saw nothing in the legislative text or context to exclude emotional distress from the types of 'loss or damage' for which relief could be provided. Three points are important for our purposes. It was said that the legislature was perfectly able to provide a remedy for damage that the common law did not recognise.[44] This, while uncontroversial, is valuable for making us ponder the distinct possibility that the common law might be found hapless in a given case. Would a data rights incursion, for instance, fall within that problematic category? Interestingly, the Court considered that, with the common law heads of actionable damage shaped by questions of policy, emotional loss *could* found compensation in an appropriate case.[45] Indeed, in data rights incursions it thought that not uncommonly emotional distress would be the *only* loss or damage suffered.[46]

Next, in response to the defendant's submission that recognising emotional distress as actionable damage would open the floodgates to frivolous lawsuits, the Court said that imposition of a strict causal link (eg that loss must have resulted directly from the breach) together with the operation of the *de minimis* rule (so that trivial annoyance or negative emotions forming part of the vicissitudes of life were non-actionable) could represent reasonable controls on usage of the cause of action.[47] Although this was uttered in the context of interpreting particular statutory language, there seems little reason why the *common law* cannot organically develop in that way to accommodate recovery in data rights incursions.[48] Compare also this treatment of the floodgates argument with *Shaw v Kovac*.[49] There, a deceased claimant's estate had sought a conventional award for

[43] ibid paras 27, 33 and 71.
[44] ibid para 73.
[45] ibid paras 74–75.
[46] ibid para 99.
[47] ibid paras 90, 93, 102 and 116.
[48] To the extent that the Court of Appeal viewed the causal inquiry as one dispositive way to limit relief for emotional distress in data rights incursions, that approaches the analysis adopted in a nuisance context by Sir Thomas Bingham MR in *AB v South West Water Services Ltd* [1993] QB 507 (CA) 532–33.
[49] *Shaw v Kovac* [2017] EWCA Civ 1028, [2017] 1 WLR 4773.

invasion of the claimant's personal autonomy by reason of certain surgical procedures being performed in circumstances where his informed consent had not been obtained.[50] Davis LJ, with whom the other members of the Court of Appeal agreed, rejected that claim expressly on policy grounds. In his view, awarding substantial compensation for a mere infringement of autonomy would carry the risk of unleashing a flood of claims in a variety of situations and lead to very real (if unquantifiable) financial, practical and other implications, especially in the 'current climate of claims farming'.[51]

It may be contended that incursions of data rights are not directly comparable to acts causing physical injury.[52] The true difference in the application of policy factors which appears to have moved the *Reed* and *Shaw* courts in opposite directions is that such incursions result in loss that is primarily emotional and mental in nature *and which, if not legally cognisable, would leave affected individuals without meaningful redress* – a net-negative scenario which the law should if possible adjust, and which means that the floodgates argument is much less consequential so far as concerns recovery following such incursions. This is unlike other types of infringements where the primary harm is physical (or psychiatric) and *already* compensable, with any emotional loss occurring on top of that harm. In any event, taken together the *Reed* and *Shaw* cases demonstrate the need for great sensitivity when judges take policy considerations into account, even one (the engagement of the floodgates argument) which looks well canvassed at first glance.

Finally, apart from overcoming the aforesaid policy arguments that sought to defeat a claim relating to emotional distress, the Court of Appeal in *Reed* referred to policy considerations that, in its view, positively compelled a conclusion that such loss could be recovered under the statutory action. The considerations (which had been briefed to Parliament) were:

- The vast amounts of personal data collected, used and transferred for a variety of reasons.
- The use of info-communication technologies like high-speed computing and business analytics, which was expected to grow the amount of data used exponentially as organisations acquired the ability to process large amounts of personal data.
- That any failure of the data protection regime to adequately govern the collection, use and disclosure of personal data might result in individuals losing trust in organisations that managed data; and if individuals lost trust in data controllers and withheld such data from organisations, the legislative aim of enhancing Singapore's status as a trusted hub and choice location for global data management and processing services would be undermined.[53]

This context led the Court to find that the vast and ever-increasing volume of personal data being collected and processed increased the risk of misuse of personal data. One can add the observation that some of these enumerated policy considerations carry relevance regardless of the jurisdiction or whether it is a statutory or common law

[50] ibid para 58.
[51] ibid paras 81–82.
[52] See also *Lloyd v Google LLC* [2019] EWCA Civ 1599, [2020] QB 747, para 63.
[53] *Reed v Bellingham* (n 28) para 98.

action that is in issue. At the very least, it seems hard to argue that no broader or external justification exists for refining the causes of action currently available under the common law.

IV. Proving Loss in Widespread Data Rights Incursions

A massive data rights incursion captures the headlines. It could be a security breach where the data of consumers collected by an enterprise is unlawfully accessed, such as the 2022 server hack of Optus, an Australian telecommunications company, resulting in the personal data of millions of customers being compromised. Or it could be the enterprise itself using data collected from its customers in a way that is wrongful or against its data policies. In each case the data rights incursion affects many people, but the impact is likely to vary from person to person. The effect will be relatively trivial for some, making a claim infeasible on cost-benefit grounds. Others may suffer severe emotional distress but that could be difficult to prove for various reasons, such as the rigidity and complexity of rules (substantive and procedural), the opacity of the technical and business operations, the imbalance of resources, and the vagaries of dispute resolution (eg lapse of time and non-availability of witnesses and evidence).

An individual may find any of these hurdles to be a significant barrier to issuing a claim against an alleged wrongdoer. Not infrequently, the procedural innovation of a representative claim is enlisted: a suit is brought on behalf of a class of persons comprising the affected individuals. The key question is whether pursuing that course of action – or some similar procedure – realistically provides any meaningful recourse for the affected individuals.

The English litigation in *Lloyd v Google LLC* has cast a harsh light on the problem.[54] Between August 2011 and February 2012, Google allegedly installed third-party cookies in Apple iPhones without the consent of their users. The cookies were said to have allowed Google to collect or infer a gamut of information relating to the users, such as their internet surfing habits, location and other personal information including age, gender, race, ethnicity and religious beliefs. Many such users were resident in England and Wales at the time. Mr Richard Lloyd, claiming both to represent them all and an entitlement to obtain damages on their behalf, sued Google under the Data Protection Act 1998 (DPA 1998) to recover compensation for damage suffered by reason of Google's contravention of its duties as a data controller.

Because Google was incorporated in Delaware, Mr Lloyd had to apply for permission to serve the claim form outside of jurisdiction. Warby J rejected that application at first instance, but the Court of Appeal allowed Mr Lloyd's appeal. Google appealed further to the Supreme Court. Lord Leggatt's judgment, with which the other judges agreed, focussed primarily on the claim issued under the DPA 1998 but there are aspects of the reasoning which lend themselves to potentially wider application and require contemplation.

[54] *Lloyd v Google* (n 5); noted J Skillen, 'Damage in the Supreme Court' [2022] *CLJ* 14; V Janeček, 'Mass Compensation Claims for Illegal Online Tracking' (2022) 138 *LQR* 205; Y Goutzamanis, 'Closing the Floodgates on Privacy Class Actions' (2023) 86 *MLR* 249.

The specific complaint of Mr Lloyd was that Google had breached the DPA 1998. As a preliminary point, Mr Lloyd could in his own right have conceivably issued a claim under the tort of misuse of private information as well, without having to show that material damage or distress had been caused. But Mr Lloyd had issued no such claim, whether for himself or for the iPhone users whom he purported to represent. Commenting on this omission, Lord Leggatt wondered whether the claimant had taken the view that, in order to establish a reasonable expectation of privacy to substantiate a claim for misuse of private information, it would be necessary to adduce evidence of facts particular to each individual user, and that was not something that could fairly or effectively be carried out without the participation of those individuals in the representative action that Mr Lloyd sought to commence.[55] Lord Leggatt went on to explain:

> If liability is established, the ordinary application of the compensatory principle would therefore result in different awards of compensation to different individuals. Furthermore, the amount of any compensation recoverable by any member of the class would depend on a variety of circumstances particular to that individual. Individualised assessment of damages would therefore be required.[56]

This was, put shortly, not a case where the putative breach had had a uniform impact on the affected individuals.

Pause to consider the irony. Google's alleged wrongdoing was said to have been committed on a massive scale and to have affected many people. Yet that same fact might have been a cause for the claimant's reluctance to pursue recovery under the privacy tort. Lord Leggatt's judgment points to a mismatch between what a just outcome may require and what existing legal processes and procedures can achieve in practice. Even accepting that loss or diminution of a right to control the use of private information is *per se* compensable without material damage or distress – already a relaxed posture other jurisdictions may yet choose to qualify or reject[57] – an English court has still to consider the impact of the wrongdoing on each affected party, unless the wrongdoing is shown to have affected all of them in a common way (which, at present, excepting *de minimis* effects, seems probable only in a minority of cases).

Ordinarily, therefore, the 'individualised assessment' must still take place. And that is often highly infeasible where a data rights incursion has occurred on a widespread scale and variably affected the data subjects, many of whom often have little to no ability to obtain redress on their own. The existence of substantive rules which theoretically make it easier for claimants to obtain a remedy cannot alone guarantee that outcome on the scale and regularity desired by the architects of the rules.[58] Effort and imagination has to be devoted to accompanying reforms in civil procedure and evidential rules,

[55] *Lloyd v Google* (n 5) paras 105–106.

[56] ibid para 87.

[57] See, eg, J Gligorijevic, 'A Common Law Tort of Interference with Privacy for Australia: Reaffirming *ABC v Lenah Game Meats*' (2021) 44 *University of New South Wales Law Journal* 673, 699–700; A Lerch, 'The Judicial Law-Making Function and a Tort of Invasion of Privacy' (2021) 43 *Sydney Law Review* 133.

[58] The suggestion that *Lloyd v Google* preserved an avenue for future claimants to pursue redress in similar circumstances so long as the representative action is differently framed has been made elsewhere, but with an acknowledgment that recourse in that form would face limitations and might not be attractive to claimants: Janeček, 'Mass Compensation Claims for Illegal Online Tracking' (n 54) 210.

for example, a review of the representative action process to identify the issues unduly hampering recovery by meritorious claimants in the scenarios painted above.[59]

Turning to some of the substantive issues that featured in *Lloyd*, in an apparent attempt to side-step the difficulties in calculating the quantum of damages for each affected individual absent their participation in the representative proceedings, Mr Lloyd submitted that damages under the DPA 1998 could be awarded on a 'uniform per capita basis'. It was argued that the Court could determine a fixed amount – without the need for proof of facts particular to an affected individual – which reflected the serious nature of Google's breach, including the 'lack of consent or knowledge of the [affected individuals] to [Google's] collection and use of their personal data'.[60] Alternatively, damages might be assessed as an amount which the affected individual could reasonably have charged for releasing Google from the duties it breached, this being (again) a fixed amount to reflect the standard terms on which Google did business.[61]

These contentions did not want of creativity but found no favour with Lord Leggatt, who thought that the quantification exercise necessitated consideration of the extent of unlawful processing in each individual case (the same obstacle on which any potential representative claim under the privacy tort would have foundered). According to him, the relevant factors to be considered when quantifying damages here included:

- The period of time over which an individual's internet browsing history was tracked.
- The quantity of data that was unlawfully processed.
- Whether any information unlawfully processed was of a sensitive or private nature.
- The use made of the information and the commercial benefit, if any, obtained from such use.[62]

Consequently, Mr Lloyd's attempt to circumvent this exercise by identifying an 'irreducible minimum harm' suffered by every affected individual was flawed because the facts that *could* be alleged in the representative claim – without the participation of the other affected individuals – went towards showing only a given individual's membership of the represented class, and not proving the wrongful collection and use of the individual's data.[63] This led to an unsurprising conclusion:

> The fundamental problem is that, if no individual circumstances are taken into account, the facts alleged are insufficient to establish that any individual member of the represented class is entitled to damages. That is so even if it is unnecessary to prove that the alleged breaches caused any material damage or distress to the individual.[64]

A similar problem plagued Mr Lloyd's argument for awarding an amount representing the fee which affected individuals might reasonably have charged to release Google

[59] See also chapter 14 of this volume, where Normann Witzleb discusses improving the effectiveness of representative actions.

[60] *Lloyd v Google* (n 5) para 88.

[61] ibid para 89.

[62] ibid para 144.

[63] ibid paras 148, 149 and 153.

[64] ibid para 147. See also E Descheemaeker, 'Claimant-Focused Damages in the Law of Privacy' in Varuhas and Moreham (eds), *Remedies for Breach of Privacy* (n 3) 152.

from its duties. It was necessary to establish what unlawful processing by Google of their personal data had occurred; only when Google's wrongful use of such data was known was it possible to estimate its commercial value. Absent individual assessment, however, no evidence was before the Court to show that Google had, through unlawful installation of the third-party cookies, collected or used any personal data of an individual in the represented class. According to Lord Leggatt, therefore, if one were to utilise the relevant valuation construct – the fee that would hypothetically have been negotiated for a licence to place the third-party cookie on an individual user's phone, but without releasing Google from its obligations not to collect or use any information about that user's internet browsing history – it was plain that the licence would be valueless and the fee accordingly nil.[65]

Although expressed in relation to the DPA 1998 claim that was before the Court, the views in *Lloyd* that have been discussed above possess clear relevance to any parallel action at common law. A lesson – unintended but no less stark for that reason – is to highlight that not all our received notions of 'loss', 'damage' and 'compensation' may adjust well to a coming reality where data rights incursions occur on a recursive, invasive and pervasive basis.[66] Lord Leggatt's analysis, which required the affected individuals to prove their loss following the incursion and sought then to match the individual losses suffered with the extent of the resulting compensation, is consistent with orthodox understanding. There is also the sense of an unspoken fear that claimants might exaggerate their condition if the rules were otherwise. But the necessity for cautiousness in the assessment of loss, whilst not to be trifled at, ought to be viewed against the (non-) acceptability of a hyper-individualised approach.[67] More broadly, the failed outcome, together with the questions raised, represent an early warning sign of the difficulties that presently exist within the common law and militate against loss recovery on a wider scale in the unique environment of today's data-intensive world.

There is therefore some concern that, in treating individuals affected by a data rights incursion in the same way as claimants affected by other types of events having real-world consequences (primarily physical and economic, although there are of course other tangible consequences), the traditional common law rules of loss (including in relation to burden and standards of proof) could lead to under-compensation and, symmetrically, a growth in undesirable behaviour on the part of data collectors, processors and users that will chiefly be checked only through a legislative scheme (ideally policed by an active, well-resourced regulator, but that is hardly a certainty). The placement of such a burden on the regulatory machinery is not itself an unacceptable result, and legislation is sometimes better placed to embrace collective harm (in its various conceptions) and the ensuing remedies. But the choice between legislation and common law should also be informed by the suitability (or not) of the common law as a vehicle for loss identification, recovery and apportionment in data rights incursions.[68]

[65] *Lloyd v Google*, ibid, para 157.

[66] See also Skillen, 'Damage in the Supreme Court' (n 54) 15–16.

[67] See, eg, Lord Justice Leveson, *An Inquiry into the Culture, Practices and Ethics of the Press* (London, Stationery Office, 2012) para 5.7.

[68] See the other chapters in this volume discussing the potential actions in tort, contract, breach of confidence and intellectual property.

Arguably the *Lloyd* case has been most significant in bringing many of the present limitations to the forefront of this ongoing debate.

Upon reflection, there can be cautious optimism that the common law is capable of *not* becoming effete and self-defeating in a future world dominated by data. Anomalous issues of foreseeability, causation and proof of loss have been confronted in the mesothelioma cases, while recovery of compensation for regularly occurring types of loss following a breach of some legal duty is common in defamation or personal injury claims, where compensation schemes may provide guidelines to be applied by courts and tribunals in the course of determining the appropriate award. Notably, in the privacy context the Court of Appeal in *Gulati v MGN Ltd* demurred from setting a tariff for damages because of a lack of history of compensation awards for misuse of private information and because it believed any such tariff to be of little use given that the circumstances could vary greatly.[69] To the extent that these reasons currently find traction in the context of a data rights incursion, they could well also fade in relevance, the first with the passage of time and the second with the realisation that some (and possibly even much) overlap in the types of emotional distress suffered is expected to result from a data rights incursion, which ordinarily affects a sizeable population in a baseline way.

V. Conclusion

I have been anxious in this chapter to highlight the resilience of the common law through an illustration of its evolutionary ability when protecting the compensatory interests of individuals who have suffered some novel type of loss. That generally behoves courts to take into account any policy considerations bearing upon the question in a way that is explicit, transparent and sensitive. Specifically in the context of data rights incursions, the relevant policy considerations justifying the development of rules surrounding recovery of damages are significant and pressing. Although the concerns stemming from the floodgates argument have been articulated before, they do not, and should not, entirely forestall recognition of other important considerations such as the vast and ever-increasing volume of data being collected and processed (thereby increasing the risk of misuse), as well as the realistic possibility that meaningful redress will be unavailable should the rules of recovery and civil procedure not be further developed.

In a number of common law jurisdictions this debate has been steadily advancing. That is not the same as saying that the common law will evolve to respond to the particular characteristics of a data rights incursion, and certainly not to suggest that a solution based primarily on common law principles is preferable to a statutory model when it comes to the recovery of damages.[70] Indeed, all reasonable alternatives can and

[69] *Gulati v MGN* (n 34) para 77; *cf* E Descheemaeker, 'Pecuniary and Non-Pecuniary Loss: A Reinterpretation' (2022) 138 *LQR* 79, 90–92.

[70] For a discussion of the overlapping regimes (albeit focussing on English law and taking place prior to the UK Supreme Court's decision in *Lloyd v Google*), see F Brimblecombe and H Fenwick, 'Keeping Control of Personal Information in the Digital Age: Efficacy and Equivalence of Tortious and GDPR/DPA Relief?' (2022) 138 *LQR* 456.

should be explored,[71] canvassing the different strengths of regulatory and private law responses. But a choice may have to be made soon; and we should also remember that what is possible will vary from moment to moment, some options being outmoded for their time and others simply unavailable owing to technical or other reasons. The incipient challenge for judges, lawmakers and regulators, viewed in that light, is to arrive at an appropriate balance as civil society more fully appreciates the conditions – and implications – of living in the massively data-centric world that is upon us.

[71] '[A] specific law should take the existing imbalances in power relations into account. Privacy's freedom and the resistance of the individuals concerned need to be reinforced to make them stronger when they face their powerful opponents. When it comes to data processing, the imbalance in power is often poignant. Information processors usually have more power than their data subjects and influence their behavior. *This process has to be anticipated, for example, by providing a whole range of effective ways to resist interference, keep the procedural threshold low, create a powerful entity which can, on its own initiative, defend the interests of the data subject's privacy, et cetera*': S Gutwirth, *Privacy and the Information Age* (Lanham MD, Rowman & Littlefield, 2002) 86 (emphasis added).

INDEX

www.ingramcontent.com/pod-product-compliance
Ingram Content Group UK Ltd.
Pitfield, Milton Keynes, MK11 3LW, UK
UKHW020141050425
456990UK00006B/348

9 781509 966028